PEACE

PEACE
A World History

Antony Adolf

polity

First published in 2009 by Polity Press
Reprinted 2010

Polity Press
65 Bridge Street
Cambridge CB2 1UR, UK.

Polity Press
350 Main Street
Malden, MA 02148, USA

ISBN-13: 978-0-7456-4125-6
ISBN-13: 978-0-7456-4126-3(pb)

A catalogue record for this book is available from the British Library.

Typeset in 10 on 12 pt Sabon
by Servis Filmsetting Ltd, Stockport, Cheshire
Printed and bound in Great Britain by the MPG Books Group

The publisher has used its best endeavours to ensure that the URLs for external websites referred to in this book are correct and active at the time of going to press. However, the publisher has no responsibility for the websites and can make no guarantee that a site will remain live or that the content is or will remain appropriate.

Every effort has been made to trace all copyright holders, but if any have been inadvertently overlooked the publishers will be pleased to include any necessary credits in any subsequent reprint or edition.

For further information on Polity, visit our website: www.politybooks.com

For Ioana, our families and friends,
To whom I owe my life and peace of mind;

For peace workers past, present and future,
To whom we owe the world and this book is a tribute;

For teachers, mentors and colleagues,
To whom more is owed than can be recognized;

Thank you.

Contents

ᏪᎣ

Acknowledgments

This book would not have been possible without the outstanding work of researchers, writers and publishers it would take volumes just to name, before whom I remain in awe and gratitude. The editorial and production teams at Polity have not only been a pleasure to work with, but are also to be merited with a professionalism and expertise for which credit here does slight justice; my appreciation to Andrea Drugan, Jonathan Skerret, Neil de Cort and Susan Beer. The anonymous reviewers of the book's early drafts provided insights for which I am thankful, as I am for those who commented on them at other stages. I value the enthusiastic support of George, Catherine and Christine Adolf, Matt Norman, Cheryl Zaleski, Rachel Hurst, Nick Smaglio and Stephanie Studzinski, among many others. All acknowledgments share the inherent deficiency of leaving out more than they can possibly include, and this one is no exception. But a constituency no acknowledgment should overlook is the most obvious: readers, thank you.

Introduction

How Does Peace Have a World History?

An analysis of the history of mankind shows that from the year 1496 BC to the year 1861 of our era, that is, in a cycle of 3357 years, there were but 227 years of peace and 3130 years of war: in other words, thirteen years of war for every year of peace. Considered thus, the history of the lives of peoples presents a picture of uninterrupted struggle. War, it would appear, is a normal attribute of human life.

Ivan Bloch[1]

As the industrialist, internationalist peace activist Bloch goes on to contend, we no longer have the luxury of seeing the actualization of peace as a noble if naive vision of how things could have been or can be. His argument in *The Future of War* is that the historically unimaginable destructive capacity of modern weapons, coupled with the inclinations of those who use them, have made risking war morally impermissible as well as rationally unthinkable. He put forth his unheeded advice at the turn of last century, in the midst of the technological, socio-economic and political upheavals leading up to the First World War. But the promises of and perils to peace today make his point as valid and vital at the turn of our own.

The problem with Bloch's shorthand world history of peace is his narrow definition of it exclusively as the absence of war, also a dominant one contemporarily. Convenient for quick quantitative analyses, this confinement makes qualitative approaches based on the many other meanings of peace proposed and practiced throughout world history practically impossible. Two millennia ago, as the Roman Republic became an Empire and the Pax Romana dawned, the historian Livy asserted that "war has its laws as peace has."[2] What Livy here allows for and Bloch does not is that just as some ways of waging and winning wars are constant and others change over time, depending on what wars mean for participants and the means at their disposal (to name just two factors), so it is with ways of making and maintaining peace. Peace and peacemaking are not a line of pharmaceutical products the only functions of which are to treat symptoms and diseases of war, nor are they merely preventative vaccines. What are they?

Three basic heuristic categories of peace and peacemaking can serve as aids in capturing a panoramic view of their history across cultures and centuries, while also permitting us to zoom in on issues of permanent or periodic importance, subjectively and objectively:

1. **Individual Peace:** How individuals become and stay at peace with themselves;
2. **Social Peace:** How groups become and stay at peace within themselves; and
3. **Collective Peace:** How groups become and stay at peace between each other.

The purpose of this book is to show how peace and peacemaking along these and other lines have evolved in and transformed their/our historical contexts. My hope is that this pedagogical exercise in the recent, distant and primordial past can improve their prospects in the present and future by emphasizing that taking cultural contingencies and diversities into consideration is a necessary choice for peace and peacemaking to be actualized based on a set of imperatives.

The purpose of this introduction is to explore how radically different forms of peace and peacemaking throughout world history coupled with our (mis)understandings of them were both causes and consequences of cultural change, and why this makes putting forth a static definition of either at the outset counterproductive. Individual, social and collective peace as described above are not intended as definitions in this sense, but as dynamic paradigms in which culturally specific meanings of peace have historically been proposed and practiced. The value of these meanings-in-action within and across cultures, as focal points of this book, lies in the ways in which they have influenced those of today and can better those of tomorrow.

Peaces of World History

Three years into the US Civil War (1861–5), in a private letter, President Abraham Lincoln as cleverly and concisely as ever confided:

Peace does not appear so distant as it did. I hope it will come soon, and come to stay; and so come as to be worth the keeping in all future time. It will then have been proved that, among free men, there can be no successful appeal from the ballot to the bullet; and that they who take such appeal are sure to lose their case, and pay the cost.[3]

Here, he does not use the word "victory" to describe the aim of the Northern Unionist States he was leading against those of the separatist South, and his absolutist first use of "peace" as the cessation of the ongoing war is balanced by his conditional aspiration thereafter. Upholding confederate constitutional principles and affirming the abolition of slavery throughout the country were not secondary considerations to Lincoln in this appeal, but part and parcel of the meaning of the *worthwhile* peace he hoped the war's end would bring about. No doubt, the peace imagined by his slave-holding opponents was different in these respects and others.

The second part of Lincoln's statement, in which the coming peace would "prove" that successful democracy is innately a deterrent of and cure for war, is somewhat more problematic. A shift has occurred from peace being a post-war condition meeting predefined criteria to the justification of a political system, however positive. Peace in world history has rarely if ever been an apolitical topic, but to lose sight of its non-political meanings is to overlook many of the other drivers of, and advantages derived from, peace and peacemaking. Religion, economics, philosophy and law have all been active arenas of pacific endeavors, to name a few. "War," in the famous words of German military strategist Carl von Clausewitz, may be "the continuation of politics by other means;" in world history peace has been only partially so.[4] Monarchical, theocratic, socialist and totalitarian governments as well as non-governmental societies have all also claimed to act in the name and for the sake of peace. States that have actually done so with "proven" results share more than their propaganda would ever allow them to admit.

What are the proofs of peace and how can they be identified, evaluated and applied? If clear-cut answers to questions like these existed then making and maintaining peace would be cumulative scientific enterprises, and this book would be a purely empirical study. They are not. Grasping how peace and peacemaking have shaped and been shaped by world history calls not only for a selective re-presentation of "facts" (in our case, events, ideas, individuals, movements, etc.) in their light, but also for a comprehensive re-interpretation of them outside the shadows in which they have previously been cast. History, it is often said, is written by the victors in war, and as a general rule this tired dictum may hold true. The champions of peace, momentous and everyday, intellectual and activist, expert professional and lay, have for too long been considered exceptions that prove this rule, when in actuality without their efforts there may not have been a history to live, let alone write. Their stories are put together here as vital pieces of the puzzle of world history so that we can better piece together the present and future (puns intended).

The dire dichotomy of war and peace portrayed in Tolstoy's novel of that title cannot be sidestepped because it is inseparable from the human experience, documented from prehistory to the Cold War's hot rhetoric and beyond. However, following this narrow chasm to the exclusion of other paths leads us neither to the purgatorial point at which humanity finds itself today nor to a more accurate overall picture of how we have survived ourselves thus far, to say nothing of what we have overcome. The devastation and desperation wars leave in their wakes preclude calling most post-war periods peaceful until long after peace has been proclaimed. Yet, such proclamations, the preparations that come before and the implementations that in the best of cases follow are as imperative to peace as any other factor in its actualization. Even taken alone, the full story of these happenings would require a book several times the length of this one. Add to them forms of peace and peacemaking not directly tied to war, but still inextricably tied to the twists and turns of history, and you would get an encyclopedia. A static definition of peace and peacemaking at the outset would be counterproductive to the comprehensive, concise and practical account of the world history of peace I have striven for because definitions without contexts are half-empty glasses. Seen through the lenses of individual, social and collective peace, which require contexts for accurate perception, humanity's glass appears half full – and fillable.

Individual, Social and Collective Peace

Individual peace is in one way the most tangible, widespread experience of the three because nearly everyone has, in one form or another, a degree of familiarity with it. In another, its experience is the most difficult to discuss because it is so close to being completely internalized, as it is commonly called "inner peace." Prayer in Judaism, Christianity and Islam, and meditation in Hinduism and Buddhism as vehicles of inner peace are, for example, subjects of thousands of treaties and used by billions of believers to reach inner peace as well as with their deities. Stoic, Confucian and Utilitarian philosophies of peace are similar, though secular, in these regards. While their respective prescriptions are discussed here within the cultural contexts in which they were put forward, practiced and spread, knowing this brings us only slightly closer to knowing why exactly, centuries later, they continue to work for some and not for others. Testimonials can give glimpses of inner peace, associated rituals outward glances; explaining the principles and growth of such experiences for individuals and as historical forces does them only limited justice. What distinguishes these works from today's bestselling self-help books that guarantee inner peace in thirty days or your money back are the test of time they have been proven by, the extended critical traditions they have been developed through, and the material effects they have had on the people and world around in addition to the individuals devoted to them. Patterns of behavior are the apparent entries into the mechanics and manifestations of individual peace, but in all the cases mentioned above (religious and/or secular) they usually involve interactions with others and the world reaching beyond the tipping point of sociality.

Social peace is slightly easier to identify and discuss in theoretical writings as well as in historical periods. The difficulty here lies in breaking molds cast by another prevalent split in peace studies and practices throughout history. As sociologist Brian Fogarty summarizes the unfinished debate, notions and applications of social peace generally belong to either of two antithetical traditions.[5] One is guided by the principle that humanity is essentially bellicose or, in Fogarty's words, that "the civilizing veneer of society is all that saves us from chaos and self-destruction," a view crystallized in the seventeenth century in British political theorist Thomas Hobbes' *Leviathan*. A world history of peace along these lines would begin at the first moment when a group agreed to disagree with enough force to sustain stalemate. Since chaos, another concept peace tends to be defined in the negative against, is the substance of humanity from this perspective, the accidental history of peace traced along its lines would structurally look much like that of Bloch. Substituting chaos for war changes what peace is in addition to what it is not. From absences of violence, peace becomes presences of authority and stability embodied in all-powerful dictators capable of keeping chaos at bay, which is in the end the very social peace Hobbes argued for. His thesis helped bring about the monarch's Restoration, who as a child was tutored by him, after the chaos following the English Civil War. Dictators throughout history – Augustus in ancient Rome, the Tokugawa Emperors in medieval Japan, and Tito in modern Yugoslavia among them – have proved Hobbes right, and wrong.

At the other end of the social peace spectrum is what Fogarty bathetically describes as the view that humanity is somehow "endowed by nature or God with an innate desire to cooperate and nurture." A classic expression of this tenet is that of the eighteenth-century French social theory of Jean-Jacques Rousseau, who personifies the Romantic era and the spirit of republicanism in *The Social Contract*. For him, humanity's primordial condition was pristine, untouched by say war or chaos, which in his recount arose only when the few began oppressing the many without mutual consent. This unrecoverable condition falls short of peace for Rousseau because the bonds upon which the latter is built have not come into being. As consensual association, not a single strong hand, sustains sociality from this perspective, abuses thereof are reduced to passing aberrations. Correspondingly, peace becomes humanity's substance and its contraries accidental, a position poles apart from Hobbes but no more tenable. Primatologists, archaeologists and anthropologists concur that social peace is evolutionarily speaking a necessity rather than a choice, and differs between species as between cultures. Evidence on this scale points to what I dub "survival of the peaceful," which works symbiotically with Charles Darwin's notion of survival of the fittest, as he and his early followers were the first to admit. On the scale of historical periods, the hazards of Rousseau's construal become clear in the revolutions justified by concordant social peace he inspired, anti-monarchical, anti-colonial or otherwise. As in ancient Athens, the birth pangs and erosions of democratic social contracts, by which votes cast constitute less and less of mandates for than sign-offs on the activities of officials, call into question blind faiths in them and in so doing also give answers as to how they can be improved.

Of course, Hobbes' and Rousseau's politically motivated contrivances cannot be used as devices for telling or analyzing global stories of peace and peacemakers. They are nonetheless representative of nearly universal narrative and interpretive undercurrents that have pulled both history and historians towards their means and ends, and are thus constitutive of these stories. As Meredith Weddle states in her study of Quaker pacifism, a prime example of how such tides can be taken into consideration without swaying methodologies or conclusions, histories of peace "have been few and have often suffered from oversimplification and a restricted scope."[6] These studies, the proverbial shoulders upon which this book stands, are still stunning in their array and expertise, generally taking one or a weighted mix of four forms I have tried to integrate:

1. **Topical**: Examining specific types of peace and peacemaking, such as non-violence, diplomacy, anti-war protests, literary and artistic expressions, etc.;
2. **Geographical**: Covering peace and peacemaking in or between specific locations, such as empires, continents, regions, nations, cities, etc.;
3. **Durational**: Dealing with loosely or strictly delimited timeframes tied to peace and peacemaking, such as regimes, eras, centuries, decades, events, etc.; and
4. **Personal**: Exploring the experience and actions of one or more persons linked to peace and peacemaking, such as leaders, activists, thinkers, ambassadors, etc.

Important sources aside from these and primaries such as laws, treaties, declarations, statements, records and the like is research directly or indirectly related to peace and peacemaking, including but not limited to sociology, international relations, political science, historiography and cultural studies. How close this book comes to transmitting the extent of this knowledge is immaterial compared to the extent that is, inherently by its parameters, beyond its scope.

Collective peace requires careful combinations of these approaches and materials to be pragmatically comprehended. From arbitrations by one neutral city between conflicting others in ancient Iraq, which may be the origin of state formation, to organizations such as the United Nations, which may depend to a debilitating degree upon its member-states, inter-group peace is determined equally by characteristics of its participants and specifics of its processes. How groups are structured, whether as tribes, classes, ethnicities, nations or parties, is a variable of social peace too, but becomes a collective issue when two or more groups interact or are unable to. Influential examples, the consequences of which continue to ensure or imperil peace today, are colonialism (periods of initial contacts between colonizers and colonized) and imperialism (periods of continued relations between them). In antiquity, Babylonian and Persian, Greek and Roman, Chinese and Indian Empires each had their own peace strategies to advance and protect conquests grounded in their own resources as well as those of their targets; likewise in modernity Spanish, Portuguese, Dutch, English, French and American Empires. Ever-present asymmetries of power can be impediments to peace, but those who have used them to prevent it have usually been making excuses with ulterior motives. Counter-examples are Bartolomé de las Casas, conquistador turned imperial peacemaker, and Gandhi, lawyer turned anti-imperial peacemaker. The achievements and setbacks of such outstanding figures are not far in importance from the anonymous blueprints for collective peace on various inter-group levels drawn up across the ages, from which those of today descend and those of tomorrow will.

In the majority of cases, idiosyncratic intra-group traits – linguistic, economic, political, traditional, religious and so on – are historically not barriers to or conduits of inter-group peace in themselves, but they are not peace-neutral either. Identity markers become so through the uses or misuses of them by those in power and the willingness or refusal of those over whom they exert it to go along. In the worst cases, genocides, systematic sufferings, disenfranchisement, it is usually over-perpetuation in duration and degree or a *deus ex machina* that triggers intercultural change. Emperor Ashoka's temporary reversal of the caste system in ancient India and struggles for social justice based on race and gender more recently (as in the early movement against Apartheid in South

Africa, against segregation in the US, for woman's suffrage worldwide and for an equitable globalized economy), belong to the history of collective peace insofar as they are transformative non-violent catalysts for change. Their peace strategies did not come about in a vacuum, they were outgrowths of pacifist, civil disobedience and other traditions that predate and inform them. In their many forms, anti-war and pro-peace activism (not to be confused) also belong to the history of collective peace insofar as they seek to recreate and reconcile groups internally and externally. Those that have thrived were and are based partially on what makes groups what they are, partially on what they can be, and wholly upon what cultural contingencies and diversities in place will or will not permit.

Trying to disentangle the webs between material conditions and conceptual paradigms is futile for our purpose because outside one or the other peace and peacemaking lose most of their applicable meanings. Obviously, concerted efforts to limit the use of specific arms and warfare in general on moral or legal grounds are dependent upon them being in use. Less obvious is how, under lustrous guises of isolationism or impartiality, weapons are manufactured and shipped, preparing the grounds for wars these positions are in theory meant to prevent. Evaluating the shock-waves of singular events (the only two offensive uses of atomic weapons, for instance) on the history of peace against epoch-making circumstances as the Pax Islamica and Pax Britannica is likewise not as insightful as appraising them on their own. So ignoring pacific ways of life and states of affairs that no longer exist to focus solely on those that continue is to enact a selective amnesia that can cost us more than we stand to gain by drawing lessons from both. Delicate balances between material conditions and conceptual paradigms, singular events and overarching circumstances that I have attempted to keep in check are meant to be measured by what they can teach us. For it is only within holistic frameworks that the possibilities and limits of peaceful individual, social and collective agency can be assessed and harnessed.

World History in Peaces

It may come as no surprise that the major architectonic shifts in world history have also made indelible impacts on the history of peace, as they have on every aspect of human life. What may be surprising is the wide divergence of directions in which the very same shifts have pushed peacemakers and their opponents, sometimes also peacemakers in their own terms. By way of closing this introduction and opening the analytical narratives that follow, four pronounced punctuations in global historiography will be briefly considered in relation to fruitions of peace and peacemaking: prehistory, antiquity, modernity and contemporaneity.

That peace predates warfare in humanity's evolution is attested in the morphological development of our primordial ancestors. Pre-human peace and peacemaking, as discernable in prehistoric remains and primate conduct, point to the irreplaceable roles they played in making us as a species who we are, and without which we would not exist as we do. The peace practices of simple societies such as the Semai and Tasaday, from reconciliatory feastings to sanctuarial immunity, tell us as much about their societies as they do about the roots of more complex peace-oriented activities, which is not to say more successful. Characteristics that came about in conjunction with evolutions of means of subsistence are also keys to unlocking prehistoric peace: with gathering, communication and conscientiousness; with hunting, planning and coordination; and with agriculture, organization and surplus management. Between the facts that primates share 99 percent of our genes and that the hunting-gathering phase accounts for 99 percent of our temporal existence lies the impossibility of not discussing the prehistory of peace as related to the early history of peace, demarcated by the use of writing. Transitions from prehistoric home bases to villages, from villages to cities, and from cities to states in Mesopotamia are inextricable from the use of writing to establish private and public legal agreements, economic partnerships, and defensive alliances, which in turn are tied to the history of peace from then on.

Following Karl Jaspers' well-known study of what he called the "axial period" in world history, trajectories of two "axes of peace" in antiquity are traced here, which in his terms gave rise to the "fundamental categories within which we still think today, and the beginnings of the world religions, by which human beings still live."[7] Offshoots of one became foundations of peace in Western culture – ancient Egypt, Greece and Rome; the other, in Eastern culture – ancient India, China and Japan. Though separated by vast distances and times, these evolving civilizations engendered comparably significant religious, political, philosophical and economic metamorphoses that forever changed peace and peacemaking. To sketch just one side of one of these themes: the organized religions of different kinds that congealed in antiquity were at the forefront of pacific enterprises over the courses of these societies. In Egypt, Pharaohs were considered guarantors of peace in as well as between this world and the next by the systems of belief they embodied. Greek Olympic Games were celebrations in honor of the gods during which a cessation of all hostilities was also honored, and the many Greek leagues of city-states all trace their origins to that of Delphi, the most important Hellenic oracle. Romans rarely made peace without consulting augurs and ushered in periods of peace by closing the doors of Janus' temple, a two-faced god of beginnings and endings. From and against these polytheistic religious peace traditions emerged those of two of the world's three major monotheisms, Judaism and Christianity, and from these the third, Islam. The gods, it appears, have historically been among peacemakers' greatest friends, but paradoxically also among their greatest foes.

Three modern cataclysmic occurrences in world history formed contours of contemporary geo-political and economic peace: colonialism and imperialism, the rise of nation-states, and the industrial revolution. For investigative purposes, they are examined in separate chapters here, an artificial division of deeply intertwined issues useful only insofar as it allows sharper focus on each. In the case of colonialism/imperialism, peace was made and maintained on linked levels of the colonized between themselves, between the colonized and the colonizers, and between the colonizers themselves. Brazil's slave republics, Native North American "forest diplomacy" like peace pipe practices, peacemaking powers vested in the Dutch East Indian and other chartered companies, tied geographically based settlements between imperialists on and off the European continent fall onto one or more of these levels. In the case of nation-states, parallel divides were how peace was made and maintained within, between and despite them. Building on medieval treaty and legislative models, the Peace of Westphalia (1648) is taken as a starting point for nation-state based peace along these lines. Grotius' proposed limitation of war, Enlightenment peace theories, natural and scientific approaches to international law and the organized peace movement fit both within and across these archetypes. In the case of industrialism, the equally reactionary courses followed are those of capitalists on the one hand and socialists on the other. Capitalist peace practices tend to support private property, competitiveness and replacing war with economic sanctions as optimal responses to industrialism; socialists tend towards collective ownership, cooperatives and the elimination of classes. Collective bargaining and other peaceful negotiation techniques stem from the resolution of disputes between these positions.

The verdict is still out as to whether the preceding pacific forces and factors were causes of the First World War by their failures or by their designs. However, given continuities in peace and peacemaking up to and including the Second, this may not be the most insightful judgment to make. While no one doubts that the Wars were formative of the first half of the twentieth century, the benefits and drawbacks of these continuities are habitually less acknowledged, including the Commonwealth and League of Nations, patriotic conscientious objecting and the Woman's International League for Peace and Freedom. Specters of poor peaces' past such as the Versailles Treaty (1919), the appeasement of Nazi Germany and the "parchment" peace with Imperial Japan reflect the precariousness of peacemaking today. The defining conflict of the second half of the twentieth century, the Cold War, similarly defined how peace was made and maintained on worldwide levels. Old notions such as balances of power took on new meanings, now in relation to two "superpowers" and their affiliates, the US and USSR, as did notions of neutrality with the Non-Aligned Movement. How the nuclear weapons-backed deadlock never went "hot" is one of the wonders of the world history of peace, spearheaded by scientists, diplomats, professionals, activists and their non-violent tactics, political, popular and direct. With the fall of the Soviet Union (1989), some intellectuals claim a new paradigm came into place, but even with advents of globalization, technology, terrorists, rogue states and new media, and peacemakers' responses to them, there seems to be a way to go before we are clear of the twentieth century's wake.

A danger often mentioned about attempting to draw lessons from history is that doing so sacrifices the objectivity of historians, implying a disservice to their audiences. If by objectivity is meant a dispassionate approach and taking no stances in regards to my subject then, in the belief that failing to learn is still more rewarding than refusing to, I have made this sacrifice with open eyes. I would even go as far as saying that historians who disclaim this sacrifice in treating any of this book's subjects have their eyes closed. The aged adage of the blind leading the blind begs another, the blind leading the sighted, which may be the greatest disservices to historians' audiences. Being wholly committed to the actualization of peace in the present and future does not prevent but rather presupposes faithfulness to its pasts. The world-historical problematizations and their resolutions I offer here are intended less as guidelines than signposts: one tells you *how to do something*, the other that you are *on the way to somewhere*. World peace cannot be this book's subject, despite the best of plans to present it this way, because it has not yet been actualized – it is, however, the objective.

I

Survival of the Peaceful:
Prehistory to the First Civilizations

ᗝ

Pre-Human Peace and Peacemaking

When did the world history of peace begin? How did peace and peace-making originally evolve? Establishing the basic characteristics and chronology of peace from prehistoric times to the origins of civilization has been a considerable challenge for researchers across a wide array of disciplines. Yet, their combined and contentious results present serious challenges to received notions about what peace and peacemaking are and where they come from. Answering these primary questions is the first step on the path to understanding what comes afterwards and effectively continues to this day. Primates are relevant to the early prehistory of peace because, as anthropologist Leslie Sponsel states in *A Natural History of Peace* (1996), "whatever else we are, we are also primates."[1] Evidence that human predispositions and behavior evolved from those of primates does not prove that we are nothing but primates or that we have not since evolved in very different ways. Nevertheless, recent research on primates does provide grounds for the argument that peace as a social condition and peacemaking as an instinctive process among primates set the stage for their counterparts among humans.

Whether the world was more peaceful before humans evolved is impossible to say, but that peace and peacemaking in certain forms then existed is clear. Although firsthand stories are unavailable, primatologists offer practical secondary windows. After studying chimpanzees in their natural Tanzanian habitat for over twenty-five years, for instance, Jane Goodall attested to their inclination towards peaceful coexistence:

Aggression, particularly in its more extreme form, is vivid and attention catching, and it is easy to get the impression that chimpanzees are more aggressive than they really are. In actuality, peaceful interactions are far more frequent than aggressive ones; mildly threatening gestures are more common than vigorous ones; threats per se occur much more often than fights; and serious, wounding fights are very rare compared to brief, relatively mild ones.[2]

The idea that social peace is a matter of proportions, the variables of which can be changed, thus starts with primates though it does not end with them. Nor are chimpanzees the only primates to exhibit predominantly peaceful interactions and the intentions underlying them. Summarizing field observations, another primatologist points out that among bonobo in Congo "encounters are characterized by cautious mutual tolerance. . . Bonobo have evolved systems of maintaining, at least on the surface, a pacific society."[3] Still others have found that "far from being ruled by aggression and powerful individuals," baboons "place a premium on reciprocity, and individuals act out of enlightened self-interest. Baboons must be nice to one another because they need one another for survival and success. It is a finely tuned system."[4] That the genesis of primate *modus operandi* for peaceful coexistence is unknown does not detract from the undeniability that they echo through to the ways of life, as well as survival, of our species.

Given the absence of developed reasoning and language skills in primates – with whom we otherwise share 99 percent of our genes – their capacity for peaceful coexistence most likely has a biological basis, reinforced by environmental adaptation and enculturation processes necessary to pass on peace instincts from one generation to the next. Primatologist Frans de Waal, author of the path-breaking *Peacemaking among Primates* (1990), sees peaceful coexistence among primates whether in the wild or in captivity as stemming from intuitions necessary for survival or, in a word, *peace instincts*. Whenever two or more primates compete for a single resource, both the value of the resource itself relative to the risk of harm or death and the value of their relationship with the competitor must be taken into consideration if the individual and group are to survive. "Sometimes the resource may not be worth the straining of a cooperative relationship, even if an individual could easily win the fight."[5] Peace instincts, distinct from inner peace in being less of a conscious state than a predisposition of which one can be unaware, play important roles in the everyday lives of primates. As with humans, two constant sources of social tension in primate groups are the drives for and necessity of food and reproduction, which spur conflicts between individuals of the same and other species. However, where primates have developed species-specific processes geared towards resolving conflicts and reducing tensions, humans have developed culture-specific processes to accomplish the same. Primatology, then, reflects and adds to the tools of peace studies disciplines that examine other periods.

For example, mating often "works to ease anxiety or tensions and to calm excitement" and so to "increase tolerance, which makes food-sharing smooth."[6] Another primate approach to peaceful coexistence is found in restorative behavior, which occurs after conflicts regardless of the amount and direction of previous aggression. The restorative behavior of rhesus monkeys includes a dramatic increase in lip-smacking and embracing during post-conflict reunions as compared to control contacts, whereas reconciling stumptail monkeys engage in the hold-bottom ritual, where one individual presents its hindquarters and the other clasps the other's haunches. Stumptail post-conflict behavior is called *explicit reconciliation* because conspicuous behavior rarely performed outside this context refers directly to the conflict, while peacemaking among rhesus is called *implicit reconciliation* because ordinary behavior is simply modified, thus only indirectly referring to the same. The restorative behavior of chimpanzees involves kissing, embracing, outstretched-hand invitations, and gentle touching. In contrast, reconciliation among bonobos typically involves mutual penis thrusting between males, genitor-genital rubbing between females and ventro-ventral and -dorsal mating between sexes. So for chimpanzees, post-conflict peacemaking means taking part in what may be called *affective reconciliation*, while for bonobos doing likewise means engaging in *sexual reconciliation*. A distinction emerges between two complementary kinds of peace-oriented activities among primates and later humans: one aims at sustaining peaceful coexistence, the other at restoring it after a temporary breach. The two together take on the characteristics of an *instinctual imperative* for peace.

Despite that its performance differs dramatically between species, in each case primate peacemaking through tension relief and restorative behavior serves the function of reconciling the parties involved in a conflict, reinforcing their peace instincts. If primates have developed ways to relieve tensions and use restorative behavior to sustain peaceful coexistence, what can this tell us about the history of peace among humans? Peace and peacemaking predate humanity in the sense that they evolved from those of primates from which our species descends. Taking a wider view, "evolution has led intra-species aggression, in the overwhelming number of species. . . to a non-lethal and non-violent form of behavior."[7] Humans inherited these innate peaceful capacities and learned abilities from primates, and only afterwards developed them distinctively for ourselves. Moreover, inter-species disparities in primate peacemaking parallel sharp contrasts between their equivalents among human cultural groups. One can easily imagine what would happen if a chimpanzee attempted to make peace with a bonobo, or a rhesus monkey with a stumptail, if neither party changes their peacemaking behavior: misinterpretation would lead to serious misunderstandings, putting the whole peace process in jeopardy. As heuristic models, such hypothetical situations among primate species are of great import to actual peace and peacemaking among different human cultures in that each demands the recognition of and adaptation to different conditions and participants to be successful.

Prehistoric Evolutions of Peace

Broadening primate instincts and social behavior into the early human realm, between our appearance as a species and our earliest prehistoric remains, several significant signs point to peace also being an advantageous, necessary and prevalent feature of human life and survival, even taking into account isolated evidence to the contrary. A standard definition of the earliest hominids posits two criteria: habitual bipedalism and a smaller dental apparatus relative to primates. Surprisingly, these two features may unlock the secrets of the origins of war and peace, confirming that peaceful cultural characteristics were prevalent throughout our early past and at least could have predated warlike ones. Walking upright, made possible by locking knees and a specific spinal structure, may arguably be the earliest origins of organized warfare as we know it, making its appearance with *Homo erectus* roughly 1.5 million years ago (MYA). Significantly smaller molars than primates, perhaps the earliest physiological evidence for peace among humans, as will be explained, made their appearance almost a million years earlier than walking upright, during the transition from ape-like Australopithecines to toolmaking *Homo habilis*. This second morphological modification in early humans, first chronologically, points to drastic changes in social relations and technology from those of earlier primates.

Early human social life probably resembled that of primates, who also form long-term relationships, actively engage in bonding and form strategic coalitions. However, primates are mostly nomadic and use their larger teeth for protection and as safeguards against changing food sources. *Homo habilis'* smaller molars are ineffective ways to threaten and masticate food from unpredictable sources. Such a pronounced adaptation implies that social relations and food sources had become and/or were made more stable and secure. Irenaus Eibl-Eibesfeldt's *The Biology of Peace and War: Men, Animals, and Aggression* (1979) suggests there is one way this anatomical change could have occurred: the development, over many generations, of cooperation and peaceful coexistence along with tool-making. The social patterns that permitted smaller molars, arguably the earliest evidence for peace, extend to more than 3 MYA, thus predating the possibility of recognizable warfare, walking upright, by at least 1.5 million years. Since the first humans who migrated out of the African continent came after the arrival of *Homo erectus*, it follows that a physiological basis for the existence of peace can be established before humans began populating the world. Even when violence becomes part of our paleontological record, in only four out of more than 110 Pleistocene (2.5–2 MYA) hominid fossil sites, "the known data is not sufficient to document warfare," taken as systemic rather than sporadic.[8]

Some archaeologists see the earliest evidence of warfare in fortifications around Jericho about 9500 years ago, probably for control over hunting-trading routes. Others see the first documented war, most likely over disputed hunting grounds, taking place in Bavaria roughly 8500 years ago, as evidenced in the Ofnet cave in Southern Germany, where decapitated skulls of women and children were found. Although lack of proof cannot in itself prove the absence of war in prehistory – as these sites show, war no doubt did exist in some form and for some time – the tremendous time lapse between the first available evidence of peace and that of war distinguished from violence is highly suggestive. The imagined warlike qualities of early humans put forth by influential social theorists such as Thomas Hobbes thus prove to be less than factual, while romantic theories of peace such as that of Jean-Jacques Rousseau, resting on peacefulness as the defining characteristic of early human societies, turn out to be no less fanciful. In his review of the relevant literature, Sponsel put forth the provocative principle that the potential for peace is latent in humanity or, more succinctly, that "peace is natural."[9] But to say that peace is natural in no way implies that it was or is easy, effortless or straightforward. Conversely, Charles Darwin and followers advance that it is precisely because peace is natural that its fulfillment requires overcoming the stressors, obstacles and complexities intrinsic to nature.

"Survival of the fittest," an expression coined not by Darwin but Herbert Spencer, is seen by theorists of evolution today as constantly working on at least two related levels, both of which are inextricable from the evolution of peace and peacemaking among humans from prehistory to today.[10] The expression commonly conveys individual organisms' ability to compete with other organisms of the same species for mates and with individual organisms of other species as well as their own for limited resources. But the expression also refers to "super-organisms,"a term also coined by Spencer to designate groups that function as organic wholes, such as ant colonies and human societies.[11] Survival of the fittest in relation to super-organisms means that the most competitive ones for resources on an inter-group level are those that function best on an intra-group level. Peace-related factors in optimal internal cooperation and external competitiveness include sympathy, mutual aid and social cohesion, as exemplified inhuman evolution. In *The Descent of Man* (1871), Darwin proposed that sympathy was and is what gives our species its definite super-organic advantage over others. "Those communities," he explains, "which included the greatest number of the most sympathetic members would flourish best, and rear the greatest number of offspring."[12] By this statement and others, Darwin opened the door to an evolutionary perspective on peaceful traits increasing the likelihood of survival. Peter Kropotkin was one of the first to elaborate upon this perspective in *Mutual Aid: A Factor of Evolution* (1902). Building on Darwin's work, his major contribution lies in the evolutionary model of mutual aid he put forth: "the fittest are not the physically strongest, nor the cunningest, but those who learn to combine so as mutually to support each other, strong and weak alike, for the welfare of the community."[13] Mutual aid and competition are complementary forces in natural selection in that they bring about interdependencies between individuals within a super-organism which simultaneously benefit the peace and survival of a species. Peace is problematic precisely because it is national.

A more recent analysis of human evolution relative to war begins by acknowledging that sympathy and mutual aid have been invaluable traits in defense and offense at all stages of humanity's evolution in bolstering social cohesion.[14] For most species, social cohesion simply signifies super-organic unity when faced with scarcity and adversity; for humans, it has the added significance of being united in principles, interests and goals. Social cohesion is an evolutionary advantageous trait insofar as it fosters day-to-day and strategic cooperation, making human groups and individuals more competitive relative to other species. Sympathy, mutual aid and social cohesion are now widely recognized by biologists as primary human evolutionary peace processes under the rubric of *mutualism*, the principle of interdependence as a condition of individual and group survival and welfare. The neologism *survival of the peaceful*, then, denotes that peaceful individual and group traits are more than bio-genetically advantageous; culturally, they are necessary for humanity's survival. In other words, just as individual human beings are how the fittest genetic systems are propagated, human societies are the vehicles through which the most peaceful cultures do the same because two imperatives in addition to the instinctual have jointly shaped human evolution and the evolution of peace.[15]

On the one hand, *bio-genetic imperatives* such as food and reproduction maximize self-interested behavior. On the other, *cultural imperatives* such as sympathy and mutual aid maximize pro-social behavior. Some socio-biologists have rationalized why self-interestedness works with, not against, pro-sociality by postulating a theory of reciprocal altruism, the truism that I scratch your back because and only because you scratch mine. However, by focusing on bio-genetic imperatives to the neglect of cultural ones, reciprocal altruism only partially resolves the "conflict between altruism as a necessary condition of social peace and self-care as a necessary condition of individual preservation."[16] A seminal anthropological analysis outlines group traits that usually either enhance or inhibit peaceful cultural imperatives.[17] Traits generally present in peaceful cultures include dynamically structured groups, ubiquitous face-to-face interactions, established enculturation mechanisms, collective action through group consensus and an overall egalitarian ethos. Traits generally absent from peaceful cultures include inter- and intra-group feuding, endemic external threats, social stratification, centralized authority and military or police organizations. Concurrently, cultural transformation theory proposes that two social structures underlie peaceful and non-peaceful cultures, respectively.[18] The partnership structure is non-hierarchical and egalitarian, generating cooperative and nurturing societies. The dominator structure rests on hierarchies backed by authoritarian threat and force, beginning with male and female, generating cultures of fear and repression.

Although bio-genetic imperatives have historically caused dominator social structures to spring up temporarily, cultural imperatives ensure the survival of partnership social structures in the long-run. So while peace is advantageous in the bio-genetic survival of all species, it must prevail in order for human cultures to survive. To be more precise, both bio-genetic and cultural imperatives have and will continue to play a catalytic role in the evolution of humanity and peace, without which we would not have survived as we did, if we would have at all. In conjunction with bio-genetics and culture, feeding behavior and habitat were driving forces behind human evolution. The development of gathering, hunting and agriculture can be taken as extending the evolution of peace from a survival strategy into one of subsistence as well. Sometime after 1.7 MYA, the first home bases appear in the archaeological record. The structure of this semi-sedentary social system was threefold, arranged around: (a) field camps for short stays on food expeditions, (b) collecting or kill sites where food production took place, and (c) home bases proper, where food was collectively consumed. Compared to eons of quasi-primate nomadism that came before, home bases were perhaps the most important social units in prehistoric times, and certainly are in the evolution of peace, because they integrated traits central to peaceful human behavior and social life from then till now, including "reciprocity systems, exchange, kinship, subsistence, division of labor, and language."[19] Pragmatic proposals for peace since that have not drawn upon one or more of these traits are few and far between.

The earliest mode of subsistence based on the home base social structure, gathering, laid the foundations of two features integral to future peace and peacemaking: conscientiousness and language-use. With gathering, humans stopped eating on the spot with whoever happened to be participating in the expedition; instead, we began making premeditated decisions to take others into consideration, to be patient and self-restrained, because we consciously had secure enough relationships to make the trade-offs worthwhile. Gathering could only be effective if information was shared, which is why both linguistic communication and the larger brain size language-use requires are considered its derivations. The symbolic systems used later in peacemaking were thus not add-ons to peaceful human behavior, but extensions of it. Synthesizing scavenging and tool-making, early hunting economies were usually mixed with gathering. This hunter-gatherer mode of subsistence is unique to our species, represents 99 percent of our existence so far, and so may be "the single most important factor in the emergence of mankind," as well as in the evolution of peace.[20] Some of the earliest evidence of hunting was found in Boxgrove, England, where about 500,000 years ago hunters trapped many large game animals between a watering hole and a cliff, where they were finally killed. Violence aside, these tactics display at least two other elements essential to ensuing peace and peacemaking: planning and organization. The choice between using such tactics for food or against other humans was based on bio-genetic and cultural imperatives of survival, and our existence attests to the choice made more often.

Planning and organization were also necessary in the emergence of agricultural modes of subsistence, such as the seasonal growing of crops and the herding of domesticated animals, which only began roughly 10,000 years ago. Early agriculture advanced two other traits central to the evolution of peace: stable surpluses and the effective management they require. Regular use of coercive force becomes part of the structure of human societies only after the advent of agriculture and its cultural characteristics. But this statement should not be mistaken for saying that agriculture is the origin of warfare. On the contrary, like hunter-gatherers before them, prehistoric agriculturally based societies most likely lacked the time, resources and leadership necessary to sustain or withstand extended modern warlike endeavors. By making food surpluses more stable than hunting and gathering alone, agriculture facilitated rather than impeded subsistence peace among prehistoric and modern humans. It is thus both plausible and probable that prehistoric subsistence societies were as predominantly peaceful. Standing armies and police organizations only make their appearance about 5000 years ago, when irrigation and trade intensified agricultural practices. But the former would not have been possible or necessary had not the latter led to a material abundance permitting settlements tens to thousands times greater than home bases – the first cities, states and civilizations, on which more below.

Given the dearth of records of human social life in prehistoric times, the cultural profiles of certain contemporary societies may in hindsight provide the "widest window on the largest part of our species' history," and that of the prehistory of peace.[21] Without projecting backwards, anthropological studies of peace substantiate the claim that simple societies are or at least can be, more peaceful than complex ones and thus have a lot to teach them. One of the uncommon but astonishing features of such societies is that peaceful cultural imperatives such as altruism coupled with propitious ecological conditions have made them as close to totally non-violent as societies may probably ever be. The Tasaday of the Philippines, for example, are said to have no weapons and no words for anger, murder, war or enemy. For this reason, their way of life has been interpreted as reflecting the "elemental pacific qualities of human nature," in Sponsel's words.[22] Of course, violence breaks out in all simple societies, but malevolence aside the intent behind its use generally tends to be to restore peace. To this end, another striking feature common among simple societies is *counter-dominant behavior*, by which individuals whose self-interested, bio-genetic imperatives outproportion their pro-social, cultural imperatives are systematically shunned and stripped of their prerogatives. Among the implication of these exemplars is that while peace as a state and peacemaking as a process can transcend cultural contingencies and diversities, they are also immanently within them.

To prevent the necessity of counter-dominant behavior, the enculturation process of the Semai, considered the best-documented case of a pacific simple society, includes children learning to become peaceful through the games they play. Rituals and ceremonies also play vital roles in keeping the balance between the benefits of partnership and drawbacks of domination. Facing their abolition by Christian missionaries in the nineteenth century, the chief of the Hokianga of New Zealand was quoted as saying that ritual feasts "have many times been the means of keeping the peace between us, and may be of service again."[23] Early in the twentieth century, the Murngin of Australia continued to practice *makarata*, or what an anthropologist describes as "ceremonial peacemaking fights" in which aggression was condoned as a means of releasing anger and restoring peace.[24] When hierarchical social structures are present in pacific simple societies, practices such as the doubling of political roles and places are typically in place to counterbalance the dangers of their abuse. The widespread Polynesian practice of chiefs acting simultaneously as the agents of war and as dispensers of peace fits this model, as do concepts of sanctuary and asylum in chief-designated locations for native Hawaiian peoples, places and timeframes of absolution for transgressors. This body of anthropological research also supports Eibl-Eibesfeldt's conclusion to his monumental ethological study of humanity: "war, defined as strategically planned, destructive group aggression, is a product of cultural evolution. Therefore, it can be overcome culturally."[25]

Peace, Peacemaking and the First Civilizations

The roles peace and peacemaking played in the ancient cultures that arose around the fertile valleys of the Tigris and Euphrates Rivers have just begun to be unraveled. It is not only peace that is lost in war in what is now Iraq, where the first historic cities, states and civilizations emerged *c.* 3500 BCE, but history itself. At the threshold of history, peace is still to be grasped as evolving, though in an even more cyclical sense than in prehistory. Changing conditions and participants – actively recorded for the first known time – shaped peace and peacemaking, which in turn altered conditions and participants, and so on. Studying the history of peace in this evolutionary way reveals as much about the origins of civilizations as their ongoing traits. Such a comprehensive perspective on Mesopotamian ("between rivers") peace practices can be drawn from the French historians of the Annales School. Integrating geography, social sciences and historiography, they saw warfare as only one of many factors contributing to the overall makeup of an era (*sic*), focusing instead on long-term structural and cultural changes. This perspective is valuable in exploring the transformation from geographically isolated, culturally homogenous home bases and villages to economically interconnected, culturally heterogeneous cities that sponsored states and made possible *civilized peace*: an ideal, a means to an end and an end in itself. Inasmuch, civilized peace was concurrently the *raison d'être* of Mesopotamian states as well as the prerequisite and underlying motive for their wars.

The identifying traits of Mesopotamian villages before 3500 BCE are their subsistence-level surpluses, economic autonomy, little differentiation between town and country, communal property, local gods and despotic rule. In contrast, the city of Mari's archives (fl. 2900–1750 BCE), for example, point to economically and politically interdependent centers characterized by overall material abundance due to irrigation; distinctions of class, occupation, place of origin, as well as public and private property; trade networks; organized religions; and shifting cooperative and defensive alliances. The meanings of peace and peacemaking at the cusp of village and city life are captured by its first known word in a written

Indo-European language, Hittite. In village contexts, making and maintaining peace meant to protect, guard and keep things or people safe as well as defending them against internal and external dangers, meanings equally applicable to the subsistence peace of home bases. In city contexts, however, peace and peacemaking took on the added meanings of being tolerant, observing agreements, laws and customs, keeping oaths and heeding advice, meanings which apply unevenly to home bases and villages, if at all.

The village-linked meanings of peace are predominantly reactive and protectionist; those specifically tied to cities, proactive and integrationist. A clear sign of this fundamental change in peace and peacemaking can be found in the earliest evidence of *urban imperatives for peace* in its Hittite sense, cylinder seals, the imprints of which were used to authenticate documents and reproduce standardized statements. Cylinder seals were unnecessary and unused in village life, in which verbal agreements between close relations were adequate to prevent and resolve conflicts. In cosmopolitan city life, however, written agreements tendered by cylinder seals were necessary tools in legitimizing and preserving ties between parties whose relationships were much less secure. That is, shared identities and interests of tight-knit village communities were sufficient to safeguard kin-group solidarity and non-kin affiliations, also essential to sustaining peaceful coexistence in cities. But the meanings of urban peace embodied in cylinder seals were crucial survival and subsistence strategies of Mesopotamian cities and their citizens insofar as they facilitated cooperation and averted war between individuals and groups with different identities and interests. Without these social and collective functions being expressed in a permanent way, fulfilled legitimately on previously agreed upon terms, it is doubtful that Mesopotamian cities could have borne the more abstract formations of states and civilizations.

A graphic entry point into the coterminous worlds of peace and war in Mesopotamia can be found in the earliest mosaic yet unearthed, set on a trapezoidal stone (presented on the following page). The archaeologists who discovered the mosaic while excavating graves in the Sumerian city of Ur identified it as a standard, carried like a banner before the state's army. This function explains the "war side" (above), in which donkey-drawn chariots charge over fallen enemies, spearmen in helmets and cloaks seize prisoners, and captives are brought before a centralized authority figure. By making clear what would happen to enemies if battles were won, or to allies if lost, this fearsome sight may have been part of "the earliest and crudest means to avoiding war," deterrence: the prevention of aggression by threat of retaliation.[26] The high value of the materials and workmanship involved suggests that the mosaic was emblematic of Sumerian economic and political prowess in

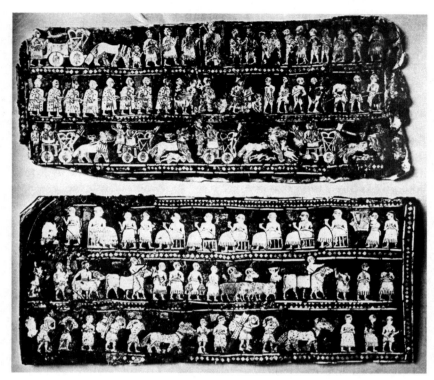

The Mosaic of Ur, *c.* 2650 BCE

Mesopotamia at the time. Sumerians were, after all, the first to found cities like Ur, the cornerstones of Mesopotamian states, which were nearly always ruled by one male leader. Such a leader is symbolized by the centralized authority figure on the war side but conspicuously absent from the "peace side" (below), portraying a lively banquet with leisurely attendants serenaded by lyres, enjoying each other's company and the gifts of the rivers, such as grains, sheep, goats and fish. This pointed detail launches one of the oldest debates in peace studies, whether "war helps to make states, states make war, and therefore states are in part, and always must be, war machines."[27] Archaeologists since the mosaic's discovery have interpreted its function as the sound box of a musical instrument, a credible rationale for the peace side. Either as a centerpiece at a feast or a rallying point in battle, this reassuring sight and its possible sounds likely were a strong reminder of the shared experience and vision of the civilized peace Sumerians considered worth celebrating and fighting for.

The mosaic's mixed messages regarding the relationships between states, war, civilization and peace echo across two millennia of Mesopotamian history and beyond. Namely, that the constructive ideal of civilized peace, lived or striven for, may paradoxically be the only force capable of sustaining as well as counteracting the destructive actualities of state warfare. In any case, the mosaic's juxtaposition of state warfare and civilized peace is the earliest evidence of the two being put into close material and conceptual proximity, inaugurating one of the longest running analytical traditions in the history of peace. Like villages before them, "no city can exist if it does not draw on surpluses of food, and in most cases this comes from the surrounding land;" it was the hydraulic revolution of irrigation that converted the sporadic, subsistence-level surpluses of Mesopotamian villages into the material abundance needed to sustain their cities, states and civilizations.[28] War was comparatively rare in Mesopotamia before the hydraulic revolution, and so the advent of irrigation tends to be seen as spurring integrations of military or police forces (a distinction which tended to be blurred) into local political systems, though only at minimal levels, when at all. But before two or more cities would go to war, other cities often attempted to diffuse the situation, resulting in unexpected unions between the cities concerned. If this juncture is taken as the starting point of regional state systems, as some historians of the period concur, then the peace-oriented concept of neutrality and role of moderator must be recognized as primary channels of inter-city relations and statehood.

Intra-city peace and prosperity were primarily predicated upon links between land and social structures, or *geo-social configurations*, significantly more complex than in villages. Sumerian land was divided into that belonging to the state, given temporarily to officials as part of their salaries and rented out. Babylon, which succeeded Sumerian hegemony, had three classes: those to whom the leader granted full liberty and all privileges of citizenship; those who, though free, were subject to legal restrictions related to land; and those who had no rights or freedoms, or slaves. As one's place in the social order was synonymous with one's place in the land, one's obligations towards and benefits from state warfare or civilized peace were entrenched in the earth. Geo-social configurations were top peacekeeping priorities in Mesopotamia because they kept conflicts of interest in check by balancing (or not) public and private needs. Nowhere is the import of this balance to peace and prosperity more clear than in the rises and falls of Babylon's religious centre, Nippur. The city flourished in peace for centuries by balancing between being an integrative public place and a social space delimited by distinctions based on private property. Granting land to government officials as salaries led to the privatization of public property, the principal cause of the city's decline into the disorder of civil war. When the balance was restored through geo-social engineering, Nippur's peace and prosperity returned. At the other end of the public-private spectrum, the Jewish prophet Isaiah (*c.* 700 BCE) protested to his fellow Mesopotamians: "woe to those who join house to house/ who add field to field/ until there is no more room."[29] Latifundization, creations of progressively larger public estates by dispossessing private landowners usually tied to an increase in social stratification, was as potent a sign of cities' decline as over-privatization. The Assyrian and Persian states began declining after systematically expunging farmers from their lands, who were frequently sold into slavery to recover their debts in order to assuage their life-threatening poverty.

Researchers studying social stratification agree that with it comes a form of *structural violence* which can compromise peaceful coexistence, such as systemic inequality and injustice, and on this point Mesopotamian cities are no exception.[30] Textual evidence suggests that the distinctions between slave/free and native/foreign may have a common origin. While slaves and foreigners were denied many of the privileges of civilized peace citizens took for granted, native freemen could enjoy them in full. Yet, slaves and foreigners were often conscripted or otherwise forced to participate in state warfare regardless of their non-citizen status, creating a dangerous double standard states depend upon like a thorny crutch. The crippling effects over-privatization, latifundization and structural violence had on the welfare of Mesopotamians were similar. Balanced geo-social configurations offset them in the short term by sustaining the material abundance necessary to the very existence of cities, states and civilization. In the long term, only by balancing public and private needs did Mesopotamians enjoy peace, prosperity and technological advances unrivalled in the world at the time. Snippets of economic theory show that they knew equitable economic policies are directly related to domestic peace. Rulers attempted to prevent civil war by issuing edicts, like one by a king of Babylon (*c.* 1600 BCE) which declared certain loans illegal and some taxes temporarily suspended. A millennium earlier, a ruler issued similar edicts just two years after he came to power. He sought to restore prosperity by prohibiting the exploitation of the poor, ending oppressive taxes and limiting state regulation of the economy, described as necessary in wartime but detrimental in times of peace.

In the Sumerian tradition, leaders' activities "concentrated upon the works of peace," already discussed, and "the building of temples;" one complemented rather than contradicted the other.[31] By far the largest buildings in Mesopotamia were steppe temples, or ziggurats, religious and administrative centers of cities and states. The organized religions they represented created new justifications for war, but also new possibilities in peacemaking. Secular life and religious life were apparently inseparable, as officials combined "what we would see as priestly and civil authority."[32] Yet, organized religions contributed to the history of peace in their own right. Leaders customarily doubled as religious and political, leveraging their war- and peacemaking powers. Leaders backed military campaigns with the joint forces of Church and State, but they also prevented and resolved conflicts in the same way. Another major consequence of expanding inter-city relations was that local gods, who had reigned supreme for centuries, now had to contend other religious beliefs, practices and figureheads. Peacemaking among competing organized religions frequently took the form of two or more local gods being fused into one regional god either at once or over time, as in the prominent god Ahura-Mazda. As long as regional authority rested with the religious and political representatives of Ahura-Mazda, local beliefs could go on as they had for centuries.

Degrees of religious amalgamation ranged from all-inclusive religious synthesis, known as *syncretism*, to worshiping one god without denying others, or *henotheism*, which generally outproportioned syncretism in Mesopotamia. When they failed preemptively, such procedures could further post-war peace. Typical of these religious peace processes, Assyrian armies would return religious objects to the citizens of a conquered city, and post-war peace terms were finalized by oaths evoking both Assyrian and non-Assyrian gods. Following anthropologist Claude Levi-Strauss, who proposed that a civilization's myths can serve as allegorical maps of its social structures and cultural assumptions, multiple versions of the same Mesopotamian myths can be read as reflecting the pacific fluidity syncretic and henotheistic peace processes imply. For instance, many editions of *Enuma Elish* (c. 1200 BCE), the era's most widespread cosmogony, from different places and in a variety of languages have been found, each adapted to local traditions, indicating that a conscious effort was made to foster common regional identities through rather than against local ones. An earlier narrative loosely based on a Babylonian ruler, *Gilgamesh* (c. 2700 BCE), was passed down orally in the region for seven hundred years before it was set in stone with local variations. The moral of *Gilgamesh* is that violence, whether structural or outright, by rulers like the story's namesake, leads inevitably to their downfall. Conversely, those who live and lead peacefully can avert disasters as great as floods, as did Utnapishtim, the man Gilgamesh takes as his mentor but from whom he does not learn.

In Mesopotamia, then, "king and god reinforced each other's legitimacy," if legitimacy is taken to mean the perception that power is moderately exercised according to moral and cultural norms.[33] Sociohistorical studies show that the legitimacy of leaders generates socially cohesive group loyalty and collective identity so that, statistically, warfare occurs less frequently in the earlier than in the later stages of states, when the legitimacy of leaders is less likely to be fully intact. The centripetal propensity of political legitimization was of particular importance to the peace and peacemaking of the early large-scale empires in Mesopotamia. For example, at its zenith, the Persian Empire founded by Cyrus II (r. c. 559–30 BCE) covered roughly 6 million kilometers in size, enclosed about 35 million people and lasted for more than 200 years. In order to maintain peace in such vast territories and among such a diversity of people, leaders like Cyrus sought legitimacy in meaningful and effective ways. This meant affirming "strength in peace and war, by his justice in upholding a fair and benevolent law, and by sharing and investing the enormous capital at his disposal to the benefit of his poorer subjects."[34] The issuance of coins by the state was also developed as a way to reduce transactional friction and for non-violently "asserting its fiscal if not political independence," the designs of which could serve as propaganda for takes on civilized peace.[35] But implementing these plans and public relations campaigns for the prosperity upon which peace depends were inadequate on their own.

Overextended empires without effective political systems and leaders who promised more than they could deliver often fell in civil war or by invasion, precluding any kind of peace. Governmental decentralization, balancing regional authority and local autonomy, was one way leaders of larger and more complex states maintained peace and power legitimately. To this end, the Persian Empire was divided into twenty administrative districts, each of which kept its own surpluses, records and police force. Persian rulers earned the loyalty of foreign subjects by leaving their traditions intact, making selective non-interference another legitimate cross-cultural peacekeeping option. Post-war political integration was perhaps the surest path to peacemaking taken by Cyrus. Not only did he adapt Persian practices to foreign customs, he cultivated natives capable of wielding power on his behalf. Cyrus is also credited with being the first known ruler to enlarge his holdings not by attacking neighbors, but by being attacked by them. The clichés that the best offense is the best defense, and that preparing for war is the best way to prepare for peace, can thus in retrospect be validly applied as far back as the first civilizations.

More than a thousand years before Cyrus was Hammurabi (c. 1810–1750 BCE), first emperor of the Babylonian Empire he founded. An early study claims that "peace and prosperity prevailed during his reign," though more recent research confines this preponderantly peaceful period to the first two decades Hammurabi ruled.[36] He improved agricultural practices, balanced geo-social configurations and put equitable economic policies. The god Marduk's syncretic and henotheistic ascendancy has also been attributed to Hammurabi. The earliest known non-military uses of military personnel are his army's expeditions aimed not at defeating enemies, but at collecting materials for ziggurats. Successes in these respects prompted the military expansion of the second half of his reign, but conquests complete he continued to rule according to peaceful principles. Hammurabi set forth these principles in his famous *Code of Laws* (*c.* 1780 BCE), carved on black stone monuments eight feet in height and strategically placed across his empire. The importance of Hammurabi's legislation lies in its codification of Mesopotamian legal tradition rather than in the originality of its content. While literacy was far from common, all Babylonians were subject to the *Code*, which broadly regulated society and prescribed specific punishments for particular crimes. Laws cover theft and bodily harm, pastoral practices, as well as the rights of women, children and slaves, among other issues, which invaluably contributed to the future history of peace by influencing "all subsequent legislation."[37]

2

Peace in the Ancient West:
Egypt, Greece and Rome

A Tale of Two Worlds: Peace and Peacemaking in Ancient Egypt

If the peace and peacemaking of Ancient Egyptians seem infeasible or impracticable in retrospect, the rift between modern mindsets and their religious beliefs accounts for much of this perception. *Maat* and *Ka*, the two religious concepts most relevant to the history of peace in Ancient Egypt, may serve to bridge the gap. According to the religious beliefs that permeated Ancient Egyptian life, peace and peacemaking in this world were directly related to those in the next. Pharaohs were considered gods who protect the heavens but also ones who maintain peace on earth. *Maat*, initially the word for truth/justice and later personified as a goddess, invoked the idea of cosmic order and was considered the Pharaoh's primary duty to uphold. *Maat* was the Pharaohs' active and ongoing pledge that the universe would be conducive to their subjects' welfare by their transformation of the "cosmic divine *Maat* into the *Maat* of a firmly established social order with good government maintaining peace, justice and stability."[1] This pledge to defend their people's peace and prosperity became the justification for Pharaohs' absolute power over them, the consistent logic of *oppressive peace* ever since and everywhere.

While *Maat* was a collective force mediated by Pharaohs, *Ka* was the Ancient Egyptian term for the peaceful life-force tied to an individual's body. Spectacular sepulchers like the Pyramids and highly elaborate burial rites represent Ancient Egyptians' attempts to assure *Ka*'s individual, and *Maat*'s collective, spiritual peacebefore and after physical death, the two being as inseparable as life and the afterlife was for them. Texts like *The Loyalist Instruction from the Sehetepibre Stela* (*c.* 1800 BCE) substantiate the links between the eternal life-force (*Ka*), an orthodox way of life (*Maat*) and physical as well as spiritual peace. In the case of Pharaohs, *Ka* was in addition seen as the divine essence of their authority and the source of their power to which all their subjects owed allegiance, the spiritual element of which partly continued to exist independently and partly transferred to the successor upon a Pharaoh's physical death. When Pharaohs died, they became Osiris, who presided over peace on earth. Like their predecessors, new Pharaohs then became Horus, protector of the heavens, completing a conservative cycle symbolized by the rising and setting of the sun. While earlier and later monarchs were often considered their deities' representatives or petitioners in the physical world, Pharaohs were believed to embody them. So whereas the god Thoth acted as *moderator* between conflicting deities as among humans, Pharaohs were first and foremost *mediators* between the spiritual and physical realms. Pharaohs' legitimacy, and with it the peace of the people, started and ended with fulfillment of their cosmically indispensable role through the performance of prescribed rituals and the implementation of particular policies, upon which two worlds' prosperity rested.

Ancient Egyptian religious beliefs further backed pacific uses of Pharaonic authority and power by fusing the temporal, physical conditions of control and influence with eternal, spiritual meanings and purposes. For the first time on record, and far from the last, peace thus became an explicit *religious imperative* where it may have been only an implicit one before. In keeping with this principle, Pharaohs realized early on that rallying the support of their subjects and gods in pursuit of immediate physical and everlasting spiritual peace could be greatly facilitated by representations as far from ephemeral as possible – one reason why, as Egyptologists today hold, the Pyramids were not and could not have been built solely by slaves. "The Great Pyramids are not only impressive monuments to the kings who built them; they are even more imposing as monuments to an age of peace and security."[2] Although this statement plays up oppressive peace, the construction of the first pyramid at Memphis under the Pharaoh Djoser (*c.* 2668–49) nonetheless marks a sharp turning point in the history of Western peace. From the Pyramid Age onwards, Western religious rulers and activists alike have almost universally tied spiritual peace to the physical world and peace on earth to the spiritual world through more or less lasting symbols of collective beliefs. However, recent research indicates that the history of peace in Ancient Egypt predates the Pharaohs. Predynastic unification by social, economic and political conciliations set precedents Pharaohs sidestepped only at their peril.

Pharaohs' position as religious mediators between spiritual and physical worlds reflected and enhanced their roles as conciliators between what became Upper and Lower Egypt. In this context, *conciliation* can be understood as overcoming apprehension, making compatible and/or settling disagreements by mutually beneficial arrangements. Archaeologists speculate that the peoples of the Nile passed through three distinct conciliatory phases culminating in the unification of Ancient Egypt under the dynastic rule of Pharaohs. During the first phase, complete by 5000 BCE, three separate societies developed along the Nile: one centered at This, the other two at Naqada and Hierakonpolis, respectively. In the second phase, ending a millennium later, rulers of these capitals strengthened and secured their respective dominions. How This gained control of the whole Nile over the course of the third phase remains unknown, but the "annexation of neighboring territories must have involved negotiation and accommodation at the very least," a supposition backed by an as of yet unexplained dearth of coercive force in the formation of the unified Egyptian state *c.* 3000 BCE.[3] The conciliatory dynamics of predynastic Egypt ultimately led to the unified Pharaonic state, calling into question the assumption that warfare is inevitable in state formation. Whatever forms they took, and only further research can tell, social, political and economic conciliations were so effective in uniting Upper and Lower Egypt, they superseded the use of coercive force past and future potentates frequently found necessary or desirable. The ruling families at This steered Upper and Lower Egypt into a twin state system, and like that of the two worlds, its unified existence depended on peace among its parts.

The divisions Egyptologists ascribe to the Dynastic periods correlate to the *unitive peace* Pharaohs were able to achieve. Early and Old Kingdoms Pharaohs further advanced conciliation in their administrative practices. Titles such as "The Two Powers are at Peace" and evidence that Pharaohs paid foreigners for domestic peacekeeping, presumably to avoid pitting Egyptian against Egyptian, suggest that they tried to limit friction in centralizing power. To concentrate channels of power from the top downwards and from the centre outwards, the capital was established on the border of the two lands. Legitimization thus took on centrifugal tendencies, whereas in Mesopotamia they had been centripetal. Thanks to these efforts, one emphatic historian claims this was a time of "unexampled prosperity for Egypt, a supremely tranquil time of peace."[4] A rhetoric of peace also developed, as both official and lay records of the age are "full of praises of peace and almost pacifist formulations."[5] A didactic work on statecraft, for example, posits: "If you are a leader of peace, listen to the discourse of the petitioner."[6] Similarly, the refrain of a poem in a prominent magistrate's autobiography reads "This army returned in peace" – not in victory or defeat.[7] So while armies no doubt did exist, their primary purpose may have been to keep the peace rather than to break it.

Seven centuries of unitive peace ended when Upper and Lower Egypt split in only one or two generations. Archaeologists surmise that an ecological catastrophe created a hungry, riotous population that remained so for another seven centuries in the First Intermediate Period. If *pacification* is taken to mean the creation or restoration of peace by coercive appeasement and forced submission, the assassination of the first Pharaoh of the Middle Kingdom is a sign that he was perhaps too great a pacificator. By paradoxically waging domestic wars to bring back unitive peace, Amenemhet I achieved his ends but also met his. He promulgated oppressive peace by pacification in *The Teaching of King Amenemhet I to his son Senusret*, who like his successors "reaped the benefit of the peace and prosperity" of previous reigns. That this policy was a constant throughout the period can be surmised in its capital's name, "Seizer of the Two Lands," and of its only woman and last Pharaoh, "Beauties of Sobek," a god whose cult was dedicated to pacifying crocodiles.[8] She died without an heir and the ensuing scramble for succession started the disarray of the Second Intermediate Period, ending with the Hyksos' successful invasion and foreign rule. Native rulers of Thebes carried out campaigns to liberate Egypt, resulting in a reunified New Kingdom with them as Pharaohs. Cyclic nadirs of divisive decline followed by pinnacles of prosperity repeated in the Third Intermediate Period and Late Kingdom, proving unitive peace was essential to the survival of the Pharaonic state.

However, two developments in Egyptian internal and external affairs require attention at this point. Theban domestic peace policies took on reconciliatory tones before liberation was complete, distinguishable from conciliation in that *reconciliation* has the benefits and drawbacks of established precedents. As mentioned, such precedents included religious, cultural, social, political, economic and administrative conciliations. New and Late Kingdom Pharaohs re-achieved unitive peace by reconciliation, not conciliation. The trouble with attempting internal conciliation with such a considerable reconciliatory toolbox at hand is exemplified in the rapid rise and fall of Atenism, the first known attempt at a universal monotheistic religion. According to an early twentieth-century appraisal of Atenism's first and only prophet, the Pharaoh Akhenaton (*c.* 1352–36 BCE): "When the world reverberated with the noise of war, he preached the first known doctrine of peace. . . He was the first Pharaoh to be a humanitarian."[9] Had this been true, he and Atenism would probably not have been almost completely erased from the official records soon after his death. Historians today claim that Akhenaton brought about the downfall of Atenism himself by working against the grain of Egyptian religious traditions while heightening instead of resolving tensions between the kingdom's centre and periphery. Along these lines, Akhenaton outlawed local languages and forced the adoption of the contemporary Egyptian one throughout the reunified kingdom. Akhenaton's linguistic policies mirrored his religious ones: in the past, new or renewed gods were henotheistically or syncretically absorbed into extant traditions rather than displacing them outright. The sun god Aten appears in centuries-old texts, and so could have been used to further religious reconciliation. Akhenaton's attempt to impose Aten as the two kingdoms' one and only god was thus at best misguided. At worst, his conciliatory policies dereconciled his people from their deities and each other, shaking the very foundation of unitive peace between the two worlds as between the two kingdoms.

The second notable development is that, as part of their foreign peace policies infused with lessons from the past, New and Late Kingdom Pharaohs created buffer zones between their territory and those of potential invaders by establishing extra-territorial trading posts, diplomatic outposts, way-stations and even permanent settlements, all of which were required to pay tribute to the Pharaoh. This tributary system was an important economic means of supporting oppressive peace and reconciliation within the kingdoms. But it was also vital in maintaining cross-border control in serving "to pay respect, to display deference, to give an earnest of peaceful intentions, and to placate the distant and more powerful sovereign in the hope that peace will continue to prevail."[10] The system's strength was its creation of bonds of loyalty and protection between distant and different peoples; its weakness was that these bonds were themselves weak despite the dependencies they created. Due in part to the system's effectiveness, a relative unimportance of warfare to Pharaohs' foreign policies is discernable in their outdated arms and ritualistically docile tactics compared to better equipped and fiercer foreign contemporaries. But this military asymmetry also explains how first the Libyans then the Nubians conquered Egypt. Their failures in sustaining foreign rule where Pharaohs' tributary systems succeeded show that, then as now, military might alone is not enough to guarantee post-war peace.

The historic actions of one Pharaoh make clear how this peace principle can be and was applied. Ramses the Great (c. 1279–13 BCE) is said to have lived to be 96 years old, had some 200 wives and concubines, 96 sons and 60 daughters. His prowess in familial affairs is of direct import to peace. As in past and later times, marriages between rulers and the installation of their children in high posts were key means of preserving the socio-political stability oppressive peace required, especially after successful foreign wars, even at the risk of rivalries that could lead to civil war. The import of actual or symbolic kinship ties on diplomatic relations is clear in a letter sent by Ramses to another ruler: "Know that in the true condition of *peace and fraternity* in which I now am with the great King of Khatti, I will abide therein for all eternity."[11] This avowal is verbatim to one made by his wife to a queen she calls her "sister," in which she describes the "situation of true peace and true fraternity of the great king, the King of Egypt, with the great king, the King of Khatti, his brother."[12] The coordinated rhetoric implies an unprecedented, consciously concerted campaign for peace, which Ramses coupled with first-time war tactics in the earliest major military campaign for which extensive records exist. He was in his twenties when he succeeded his father, whose battlefield exploits he experienced firsthand and emulated. They taught him that quick, successful battles or the appearance thereof could further the cause of post-war peace, a climax of which was the Battle of Kadesh (*c.* 1285 BCE) against Hittites over whom the King of Khatti later ruled.

If the "major problems in war and politics are how to end a battle and how to end a war" then Ramses' solutions in this case were groundbreaking.[13] During the battle, he revolutionized military logistics by introducing the quicker ox-drawn cart instead of standard donkey-drawn ones, probably in an attempt to provide faster aid to the injured so as to limit casualties as well as to hasten the battle's end. Although it was indecisive, both sides came to realize that the rise of Assyria demanded a coalition to be deterred, so enemies became allies to offset a common threat. The peace treaty between Ramses and the Hittite King that inaugurated this alliance has been called "the first diplomatic instrument of international high policy that human archives have preserved to us," negotiated by plenipotentiaries about fourteen years after the battle.[14] Many conflict-ending and alliance-forming agreements had been reached in the past. What makes this post-war peace treaty the first is its articulation of conciliatory and collaborative intents both to end present hostilities as well as to foster peace in the future:

> Present Treaty – Then Khattusil, the great chief of Khatti, has himself made a treaty with the great ruler of Egypt, Usermara-Setepenra, to date from this day to establish a real peace and a real fraternity between us for ever. And he is in fraternity with me and at peace with me, and I, I am in fraternity with him and at peace with him for ever. . .
>
> And the children's children of the great chief of Khatti shall be in fraternity and at peace with the children's children of Rameses-Meriamon, the great ruler of Egypt, being in our position of fraternity and peace. And the land of Egypt with the land of Khatti is at peace and in fraternity, and hostilities shall exist no more between them ever.[15]

Displaying a narrative flexibility considered unpardonable by later writers of peace treaties, the texts are identical except in their attribution of peace initiatives, which each side claims in their version. One likely reason for the discrepancy is that making both rulers heroes of peace in their peoples' eyes greatly assisted in gathering support for the alliance on either side, strategically instating foreign peace while safeguarding it domestically. "For the first time, to our knowledge, in the world's history men awoke to consciousness of the advantages of universal peace and felt the benefits of a common policy," which lasted fifty years.[16]

Ancient Greece, Cradle of Western Peace and Peacemaking?

Peace and peacemaking in Ancient Greece continued to be strategies of survival and subsistence, as in prehistoric times, as well as basic components of prosperous and unified cities, states and civilization, as in Mesopotamia and Ancient Egypt. In previous eras, however, the means and ends of pacific enterprises were dictated almost exclusively by necessity, tradition and from the top-down. Ancient Greek mythology, politics, literature and philosophy challenged such peace praxes by positing ideas and individuals as sources of peace as well, and the city-states (*polis*) of Sparta and Athens and leagues they supported continue to provide competing, contrasting peace paradigms. Mythology provided contemporaries with a common cultural framework that reflected and influenced how peace was or could be made and maintained. Tracing mythological developments brings the evolution of Ancient Greek peace practices into relief by assisting in placing them in their changing historical contexts. In this respect, divine genealogies are particularly revealing because of the conceptual webs the gods personified, indicating how they and the relations between them changed over time.

Of all mythological families, none illustrates the evolution of peace in Ancient Greece better than that of Themis, whose name evoked the "regularity of nature, the peaceful law shared by all its creatures."[17] She had triplets with Zeus, god of thunder and king of them all, called the Horae, meaning "rhythmic periods of the world's unfolding," root of the word hour. They initially controlled time spans related to rural peace and prosperity: Thallo, "blossom-bringer," was the goddess of spring; Auxo, the "increaser," of summer plant growth; and Xarpo, "food-bringer," of ripening and the autumn harvest. However, the Horae took on new names and profiles over time. The second generation of Horae, chronologically not genealogically, was: Dike, who presided over social justice, just as Themis did natural justice; Eunomia, who oversaw human laws and legislative processes; and Irene, goddess of peace and basis for the Greek word for it, also strongly associated with wealth. As seasonal goddesses, the first generation reflects the peace-related concerns of an agricultural society, which early Ancient Greece exclusively was. As socio-political/economic goddesses, the second generation of Horae reflects the peace-related concerns of a more urban society. Whereas the first generation controlled peace by the natural order of crops, Themis' ecological bequest, the second did by the human order of society, Themis' law-making legacy. One reflects bio-genetic imperatives, the other cultural imperatives, but both generations were entrusted with the guardianship of heavens' gates. Thus, as conditions of peace and peacemaking evolved, so did what Ancient Greek mythology reflected.

The literature of the Ancient Greeks exemplified the pragmatics of peace reflected in their mythology. In effect, Ancient Greek literature presents the first comprehensive corpus of anti-war and pro-peace literature in the West, of which preeminent instances are the Homeric and Hesiodic epics. Passed orally by peripatetic bards for centuries, Homer's *Iliad* and the *Odyssey* were already keystones of literary culture by the time they were inscribed *c.* the eighth century BCE. The *Iliad* revolves around the Greek armies' greatest soldier, Achilles, in the last of a ten-year war against Troy. After his commander breaches the boundaries of his authority in his eyes, Achilles defects in an early literary instance of civil disobedience. Only when his best friend is killed does he rejoin the war, dying bravely in the process of securing a triumphal Greek return – except for the cunning Odysseus, who faced ten more years of unearthly misadventures narrated in the *Odyssey* before reaching home. Graphic depictions of battles everywhere temper their glorification in these two sidelong parables. "A surgeon who can cut out an arrow and heal wounds. . . is worth a regiment," we are told in the *Iliad*, which ends with a truce between the two armies.[18] At one point in the *Odyssey*, the warriors agree to ban poison arrows. The devastating domestic impact of drawn-out foreign wars like that of the *Iliad* is the *Odyssey*'s starting point, as its hero returns home only to find his kingdom in disarray. Ares, god of war, is described as being without *themis* and even Zeus denounces him, saying "Most hateful to me art thou of all gods. . . for ever is strife dear to thee, and wars and fighting."[19] Achilles and Odysseus stand out as champions of what scholars call *heroic peace* by their bravery and cunning in hastening war's end and soldiers' homecoming.[20] Achilles' resistance to war and Odysseus' cautionary struggle with its aftermath make them paramount though unlikely anti-war heroes.

The moral of Homer's stories, in the *Odyssey*'s last words, is to "let the mutual goodwill of the days of old be restored, and let peace and plenty prevail."[21] Which days of old are being referenced? According to Hesiod's didactic epic, *Works and Days* (*c.* 700 BCE), humanity has passed through five Ages including the present. During the Golden Age, humans were at peace, living in harmony with worldly and cosmic spirits. In the subsequent Silver Age mythological deities arose, humans lived as children for a century, then aged rapidly and died. A great flood inaugurated the Bronze Age, when humans were fierce warriors consuming themselves in war. Achilles and Odysseus lived in the Heroic Age, in which demigods and heroes, often one and the same, roamed and ruled the earth. The current Iron Age is one in which gods no longer interact with humans and it seems our only escape from war and suffering is death. However, Hesiod does not leave humanity without hope. His foresighted formula placed a premium on strong work ethics and justice, leading from inner to social peace: those who "go not aside from what is just, their city flourishes. . . Peace, the nurse of children, is abroad in their land."[22] Foreshadowing modern economic theories of peace, he stressed two kinds of strife: one military and destructive, the other commercial and productive, advising that the latter replace the former. Thus peace belongs to a distant past which can only be secured for the future by immediate action in the present. For Homer's heroes, such actions involve incredible feats of mind and body exhibited in heroic peace. Humans can seek to emulate heroes, but in Hesiodic terms heroic peace can never be replicated because its Age has forever passed. The less illustrious though equally powerful definition of peaceful action in our times is, as individuals, to fulfill our duties as we understand them diligently and, as societies and collectives, to treat each other justly.

In historical terms, there was in fact a proto-Greek culture located on the island of Crete that, if not fitted, then at least shows striking signs of being a possible wellspring of inspiration for these literary depictions of peace in the distant past. Archaeologists refer to this period as the Minoan Peace because they have found little (some argue, no) remains of warfare. Politically autonomous Minoan towns cooperated nonviolently and as peers on an economic basis and on a scale unamtched in Europe until then. But no data suggests Minoa came close to the complex networks of Greek city-states a thousand years later. Although the Oracle of Delphi dates back to prehistoric times, first as a centre for the worship of the earth goddess Gaia, then her daughter Themis, in time it was housed in the temple of Apollo, god of healing, truth and defender of sheep flocks. Apollo's brother Dionysus, god of wine, took his place in winter, as both were also known as promoters of peace. Knowledge priests gathered in consultations probably informed the chief priestesses' prophecies, which guided the fate of Ancient Greece. The range of topics upon which they gave predictions, from individual pursuits to the fate of cities, and the gravity with which they were considered, gave Delphi its clout. Inscriptions at the Oracle's entrance – "know thyself," "nothing in excess" and "give a pledge and trouble is at hand" – mirror

the notoriously enigmatic predictions pilgrims received.[23] This equivo-
calness makes it difficult to discern whether actions stemming from the
Oracle visits should be attributed to its predictions or their interpretation, though in two cases peace was a direct result of both.

By around 1100 BCE, Delphi had become the centre of a religious
league of all major Greek cities. Known as the Amphictyonic or simply
Delphic League, its aims were to ensure that sacred sites and personnel
were protected, that no city was wiped out in war and that water supplies
were never cut. Offenders, whether members of the League or not, faced
joint attacks if they broke its code. The League's council of heads of states
or their representatives had the power to pass binding internal legislation
and direct common foreign policy. This League outlived many of the later
Greek ones modeled upon it, and lasted in varying forms until Roman
times. By the sixth century BCE it had considerable political influence,
and the more powerful cities could control policy by pressuring the lesser.
Legend has it that late in the ninth century BCE, a League member, King
Iphitos of Elis, visited the Oracle with the aim of ending altogether hostilities between his compatriots. The priestesses advised him to establish
a special truce between local rulers like himself, a bold and unparalleled
venture in which Iphitos was ultimately successful. The terms of the truce
provided that, every four years, all fighting between Greeks would cease
from twelve days before until twelve days after a sporting competition celebrating the gods, in which all Greeks could participate and travel safely
to and from. On this premise, the first Olympic Games were held in 776
BCE at Olympia, a central city named after the gods' dwelling.

In time, the Games included literary competitions, diplomatic meetings and trade summits. Winners in each event were revered as heroes
in their homelands and received an olive-branch crown, ever since a
prominent symbol of peace. According to myths, Athena, goddess of
wisdom, and Poseidon, god of the sea, competed to see who could give
humanity the most useful gift. Poseidon presented the horse and Athena
the olive tree. Athena was judged the winner because her gift provided
a stable source of nourishment in mountainous regions such as Greece
and a shelter from their harsh sun and wind. Embodying the third staple
of Ancient Greek agriculture aside from flocks and wine, the olive-
branch crown was "uniquely suited to represent peace and social
concord" because olive trees required one or two generations to bear
fruit, which assumes a stable state able to withstand external and internal threats.[24] The Games became such an important element of Greek
culture that the four-year cycle of prescribed periods of peace, an
Olympiad, became a basis of classical chronology. The ancient Olympic
tradition continued unbroken for nearly a thousand years, until suppressed during the imposition of Christianity throughout the Roman

Empire, by then including Greece. The Olympic peace tradition was renewed in 2006 with the UN's Olympic Resolution, by which 179 nations agreed to halt hostilities during the Winter Games in Turin, Italy, that year.

By 800 BCE, Ancient Greece was a network of prosperous agricultural and maritime trading communities, when they were not fighting over rights to land, sea and trade. Two of the largest, Sparta and Athens, began annexing proximate towns by force and diplomacy, a process they called *synoikismos* ("bringing together in one home") while founding others of their own. Before long, the conflicting paradigms of peace these two city-states developed and had to offer brought all of Ancient Greece to war. For both Sparta and Athens, *synoikismos* was limited to Greek-speakers, the rest of the world were barbarians ("those who say ba-ba"), who could feel the wrath of their warfare but could never enjoy their peace. The reason for Sparta's awkward appearance in a history of peace is that the militarism by which the city-state came to rule most of continental Greece also adeptly obviated domestic conflicts. After a series of skilful reforms by the legendary lawgiver Lycurgus (seventh century BCE), Sparta soon controlled two-fifth of the Peloponnese as its foremost polis. The central document of these reforms, the *Great Rhetra*, set a societal structure that for eight centuries sustained external warfare and, paradoxically, internal albeit oppressive peace. At the apex were hereditary double monarchs who could check each other's actions and declare war, a power later transferred to the popular assembly, in which all citizens could vote directly on proposals and elect members of the elder and executive councils, an innovative form of mixed government Plato would later laud. The *agoge* system, among the most rigorous, military-oriented mandatory education system ever instituted, was so effective in producing able, cooperative and obedient soldier-citizens of both sexes that Sparta was the only polis which did not find defensive walls necessary. The general Xenophon (*c.* 431–355) explains Sparta's social cohesion in saying that "good order seems to provide safety while disorder has already destroyed many."[25] Until they broke down in 4 CE, Sparta's mixed government and the *agoge* system fostered an authoritarian society that was as internally peaceful as it was warlike to outsiders – especially as compared to its internally tumultuous rival.

Athens is generally considered the cradle of Western civilization. But whether or not it is the birthplace of Western peace and peacemaking is questionable at best. Originally limited to the fortified tip of the Acropolis, *synoikismos* soon made Athens a maritime superpower second only to land-backed Sparta. Noble-born hereditary rulers of four prominent local clans once met atop the indicatively named Mount Ares in a council known as the Areopagus to deliberate upon war, peace and affairs of state. As Athens' fleets and economy grew, so did the power of the merchants and tradesmen, threatening the nobility. The exclusivity of the Areopagus caused internal strife in the seventh century BCE, only temporarily quelled by Draco's harsh laws. So serious was this strife that the historian Thucydides describes it as a danger to day-to-day polis life. The severity of Draconian policies precluded even oppressive peace, so were followed early in the sixth century by Solon's reforms. These reforms changed the Areopagus' hereditary membership to land ownership requirements; bolstered the Boule's power, a lottery-based legislative assembly initiated by Draco; developed a popular assembly similar to Sparta's; and divided the population into classes upon which punishments and levels of political participation were decided. However, the more direct democracy instituted by Solon's reforms only inflamed Athens' class conflicts, which reached epidemic proportions again in the late sixth century. Once more, exclusivity was the cause of strife, since citizenship was still the privilege of a narrow minority of Athenians, landed males over the age of eighteen. The women, foreigners, landless and slaves who constituted the crestfallen majority were never citizens and so could not participate in political processes, notwithstanding that Athens could not have existed as it did without them.

Tyrants, not necessarily cruel rulers, but who took and held power by force, barely ruled chaotic Athens through the fifth century. One of their progeny, Cleisthenes, ushered Athens into its golden age by continuing the reforms Solon had started, though he self-consciously styled them *isonomic*, equality in law, rather than *democratic*, rule by the people. Other city-states then began emulating Athens' isonomic model or were made to by Athenians, which Spartans started to see as a threat to their authoritarian ways. The Athenian rhetorician Isocrates (436–338 BCE) said of his polis' political prowess during this period:

> . . .we established the same polity in the other states as in Athens itself – a polity which I see no need to extol at greater length, since I can tell the truth about it in a word: They continued to live under this regime for seventy years, and, during this time, they experienced no tyrannies, they were free from the domination of the barbarians, they were untroubled by internal factions, and they were at peace with all the world.[26]

In the same rhetorical vein, the age's great charismatic leader Pericles (*c.* 495–429 BCE) called the Athens he knew the "School of Greece," though it was only partly the school of domestic peace, if at all. At its worst, Athens under Solon's exclusivist democratic system was detrimental to domestic peace because it vested too much power in the whims of a minority while prohibiting the majority from participating in the very political processes by which they were excluded. The result was a cycle of coups and tyrannies through which "lawless ferocity and violence" became the norm in historian Polybius' words (*c.* 203–120 BCE).[27] At its best, Athens under Cleisthenes' isonomic restructuring promoted peace by turning potentially violent conflicts between opposing constituents into non-violent political struggles.

Sparta, not Athens, was the guiding light of the many leagues between Ancient Greek city-states, for the only valid pretext for inter-polis peace proved to be uniting to face a common enemy, as exemplified in the Peloponnesian, Hellenic and Delian Leagues. The first of these, which flourished during the sixth and fifth centuries BCE, was formed by Sparta to stop a rival from regaining power after defeat and to curtail another's ascendancy. To these ends, Spartans used their skill in war as a bargaining chip, bringing Corinth into the League by overthrowing its tyrant upon request and securing Elis' control over the Olympic Games by trouncing all of its competitors. A turning point in the history of Sparta's foreign war and peace strategies came when war broke out with Tegea (*c.* 560 BCE). Sparta strategically limited the decisive battle to the frontiers in order keep the polis intact as a League ally after submission, which Tegea then became – among the earliest known instances of intentionally limiting warfare for the sake of post-war peace. In return for accepting Spartan hegemony, particularly but not only in matters of foreign policy, League members were promised protection from non-member aggressors, which now principally meant Persia. The Greco-Persian Wars (*c.* 500–450 BCE) showcased many of the League's strengths, notably the effective cooperation, determination and military might of Greeks if and when they worked together. But the Wars also exposed many of the League's deficiencies, including its erratic gatherings usually called only by Sparta, inconsistent financial and material support and disproportionate participation in its missions.

Towards the Wars' end, the Peloponnesian League gave way to the short-lived Hellenic League, which of necessity combined Sparta's army and Athens' navy to amphibiously deter Persia. When Pausanias, the new League's Spartan military commander, was stripped of power for conspiring with the Persians (*c.* 478 BCE), Athens was handed the Hellenic helm and proceeded to reform the League along more isonomic than authoritarian lines. Seeing Athens' hegemony as a threat to its power, Sparta broke away from the Hellenic League and reformed the Peloponnesian League along its original lines. In 477 BCE, city-states faithful to Athens reunited in the Delian League, so-called after the sacred polis Delos where it originally met and collected its wealth, in the tradition of the old Amphictyonic League. With Athenian wisdom, Delians called for the termination of hostilities between members, regular meetings and commensurate contributions. But Delians remained Spartan in spirit. Though early on they deployed diplomats around Greece to enlarge the League, they soon began doing so by force; its isonomic principles faded and began to favor larger members. That the Delian League had become an Athenian Empire became clear when Pericles moved its financial centre from Delos to Athens in 454 BCE, putting the golden in Athens' golden age. An Athenian delegate, Callias, negotiated a peace treaty with the Persians on behalf of the Delian League in 449, by which "all might sail without fear and be at peace," in Plutarch's account.[28] The operative word here is "sail," symbolizing Athens and its naval allies. The Peace of Callias was not binding on Sparta and its continental allies, who arguably betrayed Athens in a separate peace with Persia in 387, the King's Peace or the Treaty of Atlantidas, forfeiting centuries of Greek maritime gains.

The benefit of these Leagues, called *symmachiae*, offensive and defensive accords by which both friends and enemies are shared, was that Ancient Greeks explicitly agreed not to fight and to settle disputes diplomatically within them. Permanent ambassadors called *proxenos* represented their city's interests abroad, acting as arbiters and tendering trade treaties. Perpetual war with Persia precludes calling these alliances peaceful, but they were nonetheless among the few ways inter-polis peace was achieved. With the Persian threat temporarily dissipated, the divergence in the Leagues' interests, one land and the other the sea, made each the convenient common enemy the other needed to protect their respective inter-polis peace. In a vain attempt to preserve the status quo, the Leagues agreed to the Thirty Years Peace in 336 BCE to prevent an escalation in ongoing armed conflict. Within five years, however, friction between Sparta and Athens reached a boiling point, Persia sided with Sparta and diplomatic relations deteriorated. The resulting Peloponnesian War (431–404) was a series of indecisive battles, pitting sea against land power, punctuated by brief periods of peace. Less than halfway into the war, the Athenian spokesman Nicias and Sparta's king negotiated a truce. The events leading up to the Peace of Nicias, which historian Thucydides (*c.* 460–395) aptly called "hollow," were satirically portrayed in *Peace* by Aristophanes, who pioneered anti-war theatre.[29] Delegates from each side decided its terms, reflecting "the results of a war which neither side had won," that is, this was more a proclamation of stalemate than peace.[30] In Thucydides' words, the Peace "cannot be reasonably defined as a real peace, since in that period they did not reciprocally return and recover all the things they pledged to do."[31] Neither party to the Peace was satisfied with the performance of the other and, as if inevitably, war flared up again five years later. In the end, downtrodden Sparta and destitute Athens both fell before the region's rising star, Macedon and its Corinthian League. The conquests of Alexander the Great are worth noting here only insofar as they ushered in Ancient Greece's last great territorial grab, which wholly un-peacefully paved the way for the Roman Empire and, in its footprints, medieval and modern Europe.

The sharply jagged line of political peace in Ancient Greece should not detract from the smoother though no less curved one drawn by its famous philosophers. Thucydides argued that "speaking as they do the same language, [Greeks] should end their disputes by the means of heralds and messengers, and by any way rather than fighting."[32] Philosophy proved to be one of those ways. How peace principles, if they exist, should be put in practice by individuals in society, if they can, are just a few of the questions raised and divergently answered. Philosophers before Socrates are usually grouped together for their materialist rather than mythological (as in Hesiod's) explanations of the universe and humanity's place within it. Thales, credited with being the first such thinker, devised a scheme to unite Greek cities into one state, keeping their autonomy but coordinated from a capital. Empedocles developed the theory of the four universal elements (water, fire, earth and air) being united by the attractive force of love and separated by the repulsive force of strife. Relations between these elements as between humans unfold in four phases. In the first love dominates, in the second love and strife compete for supremacy, in the third strife triumphs and in the last love trumps strife, an unending cycle. In Pythagoras' theory of universal harmony, based on the study of rigorous yet mystic mathematical formulas and astronomical observations, violence and war are aberrations of a creative cosmic order he called the One, which humanity can learn about and live by. An early biographer claims "So much did he hate killing and killers that not only did he refuse to eat the meat of slaughtered animals but he avoided the company of cooks and hunters."[33] Thus Western philosophies of peace were born.

The historian Herodotus developed a similar concept of universal patterns (eike) that, when recognized and acted upon, can improve humanity's lot. He correspondingly sees peace as a universal pattern and war its aberration: "In peace children bury their parents; war violates the universal pattern, causing parents to bury their children."[34] Heraclitus, in contrast, contended that the universe's true being is flux and that permanence is an illusion. From his metaphoric river, which can never be stepped in twice, it can be inferred that peace and peacemaking violate universal law to the extent they resist change, while "war is the father of all things" insofar as it sires change.[35] The famed Oath of the physician Hippocrates, still invoked today, did more than make medicine a profession distinct from theurgy. Swearing to work "for the benefit of the sick according to my ability and judgment," physicians must also promise to "keep them from harm and injustice" and "neither give a deadly drug to anybody if asked for it," nor "make a suggestion to this effect."[36] His medical law prescribed both a non-violent code of conduct for practicing medical professionals and collective moral guidelines – also the ethical agenda of modern organizations and conventions. Encapsulating individualistic pathos and collective ethos of pre-Socratic philosophers is Protagoras. He practiced Sophistry ("to become wise"), and was hired as a private tutor or to plead on his client's behalf. The relativistic reasoning and rhetorical skills Protagoras engaged in could be used to argue all sides of any dispute between individuals or groups. A fellow Sophist once remarked that "Philosophy is a machine for attacking the laws," a non-violent alternative to weapons.[37] Replacing armed conflict with debate, preventing violence by compromise, and expediting reconciliation through agreement, Sophistic abilities fetched a high price in turbulent Athens. But the open, critical dialogue Protagoras practiced has proved invaluable to peace and conflict resolution throughout history.

Socrates' crux status in the *philosophy of peace* derives from the intellectual and pedagogical traditions culminating in and inaugurated by his star student, Plato. His place in the *history of peace*, however, derives from how he lived and faced his death. Like Protagoras, Socrates promoted open, critical dialogue, took on students and argued cases. Xenophon quotes him saying that "enmities and dangers are inseparable from violence, but persuasion produces the same results. . . who would rather take a man's life than have a live and willing follower?"[38] But unlike Protagoras, he disparaged payment and titles, living as an urban itinerant with an uncanny knack for conversation, fountainhead of his fame and downfall. The Socratic Method named after him consists of pointed questions and answers which aggregately reveal truths or ideas. Directed by individuals, actualized in collective collaboration, the dialectical process Socrates practiced still stands as a paradigm for studying and teaching peace, as well as for making and maintaining it. However, reducing the Method to a formula blinds us to the social significance of his way of life. Socrates' quest for wisdom, and the "good life" lived accordingly, is radically democratic in that anyone can do likewise, regardless of their background. The Socratic paragon is also seditiously isonomic in that everyone begins on an equal footing with the same rights to wisdom and its benefits, like peace. The path Protagoras trampled, Socrates made his own: a total replacement of force with dialogue in daily affairs, used towards social-, not just self-improvement and -empowerment. Harassed but unharmed during the Thirty Tyrants' reign, when Athenians were convicted and executed without trial, only after democracy was restored was he charged with disruptive behavior and corrupting youth. He defended his cause and was found guilty of these capital crimes. Friends tried to convince him to escape; he tried to convince them that injustice, inherently antithetical to peace, cannot be overcome by further injustice.

As his final remonstration, Socrates silently drank the fabled hemlock, making the greatest irony of his life his death. Not an act of civil disobedience, nor passive or non-violent resistance, since he carried out the sentence of killing himself; rather, Socrates' distinctive form of peaceful protest, if it can be so called, turned silence into statement, complicity into defiance, submission into rebellion and surrender into victory.

Socrates' philosophy of peace cannot be discussed separately from that of his student, Plato. Only after meeting him did Plato embark on his own quest, the crowning achievements of which are his Dialogues, the Academy he founded and his prodigy, Aristotle. Plato's ostensibly open *Dialogues* are never open-ended. Instead, Socrates, usually their main character, skillfully steers the conversation. In *The Republic*, for example, discussion springs from Socrates' deceptively simple question: What is *dike*, the source of concord and a determinant of polis peace since mythological times? One of the "discoveries" made through the Socratic Method is that war is "derived from causes which are also the causes of almost all evils in states, private as well as public."[39] Thus, in *The Laws*: "every one of us should live the life of peace as long and as well as he can" and "cities are like individuals in this, for a city, if good, has a life of peace, but if evil, a life of war within and without."[40] But what are good and evil in this context? While this question has been debated ever since Plato, for our purposes they correspond to pursuing perfect and eternal Ideas, adopting them as ideals and implementing them, or not. *The Republic*'s famous Allegory of the Cave, in which Plato illustrates this idealism, begins with people who live confined inside one, forced to stare at its back wall from birth. A fire behind the captives casts shadows of moving statues shaped like worldly objects onto the wall, figurative of sensory perceptions that always fall short of the Ideas they represent. One breaks free, uncovers the ruse but is blinded as he makes his way past the firelight into sunlight, symbolic of rational inquiry, the pursuit of Ideas. Outside, he eventually regains sight and sees the actual world, representing Ideas. Whether he re-enters the cave to "enlighten" his people and if he does whether they embrace, ridicule or reject him are the Allegory's closing questions, leaving the problem of implementation unresolved.

Peace fits within the Allegory's conceptual framework in three metaphoric places. As a shadow, peace is not an Idea but an image, "in fact only a name."[41] The consequential paradox of Plato's contribution to the philosophy and practice of peace lies in the light. As the firelight, peace is pursuable by our bodies and an implementable ideal, but is not an Idea. As the sunlight, peace is an Idea pursuable by rational inquiry, but cannot be implemented otherwise. Plato's Cave thus construes the conditions, experience and ideals of peace inside and outside as mutually exclusive and hierarchical. Humans can adapt to and adopt both, but pursuing or implementing peace inside will *a priori* always fall short of doing so outside. In other words, the Idea of peace is accessible by our minds, but un-implementable with our bodies; all we can do is try. Rather than resolve this paradox, the socio-political model Socrates goes on to construct builds upon it. Placed at the apex of Plato's ideal state is a class of philosopher-kings who, though vested with near-absolute power, are enlightened and so rule with prudent reason. Fortitude and vigor are the defining traits of the guardian class that takes and executes philosopher-kings' orders. The laboring class under their combined control, farmers and craftsmen who provide for themselves and their rulers, is characterized as tempered by their work despite being temperamentally inclined. Plato, through Socrates, contends that in this state, the Ideas of *dike* and peace come closest to being enacted by the complementary qualities each of the three classes embodies in fulfilling their prescribed roles. The possibilities and limits of peace Plato congealed have shaped the history of peace and peacemaking in the West and, through the West's influence, the world. But there can be no doubt that without Rome's espousal of Ancient Greek culture, Plato would not have had the same influence on pacific thought and practices as he did.

One Empire, One Peace: The Rise of Rome to the Pax Romana's Decline

Although peace and peacemaking took very on different forms and functions during the twelve centuries Rome emerged from obscurity to conquer the Mediterranean region, when they did at all, peacemakers almost always played second fiddle to warmongers. Yet, Romans left such an indelible mark on the history of peace that they cannot be ignored. The inseparability of war and Roman culture made peace and peacemaking into what Gerardo Zampaglione calls an "ideological imperative" in *The Idea of Peace in Antiquity* (1955), overshadowing them as bio-genetic and cultural imperatives but unable to replace them as such.[42] The Roman history of peace is, in the end, more of forms than substance, in which lies its significance. The chronicles pertaining to the origin of Rome are less valuable as accurate records than they are as insights about what later Romans believed or wanted to believe about themselves and their past. Nevertheless, what we know of the violent early history of Rome is for this very reason both self-revelatory and prophetic, if a study in un-peacefulness overall.

The high esteem Romans came to hold for the Greeks who came before them is evident in that the twins Romulus and Remus, legendary descendants of the Trojan War hero Aeneas, are said to have founded their city

(c. 753 BCE). Archaeologically, Rome seems to have resulted from a vicious struggle for supremacy over the northern Tiber River region between three tribes: Latins, Etruscans and Sabines. They were apparently influenced by Sparta's Sicilian colonies, visible in their aggression towards one another as recorded in their remains as well as stories. Romulus killed Remus over who would be the namesake of what was to become Rome and went on to grant asylum to the region's brigands and outcasts, all warlike men like him. So while the first Romans soon partially pacified the Etruscans, at one time more powerful, they also suffered a shortage of brides. The episode that ensued, called the Rape of the Sabines, brought about the first known instance of Roman peacemaking, uncharacteristic as it was. The Romans invited the rival Sabines to celebrate a festival, which they accepted in good faith. However, once their guests were inside their walls, the hosts abducted the visiting women and made them unwilling wives. The Sabines took months to prepare for war against the Romans. Just as the two armies were about to annihilate each other, the abducted women and by-now mothers rushed between them to plead for peace. They declared that death was preferable to losing both their fathers and the fathers of their children to one war. This Peace of the Sabines, often overlooked in favor of the more graphic Rape, brought about not only the immediate end of hostilities, but also lasting concord between the Sabines and the Romans. Thus, conceived and gestated in violence, Rome was born in peace. Unnecessary loss of family members remains one of the most widely used anti-war pleas for peace to this day.

The first decades of the Roman Republic (c. fifth–first centuries BCE) set the tone for war- and peacemaking for the rest of its existence. The final local war of significance between Rome and its tribal rivals was the Battle of Lake Regillius (c. 496 BCE). This battle's concluding peace terms, which formed the Latin League, marks the start of Rome's regional consolidation and inter-regional conquests. The League was similar to Spartan predecessors in most respects, and like them was discarded when convenience outweighed necessity:

> Let there be peace among the Romans and all the Latin cities as long as the heavens and the earth shall remain where they are. Let them neither make war upon one another themselves, nor bring in foreign enemies nor grant a safe passage to those who shall make war upon either. Let them assist one another when warred upon . . . and let each have an equal share of the spoils and booty taken in their common wars.[43]

Here emerges the antipathetic Roman practice of using war to prepare for peace, and peace to prepare for war. Employing this method as well as divide-and-conquer, Rome subjected the last independent peoples of Italy and those of Gaul and Hispania, roughly modern France and Spain, making limited partners of the conquered where this could be done and annihilating them when not. These principles are the basis of the historian Tacitus' (c. 56 -117) statement, centuries later, that Roman leaders "create desolation and they call it *pax* (peace)."[44]

Etymologically, the Latin word *pax* is linked with *pacisci*, to conclude a pact. But whereas for Greeks pact-making at least aspired towards isonomic convergences of free people, for Romans it was from the start either synonymous with the unconditional surrender of the defeated to their will or a means to this end. Conquered lands and peoples were "Romanized" by victorious governors, soldiers and settlers to which they were granted as plunder. At best, Romanization meant "assimilation to Roman customs and habits and promotion of an identification with Roman interests," and at worse the militarily manageable animosity of the enslaved. Either way, it was Romanization that gave Europeans of the future, both as individual nations and as a whole, their identities and interests. The flipside of Rome and the Latin League's foreign policies is made clear in the case of Pyrrhus (c. 318–272), the last Greek general to seek control over southern Italy. After defeating the Romans several times, his peace proposals were rejected. Following another series of battles, he is said to have exclaimed: "Another such victory and I shall be lost!" hence the expression Pyrrhic victory, by which the vanquished (in this case, the Romans) reverse their losses by dictating peace terms. Pyrrhus' capitulation led directly to Latin League control over Greece and so brought the Romans to the attention of the Eastern Mediterranean powers from Persia to Egypt and vice versa.

A powerful city in northern Africa, Carthage, tried to replace Greeks in Italy as their control waned. Rome, always recovering from or preparing for local wars, signed trade and cooperation treaties with Carthage, stalling a regional war it could not yet win. These strategic peace tactics outlived their usefulness when Pyrrhus fell, and Rome took Carthage head on. Janus' temple doors were closed at the end of the First Punic War (264–241) between them, for a few days. By the third and last Punic War (149–146), Carthage was ruined. Ending its League, a nearly ruined Rome now ruled the Western Mediterranean. "At one time bringing their wars to rapid conclusion by invasion and actual defeat, at another wearing out an enemy by protracted hostilities, and again by concluding peace on advantageous terms, the Romans continually grew richer and more powerful," praised Machiavelli centuries later.[45]

The Roman Republic, despite its many shortcomings, is the second longest-lasting form of government in world history. Understanding the dynamics of domestic peace during this era requires reviewing republican socio-political structures because they were often the causes of recurring class struggles and civil wars, as well as used in their resolutions. Pax thus evolved from being an asymmetrical pact-making process to a social condition devoid of violence. With this redefinition of peace came a re-characterization of war. The Rex or king, like Romus, had been granted lifelong *imperium*: absolute authority over and immunity from his actions or inactions as chief legislator, executive and adjudicator. These powers were at first divided between two elected Consuls in the Republic for one-year terms and *imperium* lasted only while they held office. Consular duties were later subdivided into judicial posts (Praetors), legislative assemblies and an extensive network of administrators for tax collection and other tasks, with the Consuls acting as appointers and overseers. The primary assembly, the Senate, was a patrician body that controlled state finances, passed laws and elected officials among its ranks. Finally, the Pontifex Maximus was high priest of Rome, conducting as augur the aus-pices required for nearly every undertaking, especially war- and peace-making. Consuls levied the military's legendary legions and conducted their campaigns, a mandate they came to share with provincial Governors. By these martial powers and the revenues they raised, Governors later became threats to the central government. The legions were initially not a standing army, but one composed of landed citizens called on seasonally by Consuls to carry out foreign expeditions or as necessary for defense. Only after the Consul Gaius Marius' reforms of 107 BCE did the legions become permanent conscripted bodies of landless cit-izens and slaves, somewhat separating military and civilian life, making the Pax Romana possible. In emergencies or in gratitude for services ren-dered, the Senate could elect a Dictator who could wield all the powers just described for a strictly limited six-month term, at least by the letter.

The basis of early Republican law, the famed Twelve Tables (*c*. 450 BCE), do provide specifically for the pacific settlement of disputes:

> When the litigants settle their case by compromise, let the magistrate announce it. If they do not compromise, let each state their own side of the case. . . before noon. Afterwards let them talk it out together, while both are present. After noon, in case either party has failed to appear, let the mag-istrate pronounce judgment in favor of the one who is present. If both are present the trial may last until sunset but no later.[46]

However, the legal tradition the Twelve Tables represent and the early Republic's socio-political structures distinguish between patricians and plebs, openly discriminating against the latter. As the number and wealth of plebs grew, so did their contribution to the state. Their dissatisfaction became the first of two major threats to domestic peace. Within twenty years of the Republic's founding, the plebs led the first known successful campaign of non-cooperation against the patricians, refusing to work for or pay them taxes. A compromise was reached when a Plebeian Council was formed, led by two elected Tribunes who could overturn patrician magistrates' discriminatory pronouncements. But this Council's legislation was binding only on the plebs. A quarter-century later, the plebeian cause was furthered by a similar campaign, after which ten Tribunes with wider powers were elected. Only after a third campaign (*c.* 287 BCE), this time more violent, did the Council's decrees (*plebiscites*) become binding on all the people of the Republic, including patricians and non-citizen residents. In these ways, the Republic's socio-political structures were modified over time to mitigate civil wars.

The historian Polybius (*c.* 205–125 BCE) captured the plebs' isonomic impulse for peace and highlighted its flaws: "Peace is a blessing for which we *all* pray to the gods; we submit every suffering from the desire to attain it, and it is the only one of the so-called good things in life to which *no man* refuses this title."[47] Some Senators began bribing the Council to achieve their goals, creating rifts among plebs' and patricians' factions. The Senate's continued control over finances and individual Senators' over most of the land led to mob violence instigated by the Tribune Gracchus (*c.* 133), the first of two major internal forces that prevented domestic peace in the late Republic and in contrast to the intransigence Romans displayed in external affairs. Shortly after the plebeian uprising came that of non-citizen residents, whose numbers increased exponentially from early Roman expansion onwards. Their plight was similar to the plebs in that they were excluded from socio-political structures of a state in which they played essential economic roles. Since defeating Carthage, Romans tried to alleviate their dissatisfaction by selectively granting citizenship to conquered peoples as an incentive for Romanization and for them to compete among themselves instead of turning against Rome's authority. The Social War (91–88 BCE), the Civil War (88–83 BCE) and the Cataline Conspiracy (65–63 BCE) show these policies failed, but also redefined what it meant to be Roman, and what Rome itself meant.

The main antagonists of the Social War were Marcus Drusus and Lucius Sulla. Drusus, a Tribune, was murdered as he was preparing to pass a law granting citizenship to all Socii, Roman allies of the Italian peninsula, which incited a *social* revolution among the depraved. Now, citizenship was used as a bargaining chip during the Roman's peace negotiations with the Socii. Most accepted it gratefully, and Senator Sulla's legions crushed the rest; he was elected Consul the next year. The Senate demanded that Sulla revenge the ravages Rome suffered, but as he was raising legions in the south his military powers were revoked by the retired Consul Gaius Marius, who bribed the Plebian Council for this purpose. This time, Sulla led his legions against Rome itself, bringing Civil War battles to city streets and the countryside. As wealth became a greater determinant of power than the pedigree of one's social and citizen status, Senators whose strength rested on the nobility of their names and whose fortunes had waned feared for their families' future. One of these, Cataline, led a conspiracy to kill the Consuls after he was denied the right to run for the office once, losing a second time. Had it not been for Cicero (106–43 BCE), the great orator to whom Cataline had lost, the conspiracy may have succeeded. In a series of brilliant speeches, which he was given dictatorial powers to implement, Cicero expressed ideas about war and peace that were to dominate the last oligarchic rulers of the Republic, the first Emperors and many Western leaders ever since. Coining the term "peace with honor," he articulated the principles of just wars and their rules of engagement.[48] "Those wars are unjust which are undertaken without provocation. For only a war waged for revenge or defense can actually be just. . . No war is considered just unless it is has been proclaimed or declared, or unless reparation has first been demanded."[49]

Among the few popular pacific forces at work in the late Republic were philosophical practices of inner and social peace developed in two schools of Greek lineage: Epicureanism and Stoicism. Their predominance was already established by the early Roman Empire. Epicure (341–270 BCE) was an Athenian philosopher whose gathering place, the Garden, is often mistakenly associated with debauchery. He did preach for pleasure and against pain, which were for him and his many Roman followers the moral compass points of individual and social existence. But the psychic rather than physical pleasure they aimed for was limited to fostering freedom from, or indifference to, worldly worries (*ataraxia*). Epicureans claimed that a total absence of pain (*aponia*), their version of perfect inner peace, could be brought about by focusing on the everyday, as on mealtime conversations; forestalling in their eyes futile fears, as of death or the gods; and foregoing vainglorious ambition, as for status or glory. Withdrawing from political life, as Epicureanism all but required, was perhaps even less of an option for Romans than for Greeks, so more pragmatic later devotees like Lucretius (94–55 BCE) advocated a more committed Epicureanism. Military societies like Rome, he held, could be reformed by wise individuals, starting by actively uprooting war, the paramount pain. This idea was instituted in the form of Irenarchs (from Irene) an office that began in Hellenistic Greece and spread across the Roman Empire. These minor magistrates, respected elderly members of the communities in which they served, were often the only ones in remote areas and prevented disputes from escalating into conflicts through mediation.

Stoicism, named after the Athenian porticos (*stoa*) where its founder Zeno (333–264 BCE) taught, is generally seen as the superseding counter-philosophy to Epicureanism. Stoics rejected the passions (lust, greed, anger, etc., later called vices) where Epicureans did pain. They held that the surest path to inner and social peace was not withdrawal but self-discipline, and that solidarity with those who practiced it could bring peace to the world. The effect of Stoic thinking can be traced in the word *virtu*, originally a quality of manly courageousness in battle, only later being associated with the pacific virtues of moderation and magnanimity. This significant semantic shift took shape with Panaetius (189–109 BCE), who argued that no one can be virtuous as long as they participate in, or even condone, war. In the same vein, Seneca (4–65 CE) assailed fellow Romans for being "mad, not only individually but collectively. We check manslaughter and isolated murders; but what of war and the much vaunted crime of slaughtering whole peoples?"[50] Stoicism, the former slave Epictetus (50–130 BCE) claimed, could bring "friendship in families, concord in cities and peace in states."[51] The limited extent that it did so is due to the Roman addition of selfless duty to self-discipline, which made Stoicism a favorite pose of the powerful and their staffs' unofficial code.

A writer who straddled these schools is Marcus Terentius Varros (116–27 BCE), whose *Logistoricus de pace* is the earliest known historical study of peace and the model for this book. Based on past and present examples, a *logistoricus* articulated practicable principles, in this case on peace. By such methods, Varros put forth the concept that individuals are citizens of two societies at once: one universal, embracing humanity and divinities, the other circumstantial, based on birth. In his view, peace is not an exclusive or independent property of either society, but stems from all dual citizens asserting their rights and meeting their responsibilities. The influence of Epicureanism and Stoicism can be discerned in the number of officials, from Irenarchs to Emperors, who adhered to their pacific principles without relinquishing the primacy of mythological practices (until the rise of Christianity), also adapted from the Greeks. Pax thus came to indicate a state of mind as well as a social condition; more precisely, even in the midst of war, inner/internal peace became not only a possibility, but an actuality. Epicureanism and Stoicism were also reflective of the dichotomous basis of peace in the early Roman Empire, internality and externality, established after the high-level power struggles of the First and Second Triumvirates that set the stage for the Pax Romana.

Military might was the two Triumvirates' origin and end. The First was formed by secret concords between three Consuls in 60 BCE: Pompey, Crassus and Caesar. While Caesar was governing Gaul, enriching himself and his legions, Crassus died invading Parthia, Rome's main rival in the East. Fearing the end of his *imperium* in face of a Senate who now feared him, Caesar was blocked from running for Consul again. As he led his legions into Rome in revenge, Pompey was made Dictator to stop him. In the civil war that ensued, Caesar chased Pompey into Egypt then conquered it. Within months of his triumphal return, secured by strategic clemencies and gifts, Caesar was made Dictator-for-life (de facto emperor), assassinated and deified. Caesar named his adopted son Octavian (63 BCE–14 CE) as heir. He formed the Second Triumvirate with Mark Antony and Lepidus, openly dividing control over Rome's cumulative conquests. Antony took the rich eastern provinces from Greece to Egypt; Octavian the western, where the best legions were levied, from Britain to Italy; and Lepidus the less valuable ones of northern Africa. After bribing Lepidus' legions away from him, stripping his power, Octavian waged war against Antony, who had moved to the cosmopolitan city Alexandria, married Queen Cleopatra and named their children his heirs. More than an affront to Roman pride, this was a serious threat to a major source of grain. At the Battle of Actium (31 BCE), Octavian's forces defeated those of Antony and Cleopatra, who committed suicide.

Octavian was elected Dictator upon his return. Calming worries about renewed civil war, he soon reduced the number of legions by almost half. He placed most of the remaining along the borders where invasion was most likely and away from population centers, thus relieved of much of the burden of supporting a standing army that could be turned against them. The rest he used to keep internal order by creating special cohorts. As the poet Ovid wrote in praise of his patron, now the "soldiers bear arms only to check the armed aggressor."[52] Given the unending series of civil wars in the past century, Romans were delighted with the peace Octavian's reign seemed to be ushering in and did not hesitate in showing their appreciation. By closing the gates of Janus' temple an unamtched three times, Octavian earned three titles from the Senate: Imperator, from which "emperor" is derived, an honorific for victorious commanders; Princeps, from which "prince" is derived, a deliberately ambiguous noun close to "first-citizen," which Octavian preferred to Rex; and Augustus, hence the month of August, meaning "revered one," which he adopted as his everyday name. In the years to come he was also made Tribune, Praetor and Pontifex Maximus, all for life. Although one wonders how many titled roles it takes not to call a king a king, by ensuring that republican socio-political structures remained intact despite his de facto monarchical powers, Augustus founded both the Roman Empire and the Pax Romana, known to contemporaries as the Pax Augusta.

Augustus made guaranteeing internal peace and the rule of law the purpose of the state. His far-reaching reforms ranged from revitalizing the arts by patronage to renovating roads, which made transportation and postal communication the most efficient they would be until the invention of railroads. Making taxes more equitable, he also redirected their flow from the Senate to a Fiscus under his direct control, using funds to foster industries and encourage trade within the Empire. He reorganized the city of Rome's relations with its provinces, dividing them between rulers who reported to him and others to the Senate, both with higher degrees of administrative autonomy than in earlier times. Peoples having no previous ties were now under a single, effective authority, yet local traditions were allowed to flourish like never before. The *Ara Pacis* or Temple of Peace, built on the Field of Mars (god of war known in Greek as Ares) at the Senate's request in honor of Augustus near the end of his life, testifies to the success of his peace policies. As the Pax Romana was coming to a close two centuries later, the Emperor Probus looked forward to when "the soldiers would no longer be necessary."[53] This statement perplexed the historian Falvius Vopiscus, and his retrospections on it are an accurate description of what the Augustan period of the Pax Romana in some ways was, in others tried to be:

> It was as if he had said "There will no longer be a Roman army; the state, guaranteed by its own security, will dominate everywhere, will possess everything. Supplies will not be accumulated for war; the oxen will stay harnessed to the plough; the horse will be born for peaceful work. There will be no more wars and no more prisons. Peace will reign everywhere, as will the Roman laws, as will our judges."[54]

Compared to the century of civil war that preceded it, falling short of this description of peace was infinitely better than having no peace at all. In the same spirit, the contemporary writer Velleius Paterculus (19 BCE–32 CE) pandered that the "Pax Augusta, which has spread to the regions of the east and of the west and to the bounds of the north and south, preserves every corner of the world safe from the fear of brigandage."[55]

The post-Augustan parameters of the Pax Romana were twofold. On one hand, internal peace was maintained by economic prosperity and an effective socio-political infrastructure, when it was at all. On the other, incessant external wars kept invaders out, the legions busy and brought in plunder by the conquest of new territories, when they were successful. This internal/external infrastructure barely survived the Emperors in Augustus' line: of the four, three were insane or became so with power, feared as cruel tyrants who disregarded law and lived lavishly. That Nero (r. 54–68), the last, was even accused of starting a fire that razed Rome is indicative. The founder of the brief Flavian Dynasty that followed rose in military ranks and was a general in Judea when he was proclaimed Emperor by his soldiers, the first but far from the last to be so honored. Vespasian's reign (r. 69–79) brought a return to legal and fiscal order, and he built another Temple of Peace (*Templum Pacis*). His two sons and successors, the first benign, the second prone to paranoia and persecutions, staunchly defended the Empire's borders. But they also bolstered autocratic rule by expanding the military. The so-called Five Good

Emperors of the subsequent Antonine Dynasty presided over the post-Augustan apex of the Pax Romana. Coins of the era celebrate *pax*, which by now did not mean "a restoration of external peace," a dream long since forsaken, "but the imposition of internal peace," well within the Emperors' power.[56] Nerva, the Dynasty's founder, reigned for only 15 months (96–98) but a reputation for tolerance, benevolence and respect for law preceded and outlived him. The Empire reached its territorial zenith during the reigns of Trajan (98–117), first ruler to officially spare women and children in battle, and Hadrian (117–138), who pulled back borders in Mesopotamia and Britain to better defend them. Antoninus Pius (r. 138–161) and the Stoic Marcus Aurelius (r. 161–180) made Varros' dual citizenship their unofficial ideology, save that the two were with good reason believed to be united in Rome. They instituted the idea of "one empire, one peace" by which a small sect was steadily ascending, and their reigns became "bywords for peace and prosperity," commonly referred to as the Empire's golden age.[57]

The anarchic third century exposed the fatal weaknesses of the Pax Romana's internal/external infrastructure, leading to its decline and fall as well as that of the Roman Empire itself. Internal peace was periodically broken by revolts against despotic Emperors, derailing the economic prosperity and destabilizing the socio-political structures by which it was maintained. Dozens of "Soldier-Emperors" came to and stayed in power such as Vespasian, while not even universal citizenship for imperial residents was enough to quell their growing dissatisfaction. Externally, the languishing legions stationed on the borders could no longer hold back Germanic and Asiatic tribes, which continuously raided and invaded, eventually sacking Rome. Its last single leader, Diocletian (245–312), divided the Empire in two along a linguistic line, the Greeks of the East and the Latins of West, then the Emperor's power into four (the Tetrarchy), two seniors called Augustus and two junior Caesars. Ironically, it is by these titles that Roman Empire finally shed its Republican forms. The seat of imperial power would totter from the Western to the Eastern Empire, now known as Byzantium, until this as well as other struggles for supremacy toppled the former (456) and the latter a millennium later. But as the namesake of the Eastern capital, Constantinople, became a convert to Christianity and began its incremental integration with the state, this major thread in the story of peace and peacemaking will be taken up again in Chapter 4.

3

Peace in the Ancient East: India, China and Japan

ᠺᠥ

The Many, the Few, the One: Peace and Peacemaking in Ancient India

The vast array of circumstances and lifestyles that have defined the Indian subcontinent's identities also bring together a core strand throughout its ancient history: *harmony*. As in Ancient China, harmonic policies and practices effectively promoted peace by laying grounds for unity in diversity. Building on differences whenever possible, overcoming them when not, at one time thousands of indigenous villages sprawled across the Indus River Valley (*c*. 3300 BCE). Finding defensive walls unnecessary, they devoted their considerable resources to securing social peace by meeting the basic needs of the many rather than of the few, putting in place the world's first sanitation systems and gridded town structures, in which sectors were based on occupation and equally provided for irrespective of wealth and status. The partnership model thus seems to have prevailed in Ancient India until the Indus Valley's extended drought-related decline, after which the dominator model took root *c*. 1500 BCE. This change resulted from the arrival of nomadic Aryans ("noble ones") of the eastern Eurasian steppes. By literary conjectures, scholars debate whether they came in a sudden invasion or in migratory waves. In any case, that Ancient Indian life was forever transformed by them, less towards than away from peace, is indubitable. The potentials of Ancient Indian peace and peacemaking came to be circumscribed by structurally violent socio-political structures, namely the caste system, and ongoing warfare on two levels: between local chiefdoms for direct rule and regional kingdoms for hegemony.

A mosaic of chiefdoms (*rashtras*) arose between the Indus Valley and the Ganges River Valley to the east, in which natives were generally subordinated to the more or less unwelcome newcomers. However, bio-genetic, cultural and ideological imperatives required that their ways of life be fused together or doomed to die apart. The nearly impenetrable forests and mountains of the two Valleys were the rashtras' natural borders, and account for the astonishing number of languages and traditions in India then as today. A multicultural proto-civilization thus emerged, called Vedic from the Vedas, its unifying foundational text and a forerunner of Hinduism. Socio-politically, a hereditary hierarchy topped by feuding Aryan chieftains (*Rajas*) and their staffs of mixed descent ascended in its early years. Rashtras then became loose confederations of capital cities, seats of religious and secular power, and satellite villages (*janas*). Later, groups of rashtrasbecame *mahajanapadas* or "great kingdoms" under *Chakravatins*, "conquerors of the world," who were entrusted with exterminating external threats more than with direct rule, which was relegated to Rajas. The direct rule of a Raja meant the ability to raise tributary revenue from his *janas*, bolstered by the plunder gained by ritualized raids into neighboring rashtras, usually with no intent to impose direct rule. The rise of *mahajanapadas* thus on the whole decreased the frequency but increased the scale of warfare in Ancient India: periodic breaks in collective peace made individual and social peace more likely.

Chakravatins and Rajas were not the only driving forces behind these individually short-lived but as a whole long-lasting Vedic states (*c.* 1500–300 BCE). They ruled by the consent and legislated with the approval of four councils of unequal weight. The *vidhata* and *gana* were elite bodies with religious and economic clout; the *sabha* and *samiti* were popular assemblies of lesser bearing. Vedic cities were also divided along occupational lines, though the strife of stratification replaced egalitarian harmony as the sustaining basis and goal of society. Hence, India's caste system originates with the Vedic civilization's socio-political structures. The Veda-prescribed castes (*varnas*) were, in declension: Brahmins, scholar-priests, bureaucrats; Kshatriya, warrior-rulers; Vaisya, farmers, traders; and Sudra, manual workers, artisans. Only centuries after the Vedas was the term *jati* used to indicate the rigid, endogamous and hereditary social group the *varnas* had by then become. The social order and continuity the caste system conferred must in regards to peace be evaluated in the shadows of the structural violence it propagated. Positive and negative examples can be found in the *Ramayana* and *Mahabharatra* epics (*c.* 400–200 BCE), part mythologies, part histories, which narrate battles as well as socio-cultural syntheses by marriage, political alliances couched in spiritual-philosophical discourse. Because of ongoing warfare between chiefdoms and kingdoms, prescribed forms of peacemaking were perhaps more fully developed in Ancient India than anywhere else at the time.

The Brahmins' *lingua franca*, Sanskrit, had a developed lexicon of peace in these overall non-peaceful conditions. Pragmatic peace terms are expounded in Kautalya's *Arthashastra* (fourth century BCE), an encyclopedic treatise on autocratic statecraft which deals with economics, education, jurisprudence, clandestine operations and peacemaking, among many other topics. A Six-Fold Policy between states is elaborated: peace (*sandhi*), war, neutrality, preparing for war, alliance, and making peace with one state while waging war with another, called double policy. To name a few of the peace processes described: peace made with a promise is called *paripanita* and with no promise, *aparipanita*; on the condition that troops along with the ruler would be turned over, *atmamisha*; on the condition that the commander would march with the army to a specified place, *adrishtapurusha*; when concluded by offering goods carriable away on men's backs, *upagraha*; when obtained by ceding all of a war-torn realm, *uchchhinnasandhi* ("peace cut off from profit"); and, when bought with an large amount of money, *kapala*. The thrust of these peace policies is economic so that, for example, if "any two kings hostile to each other and deteriorating expect to acquire equal amount of wealth in equal time, they shall make peace with each other;" and if "by making peace with one, I can augment my own resources, and by waging war with another, I can destroy the works of my enemy," then he may adopt the double policy and increase his resources.[1] A ruler situated between two more powerful states is instructed to seek protection from the stronger or to make peace with both on equal terms. Above all, relative strengths and resources must be considered in making peace and alliances or breaking them. In the end, "when the advantages derivable from peace and war are of equal character, one should prefer peace; for disadvantages, such as the loss of power and wealth. . . are ever-attending upon war."[2] The surest way for a ruler and his people to prosper was for them to unite in amity with their neighbors, creating *suvarnasandhi*, "golden peace."

Reinforcing implementations of these political peace-related terms were parallel religious ones based on polytheistic belief systems, Vedism and Hinduism, likewise formative of Indian culture, specifically in relation individual minds, bodies and spirits. Similarities between Vedism and Hinduism outweigh their differences for our purposes and lie primarily in their respective emphases within the same textual tradition, Hinduism being an outgrowth of Vedism. Of primary importance to inner peace in Vedism is the recitation of hymns and the performance of rituals; in Hinduism, bodily drills like yoga and exercises of the spirit and mind take precedence. A salient peaceful feature of Ancient Indian polytheism, aside from ongoing syncretism and henotheism, is that unnumbered gods and goddesses represented everything from elements of local landscapes and natural phenomena to everyday objects and timeless ideals were all part of one pantheon and system of belief. Ways of worshiping them included individual or group meditations, festivities, rituals and drills. War did require religious legitimatization, but this astonishing plurality meant that religion was seldom a valid pretext for war on its own. Presupposing tolerance, polytheism fostered a peaceful coexistence of spiritualities coordinated by shared pantheist concept: *atmans*, the individual souls of humans as well as divinities; *brahman*, the universal soul governing them by an eternal law, *karma*, by which atmans' actions are held accountable. In Hinduism there is a separate deity called Brahma, the creator, part of a trinity with Vishnu, the preserver, and Shiva, the destroyer, whose imports to peace are obvious. Atmans and brahman were at one time united and innately peaceful, *shanti* in spiritual senses and *manahprasada* in cognitive. Their separation stems from atmans' ties to the temporal-material world and the brahman's universal and everlasting immateriality, whose energy is the basis of this world.

In a sense, the sole purpose of Vedic and Hindu practices is to restore individual atmans' lost peace by identifying or unifying them with brahman, which is why purification rituals to "decontaminate" atmans from impurities play key roles in Hindu spiritual and bodily inner peace practices. By following the Vedas, atmans can generate qualitatively positive karma while also reducing it quantitatively; not doing so generates negative karma and increases it. Reincarnation (*samsara*) occurs through a hierarchical order of beings so that, and until, atmans become empty of karma. At that point, liberation from the cycle of reincarnation (*moksha*), identification with the brahman and immaculate peace are attained. This process was adapted, with variations, by Mahavira in the Janaist religion he founded in the fifth century BCE. Although stress is placed on the individual, karma also had strong collective connotations. The proportion and degree of the karma-free in society serve as a gauge of its general peaceful state, which in turn influences the feasibility of individual karmic pursuits. Shanti is sometimes used interchangeably with *sandi* (association, combination), the opposite of *vigraha* (separation, isolation); corollary terms are the absence of isolation (*vigrahabhava*) and absence of strife (*yuddhabhava*). Believing that our actions in this lifetime determine our state in the next is a tremendous impetus for peace, the logic being not only that the peace we bring about now will follow us, but also that violence will too. This concept may be called *reincarnative peace*, found in both polytheistic and monotheistic traditions, East and West. So while polytheistic beliefs supported social stratification, they also offered practical opportunities to transcend them.

As a rule, the preceding socio-political and religious traditions combined sustained the caste-based dynastic system through the Magadha Empire (684 BCE–550 CE) despite the Persian occupation under Darius

I, and those of the Indian Middle Ages (230 BCE–1279 CE) despite the Greek invasion of Alexander the Great. Tumultuous as they were, these mixed native dynasties and periods of foreign rule left largely unchanged the Vedic socio-political and Hindu religious forms until the Islamic Sultanates of the twelfth and thirteenth centuries CE. Two peaceful exceptions that proved this structurally violent rule were the first explicitly non-violent religion, Buddhism, and the part of Ashoka's reign based on its principles. Like those of future peace leaders, their stories mingle history, legend and allegory but with distinctively peace-oriented messages. Siddhartha Gautama, Buddha's given name, was the son of a Kshatriya prince in modern Nepal. Soon after birth (c. 563 BCE), a seer foretold that he would be a great teacher if he left the palace grounds and a great king if he did not. So his family immersed him in luxurious distractions to shield him from sufferings that might motivate his departure. But on escaping his comfortable confines, and after having married and continued the family line, he witnessed three commonplace sights from which he had previously been safeguarded: an old, a sick and a dead man. These sights made him aware of human suffering's universality, of which the unnecessary persistence, he decided, precluded individual and social peace, to which he then devoted his life.

To his family's dismay, he deserted the palace and began practicing in the most ascetic veins of Hinduism, through which he discovered that denying the spirit, mind and body can be as detrimental to inner peace as indulging them. The "middle path" between these two extremes he followed from then on was the basis of the Four Noble Truths, the Eightfold Path and the Three Jewels that govern much of Buddhist life. These he began to preach after becoming Buddha, or "enlightened one," which is said to have occurred in one night as he meditated under a tree. His first disciples quote him saying that the Truths together lead "to peace, to direct knowledge, to enlightenment."[3] Dukkha, the central tenet of these Truths, is usually reduced in English to suffering, but is more insightfully understood as the deeper meaning of Siddhartha's three sights: a needless inhibition of inner and social peace. In sum, the Truths are: Dukkha is universal and is entangled in humanity's materiality, sensory perception, cognition, habits and experience, the five aggregates; Dukkha's origins lie in expectations and attachments, to the five aggregates or anything else of this world; the cessation of Dukkha, or the state of enlightened peace Buddha reached (Nirvana), is possible for all; and the way to the cessation of Dukkha is the Eightfold Path. The Truths are principles more than prescriptions, like the Eightfold Path, which represents the Buddhist perspective on pacific wisdom, conduct and discipline.

Each of Path's eight elements are qualified as *samyanc*, usually translated as "right," but which more accurately combines the meanings of completeness and perfection, in the sense of both a state of being and a process:

1. **Understanding** of the Four Noble Truths and of the impermanence of Dukkha;
2. **Intention**, a commitment to non-violence and the pursuit of enlightenment;
3. **Speech**, to abstain from lying and divisive discourse, as well as idle chatter;
4. **Action**, specifically to refrain from killing, stealing and intoxicants;
5. **Livelihood**, not engaging in a profession that is violent or dishonest;
6. **Effort**, to always show goodwill and positivity while rejecting their opposites;
7. **Mindfulness**, being alert, clear- and open-minded to one's being in the world around; and
8. **Concentration**, the practice of meditation both as an activity and as a way of life.

Of all the overtly peaceful religious tenets ever proposed, the Path is among the simplest and most directly applicable in everyday life. It requires tremendous dedication but, like the Socratic Methods of peace, is democratic in that anyone can follow it – which in Buddha's time meant regardless of caste, a radical religious move. Yet, the Path has not once been used to justify war or conflict. Although individual and groups of Buddhists have participated in wars, its internal logic and external remedies preclude it from being so abused. The Path is also the cornerstone of Buddhism's Three Jewels: the Dharma or "teachings," the Buddha who originally taught them, and the Sangha or sodalities of enlightened who have ever since provided guidance to Buddhist individuals and the societies in which they lived.

Buddhism's pacific power is nowhere more evident in the Ancient East than in the life of Emperor Ashoka (*c.* 304–232 BCE), who came to rule lands that stretched from modern Iran to Bengal. However, had he not lived past middle age, he certainly would not have been granted the honorary title Beloved of the Gods. His father, ruler of the largest empire in Indian history, was nicknamed Slayer of Enemies, and emulating him Ashoka's abilities as a warrior-statesman made him popular throughout the empire. When, seeking his embarrassment, his elder brother and heir to the throne sent him to govern a region ripe for war, fighting ceased upon his arrival. But as it resumed, Ashoka ordered an all-too successful suppressive massacre, for which he was ostracized, a form of counter-dominant behavior also practiced by Ancient Greeks. Called back from exile to quell a rebellion against his father, who died soon after, Ashoka was injured and taken into hiding so as not to be killed by his brothers. The care he received from a Sangha was his first exposure to Buddha's peaceful principles. They did not leave an immediate impression, for when he was well enough he led another massacre, this time of the city in which his brothers lived (modern Patna), killing them off one by one. Ashoka, now Emperor by default, subjected peoples and lands beyond even his father's dreams, enriching the Empire but also earning him the moniker Chandashoka, the Cruel. These campaigns culminated in the Kalinga War (*c*. 265 BCE), a kingdom which refused to submit to Chandashoka. His army butchered 100,000 Kalingians and displaced as many. Amidst the ruins, he realized all the suffering he had caused, screaming the adage "What have I done?" in horror. Tormented, he went sleepless for days – until he recalled the benevolence the Sangha once bestowed.

From that day on, he committed himself not only to the Eightfold Path as his personal way of life, but also adopted it as his public policy. Chandashoka soon came to be known as Dharmashoka, the Good Teacher. The basis of his policy was *ahimsa* or non-violence towards humans and animals, a Hindu concept adapted by Janaism, Buddhism and Gandhi in the twentieth century. Dharmashoka prohibited outright as well as structural violence, abolishing slavery, outlawing discrimination based on caste and promoting vegetarianism. Reinvigorating the unity in diversity of Ancient Indian polytheism, he set up networks of free hostels for pilgrims of all faiths. He founded institutions of higher learning for agriculture, handicraft and spiritual studies, and secured the basic needs by sanitation, hospitals and roads, as did the partnership-modeled Vedic societies of old. He also built thousands of Stupas, temple-mounds of earth around which Buddhist devotees are meant to walk in meditation (as at Sanchi) as well as Viharas, housing for the Sangha who had put him on the Path of non-violence for the rest of his reign. These peaceful objectives and achievements, to which archaeological remains attest, are also described in Ashoka's eminent Edicts, which harken back to Hammurabi. Inscribed in languages from Pali to Aramaic on columns scattered across and beyond his vast empire, his Edicts are one of the earliest and widest known multilingual disseminations of universal isonomic law. To spread the Dharma, he sent diplomatic missions as far as Greece and Egypt in the West and modern Sri Lanka and Thailand in the East, the first ruler in recorded history to do so on such a scale. When the modern Indian state gained independence from Britain in 1949, the symbol of Ashoka's transformation from feared warmonger to beloved peacemaker, an octagonal crest representing the Eightfold Path placed atop an Edictal column, was adopted as the emblem on its flag.

Buddhism's peaceful proliferation can also be attributed to Ashoka, but requires a brief retrogression to be understood. Shortly after Buddha passed, a First Council of the Sangha was held to establish his teachings. A Second Council of this still small, regional religion was held a century later to determine the Sangha Code's applicability. The principal point of contention was whether it should be relaxed to attract more lay practitioners; the Council held that it should not, originating the subsequent schism between the Mahayana ("Greater Vehicle") schools which successfully spread Buddhism by contravening the Second Council's decree, and the Hinayana ("Lesser Vehicle") schools which did so by following it, each non-violently to the other and converts. The Ashoka-sponsored Third Council (250 BCE) sought to reunite the growing number of schools, write the Dharma down for the first time, and organize missions to spread Buddhism around the known world. All Ashoka's goals, except reunification, were achieved. A benefit of remaining rifts was that priests propagated their own schools instead of a centrally determined one, allowing for localizations that would have otherwise been limited or prohibited. Thanks to a commitment to non-violence, these Councils were peaceable despite their disputed resolutions, an example their delegates abroad followed. For centuries after Ashoka's peaceful proselytizing, Buddhism flourished in almost as many forms as places reached. Hinayana sects like Theravada spread west to modern Iran and Turkey, and Southeast to Cambodia, Vietnam, the Philippines, Indonesia and elsewhere. Mahayana sects were slower-moving but reached even farther east, including to Korea and Japan, then annexes of Imperial China.

Harmonies and Antinomies of Ancient China

Ancient China's demographic diversity and geographical immensity made harmony and authority two necessary peace principles of its political systems from their earliest days, but also made them so difficult to implement. Family and community were always and everywhere the bedrock of Ancient Chinese societies; it is only with the development of imperial political and administrative infrastructures that various peace-oriented codes came to compete for individual adherents as for social and collective control. The *Records of the Grand Historian*, attributed to second century BCE historiographer Sima Qian, and the *Bamboo Annals*, an anonymous chronicle of a slightly later date, present peace as central to the origins of Ancient China. Their historicity, like that of the records of early Rome, is questionable at best, and of less import than the ideas about peace they conveyed to those influenced by them. According to these works, the world was at first ruled by the Three Sovereigns, demigods who in their infinite insight presided over a period of universal harmony between all the cosmos' constituents: the Heavenly Sovereign, the Earthly Sovereign, and the Human Sovereign. They not only ruled benevolently in their own realms but together kept a perfect balance between them.

Among the gifts they gave to humanity were fire, fishing, agriculture and writing, the last two being of special relevance to the history of peace. Archaeologists date the first of these developments to *c.* 7000 BCE. The words for agriculture and rice cultivation are synonymous in old Chinese script, suggesting that rice was a long-time staple. More than other crops, cultivating rice in nutritional quantities for small or large societies required cooperation, coordination, social cohesion and hydrological expertise, which is why Confucius later wrote that "from agriculture social harmony and peace arise."[4] Thus, while warfare seems to permeate Ancient Chinese history, continuity in rice cultivation is a strong reminder that general populations not only needed peace to survive, but in large measure helped create, recreate and sustain it. That rice spread throughout Asia and India before the times of the Ancient Greeks is also a sign that vast trading, political and other cooperative networks must have existed, although little about them is known. Chinese ideograms developed from inscriptions on bones used in wizards' divinations for, among other purposes, war and peace. The modern Mandarin characters for social peace, the etymologies of which can be traced back to these times, are shown on the following page. The left character (*hé*) on its own means: together with, harmony or union. The right one on its own (*píng*) means: flat, level, equal, to make the same score or to tie. The character for peace in another sense is *ān*, meaning content, calm, still, quiet or to pacify, ideas as challenging to trace historically as their characters can be for foreigners to write.

The time of the Three Sovereigns passed when the Five Emperors came to power halfway through the third millennium by Qian's account. They were not demigods but sage kings who were patrons of medicine, music, calligraphy, astronomy and hydrology, all of which were practiced in and for peace. Armed conflicts occurred in this period, but the wisdom of the Five Emperors prevented as well as resolved them. Legends surrounding the Yellow Emperor, first of the Five and the mythical founder of the future Han Dynasty, relate that he used fog to fight aggressors, in which he found their leader with a special compass, sparing the soldiers. Early commentators claim that he limited warfare to achieve lasting victories and fostered peace to make his people prosperous and obedient. Emperor Shun, the last of the Five, is said to have met hostility from his family and subjects, yet continued to love and care for them until the day he died. Above all, later commentators considered the Five Emperors to be moral models for current heads of states. Later political treaties on the Yellow

和平

Emperor's rule prescribe that "Only in case of necessity will [sage rulers like him] undertake military actions," as warfare harms the economy, making people discontent and reproachful of their rulers.[5] However, these treaties also emphasize that a state without a strong army will not be able to survive. Tradition has it that the Fifth Emperor abdicated in favor of his best civil servant, Yu. Succeeding where his father had failed, Yu had expertly diverted floods for years, saving many lives and livelihoods. As a Qing emperor three thousand years later paid homage:

> Since ancient times, the model for long-lasting peace has been essentially to ensure people's livelihood. To achieve this is to have land reclaimed for farming so that surpluses are produced and income become inexhaustible.[6]

Yu ruled, if he did at all, roughly as the archaeological Erlitou culture arose. His successors, the Xia (*c.* 2205–1766) who may be more fiction than fact, were at the threshold of small warrior chiefdoms, becoming powerful palaces that could coordinate, if not yet control, others.

The Shang Dynasty (*c.* 1766–1122 BCE), China's earliest historical one, took power by coup. Their palaces included courts and their many ministers and workmen. Wizards and warriors were thus slowly being replaced with bookkeepers and bureaucrats, by training and disposition less violent, though no less cunning. But citizen-soldiers who once did battle for themselves now became paid or conscripted armies who campaigned on their commanders' behalf and behest. Before long, Shang capitals like Yin on the Yellow River became religious, administrative and political centers that could levy and expend taxes for the people's welfare, but also for conquests near and far. As in Ancient India, if the duration and quality of peace increased with the size of Shang rulers' dominions, so did the scale and intensity of warfare. With the Shang, natural spirit and ancestor propitiation developed into full-fledged systems of belief, from whom guidance, assistance and consolation were sought in peace and war alike through meditation and ritual. Sacrifices led by Shang rulers were made to the weather-god Di, without whose goodwill no enterprise could thrive, peaceful or otherwise. The labor and logistics required to produce the large number of bronze religious vessels found attest to the Shang's technical sophistication and organization. But few ties bound the traditional elite of distant regions together, and hardly any did the diverse conquered peoples to each other or to their rulers. This lack of social cohesion on a large scale led to the decline of Shang's authority in making and maintaining peace, which the Zhou Dynasty (*c.* 1122–256) that overthrew the Shang sought to restore.

The Zhou redefined statecraft and morality while revitalizing family relations during the longest and arguably the most illustrious reign in pre-Imperial China. Historians divide the Zhou Dynasty into four overlapping periods with distinct cultural profiles. Three traits unite them: the Mandate of Heaven, the Fengjian system and the Zongfa, each having a complex relationship with contemporary and subsequent socio-political peace in China. The Mandate of Heaven was a belief that a ruler's legitimacy derived directly from Tian, the god of heaven the Zhou restored from the Xia in place of the Shang's Di. Tian showed support for rulers, called Sons of Heaven, by making their reigns peaceful and prosperous. Conversely, a lack of peace and prosperity was considered proof that Tian no longer supported his Son, so that another may rightfully take his place. Divinations thus began losing ground to rituals, a reliance on precedents and continued spirit and ancestral propitiations, all aimed at maintaining peace and prosperity through socio-political order, or at least its appearance. The Fengjian socio-political structure is often compared to European feudalism for its stratified conflations of property and people, at the top of which were Sons of Heaven. Below them were aristocrats of various ranks who received their fiefs by inheritance or as gifts for services rendered and were responsible for keeping them peaceful and productive. Below them were the masses who paid dues in labor, cash or kind; professionals like doctors, scribes and clerics were somewhere in between. Fengjian reciprocal obligations and mutual limitations of action, spheres which are today seen as precursors to the "ideology of peaceful coexistence" put forth by Confucius, are discussed below.[7]

The foundation of the Fengjian social structure was its lineage system, the Zongfa or clan law, governing all but the lowest classes: ranks, titles, professions and primary possessions were passed on to eldest sons, whose families and descendents were called main lineages, while those of younger sons, minor lineages. The Zongfa entailed a jealously guarded exclusivity of ancestor worship, by which branches of the royal lineage reproduced legitimizing rites in their realms, and branches of aristocratic lineages did so within their clans. In time, the verticality of the Zongfa was supplemented with horizontal segmentations, so that the "principle of collective liability for punishment on the basis of households was the legal expression of a new institutional order."[8] Sanctions were not limited to individuals but could be collectively extended to family and clan; in the case of crimes by officials to superiors, subordinates or to those who had recommended them to office. Strict as they were, inter-class loyalty and social cohesion set in place by Mandate of Heaven, Fengjian socio-political structure and Zongfa were considerable improvements on the Shang, bolstering Zhou authority and legitimacy and so their ability to make and maintain peace, when they so chose. Until the early eighth century BCE, descendants of the Zhou's first family, the Ji, ruled from their western capital on the Wei River, Hao, near modern Xi'an. During this first period, called the Western Zhou, the three preceding traits were still taking shape and gaining ground, and the rapid and extensive territorial annexations they made possible mark the first pinnacle of Zhou power. Following a war over the Mandate of Heaven, in which Hao and the western fiefs were captured by nomads, the Zhou capital was moved east to Luoyang in 771 by the remaining Ji, a self-made Son of Heaven and inaugurator of the Eastern Zhou period.

Displaced from their stronghold, the Zhou now needed the support of local Fengjian lords and their fiefs more than ever before, which these were willing to give to keep intact the systems that also supported them. At this point the three traits became ubiquitous in, and synonymous with, Ancient Chinese civilization, and the Zhou reached their second apogee before their long decline. The Eastern Zhou period is subdivided into the Spring and Autumn Period and that of the Warring States. The former gets its name from a chronicle attributed to Confucius, about one of these Fengjian states. At first the mutual support between the Ji and the ruling clans served its purpose of maintaining the peace and prosperity of the Fengjian system in the face of internal unrest and external threats. Aside from interstice wars between the Fengjian, inter-state diplomacy and law was often successful. Hundreds of treaties (*meng*) creating trading and defensive alliances between fiefs were ratified by Fengjian ambassadors representing their lords. A precise diplomatic vocabulary came into being, with specific words for ambassadorial meetings, friendly envoys sent by one fief to another and even trust-building hunting events for visiting officials. But major Fengjian lords became overlords themselves by interventions and annexations, and power-sharing with the Ji turned into a power struggle as fiefs grew into states. The Seven Warring States that fought ceaselessly for the next three centuries were the Qi, Chu, Yan, Han, Zhao, Wei and Qin, the last of which eventually reunited all of Ancient China by employing new philosophies and practices of peace to create its lasting Imperial form.

The hostile environment of the Eastern Zhou period was the unnatural habitat of Chinese philosophy's golden age, what Sinologists rhetorically call the Hundred Schools of Thought. The Hundred Schools of Peace these schools of thought spawned were direct or indirect responses to wars happening all around them, at least four of which ineradicably influenced the rest of Ancient Chinese history and the East as a whole. Not first but foremost among them was that of Confucius (*c.* 551–479 BCE), founder of the school that bears his name. Tradition tells he was the son of a destitute nobleman who was forced to flee to the Fengjian fief of Lu before it was subsumed by one of the Seven Warring States. Fascinated by ritual from an early age, he committed himself to studying his being in the world at fifteen, holding odd jobs till his twenties, when he married, had a son and became a Lu administrator, rising to Justice Minister by age fifty-three. But he soon resigned this position in protest at the Lu's unjust policies, and travelled to neighboring states in search of a ruler who would take his advice. After several failed attempts, he returned to Lu, where he edited the *Five Classics* of Ancient Chinese literature. His teachings are collected in the *Analects* and *Great Learning*, posthumously assembled snippets of conversation and aphorisms. Far from proposing a systematic philosophy, he challenged his students to think for themselves, study the world around them, and respectfully reinterpret rather than reject tradition. If there is "single thread binding my way," as he claimed, it is the enterprise of pacific harmony within and between individuals in society.[9]

As a moralist, Confucius focused on three traditional, interconnected concepts: *li*, mores or rites; *yi*, reciprocal respect; and *ren*, humane responsibility. From these stem the so-called Silver Rule he articulated: "What you do not wish for yourself, do not do to others."[10] Of crucial importance to his philosophy of peace was social order through loyalty and meritorious self-mastery, which, as we have seen, the Zhou initiated and Confucius, building on their principles, came closer than anyone to perfecting. For Confucius, loyalty comprises duties of children to parents and, analogously, the ruled to the ruler; meritorious self-mastery is an auto-limitation of rulers' powers by the Mandate of Heaven and incentives for prescribed public service. Perhaps the clearest encapsulation of Confucius' *philosophical imperative* for peace is to be found in the following passage, of which the reverse is also true:

> When the world is investigated, knowledge is extended. When knowledge is extended, wills becomes sincere. When wills are sincere, hearts are redressed. When hearts are redressed, individuals are cultivated. When individuals are cultivated, families become harmonious. When families are harmonious, states becomes orderly. And when states are orderly, there is peace in the world.[11]

Confucius had only a small circle of students in his lifetime, but during the Warring States period his teachings were studied and debated by a growing number of intellectuals in high and low official positions, who like him were seeking a stable way out of war. One of these, Mencius (fl. fourth century BCE), codified Confucian thought and presented it to numerous Fengjian lords, some of whom began to apply it systematically early on. Mencius regarded those who engaged in war as being below beasts, proposing that they should be punished by the death they inflict on others. He also emphasized the concept of *de* or moral virtue as humanity's innate and universal quality, innately non-violent but which can and usually is corrupted by unjust institutions. By the second Imperial Dynasty, the Han, Confucianism was synthesized with the preceding Qin's Legalism and became official Imperial policy, remaining so in evolving forms until the early twentieth century CE, when nationalism, then communism displaced it. As Ancient China's sphere of influence expanded, so did Confucianism, making it and Buddhism the two most widespread peaceful forces of the Ancient East and, geographically speaking, the world.

Unlike the early Confucian school, which held that social harmony came from within individuals, the Legalist school held that it came from outside them. After Mencius, the third great Confucian countered that *de* was neither innate nor universal but developed by self-cultivation, upbringing, education and lifelong discipline. His star student, Han Fei (*c.* 280–233), was a Han prince who used this theory in building a pragmatic political philosophy of peace that made law the formative and decisive force in shaping individual behavior and social norms. Apparently Han Fei stuttered, so he presented his ideas in elegant prose instead of at court. The cornerstone of his school of peace is the legal code, which he argued should be precise, publicly available and the final word on everything for everyone. In the words of a modern scholar, the Legalist's law code was thus set up to be the "all-powerful instrument which makes it possible to guide everyone's activity in the direction most favorable to the power of the state and the public peace."[12] Accordingly, the law itself is authority, not the individual who applies it, who from high to low is bound by it, motivated by its punishments for disobedience and rewards for compliance, the basis of Legalist morality. Legitimacy, peace and power, then, rest in legally prescribed and -delimited positions, not people who hold them. It was thus a ruler's duty to heed his ministers' advice and consider his people's pleas just as much as it was for them to obey his commands. In practice, this tended to give rulers the upper hand. Legalism became Imperial policy with the Qin Emperors, whose chief minister Li Si (*c.* 280–208) competed intellectually and politically with Han Fei. Li Si bolstered state bureaucracy to administer the law and standardized as much as he could, including writing, money, weights, measures and the civil service testing system that lasted for three millennia. Though wondrous in stabilizing society after the chaotic Warring States period, his policies brought about a conformist culture that saw creativity and tradition as threats. After outlawing other schools of thought and peace, burning their books as well as historical records, and burying nearly five hundred Confucians alive, Li Si had Han Fei, who had joined the Qin court at the Emperor's request, killed. This was the negative image of the Legalism Han Fei had hoped would bring peace and harmony to where there was recently the disarray of war, a misguided authoritarianism that brought down the Qin.

Daoism, in contrast to Legalism, was as much a system of religious beliefs as a body of thought, and as anti-authoritarian as Ancient Chinese philosophies of peace could be. Its origins are traced back to the Yellow Emperor, but its locution occurred with two foundational texts. The *Dao De Ching* is attributed to Laozi, an older contemporary of Confucius and Zhou bookkeeper before becoming an itinerant sage. The *Ching*, or book's title, serves well as an introduction to the complexities of its pacific contents. Dao, usually translated as Way or Path, can be understood in three related senses: cosmic-supernatural, earthly-natural and human, uniting the universe, giving entities their identities and purposes, which can be revealed but never imposed. Essentially, Daoism aims at aligning individuals and society with the Dao, bringing about inner, social and collective harmony. In each of its three senses, Dao has strong associations with Yin-Yang, the balancing female/male, passive/active, receptive/creative forces, and omnipresent energy, Ch'i. Communing with nature, paying homage to ancestors and spirits, meditating, health-enhancing activities such as Tai Chi Chuan, and the arrangement of space according to Feng Shui are all Daoist methods of achieving its inner peace (*pu*), physical and spiritual, by balancing Yin-Yang and allowing Ch'i to flow freely. They are still practiced today, increasingly in the West. Thus, a later Daoist text explains: "The correct Dao will cause no jeopardy. . . It is useful to individuals and it is also useful to the whole country. Attaining it, an individual will succeed. Attaining it, a country will be at peace. Attaining it, a small country will be able to defend its territory. Attaining it, a large country will be able to unify All-under-Heaven."[13]

The De in the *Dao De Ching*, crossing inner strength and virtue, results from following the Dao. The central Daoist concept associated with De is *wu-wei*, literally non-action or non-interference, letting ourselves and the world be so that the Dao may take its course. The political implication of wu-wei, a kind of stoic anarchism, is that the optimal form of government is that which is least perceptible, or does the most by doing the least. Thus, "the kingdom is made one's own only by freedom from action," while "when opposing weapons are crossed, he who deplores the situation conquers."[14] It follows that not participating in, nor collaborating with, violent governments is the best way to resist them, and withdrawing from warlike cultures the best way to change them. The ideal Daoist society, then, is one in which individuals are free to follow the Dao as revealed to them, regardless of class or clan. This point is where Zhuangzi (fourth century BCE), an official of the Fengjian Meng, takes off in the book named after him, actually an evolving accretion of Daoist dialogues, narratives and essays. The Dao of the *Zhuangzi* is still universal, but takes on a less normative and more relativistic role. Pluralistically, we must find and follow our own dao within the Dao, upon which individual, social and collective peace and harmony depend. But wu-wei still plays a major part in the *Zhuangzi*:

> The inaction of heaven is its purity; the inaction of earth is its peace. So the two inactions combine and all things are transformed and brought to birth. . . heaven and earth do nothing and there is nothing not done. Among men, who can get hold of this inaction?[15]

Traditional yet revolutionary, Daoism was so popular by the seventh century CE that T'ang Dynasty Emperors gave it official sanction and has, with a notable exception discussed below, been a strong peaceful undercurrent in Chinese culture since inception.

Confucianism, Legalism and Daoism developed during the heyday of Mohism, the most prominent school of peace of the Warring States period and the only major one not to survive it intact. Little is known about its fifth-century BCE founder, Mozi, other than that he may have been a Song official and was possibly a former slave or convict. Guided by the *Mozi*, its collected teachings, the Mohist School was the first in the Ancient China to actively promote open debate as a means to mitigate conflict and build consensus, and persuasion rather than law or tradition to establish moral standards. Mohists were committed to exploring and applying what they saw as the complementary principles of universal love and utilitarian order:

> When everyone regards the states of others as one's own, who will invade? . . . If everyone loves universally; states not attacking one another; houses not disturbing one another; thieves and robbers becoming extinct; emperor and ministers, fathers and sons, all being affectionate and filial – if all this comes to pass the world will be orderly. Therefore, how can the wise man who has charge of governing the empire fail to restrain hate and encourage love? So, when there is universal love in the world it will be orderly, and when there is mutual hate in the world it will be disorderly. This is why Mozi insisted on persuading people to love others.[16]

The flexible doctrines at the *Mozi*'s core are: only meritocratic government sustains stable socio- economic and political order by being a moral model for, and accountable to, the people by the Mandate of Heaven; aggression, particularly offensive war, is to be condemned and replaced with all-inclusive compassionate care; thrift, humility and altruism lead to prosperity; and, together, these principles bring about universal love, peace and harmony.

In these veins, Mohist advocated extending familial feelings beyond the family, a frugal lifestyle of no waste, and livelihoods of collective benefit such as agriculture, instead of harmful ones such as the military. They protested against the wars of the Fengjian states both in person and in writing, preventing them when they could and, when not, participated in making strong defenses (in which they became experts) the best offense. As the most vocal anti-war and pro-peace activists of their times, Mohists were at greatest odds with the Warring States, which, along with the Imperial Qin, suppressed them. Mozi's influence was limited by his own radicalism, a lesson competing schools of peace were quick to learn and so better-equipped to overcome. As a whole, these Ancient Chinese schools confirm that times of widespread war can and have acted as catalysts of peace, both in thought and in action. Many of the merits of the long-lived Imperial system by which the Warring States were unified can be traced back to Confucianism, Legalism, Daoism and Mohism, and many of its faults to failures in either understanding or applying their pacific teachings, which were in time enhanced with those of an import, Buddhism. In the end, "Peace and unity were only possible if the political power could control and share the principal resources," which the Hundred Schools of Peace could assist in but not guarantee.[17]

As mentioned, the Qin (or Chin) unified the WarringStates and others, and are for this reason considered China's founders. Under Li Si's Legalist principles, which endorsed the use of coercive force in unification, and backed by the latest in iron weaponry as well as military strategy like Sun Tzu's *Art of War*, the Qin turned enemies into subjects with or without their consent, effectively ending divisive war by total war in 221 BCE. It was the Qin who initiated the transformation of the Fengjian into an Imperial system, intended to eliminate external threats as symbolized by their Great Wall, and quell internal strife by imposing peace and promoting prosperity from the top down and centre outwards. However, pacification complete, they did not change their ways and were therefore unable to maintain the oppressive peace they had made. A decade after Li Si's persecutions began, revolts did away with the Qin. But the indispensability of their socio-political infrastructure is evident in its surviving the civil war that ensued between provincial families for its Mandate of Heaven. The Han were ultimately victorious, defeating the Qin in 202. By learning from mistakes of their predecessors, and being traditionalist innovators in their own right, they ruled for 400 years. Early on, the Han fused Confucianism with Legalism to form their official policy, diffusing this synthesis by diplomatic and military annexations that brought close to 60 million people and most of Asia under their direct control, an era sometimes referred to as the Pax Sinica. The Han achieved this by dividing territories into administrative districts owing allegiance and paying taxes to the Emperor in return for the protection, economic advantages, the rule of law and social order they received.

A sign of this more peaceful period is found in the name the Han gave to their capital: Chang'an, or Perpetual Peace. Another is a semantic shift of the word *shih*, which once referred to warrior elite and now to literates fit for civil service. Yet another is the policy of "peace and friendship" (*he-ch'in*) the Han adopted as part of their foreign policy, by which annexations were increasingly made by strategic marriages and diplomatic mission instead of force.[18] For example, a popular story relates that Wang Chao-chün, a princess, was sent off to become the bride of a foreign tribal chieftain as part of a peace agreement, which succeeded. Gift-giving was also used as pre-emptive peacemaking, as no state "has ever made such an effort to supply its neighbors with presents, thus elevating the gift into a political tool."[19] Buddhism's peaceful rise in China dates back to the Han's opening of the famous Silk Road in the second century BCE. Traders and diplomats came into contact with the Yuezhi, a Central Asian tribe whom Ashoka's missionaries converted. By the first century CE, their Kushan Empire was formed, whose rulers sponsored a Fourth Council to formalize the Mahayana tradition, which then slowly spread from the bottom up along the Silk Road to Perpetual Peace by being adapted to local cultures rather than challenging them. Acting on a dream, a Han Emperor sent delegates to Kushan; possibly as a consenting nod to the foreign religion's growing native numbers, China's first Buddhist temple was built upon their return. The Dharma was transposed into the language of the Dao, and was for a long time a folk religion disjointed from the gentry's Confucian Legalism by its emphasis on individual enlightenment instead of service to the state.

The rise of merchant and bureaucratic classes, large landholders and mining magnates, coupled with floods, epidemics and costs of evermore distant annexations began to accentuate inequalities. By 200 CE, rebellions at the peripheries and centre of the Han Empire reached dangerous levels. Blending their brand of Daoism with this dissatisfaction, three brothers began a peasant movement called the Yellow Scarves, which they wore, soon half a million strong. They called their sect the Tai Ping ("Great Peace"), connoting a great age of equality and collective ownership. Paradoxically, and contrary to Daoist teachings, they tried to bring about their Great Peace by waging war against the Han. The Han's generals and armies called upon to suppress such insurrections did so successfully. But in the process, they became more powerful than the Han Emperor himself, and brought about his imperial dynasty's demise. Whirlwinds of warlords filled the Han power vacuum with local military dictatorships. These were consolidated into the Three Kingdoms, ruled by regional overlords whose iron fists barely fended off anarchy. Their infighting introduced the Six Dynasties (222–589), with capitals on the Yangtze River, which came to divide the northern land-backed powers from the southern naval ones, parallel to Sparta and Athens, and who like them more often than not competed violently for supremacy in the others' territories and their own. Brief periods of harmony, usually at the start of new ruling dynasties, were followed by longer discordant ones as they disintegrated, paralleling the Qin's fate. This cycle was driven by disunity and devastation due to internecine struggles and the invasions these invited, including those of the Mongols and Muslim Turks.

To counteract this threatening trend, a policy of Sinicization (Ancient Chinese equivalent of Romanization) was adopted, the idea being to align without friction the interests of those at the fringes of the Empire with its own.[20] Soon-to-be rulers of bordering states were educated at the Imperial court before returning home, while colonies became designated outposts of Imperial culture as well as policy. Instead of peacefully bringing non-Chinese into the Imperial fold, Sinicization often gave hostile outsiders knowledge necessary to take over parts of the Empire and eventually the whole. Towards the end of the Six Dynasties, the reverse of the Sinicization process also took place in that non-Chinese ways were widely adopted by Chinese peoples and their rulers. As bastardized forms of Daoism like the Great Peace became a threat to social order, the elite began to throw their weight behind Buddhism as a more peaceful alter-native. During the north–south split, the more rigidly stratified and tradi-tional south reactively resisted the imported religion, while the new and now foreign powers of the north blended it with existing ideologies to end turmoil by solidifying popular support. The north's syncretic religious policy became the norm throughout China by the Six Dynasties' end, while in India warring Hindu chiefdoms and kingdoms gradually extin-guished Buddhism's presence there. Ancient China was reunited by the short-lived Sui Dynasty (581–618) and flourished under the longer-lived T'ang (619–907). The first of these officialized Buddhism and, ironically, began its exportation as an integral part of Sinicization, such as to the nearby island satellite of what is now Japan.

Foreign Influences and Native Peace in Japanese History

In 1588 CE, during Japan's Warring States period, the Sengoku, an Imperial decree was issued ordering the surrender of weapons to the

Emperor's agents. It is the first Eastern weapons ban explicitly restricting firearms, developed in and imported from outside the Empire:

> The people of the various provinces are strictly forbidden to have in their possession any swords, short swords, bows, spears, firearms or other types of arms. The possession of unnecessary weapons makes difficult the collection of taxes and dues and tends to foment uprisings. . . Therefore the heads of provinces, official agents, and deputies are ordered to collect all the weapons mentioned above and turn them over to the government.[21]

The decree's pivotal words, *unnecessary* weapons, selectively demilitarized the people of Japan for centuries by giving the government full discretion in determining their necessity. Ostensibly, weapons were only needed for external defense. Actually, they were used to subdue and control a close to defenseless internal population. Historically, the use of imported means in maintaining oppressive peace in Ancient Japan long antedated this decree.

While the earliest historical references to Japan are in Han documents of the first century CE, prehistoric remains indicate that game-followers settled on the islands as early as 10,000 BCE. This indigenization period, which lasted until *c.* 300 CE, and its peoples are called the Jomon, who mixed subsistence hunting-gathering with coastal activities such as fishing in small, apparently egalitarian partnership-modeled villages, lacking the resources to sustain intense or prolonged conflict, and so were likely more peaceful than not. Whereas in Ancient India, nomad invasions increased outright and structural violence, a migration of agriculturalists from China and the Korean peninsula did so in Ancient Japan. Along with rice cultivation, they also brought with them metal tools and weapons; each were to become staples. The resulting Yayoi culture (*c.* 300 BCE–250 CE) quickly subsumed the Jomon, keeping its coastal but few of its other cultural traits. The absence of obvious signs of aggression during this transition remains unexplained and highly mismatches their abundance afterwards, including widespread tribal warfare, developed defenses and social stratification, but also the formation of strategic and cooperative alliances between tribes. Han references are to these Yayoi tribes, numbering in the hundreds, certain of which were Han tributaries by 57 CE.

Two centuries later, following years of inter-tribal war, a shamanistic priestess named Himiko is said to have charmed thirty of the Yayoi tribes to confederate in peace for mutual protection and prosperity, Japan's first polity. In 238, she sent gift-bearing emissaries to one of China's Three Kingdoms, who recognized her as the region's sovereign. Two years later they reciprocated, initiating a pattern of peaceful exchange between Japan and China that continued intermittently for a millennium. When Himiko died, her brother-military advisor took the throne. His militarism got him deposed and replaced by a young female relative, Iyo. It was hoped she would bring back the peace of Himiko's reign but she did not. The *Kojiki* (*Record of Ancient Times*, 712) and the *Nihon Shoki* (*Chronicles of Japan*, 720), Japan's earliest native historical records, deal largely with the rise of the subsequent and much more centralized Imperial state.

That the *Kojiki* and *Nihon Shoki* were written in a form of the Chinese script is symbolic of the other mainland traditions which were integrated as Japanese Emperors gained control of the islands, adapting foreign strengths to overcome native weaknesses. Cosmogonies establish the divinity of Emperors by tracing the Imperial lineage back to the sun god Amaterasu, blending natural spirit (*kami*) and ancestor worship in an early form of Shinto, discussed below. Divine Japanese Emperors were unchecked by their Chinese counterparts' Mandate of Heaven, one of the primary differences between the two Imperial systems. The first verifiable Emperor, Suijin (early fourth century CE), was as skilled a negotiator as he was tactician. He and his delegates "relied heavily on negotiation and persuasion – and no doubt threat and coercion – rather than simple military confrontation," as his predecessors had in annexing proximate Yayoi tribes and centralizing power.[22] Social ranks and official titles were used as blunt bait in luring them into the Imperial hierarchy, which gave new members an immediate stake in the state's fate. In this way, hostility towards the Empire was reduced when it could not be eliminated, and peace after non-military incorporations was also more secure than after military ones. Suijin's name has been used ever since by Shintoists to refer to a benevolent water kami.

The Imperial state's first phase (*c.* 250–538) is named after its early elites' burial mounds, the Kofun. These are characteristic expressions of the animism dating to Himiko's times, but also indicate the steady increase in structurally violent social stratification since the Yayoi. Elites such as the powerful Soga clan began concentrating in the Asuka region, whence the Imperial state's second phase (*c.* 538–710) gets its name. They had strong ties to the Korean peninsula, especially one of its own ruling Three Kingdoms. For military support against the other two, Japan received Mahayana Buddhism's peaceful religious know-how, adopted by the Imperial court in the sixth century, which the Soga clan used to unite and pacify subjects old and new in the Emperor's name. Another Korean import, important for its uses in both in war, as cavalry, and in peace, as transportation and labor, was the horse. Meanwhile, flurries of envoys called *kentoshi* to and from China sometimes stayed for years before returning, reinforcing centuries-old ties, keeping Japan up-to-date in legal, religious and administrative affairs. One Japanese envoy, Abe no Nakamaro (seventh century), even passed the Chinese civil service examination and became an important government official there. Dozens of kentoshi were sent during China's Sui and T'ang Dynasties, recorded in the records of both Empires. "The information they brought back was valued highly and their contributions to Japanese culture were incalculable," not least of which were ways of making, maintaining and celebrating *spiritual peace*.[23]

As mentioned, the divine Imperial lineage is traced back to Amaterasu, the Sun Goddess. What has not been discussed is how she came to represent peace and prosperity in general and, in particular, that of the Imperial state. Although Shinto beliefs and practices can be traced back to the native animism of the Yayoi tribes, historical references to them begin with the *Kojiki* in the early eighth century CE when the imperial state was taking shape. The word Shinto was used to distinguish native traditions from foreign Buddhist or Confucian traditions with which they were soon infused. According to the *Kojiki*, Amaterasu's light is what allowed rice to grow, explaining why she was worshipped as the source of all food, ultimately the source of peace. But her brother Susano, god of storms and representative of the warlike tribes the early Empire was struggling to bring into its fold, destroyed all her pacific achievements in a drunken rage. When she emerged from a cave in which she hid herself in reprisal, peace and prosperity returned to the world, implying that the Empire was conceived as the only way for this to happen in the present, notwithstanding its benefits from foreign influences.

By the *Kojiki*'s time, local kami tied to everything from rivers and mountains to animals and elements were already venerated or appeased with offerings and prayers throughout Japan. While no one kami reigned supreme in Shinto polytheism, a hierarchy of deities reflective of the socio-political order emerged. Soon after the *Kojiki*, Buddhism was imported and Shinto fables reflect this as well. In one tale, a transgressive fox kami is brought to order by a Buddhist monk depicted as the upholder of justice and peace. Around the same time, the practice of Shugendo emerged, blending Shinto, Buddhism and Daoism. Its ascetic practitioners lived alone or in small groups and sought inner peace primarily through communion with nature, which they believed could also bring social peace to the communities they once belonged. Zen Buddhist methods of attaining inner peace were more popular, of which two main schools flourished in Japan: Rinzai and Soto. Rinzai emphasized enigmatic or non-rational dialogue (*koan*) to gain immediate Nirvana such as, germane to our topic though admittedly my invention: Can peace exist if there is no one around to experience it? Soto master Dogen (1200–1253) emphasized seated meditation (*zazen*) or in daily activities to reach the same end. So "multi-layered, coexistent and syncretistic beliefs are found everywhere" in Japanese history, nearly all directly related to up-keeping an inner, socio-political or natural order conducive to collective peace.[24]

Another set of supernatural beings called *tengu*, for example, derived from Ancient India and China, came in hundreds of different forms. The most popular was a crow which was thought "to punish those who disturbed the peace of the forest or damaged the trees."[25] Yet another import, the Jaodori festival which began with Chinese residents of Nagasaki, involved a serpent or dragon paraded in the street to symbolize human "striving after peace. . . amid the noise and hardships," symbolized by the clamor of drums, gongs and firecrackers.[26] In more personal but no less supernatural terms, it was believed that the spirit of someone who died with wishes for revenge would not find peace unless "rites for the pacification of his soul were accomplished, or until his enemy had been vanquished."[27] Like the shrines that housed the kami, tombs were places where peace could be made with and for the dead. As late as the seventeenth century, decapitated heads were placed on tombs together with documents stating that the intention was to bring peace to the deceased spirit. Similarly, a common plot of No plays is a ghost who tells the story of their guilt-ridden lives and find not only their own peace of mind with the help of a priest or friends, but that of those who have survived them as well. One may doubt the beliefs upon which such spiritual peace practices are founded, but not that those who performed them believed in their effectiveness regardless of their place of origin.

Socio-politically, Confucian Legalism soon became Japan's Imperial state policy. Prince Shotoku's Seventeen-Article Constitution of 604 made Confucian morality the basis of Imperial society. His successor's Taika or Great Reform of 645–6 made Legalism the ideology of the Imperial state. The Taika was in part a response to the Soga dominance of the Imperial court, whose patriarch was killed in a conspiracy involving the Emperor the year before. In short, the Taika abolished private landholdings, which the Emperor would thereafter own and allot on a per-capita basis; ordered regular censuses for tax and policy purposes; put in place the *ritsuryo*, *ritsu* being the penal code and *ryo* the administrative code, and the bureaucracy required to effect it; and, for the first but not the last time, outlawed weapons not authorized by the state and called for a conscripted army to be levied from across the empire and centrally directed. Oppressive peace in various degrees, broken by wars to remove or impose it, was the norm in Imperial Japan from the Taika onwards, though this did not dry springs of peace in other forms.

A new capital built on the Chang'an model was established at Nara in 710, the start of the next phase of the Imperial state. Emperor Shomu's reign (724–749), who lived as a Buddhist monk after abdicating, is known as the Era of Tempyo or Heavenly Peace, for his bolstering of state and religious institutions. Temples like the Todaiji were given tax-exempt status, adding economic to religious clout by the "donations" they received from wealthy families for cost-effective safekeeping. Reacting to this religious loophole, the capital was moved to Heian-kyo ("Capital of Peace," modern Kyoto) in 794, beginning the final phase of the early Imperial state that lived up to its capital's name until the eleventh century. Rivalries between clans once located outside the Empire were now internalized in the form of courtly influence on the Emperor. In the words of one modern historian, "The Heian period was characterized by peace and prosperity. . . there was no large-scale general warfare in the country."[28] Regencies set in place by the powerful Fujiwara clan eventually reduced Heian Emperors to nominal sovereigns, and the Taika eroded as Chinese influence waned with the fall of the T'ang. Diplomatic documents now referred to Japan as the "Land of the Rising Sun" and China as the "Land of the Setting Sun," suggesting an equal or even superior footing, infuriating the former hegemons, and the last kentoshi was sent in 838. Increasing isolationism reduced external warfare, but also weakened cultural and commercial links with the mainland that had benefited internal peace in the past.

Towards the end of the Heian period, Imperial lands were increasingly privatized by an elite minority and their tax-sheltered temples while the vast majority became their vassals. These lands, known as Shoen, were exempt from Imperial law and taxes by the tenth century. With the revenue reduction and jurisdictional limitations Shoen entailed, the conscripted Imperial army that had maintained oppressive peace since the Taika had by the eleventh century become one levied by provincial governors on their own account without counterbalancing forces. A distinction thus materialized between *public wars* fought on behalf of the state and *private wars* instigated by and fought between governors' armies.[29] At first, all private wars were punishable by the Imperial state by banishment or death. But as the forces called upon to enforce these punishments for breaching the peace were increasingly involved in private wars themselves, the legitimacy of the Imperial state doing so waned with its authority. "This placed the state in the ironic position of depending on the very group most active in outlawry to preserve the peace," and ultimately led to its inability to preserve peace altogether, a lesson that costs much to relearn.[30] By the twelfth century, Shoen needed protection not only from brigands and bandits, but from each other and the Imperial state itself. An emerging class of warriors, the samurai, was eager to provide them both for profit and glory. Shoguns, warlords who ruled or tried to rule Japan until they were overthrown in the nineteenth century, did so based on the Shoen and samurai systems. Shoen lords, Daimyo, to whom the samurai owed allegiance, in turn owed allegiance to Shoguns. Their struggles for supremacy, in the Emperor's name or not, precluded the oppressive peace they sought to achieve, if and when they did at all.

Among their many maxims was that "It is a good maxim for the samurai in peace time never to forget war."[31]

The Bushi or warrior elite were often well educated and knew they contravened the spirit of the long defunct Taika and non-violent Buddhist principles. So they lived by their own code, the Bushido, formulated in the Kamakura period (1185–1333). An early Bushido master stressed learning and military arts as the guiding principles of samurai: "Literature first, and arms next to it. . . They must be cultivated concurrently."[32] Like chivalry in medieval Europe, the Bushido can be understood as an attempt to "civilize" militarism, circumscribing while justifying its use. Core Bushido virtues included honor, respect, honesty and loyalty: a Confucianism of swords instead of words. "If you have an opponent, says Bushido, beat him. . . but once you have beaten him, then see to it that you make him your friend."[33] Accommodation was vital for the Bushi both for survival and success, seen in the tradition of two leaders of warring factions seeking to let the other write peace terms. "Each considered that the other, knowing that peace would come only from a real accommodation of interests, would write terms acceptable to both sides, a policy most would consider too perilous today."[34]

Bushi lore tells of a sword kept at the Iso no Kami Shrine (modern Nara prefecture) that has "the power to maintain peace in the country."[35] It was used in a dance aimed at pacifying evil spirits that caused illness to Emperors, upon whose health the Empire's rested. They also painted a figure called Fudo on votive offerings for peace in troubled times, usually depicted with a red face, large eyes, wild hair and a halo of flames. Of all Bushi traditions, however, none is better known today than ceremonial tea drinking. Beside his famous Silver Pavilion, a Shogun of the Ashikaga period (1338–1597) built Japan's first tea room, where he and friends could experience "a few fleeting moments of peace" since, as became the custom throughout the realm, weapons were required to be left outside tea rooms, secular temples.[36] Bushi militarism did keep the Mongols, who had conquered much of mainland Asia, off the Japanese Islands, but European traders who arrived in the sixteenth century to exchange guns for goods were more difficult to resist. Shogun rule was progressively fractured by constant wars between Daimyo, in which samurai were massacred by trigger-pulling peasants enlisted en masse for the first time since the Taika. The weapons ban cited above was issued during the Azuchi-Momoyama period (1568–1600) to diffuse this dangerous and destabilizing situation, after its short-lived Shoguns militarily reunified all the Shoen. Many forms of non-armed martial arts, such as Karate, were developed underground so that the demilitarized population would not be totally defenseless. Emboldened by his successful selective demilitarization, the Shogun Hideyoshi (1537–1598) carried out the first foreign campaign in centuries. He tried to conquer the Korean peninsula with a conscripted army, but his failure resulted in his downfall and a change in military regimes.

Tokugawa Shoguns (1600–1868), with their capital at Edo near modern Tokyo, brought about a slight return of oppressive peace by building on the successes and capitalizing on the failures of their predecessors. Over the course of their extended reign, they enforced the rule of law in the Emperor's name; somewhat demilitarized the Bushido to bolster state bureaucracy; greatly reduced the number of Daimyo, granting them local autonomy for peaceable alignment with central policy; and redistributed the Shoen for political and production purposes. At first, they encouraged economic and cultural exchanges with still-new sets of foreigners, Western ones such as the Portuguese and Dutch, while renewing contacts with China and Korea. Hayashi Razan (early seventeenth century), advisor to Shogun Tokugawa Ieyasu, was a famed Neo-Confucian scholar who exemplifies the renewed interest in foreign affairs of Japanese culture and statecraft during the early part of this period. "To have the arts of peace," he wrote, "but not the arts of war, is to lack courage. To have the arts of war, but not the arts of peace, is to lack wisdom."[37] His house in Edo had a large library and came to be called the Hall of Confucian Learning. Within fifty years, it had become the official Head of State University and, after being relocated to another part of Edo and enlarged, was renamed The School of Prosperous Peace (*Shoheiko*) in 1691. These and other re-integrations of foreign into native culture have led many historians to call this early era the Tokugawa Peace.

By the 1700s, however, foreign influences were once again perceived as threats to native traditions of peace and power. A strict isolationist policy called Sakoku, punishing unauthorized departures from and arrivals to the Japanese islands by death, was enacted to preserve oppressive peace from within by selectively eliminating and channeling intercessions from without. Only the Dutch and Chinese, seen as the most peaceful foreign forces, were permitted to do business from ports at strategic distances from Edo. By the end of the nineteenth century, Tokugawa Shoguns sought to further purge foreign influences by returning to a "pure" Shinto. Religious traditions once skillfully combined to prevent and end violence were displaced by Shinto priests paid to pray for peace. With the Meiji restoration of the Emperor at American instigation and Shoguns' expense in 1868 (see Chapter 7), state Shinto was once again used to glorify the Emperor, but this time to justify policies of aggression. After two world wars in which Japan played no small part, the new national Shinto organization issued the following peaceful policy, returning to its roots:

1. Be grateful to the kami for their blessings and to the ancestors for their beneficence; devote yourselves to shrine ritual with hearts of sincerity, bright and pure.
2. Serve society and all people; as purveyors of the wishes of the kami, restructure the world and give it substance.
3. Respect the emperor as mediator of the wishes of the Sun Goddess; be sure to follow his wishes; pray for good fortune for the people of Japan, and of all nations and pray, too, that the world may live in peace and prosperity.[38]

4
Monotheistic Peaces: Judaism, Christianity and Islam

Shalom: Peace in the Torah and its Times

The Hebrew word for peace, Shalom, is today a customary Jewish greeting. But the uses of the word in the Torah, which recounts the early history, theology and principles of the Jewish people, are far more complex and are directly related to contemporary concerns. By its narratives alone, the Torah is "a violent book with an obvious bias towards strife" in line with its violent, strife-filled times.[1] As contexts, however, these narratives foreground the evolution of physical, spiritual, ethical and socio-political contents of Shalom. Caught between the rival powers of Mesopotamia and Egypt, Hebrew-speaking nomadic pastoralists of the Patriarchs' generations (Abraham, Isaac and Jacob, c. 2000–1500 BCE) were also at the mercy of nature. Originally from Ur, they set out on foot into the desert for distant Canaan, the Promised Land, after Abraham received a divine order to do so. In a very physical sense, then, Shalom first meant protection from human and elemental hostilities surrounding a people always on the run.

The spiritual covenant with God, by which Abraham's progeny would be plentiful and prosper in the Promised Land with divine protection, was in a way a conditional treaty on the tributary model. For these blessings, full submission and undivided devotion to the deity was required of them. The originality of this "covenant of peace" that God continually renewed with Abraham and his descendents is that it tied a single god to a single group of people exclusively and indefinitely, whereas syncretism and henotheism were then the main modes of religious peacemaking in the region at the time. Many gods are recognized in the Torah, one of which chooses Abraham's people, giving them and their descendents a unique identity and destiny. In return, they choose this god to be *the* God for them, demoting the rest to idols. Highly anthropomorphized, this God (Yahweh) walks and talks with Abraham, is jealous of other gods, and gets vengefully angry when he is disobeyed. As the search for the Promised Land's peaceful safe-haven continues, Yahweh inflicts atrocities on those standing in the spiritual or logistical way of his people, reinforcing their belief in Yahweh's provident omnipotence and the covenant of peace. For his part, Abraham occasionally takes on the role of diplomat, as in the non-aggression pact made with a Philistine king and his general near Canaan. "Show me," says the king,"and the country where you are living as an alien the same kindness I have shown you," a typical description of the guest–host relationship crucial to the survival of migrants in settled lands.² Abraham swears to this and offers seven ewes for access to a well, in the vicinity of which he died and where his progeny prospered for a while under his son Isaac. The peoples of all three monotheisms would later trace their peace traditions back to Abraham.

In individual terms, Shalom came to refer to inner peace qualified by health, serenity of mind and spiritual purity from sins such as idolatry. In search of this, Jacob (Isaac's son and last of the Patriarchs) fled from famine to fertile Egypt with his people, where they were eventually enslaved. There, inner Shalom became a means of preserving their faith, identity and lives in the face of ongoing oppression, without which the Jewish faith might not exist today. During the subsequent Exodus from Egypt to Canaan, the ethical principles or laws of Jewish society were made explicit by its leader, the Prophet Moses. As an adopted member of the Pharaoh's court, he had tried to make peace between the enslavers and the enslaved, as well to promote it among the enslaved themselves. When these attempts failed, he tried to negotiate with the Pharaoh for their release. The Pharaoh agreed only when Yahweh wreaked ten plagues upon the Egyptians and, with similar support, Moses and the former slaves subdued the hostile human and natural forces they met with, at great cost of lives and resources. The Ten Commandments revealed to him on the journey were meant not only to promote peace among his people, but also between them and Yahweh, who it was now believed must be punishing them for their wayward ways. The first four renew the exclusive covenant of peace discussed above, prohibiting the worship of other gods or idols and holding Yahweh and the day of worship in the highest esteem. The last six are basic guidelines for living in a stable, unwarlike society, quite the contrary of theirs at the time: not murdering or stealing, nor coveting property or people, and treating parents with respect. The "eye for an eye" doctrine put forth a few passages later complements the

Commandments as a preventative measure, but contradicts them by perpetuating instead of stopping violence in conveying a retaliatory justice confusable with the commendation of conflict. Having barely made it to Canaan, Yahweh called upon Moses to write the traditions his people had passed down orally since before Abraham's time, after which he soon died. Being a "people of the book," discussed below, further distinguished his religion from those tied to persons or things, and lent a portability and permanence to the instructions for individual and social Shalom that later provided the basis for both socio-political and Messianic Shalom.

The conquest of Canaan (c. thirteenth–eleventh centuries BCE) led by Moses' protégé and the most military of the Prophets, Joshua, was a cruel and drawn-out affair despite and because of divine interventions. It was motivated by a belief that the sought-for Shalom was tied to a specific geographical location and a God-given right to occupy it regardless of present residents. Bloody battles between the newcomers and the locals over land, resources and religion continued long after settlement started, though Joshua had "made peace with them, and made a league with them, to let them live."[3] Following his death, the settlements were divided among twelve traditional tribes descending from Jacob's twelve sons. These fractious new conditions and the infighting they brought about created a need to redefine Shalom in a more socially cooperative, politically united sense. The religious messages Shalom had carried for more than a millennium thus slowly took on the added dimensions of a socio-political ideal. Mixing legislative, judicial and religious powers, potentates called Judges (shopetim) were invested with decision-making authority for and between the twelve tribes, presiding over individual cases and over their collective activities. In the Judges' hands, Shalom came to mean an arrangement or agreement reached by mutual consent, legitimately authorized and justly implemented by established processes. Peace was now associated with power equilibriums conducive to prosperous internal order and strong defences from external threats, as when the Prophet Isaiah later proclaimed "let him take hold of my strength, that he may make peace with me."[4] As Judges consolidated their territorial gains over the course of two centuries, they began to show the same peaceable guest-host parity to strangers as their forefathers had once received in the same region. Simultaneously, attempts began to be made to consolidate previous innerpersonal into an inter-personal peace by turning wisdom, generosity, charity and patience into admirable qualities, not yet as substitutes but as additions to the warlike ones of yore.

The twelve tribes, probably drawing on the monarchical models elsewhere in the region, began agitating for a king to solidify these consolidations, only three of which ruled (c. eleventh–tenth centuries BCE) before the Promised Land was once again lost. The last Judge, Samuel, appointed the first two Kings, Saul and David. Yahweh supported Saul as he led the twelve tribes to military victories over regional rivals, but then condemned him for keeping loot for himself, and he dies in battle shortly thereafter. Under David, the twelve tribes' combined forces were able to fully pacify their foes. The internal peace David's defensive/offensive alliances conferred to the twelve tribes was offset by the external wars by which it came into being. With fewer and fewer enemies left to be united against, staying united in and for peace became more and more of a problem. David's dream of building a great temple in the kingdom's new capital, Jerusalem, was forbidden by Yahweh because David was a "man of battles" who had "shed blood."[5] Yahweh, once a staunch supporter of his people's wars, had become the protagonist of their peace. Famed for his wisdom, David's son and successor's name is a variation of Shalom and his early reign an example of its socio-political meaning. King Solomon, reaping the benefits of his forefathers' cumulative achievements, also extended them. With peace at the borders and prosperity within them, Solomon established new cities and repaired old ones throughout the kingdom while founding several colonies. He formed inter-kingdom economic alliances, as with the King of Tyre, and political ones by way of multiple marriages, as with a Pharaoh's daughter. Yahweh, approving of Solomon's peaceful reign up to this point, allowed him to build the great temple David was denied, where ancient ritual sacrifices intended to appease, give thanks to and glorify the deity continued. But he began levying disproportionately heavy taxes affecting the poor and demanded compulsory labor to execute his extensive building programme in Jerusalem, stirring dissent among the more distant tribes. He also encouraged his foreign wives in practicing their native religions, shocking his subjects' spiritual sensibilities, to say nothing of Yahweh. Shortly after Solomon's death, these policies divided the kingdom, the strength and peace of which depended on unity and justice. The ten northern tribes seceded and became Israel; the two southern, loyalist tribes became Judea. Israel, weak and war-torn, fell to the Assyrians in 722 BCE. In the same state, Judea fell to the Babylonians in 586 BCE, when the great temple symbolizing King Solomon's Shalom was destroyed.

The subsequent Exile and Diaspora or "scattering" of the Hebrew people, at first around the region then across the Hellenic and Roman Empires, stretched Shalom's meanings in new directions. Without a homeland, estranged or integrated in societies often historically unrelated to them, and a lack of military wherewithal dramatically changed perspectives on peace. Suddenly, tactical surrender as a means to Shalom began to be preferred to conflict, armed or otherwise. Power was no longer considered solely as an instrument of survival and domination, but also as a means of constructively reforming societies from within, instead of destructively from without. "Be at peace," asserts Job in the book bearing his name, "and thereby thou shalt have the best fruits."[6] Renewed readings of the Torah, now taking its final form, informed prophecies and philosophies aimed at collective transformations, Kabala enhanced the mystical elements of Judaic inner peace, while exegetical works such as the Talmud aimed at conserving peace-oriented priestly, legal and lay traditions. Genesis, the first book of the Torah, tells of a Paradise called the Garden of Eden created by God for humankind where the primordial man and woman (Adam and Eve) lived in plenty and perfect peace with each other, the natural world and the deity. However, tempted by a serpent, they sacrificed this sublime Shalom by disobeying God's only command to them: not to eat from the Tree of Knowledge of good and evil. As punishment, God cast them and their descendents out of Paradise into this world of toil and trouble. Cain, one of their sons, kills his brother Abel in a jealous rage over God's preferential treatment, the act of violence back to which the three monotheisms sharing this story trace the history of warfare. Just as the peace of Paradise was lost by the sin of its inhabitants, so it was now believed was that of its closest approximation since Solomon's kingdom. God had sent many great leaders to guide his people after their banishment from Paradise. Now that they were banished from the Promised Land, a widespread belief emerged that the peaces of the past would return in the near future through a new kind of leader.

Working within this theological paradigm, Jewish Prophets predicted the coming of a Messiah ("Anointed One") who would bring about spiritual salvation, ethical regeneration, Shalom to God's people and, through them, to humanity. The Messianic message was one of universal peace, though along strict sectarian lines. The Messiah would be a descendent of David, but part human and part divine. His wisdom and justice would pacify the earth, which would then become his undivided kingdom. His peaceful reign would be eternal; he would purify the hearts and minds of his subjects, who would then model their morals and actions on his; and God would accept his suffering as atonement for humanity's sins since Adam and Eve's fall from grace. After the Messiah's arrival, "the work of righteousness shall be peace," as opposed to the history of righteous warfare in God's name preceding it, and "the effect of righteousness quietness and assurance forever."[7] The Messiah would also be a conciliator, as "the wolf shall dwell with the lamb, and the leopard shall lie down with the kid," but would concurrently deliver divine judgment, so that "there is no peace to the wicked."[8] The Messiah would be an activist arbiter, stopping all wars at their sources:

And he shall judge among the nations, and shall rebuke many people; and they shall beat their swords into ploughs, and their spears into pruning hooks; nation shall not lift sword against nation, neither shall they learn war anymore.[9]

Through the Messiah, Shalom in all its meanings would come into being and Paradise would be restored. Combining Jewish with the Greco-Roman traditions, Philo of Alexandria (c. 30 BCE–40 CE) concluded that war is a corruption of the soul curable by living "with fellow citizens in peace and law-observance, that order of which justice is the guiding influence."[10] The peace he envisioned by synthesizing the Pax Romana's ideological imperative and the Messianic message was single, indivisible, the same for one and all. But one question the Prophets left unanswered was: When exactly would the Messiah's Shalom arrive?

"Our" Universal Peace: From Christ to Constantine

The history of Christianity from its origins to its adoption by the Eastern Roman Emperor Constantine (c. 280–337) is inseparable from the peace and peacemaking preached and practiced by its founder, Jesus of Nazareth or Jesus Christ, Messiah in Greek. Indeed, Jesus' innovative forms of pacification, pacifism and peacemaking were decisive in the early proliferation of his doctrine. However, from Jesus' immediate followers onwards, as the socio-political situation of Christians changed, so did their ideals and practices of peace, sometimes even in the opposite directions in which they were originally intended. Jesus' life and death are innermost to pacific Christian practices and beliefs. The story is recounted in the Gospels ("Good News") of the Apostles Matthew, Mark, Luke and John, the first four books of the New Testament, the Torah being the Old and the two together, the Bible. This link would prove to be the starting point of both amity and strife between practitioners of the two religious traditions, and a third.

Jesus' lineage is traced back to David, genealogically positioning him as the prophesized, peace-bearing Messiah. Son of a virgin mother and an itinerant carpenter from Galilee, once part of Judea and now ruled by the Jewish King Herod on behalf of Rome, angels are said to have greeted his birth with the words "Peace on earth to men of good will."[11] The only episode told of Jesus' youth is that his parents, having lost him for three days, found him at the local temple amazing priests with his knowledge of the Torah. The story picks up again some twenty years later as he is ritually purified by John the Baptist, who publicly attests that Jesus is the Messiah Prophets had foretold. After fasting for forty days in the desert, where he refutes temptations by quoting scripture, he embarks on his mission to prepare humanity for God's final judgment and peaceful heavenly kingdom. He grudgingly performs miracles such as healing the diseased and resurrecting the dead to prove his divinity to the doubtful of all races and religions. When met with hostility he never reciprocated, avoiding violence by subterfuge or persuasion. He is often portrayed catering solely to the sick, weak and downtrodden whom the religions of the times considered disfavoured by their deities, in proposing they would be favoured on judgment day and the first to enter God's kingdom, making him popular among them. But he also preached to soldiers, tax collectors, priests and officials whose salvation was also assured if they changed their beliefs and ways, eliciting affection as well as animosity. Jews, non-Jews and members of all sections of society became his disciples, showing that his transformation of the particular Messianic message into one of universal import was working.

Jesus set out the terms of a new covenant – one of peace not only between Jews and God, but also among all humans and with God – in a series of readily intelligible sermons and parables, accounting in part for the speedy distance of their dissemination. The most influential, the Sermon on the Mount, contains the following passages, which distinguished his message from that of the Jewish past and defined Christian non-violence, or the *law of love*:

> Blessed are the peacemakers, for they will be called sons of God. . . You have heard that it was said, 'Eye for eye, and tooth for tooth.' But I tell you: resist not evil. If someone strikes you on the right cheek, turn to him the other also. . . You have heard that it was said, 'Love your neighbour and hate your enemy.' But I tell you: Love your enemies and pray for those who persecute you, that you may be sons of your Father in heaven.[12]

By the old covenant, Yahweh had condoned his people's use of violence to pacify their way to the Promised Land. The new covenant was a commitment to reject hate and violence as evil, the doctrine of Christian pacifism, and diffuse violence by forgiving and loving deeds, the doctrine of Christian peacemaking. Similarly, the Parable of the Good Samaritan depicts unconditional kindness in helping others regardless of who they are. Fostering peace in this life by working for the benefit of others in this way became a spiritual reward infinitely more valuable than any material reward because it is the basis upon which God will judge our worthiness of everlasting, blissful peace and felicity in the next life. Jesus' so-called Golden Rule, "do unto others as you would have them do unto you," expresses the Parable's moral in prescriptive form.[13] But its proactive formula, by which what is peaceful for me is peaceful for you, can be less propitious and entail more risks than the passivity of Confucius' Silver Rule.

The inner peace Jesus proposed was as much the prerequisite of the new covenant as social peace was its result, discernable in his send-off to disciples to preach and do good works in his name: "When you enter a house, first say, 'Peace to this house.' If a man of peace is there, your peace will rest on him; if not, it will return to you."[14] Unlike the peace of the Promised Land, limited by its ties to a single people and geographical location, the peace of the heavenly kingdom Jesus proposed was open to all and not of this world, not even of this life, but of the next. Unlike the peace of Paradise, isolated in the spiritual and temporal past, the peace of the future heavenly kingdom offered peace of mind, consolation and hope in the present on the basis of reincarnation. Believers thus had a strong motivation for sacrifice and personal betterment. Hence, in one instance, Jesus says to an Apostle, "Put up again thy sword in its place: for they that take the sword shall perish with the sword."[15] And in another, he says, "I have told you these things, so that in me you may have peace. In this world you will have trouble. But take heart! I have overcome the world."[16] The overcoming Jesus speaks of here is ethical and peaceful, as in forgiveness and fellowship, rather than material and violent, as in fighting foes. He advised that rulers who are contemplating going to war with another should first seek peace, especially if they are weaker. So important was peace to Jesus' ministry that among his last words to disciples were: "Peace I leave with you; my peace I give you. I do not give to you as the world gives. Do not let your hearts be troubled and do not be afraid."[17]

Within no more than three years, Jesus' radical teachings rooted in Jewish traditions had such a following the authorities perceived him as a threat. That John the Baptist was beheaded by King Herod may have given Jesus a premonition of his suffering and death to come, called the Passion, in any case confirmed to him by God. Following a triumphal entrance into Jerusalem, the solemn Last Supper took place, during which disciples learned of upcoming events and roles they would play to their dismay. Bread and wine Jesus passed around to symbolize the passing of his body and blood also signified that the Passion would be the seal of the new covenant. That night, as portended, Jesus was arrested by the betrayal of disciple Judas for thirty pieces of silver. He did not resist the arrest, nor did he denounce his betrayer, nor did he allow the other disciples to protest on his behalf. Jesus then avowed the two crimes for which he was tried separately: first by a Jewish council for blasphemy, for not denying he was Son of God; second by the Roman authorities for sedition, for not denying he was the King of the Jews. His punishment was death by crucifixion, including a long, cross-carrying procession during which convicts like him were spat on and stoned. The people of Jerusalem, given the choice between saving Jesus or a militant insurrectionist, chose the latter. Christian faith is founded upon his subsequent resurrection and ascension to heaven, celebrated as Easter today. Jesus' self-sacrifice, and God's of his only son, to atone for humanity's sins was believed to be the final preparation for the everlasting peace of the heavenly kingdom, which must therefore be close at hand. Otherwise violent, the Passion is vital to the history of peace because it became the non-violent model for early Christian life and martyrdom, backed by Jesus' pacific teachings and theology, which made peace into the *moral imperative* it became throughout the rest of Western history.

With the missionary work of the Twelve Apostles ("envoys") after the Passion, Jesus' ministry took on the features of an organized religious peace movement, the second major one in world history after Ashokan Buddhism. Each was assigned a different group or part of the Roman Empire to proselytize: for example, while Peter was sent to the Jews of the Diaspora, Paul was sent to the Gentiles, or non-Jews. They acted on Jesus' orders, but also in his image as one who "came and preached peace to you that were far off and to them that were close," and suffered a similar fate, "making peace through his blood, shed on the cross."[18] Demonizing warfare, they preached and practiced peace. Humanity, in their view, had already been spiritually unified by Jesus' self-sacrifice, so "There is neither Jew nor Greek, there is neither bond nor free, there is neither male nor female: for all are one in Jesus Christ."[19] As "God is not the author of confusion, but of peace," they recognized and reconciled cultural differences to promote a religious unity that was almost political.[20] The peace Jesus once called his was now ours: "For he himself is our peace, who has made the two [Jews and Gentiles] one and has destroyed the barrier, the dividing wall of hostility."[21] Evangelism was peacemaking because God "reconciled us to himself through Christ and gave us the ministry of reconciliation: that God was reconciling the world to himself in Christ, not counting men's sins against them."[22]

In Philo's footsteps, the Apostles made great efforts to syncretise Greco-Roman ideas and ideals with those of Jesus' Jewish tradition, without which Christianity would not have taken root peacefully, if it would have at all. Catered to their intended audiences (such as Romans, Hebrews, Corinthians), Apostolic Epistles form Part II of the New Testament. Their unifying theme is that an imminent supernatural event would suddenly occur through which worthy believers would be selected for the heavenly kingdom and unworthy unbelievers banished from it. Upon this Second Coming of Christ, "While people are saying, 'Peace and safety,' destruction will come on them suddenly, as labour pains on a pregnant woman, and they will not escape."[23] The severity of the justice and the perfection of the peace to come made present injustices and wars ephemeral. Because the Second Coming's timing was uncertain and could not be sped up, the best that early believers could do was to pray for, participate in and propagate the pacifist and pacification principles Christ had taught, lived by and died for. The objective of the Apostolic generations of Christians was thus not to establish a new state, but to prepare themselves as individuals for the Second Coming. Roman militarism, the backbone of its cosmopolitan culture, left little room for mercy, compassion and forgiveness. Early Christianity, in counter-culturally promoting these, focused on spiritual and behavioural principles rather than organizational or theological ones. As inequalities in this world would soon be levelled in the next, no new social system was required for salvation regardless of the structural and outright violence suffered under the yoke of Roman rule. With pacification in God's hands, the prospect of the Second Coming put the urgency of involvement in worldly affairs on an early Epicurean-like hold.

Far from inciting rebellion, Jesus' well-known maxim to give to Caesar what is Caesar's and to God what is God's was taken as a call to respect and obey civil authority insofar as doing so did not conflict with his religious authority or moral precepts. Reinforced by the Apostles, this principle gave early Christians their political strategy vis-à-vis Rome: rapprochement. However, two impassable points of contention soon became obligatory: Emperor-worship and mandatory military service, impossible for pacifist Christians because they were tantamount to damnation. To the extent that the antimilitarism and monotheism of early Christians disrupted the stable paradigms of Roman imperialism and mythology, they met with suppression and persecution carried out systematically by imperial powers, arbitrarily by local powers, and sporadically by popular powers. Using violence in self-defence was out of the question not only because it went against their convictions, but because it put their very survival at risk. Martyrs, modeling their death on that of Jesus, became the first Christian heroes less for the example they set than for the idea and ideal of non-violence they represented. One of these, ironically named after the "pagan" goddess of peace Irene, was later canonized by the Catholic and Orthodox Churches as the first patron saint of peace. Breaking Roman law could bring on material, corporeal punishments that could end with death; God's punishment for breaking Christ's law of love was spiritual and eternal. Following Christ and the Apostles, the first Christians thus positioned themselves not as Rome's foes but as its victims, paradoxically the position from which they gained an Empire but at the cost of the very peaceful principles upon which this position was founded.

In the post-Apostolic era, roughly from the late first to the early fourth century CE, fervour for the Second Coming and missionary zeal subsided somewhat. The conviction that the condition of the world at large, not just preparedness of individuals, would affect God's judgment whenever it came spread slowly, so that theological questions and organizational issues once considered irrelevant now needed to be faced – and fast. The growing numbers of Christian cells, even in the Roman army, and communities as at Rome made peaceful relations between their members and with the state the top socio-political concerns. Leaders of the loose network of Christian churches began realizing that their cause could and was benefiting, at least in some ways, from its unique situation within an imperial infrastructure that had created order and stability in an enormous geographical area and among a great diversity of peoples. As critical masses were reached by the second century CE, pressing questions arose as to whether Christians could, would or should become the heirs or replacements of the Roman Empire instead of being its victims. If so, how would the transition from the Pax Romana to Christ's kingdom take place? If not, how would Christian and Roman traditions coexist?

Bishops who took over the Apostles' regional sees by succession eventually became the churches' official representatives and collectively decided policy and doctrine, while deacons managed the day-to-day of the churches, increasingly well-funded by wealthy converts. Only presbyters continued the tradition of working directly for the benefit of all. Mixed among these were intellectuals, discussed below, who exemplified the idea, popular among the upper classes, that the ideal Christian was not a blind believer, but one capable of defending Christian beliefs with their minds just as vigorously and non-violently as martyrs did with their bodies. After three centuries of pacifism, Christianity was no longer an underground religion, but was now openly competing with Romanization from the inside out and the bottom upwards. Christians won over the Empire when Emperor Constantine who, as it happened, founded a temple to Irene soon after making Constantinople the new capital, converted to Christianity and outlawed persecutions by the Edict of Milan in 313. However, Constantine also passed an ecumenical law by which any Christian who abandoned or refused to bear arms for Rome was excommunicated. In this way, he fully aligned the interests of Church and State, but also betrayed the pacifism by which this alignment had come into being. Religious persecutions continued, but increasingly it was the Christians perpetrating them against polytheists, Christian heretics, Jews and each other.

Christian intellectuals in the Western Roman Empire adopted philosophical pragmatism to address political issues faced by their churches. Saint Justin (*c.* 100–65), born in Palestine and martyred in Rome, wrote two *Apologias* addressed to the Roman Senate. In the first, he used the aphorism "You can kill, but not hurt us" to highlight both the ungodly violence Christians still suffered as well as their godly commitment to non-violence.[24] Building on this point, in the second he argued that while peace on earth could be imposed, as the Pax Romana purported to do, the peace of heaven must be earned. In another *Apologia* addressed to Roman Emperor Marcus Aurelius, Saint Melito (d. 180), a bishop of Sardis in modern Turkey, argued that the Empire was part of God's plan for the spread of Christianity's universal pacification and peace, noting that the start of the Pax Romana roughly coincided with the birth of Christ. Considered Christendom's first great Latin writer, Tertullian (155–228), echoing Saint Justin, stated the paradoxical inversion of values displayed by the martyrs whose executions he witnessed in his native Carthage: "Your peace is war for him."[25] He went on to redefine empire as a brotherhood without borders which could even include converted barbarians, replacing the internal/external dichotomy that had sustained the military basis of the Pax Romana, and brought about its downfall. Though writing in defence of one who refused to worship his commander in chief, the term "Christian soldier" was an oxymoron for Tertullian because "by disarming Peter, the Lord dismissed all soldiers."[26] Instead, he proposed not only that Christians could pray for emperors as opposed to worship them, but that Christianity itself could curb abuses of imperial power detrimental to peace by the emperor being reminded that he is not God. A later Carthaginian, Saint Cyprian (d. 285) shared Tertullian's antimilitarism: "Homicide is a crime when committed by the individual, but a virtue when it is collective. It is not innocence, but the scale of the harm they cause which ensures that rogues get off scot-free."[27] The vision of a Roman-Christian peace on earth of a third Carthaginian, Arnobius (d. 330), was put forth in an effort to refute the claim that Christianity, particularly its pacifism, was the cause of Rome's ongoing decline. Tertullian, Cyprian and Arnobius set the groundwork for their fellow North African and the most influential intellectual of the early Middle Ages, Saint Augustine.

Christian intellectuals of the Eastern Empire adopted theological speculation to address religious issues regarding the spiritual unity and integrity of individual believers and those of the doctrine of their churches. The scholastic center of Christianity was Alexandria, where Clement (*c.* 150–210) and his student Origen (*c.* 185–252), headed the catechetical school. In Clement's view, peace is the point of education, and war the result of its absence: "We are educated not for war but for peace. In war, there is need for much equipment, just as self-indulgence craves abundance. But peace and love, simple and plain blood sisters, do not need arms nor abundant supplies."[28] Yet, he uses military language to urge learning how to use peace and pacifism: "Let us therefore learn to handle the arms of peace," meaning faith and scripture, "these are our arms and nowhere will they inflict wounds."[29] Origen, on the other hand, saw peace in the negative: "You can say there is peace when no one lives in a state of discord, when no one gives way to quarrelsomeness and there is no hostility or cruelty."[30] For him, the peace and unity of humanity through Christianity was not limited by the empire or to cosmopolitan concord, but was cosmic in the name of Christ. Peacemaking was the duty of Christians as "children of peace," both by the exemplary life Jesus had led and "for the sake of Jesus who is our leader."[31] The *Apostolic Constitutions*, a collection of prayers and customs of the Eastern churches compiled shortly after Constantine's death, partly concur with Clement and Origen, and partly contradict: "Let us pray for the peace and settlement of the world and of the holy churches; that the God of the whole world may afford us His everlasting peace, and such as may not be taken from us."[32] Jesus' peace, once "his," then "ours" in a universal sense, was now reserved for "us" Christians. As this prayer suggests, the primary problem facing Christianity after making peace with the Empire was how to keep "our" universal peace for and within Christianity itself.

A Pillar of Peace: The Qur'an and its World

Though embedded in them, unlike Judeo-Christian peace principles and practices, those of Islam technically could not develop even if from its origins onwards they were manifested very differently in different circumstances. This *static dynamism* stems from the belief that the message Mohammed (570–632) transmitted in the Qur'an was God's culminating revelation to humanity. So while its core communication is one of peaceful unity through the tolerance and benevolence that come with complete submission to God, Muslims have theologically and historically held Qur'anic methods of applying these principles for peace as unchangeable as they are inviolable.

Mohammed was born in Mecca, a trade-route oasis town off the western coast of the Arabian Peninsula prone to flash floods. Aside from its commercial activities, Mecca's main attraction was a masonry structure, later called the Kaaba, to which pilgrimages were made for the tribal jinn figures it housed. He belonged to the Quraysh tribe, a local power by its control of the caravan trade with the northern superpowers, Christian Byzantium and Zoroastrian Persia, monotheist monarchies always at war with one another. Orphaned as a child, he was adopted by his uncle, a merchant of a minor Quraysh clan. Little is known of his youth other than he also became a merchant, a peripatetic profession bringing him in contact with Jewish and Christian traders, probably Arabic-speaking like himself. When a flash flood damaged the Kaaba, a dispute arose between the Quraysh clans as to who would place the honorary last stone. Mohammed is said to have spread out his cloak on the ground, put the stone in the centre and asked clan heads to place it together. His reputation for justice, trustworthiness and honesty attracted a wealthy older widow, whom he married and with whom he had six children.

Then, around 610, Mohammed's life changed. God began speaking to him through the archangel Gabriel, as his wife and a few other Meccans came to believe. The divine messages he received, sometimes in ecstatic fits, over the next two decades became the Qur'an, literally a recitation. An early recitation, the infamous Satanic Verses, seems to have allowed the worship of three jinn along with Allah, Supreme Being in Arabic, perhaps a theological effort to bring the Quraysh clans together as Mohammed had with the cloak.[33] But as Quraysh hostility increased with the number of his followers, Gabriel told Mohammed to recant this recitation and condemn the jinn. From then on, Allah's message was, on the surface, surprisingly simple: Allah is the only and almighty God, Mohammed is the last of Allah's prophets, and the Qur'an is Allah's will. The Arabic word *islam* corresponds to the English word "submit," i.e. to the will of Allah embodied in the Qur'an, and a *muslim* is one who so submits. For Muslims, then, peace was from the start both the result and the reward of this submission, individual in a spiritual sense and social in a behavioral one. "Peace is on him who follows the [Qur'an's] guidance," and those who "believe and do good are made to enter gardens, beneath which rivers flow, to abide in them by Allah's permission; the greeting therein is, Peace."[34]

Theologically, the meanings of the Arabic word for peace, *salaam* (as in the greeting, *Salaam Aleikum*, related to the Hebrew word Shalom) in the Qur'an are closely related to those of Judaism and Christianity. The peace of the next world takes on a more worldly appeal in Islam, but the process for reaching it is similar: after death, Allah will judge worthy to enter the garden abode of heaven those who believe in him and behave according to the Qur'an. In time, the basic Qur'anic criteria (*arkan ad-din*) for worthiness of the name Muslim, let alone heaven, became the Five Pillars. Each of the Pillars contributes to individual (spiritual, physical), social (economic) and/or collective (cultural) Islamic peace in its own way:

1. **Shahadah,** the declaration of faith at births, on deathbeds and by converts: "There is no god but Allah, and Mohammed is His messenger;"
2. **Salah,** praying five times daily at prescribed times, in Arabic, facing the Kaaba in Mecca, as a means of communion with and thanksgiving to Allah;
3. **Zakah:** a "religious tithe" given to the needy based on a fixed percentage of one's income, the more given the higher the spiritual reward, distinguished from charity (*sadaqa*) which is not required, but voluntary;

4. **Sawm**: fasting, if health and age permit, from dawn till dusk for the holy month of Ramadan, including a focus on sin-free living such as abstaining from violence; and

5. **Hajj**: a pilgrimage, if feasible, to Mecca once in one's lifetime to pray at the Kaaba as homage to Mohammed and the history of Islam.

Based on these and other principles drawn from the Qur'an, one of Allah's sacred names is the "giver of peace" who invites to the "abode of peace and guides whom He pleases into the right path."[35] On the right path, spiritual and behavioral submission is never to be an impediment to peace and peacemaking: "make not Allah, because of your swearing by Him, an obstacle to your doing good and guarding against evil and making peace between men."[36]

The reason for the similarities between the three monotheisms is that Mohammed, whose genealogy is traced to Abraham, is viewed as the fulfillment of the Judeo-Christian prophetic tradition preceding him. The Torah and New Testament are called *qur'ans*, though referring to Jesus as the Son of God is blasphemy because even Mohammed was not divine but a divinely selected human messenger. Many Judeo-Christian narratives are adapted, and their historical or ethical points adopted, into the Qur'an with minor or significant variations. Those who uphold these traditions are referred to as the People of the Book (*ahl al-kitab*) aligned with Islam, rather than "unbelievers" separate from it, which is why Muslims have historically been more tolerant of and benevolent to Jews and Christians than other religious groups.[37] Only later were the three religions divided by one god. Distinctions between Muslims, People of the Book and unbelievers made peace and peacemaking among them problematic. Islamic peacemaking must be carried out Qur'anically to be valid, and the complexity of its messages about this holy activity is comparable to that of the Torah, as its original audience was also a desert tribe. According to the Qur'an, peace and peacemaking must always be reciprocated: if opponents "incline to peace, then incline to it and trust in Allah."[38] With People of the Book and Muslims:

> if two parties of the believers quarrel, make peace between them; but if one of them acts wrongfully towards the other, fight that which acts wrongfully until it returns to Allah's command; then if it returns, make peace between them with justice and act equitably; surely Allah loves those who act equitably.[39]

The logic behind this process is that "believers are but brethren, therefore make peace between your brethren and be careful of your duty to Allah that mercy may be had on you."[40]

But war, peace and peacemaking need not be initiated with unbelievers unless certain conditions are met. War, in Allah's name or otherwise, can be waged against unbelievers by Muslims – "except those who reach a people between whom and you there is an alliance, or who come to you, their hearts shrinking from fighting you or fighting their own people." Peace is to be made "if they withdraw from you and do not fight you and offer you peace" because "Allah has not given you a way against them."[41] False prophets and gods were to be guarded against in the Torah and the Bible; to these the Qur'an adds false peacemakers.[42] In a prophecy that proved remarkably accurate, the Qur'an says that Muslims

> will find others who desire that they should be safe from you and secure from their own people; as often as they are sent back to the mischief they get thrown into it headlong; therefore if they do not withdraw from you, and do not offer you peace and restrain their hands, then seize them and kill them wherever you find them; and against these Allah has given you a clear authority.[43]

Yet, "When you go to war in Allah's way, make investigation, and do not say to anyone who offers you peace: You are not a believer."[44] Only centuries after Mohammed was a distinction made between territories of Islam (*dar al-Islam*) and territories of war (*dar al-harb*), in a ninth-century treaty on Islamic statecraft called the *Islamic Law of Nations*. Even then, it was made to distinguish where war could be justly carried out on religious grounds: only when non-Muslims lack "legal competence to enter into discourse with Islam on the basis of equality and reciprocity because they failed to conform with its ethical and legal standards."[45] In fact, "religion is conceived as a *limit* on war" by the majority of Muslim theologians, jurists and scholars both historically and presently.[46] In this light, Jihad – "to strive" or "to struggle," i.e., with oneself or others for Allah – as paradoxical as this may sound, is a form of *auto-peacemaking* insofar as it refers to an individual Muslim's internal quest for spiritual peace in submitting to Allah's will.[47] Jihad becomes a form of war-making only when externalized as a pacification of non-believers who threaten the faithful or as necessary for their survival. Jihad in early Muslim expansion was used more as a lowest common denominator, catchphrase rallying cry in battle than a systemic rationale for war, territorial, economic or otherwise.

Islamic peace and peacemaking are illustrated in Mohammed's life after the recitations began and Muslims' rise to local, then regional power. Persecuted by the Quraysh, Mohammed and his intermediaries negotiated an agreement with the pagan Arab and Jewish tribes of Medina, a town some 200 kilometers north of Mecca, to relocate the Muslims there. This epic emigration, in which no recorded violence was involved, is known as the Hijra. Formalized after their arrival as the Charter of Medina (c. 622), this historic agreement normalized not only relations between the newcomers and locals, but also between the locals themselves and with outsiders. Building on the long tradition of informal inter-tribal alliances based on common commercial, defensive and other interests, the Charter was innovative in its ecumenism under Mohammed's authority, whose reputation as a just mediator preceded him. He thus became an inter-religious political leader only shortly after becoming leader of the Muslims. Promoting religious freedom, the Charter also prohibited religious violence, established a judicial system for internal conflict resolution and protocols for external relations. Unfortunately, the Charter was broken before it had the chance to work. For reasons that remain unclear, Mohammed expelled one of Medina's Jewish tribes, who then aligned with the Quraysh in an attack on Medina to regain control of the caravan trade, now in Muslim hands. In protest, Muslims no longer faced Jerusalem in prayer, but instead towards Mecca.

In 628, Mohammed negotiated the Peace of al-Hudaybiyyah with the Quraysh, stipulating the war would halt for ten years, Meccans and Medinans could freely ally themselves, but also that Muslim Meccans who moved to Medina without their guardian's consent were to be sent back, while the Quraysh were exempt from reciprocating. In the words of a modern scholar: "to spread the faith by peaceful means, or at least to re-establish thereby peaceful contacts with the peninsular Arabs, who continued to revere Mecca, as well as with Mecca itself, was, after all, the Muslims' professed motivation."[48] The Quraysh breached the Peace two years later, and with the converts Mohammed gained by this peaceful policy he captured Mecca. Within a few years of Mohammed's death in 632, the Arabian Peninsula was under the control of his companion and successor (*caliph*), Abu Bakr. Pausing briefly to consolidate his gains and to solidify Muslim unity, within decades the Caliphs conquered large and important parts of the Byzantine and Persian Empires, including what are today Egypt, Lebanon, Iran, Iraq, Israel, Syria, Libya and southern Turkey. According to a modern Islamic historian, "As a result of these campaigns, for the first time in its known history a period of peace was experienced throughout the entire Arabian Peninsula," referred to as the Pax Islamica and discussed below.[49]

The rapidity of these vast early territorial gains is no less stunning than the low degree of violence Muslims used to achieve them. Weak from ongoing wars between the two Empires misruling them, the diverse inhabitants of these lands often sided with the Muslims against them, just as the Qur'an had prophesied. Some Christians, such as John of Damascus, saw Islam as a heretical sect of their own religion, which had already been infighting for centuries. Surely, when people refused to surrender peacefully, they suffered for it. But it was usually not in the best interests of Muslims to kill peoples and destroy property that, left intact, could be ruled in and for peace to greater profit. Tribes of Muslims (*umma*) thus conquered and ruled with words, not simply with swords, tending to leave economic and administrative infrastructures of the regions they conquered intact, probably because this was the most effective way to leverage their proportionately tiny numbers compared to the conquered. Far from spreading Islam by the sword, the Qur'an states: "No compulsion is there in religion."[50] Tolerance of other religions alien to Islam, called People of the Pact (*ahl al-dhimma*), was added to that of the People of the Book, and the two were gradually grouped together as *dhimmis* entitled to legal and financial privileges or protections as long as they paid poll taxes. Their members increasingly converted of their own volition, usually with mixed motives. Whether they did or not, the most able of them meritocratically participated in the new Islamic states.

However, a fateful schism among Muslims had by this time occurred, detrimental to Islamic unitive peace down to our day. The fourth Caliph, Ali ibn Abu Talib (*c.* 600–61), claimed that legitimate Muslim leadership is based on belonging to Mohammed's bloodline, not just the emulation of his piety, as was the case with previous Caliphs. His supporters became known as Shi'a Ali ("Ali's Party" or Shiites), and those who opposed him Sunni, or traditionalists. Ali was succeeded by Muawiya, Mohammed's secretary and governor of Syria and Egypt on his behalf. He was contentiously awarded the Caliphate for reuniting the Arab tribes and in so doing founded Islam's first dynasty, the Umayyad (661–750), who ruled the Muslim empire from their capital at Damascus. The general sent to capture the city negotiated a peaceful surrender with natives by promising them no harm, no theft or destruction of property and respect for their religions in exchange for recognition of Muslim rule and taxes equivalent to what they were paying before. Muawiya made good on the promise and secured a temporary truce with the Byzantine Emperor, which allowed for major internal reorganizations.

Two distinct but related processes constitutive of the Pax Islamica intensified with the Umayyad: Islamization and Arabization.[51] Islam's universality, its openness to Arabs and non-Arabs alike, and supremacy emerged with and against the official positions of other religions in the new Islamic state. At first, religious and with it socio-political integration had barriers; one had to become an adopted member of an Arab tribe (*mawali*) to be recognized as a Muslim. As these barriers broke down, however, so did early rationales for Muslim authority and taxation. In response to these developments, Abd al-Malik (685–705), the third Umayyad Caliph, embarked on Arabization campaigns by which state affairs were to be carried out in Arabic and hierarchies based on geo-social configurations, not just religion.

So while Islamization provided an impetus other than territorial-economic for Umayyad expansion of the Pax Islamica into North Africa, South Spain and Central Asia, Arabization provided a means of sustaining it.

Baghdad, known as the City of Peace (*madinat al-salam*) in its early days, became the capital of the succeeding Abbasid Dynasty (749–1258) with its second Caliph. Although they took power by overthrowing the Umayyad with a coalition of Shiites, mawali and non-Muslims, the cooperative spirit between them remained long thereafter, and gave rise to what is considered an Islamic golden age. Pax Islamica, defined as "lands under the rule of a Muslim government in which the laws of Islam are the laws of the land," took on its full meaning with the Abbasid, not least because Islamic law (*Sharia*) began to be codified.[52] The Caliph's court became a center not only of Islamic studies, but also of cosmopolitan luxury and inter-cultural learning to which no Christian city of the times came close. In 780 the Caliph al-Mahdi invited Christian patriarch Timothy I, who translated Aristotle's works into Arabic on his request, to his dinner table for a theological debate – an event unthinkable in contemporary Europe, where even theological debates among Christians were turning into bloody battles.

Under Harun al-Rashid (r. 786–809), the most famous Abbasid Caliph for his prominence in the *Arabian Nights*, violent punishment against dhimmis who failed to pay taxes was outlawed. "Rather," in the words of his judge, "they should be treated with leniency."[53] As a controversy over icons in Christian churches brought Constantinople to civil war, Empress Irene paid Harun for peace. When she was deposed, Harun sent envoys to the Franks' newly christened king by the Pope in Rome, Charlemagne (see the next chapter), seeking a strategic peace against Byzantium and the remaining Umayyad Caliphate in Spain, and Charlemagne ultimately agreed. The Islamic Sufi sect, borrowing from Buddhists and Christian monks in Khurasan, began seeking a mystical inner Salam in silent prayer or physical frenzies. Jews, persecuted in Christendom, often held high administrative posts in the Caliphates. Participation in each others' religious festivals was common, displaying what a modern historian of medieval Egypt refers to as "mutual respect and brotherhood between the religions."[54]

Harun's son, al-Ma'mum, funded a multicultural group of scholars and scientists who worked in a library called the House of Wisdom, amongst whom was the renowned Al-Kindi. Although at war, he sent envoys to Byzantium requesting Greek manuscripts. Christians began writing theology in Arabic and found common ground with Muslims in the theological utility of Ancient Greek logic. His state-sponsored translation program aimed at accessing intellectual tools ended up being one of the primary vehicles of the retransmission of classical learning into Western

Europe. The Byzantine Emperor Theophilus pleaded with him: "I have written to you to make a peace agreement. . . so that you may remove the burdens of war from upon us and so that we may be to each other friends and a band of associates, in addition to accruing the benefits of widened scope for trading through commercial outlets," but ended with a threat: "If you reject this offer I shall penetrate into the innermost recesses of your land." Al-Ma'mum rejected it, and battles between the Abbasids and Byzantium continued for centuries. Through the fifth century, each would fall to the other, Mamluk mercenaries, Mongols and then Turks.

After the Abbasid coup, the last living Umayyad re-established himself in Al-Andalus, or Muslim Spain, which had been taken from the Visigoth. As early as 713, treaties of peaceful capitulation on terms similar to those at Damascus earlier secured the cities of Murcia, Toledo and Cordoba. The latter became the Caliphate's capital, and soon was more populous than Rome, London and Paris of the times combined. As the Arab and Berber Muslim conquerors shunned farming, they hired Christians as laborers, who were better treated than those in feudal Europe. Jews acted as intermediaries not only between Muslims and Christian in the Iberian Peninsula, but thanks to their vast networks around the Mediterranean that transcended existing conflicts, as Muslim agents throughout the region. A tenth-century Jewish physician named Hasdai ibn Shaprut earned a position in the Cordoba Caliph's court. He was asked by the Caliph to negotiate a strategic peace deal with the Byzantine Emperor against the Baghdad Caliphate, and although several convoys were exchanged the deal never went through.

In the early eleventh century, the Christian Prince of Navarre signed a treaty with the Muslim ruler of Toledo to split spoils after jointly defeating the Muslim city of Guadalajara. The rulers of the latter then made a deal with the King of Leon-Castile and sacked Toledo. The King then agreed to switch sides and back Toledo for a large sum. These events exemplify how warfare based on internal divisions between Berber and Arab rulers drained the Cordoban Caliphate's resources and led to its collapse in 1031, and that warfare was rarely religiously motivated even if done under its banner. But the last Iberian Muslim stronghold only fell in the fateful year of 1492. The idea that Islam was spread and Muslims ruled solely by the sword, a fuel of today's fear and fierceness, is an inaccurate reduction of history, also unfortunate because it obscures the message of peaceful unity based on tolerance and benevolence put forth by Mohammed in the Qur'an and practiced by him and the vast majority of his followers, then as now.

5

Medieval, Renaissance and Reformation Peaces

A Tale of Two Cities: Medieval Peace and Peacemaking

This chapter's coverage of extended periods in European history, from the fall of Rome to the Renaissance rise of Italian city-states and the Reformation, is intended first to dispel the myth that there was nothing peaceful about medieval times. Contrary to popular and even some academic beliefs, it may be the Middle Ages more than any other single period that has shaped modern peace principles and practices, notably by innovations in treaty-making and through the *modus vivendi* of monasticism, but in other ways as well. Saint Augustine's (354–430) emphasis on peace through individual and social order in the following prescription, for instance, was probably a reaction to chaos stemming from the sack of Rome by Germanic tribes in 410, who eventually seized much of the Western Roman Empire:

> The peace of the body is an ordered proportioning of its components; the peace of the irrational soul is an ordered repose of the passions; the peace of the rational soul is the ordered agreement of knowledge and action. The peace of body and soul is the ordered life and health of a living creature; peace between mortal men and God is an ordered obedience in the faith under an everlasting law; peace between men is an ordered agreement of mind; domestic peace is an ordered agreement among those who dwell together concerning command and obedience; the peace of the heavenly city is a perfectly ordered and fully concordant fellowship in the enjoyment of God and in mutual enjoyment by union with God; the peace of all things is a tranquility of order. Order is the classification of things equal and unequal that assigns to each its proper position.[1]

Augustine, a well-educated and well-traveled bishop, perceived that a paradigm shift was underway that could transform the Roman way of life. So the questions he raised in the *City of God*, written soon after the sack and in which this passage appears, were how and by whom.

Two kinds of cities, he claimed, could be "created by two kinds of love: the earthly city by a love of self carried even to the point of contempt for God, the heavenly city by a love for God carried even to the point of contempt for self."[2] In earthly cities, "waging war and extending their dominion is in the eyes of the wicked a gift of fortune, but in the eyes of the good it is a necessary evil."[3] Just wars, then, are those that establish or sustain heavenly cities, in which the "voice of God is an invitation to peace. It says: 'If you be not in peace, love peace; what can you hope to receive from me more useful for you than peace?' What is peace? The condition from which war has been excluded; where dissension, resistance and adversity no longer exist."[4] Augustine's near totalitarian, dualist definition of peace as the absence of war, also Platonically absolutist and idealist in its incontestable perfection, reflects the hierarchical universality and internality of his prescription for peace. Together, the metaphors of the two cities prove to be highly predictive of the limits and possibilities of peace in the Middle Ages, which flowed from the fusion of Roman and Germanic peace traditions once considered antithetical by both sides.

Rome's ongoing difficulties in maintaining internal peace through external wars and effective socio-political structures became impossibilities as its resources depleted, its armies weakened, and Church institutions gained power. Terminal conflict with "barbarian" Germanic tribes, once considered the only solution to their threat, lost ground to compromises, bringing about a fusion of Roman and Germanic peace traditions. As in the heyday of Romanization, such compromises included offering land, enculturation and citizenship for pacts of non-aggression, taxes and military service – except they were now used for remilitarization, not pacification. Overdependence on Germanic mercenaries, as Edward Gibbon points out in the best-read history on the period of *The Decline and Fall of the Roman Empire* (1776–88), ultimately put them in a better position to make or break the peace they were paid to protect than as adversaries. To be sure, many chose to break it, and their invasions were brutal affairs. But as Gibbon also points out, the invaders had their own peace traditions, as when during their annual festival "the sound of war was hushed, quarrels were suspended, arms laid aside, and the restless Germans had an opportunity of tasting the blessings of peace."[5] Building on these traditions, some newcomers chose to make and maintain peace with locals after they arrived, and recent scholarship holds that modern Western culture derives from such collaborative efforts.

One example is Ostrogoth King Theodoric the Great (454–526), who continued Roman traditions after he invaded Italy. Two of his administrators, Boethius and Cassiodorus, greatly influenced medieval thought and education. While not all Germanic tribes found it necessary or desirable to fully Romanize, all eventually converted to Christianity. As a diplomatic instrument, conversion was of tremendous use because it conferred spiritual benefits at no cost and a unitive impetus regardless of language or race, bringing together peoples Romans had been unable or unwilling to, as in the case of the first king of a united France, Clovis I (466–511). Intermarriages created or made official socio-political, economic and emotional ties between Romans and their tribal arch enemies; without such mingling, the shedding of blood alone could not have permitted foci of power and prestige to swing from longstanding urban centers to previously remote rural areas. An apogee of this mixed system was the ninth-century Carolingians, whose celebrated leader Charlemagne (742–814) was crowned by the chief bishop in Rome, now called the Pope, enhancing the Church's temporal powers with land and military might, and evolving peace and peacemaking into feudal and religious forms with strong parallels to Augustine's earthly and heavenly cities. Gradually, the Western Roman Empire was thus transformed into a labyrinth of regional kingdoms based on reciprocal obligations and mutual recognition, including the Lombards and Ostrogoths in the Italian Peninsula, Visigoths in the Iberian, Burgundians and Franks in Gaul and Germany, and Anglo-Saxons in England. Romanticizing of medieval warfare has regrettably taken the spotlight away from the realism of the period's peace practices. They came as close as possible to actualizing peace in embodying Augustine's earthly city.

In the tenth century, a clergy-led peace movement called the Pax Dei ("Peace of God") tried to curb the feudal system's pervasive violence by prohibiting attacks on Church grounds, unarmed churchmen and peasants, their properties and families. Traders and merchants, a class also greatly reduced in size and importance since Roman times by unsafe land and sea travel, were also eventually protected by the Peace of God. By the eleventh, a Treuga Dei ("Truce of God") was added, prohibiting all violence during certain holy days and periods, signaled by church bells. As in contemporaneous Japan, a distinction was increasingly made between private wars fought between individuals and their supporters, and public wars fought between kingdoms and theirs. The Peace and Truce of God aimed to limit both private and public wars, but despite kings' nominal support in the twelfth and thirteenth centuries, after the Carolingian collapse heightened both kinds of warfare, the Peace and Truce of God were on the whole ineffective. One reason was that violators could "buy" their way back into the Church's good graces by its increasingly used indulgences, decreasing their motivation to comply. In the late twelfth century, England's King Richard I, Lionheart, began commissioning knights to ensure that his kingly obligation to keep the peace in his realm was met. At first stationed in unruly regions, by the fourteenth century these Justices of the Peace, as they were now called, were present in every corner of his kingdom. They were charged with mediating disputes, preventing crimes as best they could, and rendering summary judgments and punishments in the tradition Greek and Roman Irenarchs. Positions of Justice of the Peace still exist today in England, also in some of its former colonies from Canada and Jamaica to Hong Kong. However, in general no longer active peacekeepers, they tend to be honorary or bureaucratic posts with no power.

Feudalism derived from both Roman and Germanic sources as an agreement between landholding nobles as high up as kings to grant lands to subordinates in return for fealty and the provision of armed forces when called upon. This is why so few early medieval kingdoms had standing armies, but also how so many violent disputes erupted between them. Securing internal peace by the reciprocal obligations of homage, investiture and their chains of command also became a means of defending or extending a kingdom's borders. Below kings were barons, lords and knights, all hereditary titles, who formed the external military and internal police core of the feudal system. The chivalric codes they ostensibly came to live by, while based on martial skills and wherewithal, also required them to defend the weak and be generous to the poor. In theory, war was only justified under Ciceronian circumstances meeting certain criteria: right authority, just cause, right intention, proportionality, last resort and breached peace. Over time, the powers of the chivalric classes grew to the point where they could challenge kings who abused theirs either by revolting or, more peacefully, simply by switching allegiances. To avoid violence by negotiations and to expedite feudal affairs, kings and/or their inferiors also formed the first post-Roman legislatures, such as the Cortes of Spain (twelfth century), the Parliament in England (thirteenth century), the Estates General in France (fourteenth century) and the Diets of German and Northern European states (fifteenth century). As the basis of most European-derived political systems, these early assemblies also formed foundations for modern intra-national peace.

Medieval bishops below the Pope in Rome, but who sometimes rivaled kings in wealth and influence, could enrich themselves and the Church by using their lands for secular as well as religious purposes. By their clerical schools bishoprics came to provide literate administrators, ever-rarer after Rome fell and before the Renaissance, whom kings needed to maintain their realms in order and who also played peacemaking roles. One of them, a French monk named Pierre Dubois (c. 1250–1312), proposed an alliance of all feudal Christian powers to maintain peace by a permanent court, its sole purpose being to prevent warfare by settling disputes non-violently between its members, which did not attract any support. At the bottom of the feudal hierarchy were the peasants or serfs, whose duties were to live peacefully while providing agricultural or other labor to their lords. In return, lords were supposed to provide protection and subsistence use of their lands. While not technically slaves, the structural violence serfs suffered was often as severe, offset only by the spiritual and material solace they may have received from the Church. Although serfs' direct involvement in warfare before the Hundred Years War between France and England (1337–1453) was limited, they were often its indirect victims. It was only after peasants began to be conscripted that they rebelled *en masse* against their lords, usually after famines or plagues such as the Black Death (fourteenth century), which physically precluded the possibility of any peace, even despite the smartest treaties tendered.

Unlike under the Roman-Christian policy of "one empire, one peace", backed by a central power capable of enforcing it, the multitude of medieval kingdoms required a multidirectional approach and so formed foundations of modern international peacemaking. To prevent or end territorial wars or to affirm a kingdom's sovereignty, treaties of mutual recognition were signed between rulers, usually represented by noble delegates at each other's courts. In 803, for instance, the Pax Nicephori was tendered between Charlemagne and the Byzantine Empire, recognizing his authority and Venice as Byzantine territory. Similarly, after the Carolingians' fall, West and East Francia (roughly modern France and Germany) recognized each other by the Treaty of Bonn in 921. Treaties were also used to deal with noble family feuds. The Treaty of Alton (1101), by which Robert, Duke of Normandy, recognized his younger brother Henry I as King of England in exchange for a stipend and continental lands, temporarily diffused a succession debate that might otherwise have ended in bloodshed, ensuring cooperation between the two on pre-determined terms. However, to show how fickle all medieval treaties could be, Henry invaded Normandy four years later and jailed Robert for life.

Other pacts such as the Pactum Sicardi (836), between Italian Duchies and the Prince of Benevento, provided for temporary armistices, while still others such as Pactum Warmundi (1123) established temporary alliances, in this case between the crusader kingdom of Jerusalem and Venice. Informal leagues of a few small principalities were formed politically, as in the Lombard League (twelfth century) of northern Italy, or economically, such as the Hanseatic League of dozens of guild towns and villages which controlled trade around the Baltic Sea in the thirteenth and fourteenth centuries. Formal alliances were also set in place, as in the Treaty of Windsor (1386),which cemented Anglo-Portuguese alliance and is the oldest extant interstate treaty. Multilateral peace and defence agreements were also used, as in the Treaty of Venice (1177) between the Lombard League, the Kingdom of Sicily, and the Holy Roman Empire and the Papacy, occasionally renewed as this one was in the Peace of Constance (1183). Some treaties dealing with a kingdom's internal affairs were called Bulls, not to be confused with Papal Bulls, as in the Golden Bull of 1222 by which King Andrew II of Hungary granted noblemen and clergy the right to disobey the king if he acted contrary to law. Others were called Charters, as is the Magna Carta (1215), which bound English kings to the law while protecting certain of subjects' rights, notably that of Habeas Corpus, or protection from unlawful imprisonment. Those who straddled social and collective peace in crafting these agreements were in most cases betrayed by conditions or participants that had changed before their ink dried.

Conflicts between religious and secular potentates recurred both between and within kingdoms. They were sometimes diffused and resolved through special treaties (*reglements d'avouerie*) aimed at normalizing their relations, in which paid "devotees" acted as arbitrators. Agreements were also reached across religious and linguistic lines, as in the Al-Azraq Treaty (1245) between the Christian King Jaime I of Aragon and the Muslim commander Mohammad Abu Abdallah Ben Hudzail al Sahuir, delimiting property and revenue rights in Spain. Some treaties took on grandiose titles, such the Treaty of Perpetual Peace (1502), halting hostilities between Scotland and England and voided a decade later. While many such secular agreements aimed to end or prevent the use of armed forces, only religious ones aimed at outlawing them outright. The Synod of Toledo (693), for example, forbade duels and private wars and the Synod of Poitiers (1000) resolved that all disputes should be adjured by law, not by force. The Synod of Limoges (1031) used the most terrible spiritual punishment, interdicts, against war. But proactive rather than prohibitive intercessions were Christianity's most influential contributions to peace in the Middle Ages: the related medieval institutions of sainthood and monasticism.

Sainthood, originally reserved for martyrs, was in time granted by a council of bishops to Christians, both men and women, whose exemplary lives were modeled on Christ's and so made for models themselves. The medieval patron saint of peace, Francis of Assisi (1181–1226), founded a monastic order. While the famous "Prayer for Peace" erroneously attributed to him is probably a twentieth-century creation, it nonetheless captures many of the pacific criteria usually required for canonization, save those of a popular cult and the performance of miracles:

Lord, make me an instrument of Thy peace;
where there is hatred, let me sow love;

where there is injury, pardon;
where there is doubt, faith;
where there is despair, hope;
where there is darkness, light;
and where there is sadness, joy.

Hagiographies, biographies of saints, were one of the few ways the spirit of early Christian pacifism survived, as in the *Life of Saint Anthony*, the first Christian monk. Maybe medieval warfare would have been better tempered if more people could have read them and did.

Two forms of monasticism emerged in Western Europe based on Near Eastern modes of renouncing earthly pursuits including violence. *Eremite* monks like Saint Anthony in Egypt (251–356) lived ascetically in solitude, striving for perfect spiritual peace on scriptural principles as mendicants. Saint Pachomius (292–338) went on to found the first Christian monasteries with the same goals, but achieved communally and self-sufficiently. His followers, first *cenobite* monks and nuns, began the peaceful monastic movement that spread across Europe. In 526, Saint Benedict put forth his Rule of monastic life. Among his "Instruments of Good Works" for cenobite monks he listed not making false peace, praying for one's enemies and making peace with adversaries. He advised that cenobite monks should be under the direction of an Abbot, upon whose will the "perseveration of peace and charity" of the monastery depended.[6] In the following centuries, many monastic orders were founded with different rules, on the surface non-violent and peace-oriented but not always actually so. Among the most prominent were those of Saint Francis, or Franciscan order, stressing inner peace through poverty and chastity (est. 1210); Dominican order, emphasizing social peace through public preaching (est. 1216), but which also carried out the Inquisition; and Society of Jesus or Jesuits (est. 1534), committed to spreading collective peace through education and missionary work, but also conspired in European colonial violence. If kingdoms were as close as medieval societies came to the peace of Augustine's earthly city, monasteries were the closest to that of the heavenly city, and have inspired utopian visions of peaceful communal and spiritual life down to our times.

(Re)Births of Peace: Renaissance Revivals of and Departures from Traditions

Rebirths of peace and peacemaking that took place in the Renaissance did not replace medieval ones but synthesized them with classical ideas and ideals which came back into vogue. Such calculated combinations aside, there occurred a major development in this history of peace, its exclusive attachment to secularism, arguably for the first time in history. One of the main reasons why secularism was proposed as a political paradigm was to counter the abuses of power by Christian potentates, not least of which was their now incessant support for wars such as the Crusades and indulgences used to pay for them, which also set off the Reformation as discussed below. The ironic implication is that secular and religious revisionisms were opposing peace movements reacting to the same set of circumstances, showing yet again that ongoing military competitions can prepare the way for competing kinds of peace.

Born in Florence during the rise of rich Italian city-states which later spawned humanism, Dante Alighieri (1265–1321) was at the cusp of these trends in peace and peacemaking: on the one hand supporting the shift from religious to secular authority over affairs of state and, on the other, expressing an unwavering Christian faith. Though known primarily as a poet, he was also a political theorist and peacemaker. In *On World-Government*, written in 1309 but not published until 1559, he argued that only in peace can humanity reach its full potential and only a global government capable of resolving conflicts between local ones can secure peace. His goal: "that each nation develop its peculiar genius to the fullest extent, and in order to be able to do this, let each nation become a member of a World-State, under the guidance of a Central Court of Justice that will regulate international affairs." "Justice," he claimed "has greatest power under a unitary government; the best order of the world therefore demands world-government."[7] Just as the protagonist of his *Divine Comedy*, Dante was led by the Roman writer Virgil from the warlike pits of hell to the blinding bliss of heaven's peace, so as a peacemaker he attempted to lead fellow Florentines from conflict to reconciliation. His compatriots would have faired much better had his peacemaking exploits exerted as great an immediate influence as his poetry in posterity.

The ideological differences between the White and Black Parties of Florence originated with the Investiture Controversy in the eleventh century between the Holy Roman Empire and the Catholic Church over the right to appoint bishops and other clergy in service of the State. After civil wars across Europe, an agreement was reached in the Concordat of Worms (1122) that the Emperor could invest bishops with secular authority but not religious, which was reserved for the Pope. And on a century, White Florentines still sought to limit Papal powers, Blacks to enlarge them, repeating while prefiguring conflicts that soon swept Europe. Dante, siding with the Whites despite being a devout Catholic, tried to make peace by leading a popular movement that met with provisional success, seeking city-wide reconciliation in expelling members of both parties who advocated the use of violence to settle the ongoing conflict. Aligned with his actions and Augustine before him, Dante had earlier written:

> All concord depends on a unity of wills; the best state of humanity is a kind of concord, for as individuals are in excellent health when they enjoy concord in soul and body, and similarly a family, city, or state, so humanity as a whole."[8]

When the Whites returned, they booted all the Blacks from the city. When the Pope got word, he threatened military action, so the Whites sent a peace delegation to Rome, including Dante. The Pope, probably aware that Dante had pitched his political treatise to the Emperor's deaf ear, held him captive as the Blacks retook the city, to which Dante never returned. An admirer from Padua, Petrarch (1304–1374), followed in Dante's footsteps as a poet-peacemaker: "I thought myself blameworthy if, in the midst of warlike preparations, I should not have recourse to my one weapon, the pen."[9] Petrarch successfully negotiated a truce between Padua and Venice and also participated in other diplomatic missions around Europe, but neither he nor Dante came close to being staunch secular defenders of the peace as another Paduan.

Marsilius (1290–1342) was a soldier of that city before attending the University of Paris, then becoming its rector. While practicing medicine after his short tenure, he wrote one of the most controversial political works of the times, *Defender of the Peace* (1324). The defender Marsilius had in mind was the secular state, totally severed from and superior to all religious authority. The peace was basically that which Dante had proposed: a product of concordant unity and producer of humanity's greatest achievements. Rather than in, by and for God as Augustine claimed, Marsilius argued that states came about by the application of reason for all to benefit from peace, and in this too he was ahead of his times in presaging Enlightenment thinkers such as Immanuel Kant. In his view, it was precisely because religious authorities had meddled in secular affairs that peace was jeopardized. Free from scriptural conjectures that confuse spiritual and political spheres, only a strong secular authority can legitimately resolve conflicts and maintain peace in and among states. Even coercive force can be used to these ends, he again presciently contended, if it reflects the will of the people whose consent through refined representative legislators ought to be required for both religious and secular decision-making. Of course, the Pope took offense, excommunicated the author and censured the work. Persecuted, Marsilius took refuge with another excommunicate, Holy Roman Emperor Louis IV, to whom the *Defender* was dedicated because he refused to relinquish power on the Pope's command. Louis then deposed the Pope and installed a puppet regime including, by sham elections, himself as king of Italy, a mendicant monk as Pope, and Marsilius as vicar of Rome. Though they were soon rooted out by Papal loyalists, Marsilius thus lived to see the most radical points of his *political imperatives* for peace put into practice, however superficially and temporarily.

Contrasting in some ways with Marsilius was Niccolo Machiavelli (1469–1527), who a hundred years later pioneered a perspective on political peace and peacemaking now called *realpolitik*, based on uses of political power rather than the power of political ideals. A statesman, he entered Florence's civil service the same year its long-ruling family, the Medici, was deposed and a republic proclaimed. As a member of the city council handling diplomatic and military affairs, he served as ambassador to France and Rome, admiring the condottiere Cesare Borgia's rise to power in central Italy. When the Medici retook the city-state in 1512 with Papal backing, he was arrested for conspiracy, tortured and banished from the city after refusing to confess. He then dedicated himself to writing, most influentially, a political treatise hastily composed to curry Medici favor, never received. In *The Prince* (1532), Machiavelli advised by historical examples that feared rulers are more effective than loved ones, and that in acquiring or sustaining their power, upon which peace pragmatically depends, the ends justify the means:

> There are two ways of contending, one in accordance with the laws, the other by force; the first of which is proper to men, the second to beasts. But since the first method is often ineffectual, it becomes necessary to resort to the second. A Prince should, therefore, understand well how to use well both the man and the beast.[10]

By cruelty alone, however, rulers are not able to "maintain their position even in peaceful times, not to speak of the perilous times of war."[11] Peace is not an ultimate goal, nor is war always to be avoided; both are simply conditions to which rulers must react to be effective. But Machiavelli's masterwork is actually the *Discourses on Livy*, considered the first modern instruction manual and manifesto for republicanism. Based on the Roman model, with an eye to the Florentine city-state of which Machiavelli wrote a history, Machiavelli argued that the most peaceful form of government is that in which the powerful are checked in popular elections. So while totalitarian tactics are often traced to Machiavelli, his lifelong commitment to republican values ought not to be overlooked. Fair terms between the powerful and powerless, he follows Livy in writing, lead to "a firm and lasting peace," while "on unfair, a peace of short duration," because "safe peace" is made voluntarily, not in servitude.[12] "It cannot be that a peace imposed on compulsion should endure between men who are every day brought face to face with one another," perhaps the most realistic proposition of *realpolitical peace* ever put forth.[13]

Returning now to the trend from which the Renaissance or "rebirth" gets its name, the revival of classical traditions in philosophy and literature predictably also took place in peace writings, and at the forefront was Erasmus of Rotterdam (1466–1536). Raised and educated in a monastery, Erasmus took his vows, was ordained as a Catholic priest, then accepted a clerical position offered by a bishop. On paid leave, made permanent by the Pope, he studied theology at the University of Paris, then worked as a travelling independent scholar and creative writer, a career which put him in contact with the greatest minds and powers of his times. In opposition to Machiavelli, in *The Education of the Prince* (1516) he argues that rulers should be classically trained, biblically guided model citizens who are loved by their subjects to be most effective in making and maintaining peace within as well as between their kingdoms. In *On the War against the Turks*, regarding European retaliation in response to Sultan Suleiman's attack on Vienna (1529), Erasmus urges that "no matter how serious nor how just the cause, war must not be undertaken unless all possible remedies have been exhausted and it has become inevitable."[14] Rather than stereotyping Turks as warmongers and using Islam as an excuse for war, he urges Christians to overcome their own warlike tendencies and religious intolerance. In his collection of classical quotes and commentaries, the *Adages*, the longest is on "War is sweet to the inexperienced." This anti-war tirade aimed at deterring readers is perhaps the most gruesome depiction and scathing critique of warfare of its time. "When did anyone hear," he asks with typically poignant wit, "of a hundred thousand animals falling dead together after tearing each other to pieces, as men do everywhere?"[15] Erasmus' pro-peace tour de force based on classical and biblical sources, *The Complaint of Peace* (1517), begins with the words "Peace talks." Within the book's context, they act as stage directions indicating that what follows is a first-person diatribe by a personified Peace about abuses humanity has hurled. Within its socio-political context, they indicate the core of Peace's plea and the plan the book advocates: violence replaced and peace restored through critical dialogue. Erasmus tried to do just that by acting as an intermediary between Protestants like Martin Luther and the Pope despite disagreeing with them, but the task proved too divine. No surprise, then, that in his renowned satirical work, *In Praise of Folly*, war runs parallel to the exploitative excesses of religious powers in precluding peace.

Erasmus dedicated this last book to a collaborator, Sir Thomas More (1478–1535), who put forth an idealist perspective on peace along both Platonic and monastic lines. Son of a judge, More studied at Oxford, worked his way up England's civil service and became Lord Chancellor, the second-highest position in the land. However, symptomatically of the times, he was in the end beheaded by order of King Henry VIII on trumped-up charges, really for publically shunning the royal divorce and remarriage in his Catholic stance against Protestantism. The Church, in a now-rare non-violent act of retaliation, canonized More as the patron saint of lawyers. More began writing his most famous work, *Utopia* (1515, coining the word), during his early continental diplomatic trips. The book's title and name of the state it describes is a pun on the Greek words for "no-place" and "good-place," hinting that Utopian peace and prosperity are both perfect and impossible. In Utopian religious disputes "no other force but that of persuasion" is used, never mixed with "reproaches nor violence," unlike in Europe at the time.[16] The differences between Utopians and his contemporaries More illustrates in pointedly unsubtle ways neither start nor end there. Had the latter been more like the former, More and unnumbered other Renaissance writers critical of un-peaceful power-wielders might not have died as they did.

In Part I, More meets the only person to have visited Utopia, who critiques present-day European states in which war is prevalent because of greed, and greed is prevalent because of private property, resulting in laws that are unjust or improperly applied, punishments ineffective or disproportionate, crimes caused by poverty due to mismanagement or miseducation, and religious differences spurred or settled by military might. Part II describes Utopia, where peace prevails because property is held in common, surplus production by hard work and thrift is used as a safety net or for trade, public officials are periodically elected, and people can choose professions and faiths. Although loathed by Utopians, war is far from unknown to them because of warlike neighbors. So they practice Spartan discipline to prepare for unexpected attacks and maintain social order. Prior to war, Utopians "pray, first for peace," then for war "without the effusion of much blood on either side."[17] They pay mercenaries, but under strict rules strongly reminiscent of Cicero, Augustine and Erasmus: "to defend themselves, or their friends, from any unjust aggressors," to "assist an oppressed nation in shaking off the yoke of tyranny," and in offensive wars only when "they had found that all demands of reparation were rejected, so that a war was unavoidable."[18] Utopianism in different forms and degrees has been a mainstay of modern peace traditions, as have institutions that make their first prominent appearance in modern history of peace during the Renaissance, universities, transformed from keepers of the bellicose status quo into breeding grounds for peace thinkers and activists alike.

Reforming Christian Peace and Peacemaking

On the last day of October, 1517, a German priest named Martin Luther (1483–1546) nailed a piece of paper on the door of the local church. Like most of his contemporaries, later commentators harp about what was written on and done about it, which was indeed of immense historical importance, including a condemnation of indulgences and the admonition: "Away, then, with all those prophets who say to the people of Christ, 'Peace, peace,' and there is no peace!"[19] But the social significance of Luther's non-violent form of protest is for the most part ignored. Those who ignored it blindly carried out the wars between religious reformers and conservatives that ravaged Europe for centuries afterwards, deeply damaging the already diminished peacemaking powers of Christianity. Those who saw the value of its non-violence prototyped major modern peace movements including civil disobedience, conscientious objecting, anti-war protesting and pacifism by drawing on both biblical and more recent religious traditions.

Critiques of Church militarism occurred in Bohemia contemporaneously to Italy, France and England, where radical returns to apostolic pacifism were proposed and practiced by two protestant vanguards. Their efforts signal another shift in Christian peace and peacemaking from medieval theocentric to modern homocentric worldviews within religious frameworks, initiating an indicative though highly inconsistent slippage between Protestantism as a religious movement and anti-war protesting as a peace movement. Jan Hus (1370–1415), born in poverty, worked his way to a degree from the University of Prague and became a professor and preacher. Influenced by writings of English Church reformer, biblical translator and proto-protestant John Wycliffe (1320–1384), Hus rejected two papal prerogatives for which he was burned at the stake as a heretic: using armed forces in Christ's name and raising funds through indulgences to support them. Unlike the strict pacifist and anti-war stances of most of Wycliffe's followers and Hus himself, Hussites took up arms in revolts against both Church and State. Their violent victories, all invalidated in time, thus betrayed the non-violent spirit of Hus' lifework: in essence, that religious institutions and their officials exist for the benefit of humanity, not the other way around, and so should not condone or participate in acts of violence. Peter Chelcicky (1390–1460) shared Hus' spirit but articulated it even more radically: "The man of violence," whether of a religious or secular calling, "unlawfully enjoys and holds what is not his own."[20] In *Spiritual Warfare* and *The Triple Division of Society*, he criticized Church, State and the upper classes for precluding peace by oppressing the poor and conducting what he considered devil's works of war with profit as a primary motive. "The executioner who kills" on command "is as much a wrong-doer as the criminal who is killed."[21] Only communal egalitarianism on pacifist apostolic models, he contended, can promote and preserve peace. Practicing what he preached, he lived and died among his peasant farmer peers. Seven centuries later, the Russian writer Leo Tolstoy would draw upon Chelcicky's humanistic Christian views on pacifism in forming his own, in turn informing Gandhi and Martin Luther King Jr.

Within a generation, similar movements to reform or secede from the Catholic Church were rampant across Europe, prompting reactionaries to use both spiritual and physical violence against them. Some reformers reciprocated, others chose non-violent means of reaching their ends, sometimes under the same banner. Sixteenth-century Anabaptists are examples of these contradicting tendencies, named after their rejection of infant baptism as an involuntary and so invalid entry into Christendom, and practice of voluntary baptism as adults. At one end militant Anabaptist leaders like Thomas Munster (1490–1525) were beheaded for leading lower classes of the Holy Roman Empire in what is miscalled the Peasant's Revolt, an economically motivated anticlerical rebellion of all classes except the highest. His aim was to overthrow Church and State to establish a peaceful theocratic society based on communal equality by any means necessary, which in the event killed 100,000 people without the desired results, the deadliest European uprising until then. At the scale's other end were pacifist Anabaptists like Conrad Grebel (1498–1526), who pleaded with Munster to "use neither the worldly sword nor engage in war" while comparing them to plagues.[22] Breaking with the leading moderate reformer Ulrich Zwingli over his dependence on Zurich's city council for change, Grebel founded a radical group, the Swiss Brethren. Advocating resistance to war and oppression by civil disobedience, they refused to bear arms, hold public office and take oaths in court or elsewhere, as asserted in the seven-article *Schleitheim Confession*. Brethren were persecuted after the civil wars they may have sparked but in no way supported; Grebel escaped, only to die of the plague. Anabaptism soon spread to Poland, where Marcin Czechowic (1532–1613) defended its pacifism in his *Christian Dialogues*, arguing that the only weapons Christ used and Christians need are love, hope, patience and prayer. In Hapsburg, Wilhelm Reublin (1480–1559) protested against taxes for war, calling such funds "blood money" and debunking the "difference between slaying with our own hands and strengthening and directing someone else when we give him our money to slay in our stead."[23] A Reublin follower, Jacob Hutter, started a pacifist protestant sect on Utopian principles, for which he also was burned at the stake, rejecting even defense weaponry in the name of peace and unity. Hutterites fled Catholic persecution from Tyrol to Moravia, where they were persecuted by militant Husserites instead. Today's worldwide Anabaptist churches are mostly of pacifist persuasions, a reminder that even religious group survival still depends on peace.

Two other Protestant churches took root in pacifist grounds, Mennonite and Quaker. Menno Simons (1496–1561), the former's founder, was born a peasant, became a Catholic priest in Friesland (now a Dutch province), but turned to Anabaptism when his brother was killed for being one. He renounced the priesthood, taking up a life of poverty and peripatetic preaching with his family. His passion for peace distinguished his from other Anabaptist strands and his rapidly growing, radical pacifist followers became known as Mennonites, many of whom were killed for harboring him. Without refusing government service as did the Brethren, they rejected all inhumane punishments and warfare whether on behalf of Church or State: "Our weapons are not weapons with which cities and countries may be destroyed. . . But they are weapons with which the spiritual kingdom of the devil is destroyed."[24] In 1572, during war against Spain, Dutch Mennonites refused to participate and excommunicated those who did. They did raise funds for William the Silent, who united Dutch provinces, won the war and in gratitude granted all Mennonites full exemption from military service, the first early modern law to sanction conscientious objecting, reconfirmed by his successor. Mennonite efforts to reform Christianity by returning to its pacifist roots show that although likeminded Protestants preceded religious warmongers through whose conflicts and resolutions nation-states emerged (discussed in the next chapter) they cannot be considered their precursors.

George Fox (1624–1691) followed a trajectory similar to Simmons in England. Born of a weaver and church warden, he somehow learned to read and write as a shoemaker's apprentice. By age nineteen, he began to receive revelations or what he called "openings," in which God told him Catholics and Protestants could be reconciled if they renounced violence. For the rest of his life, he traveled the British Isles and American colonies to debate his doctrine with priests, preach it to the poor, and convince the rich and powerful of its validity: "I told them I was come into the covenant of peace which was before wars and strifes were."[25] During the English Civil War (1642–1651) he was jailed for his views, where he was offered a military command on account of his popularity and leadership skills. In refusing, Fox said he "lived in the virtue of that life and power that took away the occasion of all wars," remaining in jail.[26] He wrote letters to Oliver Cromwell, war leader and Lord Protector of England's only republican state, pleading for peace as for his life: "I was sent of God to stand as a witness against all violence, and against the works of darkness; and to turn people from darkness to light; and to bring them from the causes of war and fighting, to the peaceable gospel."[27] Cromwell asked to meet him and was so impressed that he wished they could talk more often; Fox was released, but they never did.

By this time, the pacifist Society of Friends he founded had become a popular movement called Quakerism, from their "quaking" in the peaceful omnipresence of God. In 1660, when the monarchy was restored, Fox was jailed yet again. Fearing his followers would be persecuted, he and eleven prominent Quakers signed "A Declaration from the harmless and innocent people of God, called Quakers, against all plotters and fighters in the world," opening with:

> Our principle is, and our practice have always been, to seek peace and ensue it and to follow after righteousness and the knowledge of God, seeking the good and welfare and doing that which tends to the peace of all.. . . All bloody principles and practices, we, as to our own particulars, do utterly deny, with all outward wars and strife and fightings with outward weapons, for any end or under any pretence whatsoever. And this is our testimony to the whole world.[28]

Although the Declaration failed to prevent persecutions, it remains among the most quoted pacifist testaments. Quakers were systematically killed or incarcerated in subsequent years, including their up-and-coming upper-class leader, William Penn. Like Fox, after imprisonment Penn preached across the Atlantic, foreshadowing how both Protestant and Catholic Churches became instrumental forces abroad in the coming centuries, a topic to be revisited in Chapter 7's treatment of colonial and imperial peace and peacemaking.

6

Peace, Peacemaking and the Ascent of Nation-States

Intra-National Peace and Peacemaking

The Peace of Westphalia (1648) among most of Europe's then-major powers that ended the Thirty and Eighty Years Wars also began new eras in peace and peacemaking, though a very long time in the making. Nation-states, which at this stage and for our purposes can be defined as sovereign governments of peoples sharing a common culture, quickly became primary vehicles of social and collective peace, but often at individuals' and each other's expense. Historical and theoretical dynamics of *intra*-national peace from contemporaries' perspectives will first be explored, followed by those of *international* modes of making and maintaining peace proposed and practiced through the so-called Westphalian System. Last, but in no way least, preventative and transformative efforts by those who saw the threats emerging nation-states posed to peace are surveyed. Only two developments in world history between the Peace of Westphalia and the twentieth century have had comparable positive and negative effects on the history of peace in scope and breadth, and it is knotty but necessary for analytical purposes to treat them separately: paradigm-altering events and processes of colonialism/imperialism and industrialism, discussed in the next two chapters which, with nation-states, mark the ongoing beginnings of modern peace and peacemaking on local, regional and global levels.

Like many others before and after, the Thirty Years War (1618–48) had its origins in shortcomings of a previous peace treaty, the Peace of Augsburg of 1555 between the Catholic Holy Roman Empire and the

Schmalkaldic League, an alliance of Protestant German princes, by which the Emperor conceded to the Princes the right to choose Catholicism or Lutheranism as the religion of their lands so long as their peoples, unasked, conformed. Uprisings ensued in the principalities in which foreign powers, notably the French, got involved for their own reasons, extending the war beyond the three decades after which it is named. Meanwhile, the Eighty Years War (1568–1648) was raging across Protestant Dutch provinces, some of which sought independence from Catholic Spain, while others at first did not. In 1576, by the Pacification of Ghent masterminded by William the Silent under Mennonite influence, all the Dutch provinces agreed to throw off the Spanish yoke once religious toleration was assured. The war continued until, due to depleted resources on both sides, a ceasefire known as the Twelve Years Truce (1609–21) was agreed to. While negotiations for a more permanent peaceful arrangement went on, the conflicting parties rearmed, repeating cross-purposes that have consistently proved fatal to peacemaking. The tide turned in Dutch favor when France, now the most populous kingdom in Europe, threw its conscripted military might behind them, more precisely against their common competitor in continental and colonial affairs, Spain.

By 1648, negotiations were well underway to end both wars in the Duchy of Westphalia among delegates from Spain, France, the Holy Roman Empire, Switzerland, Sweden, Portugal, the Dutch Provinces and German principalities. Rather than risk direct confrontation, parallel sessions were held for Catholic representatives in Munster and Protestants at Osnabruck, some thirty kilometres apart. In a *tour de force* for peace, identical treaties were signed in October and May, collectively referred to as the Peace of Westphalia. Cardinal Mazarin, chief advisor to the child "Sun King" Louis XIV of France, is generally considered the architect of the Peace. Borders reflecting actual spheres of influence were set, the Peace of Augsburg was reconfirmed with Calvinism as another option and the caveat that peoples could practice the Christianity of their choice regardless of their states' religion, and heavy wartime trade restrictions were partially removed. But the Peace of Westphalia's lasting results were political, for by it the intra-national principles of peace through state sovereignty, self-determination and non-intervention in internal affairs by other states were instituted and continue to be touted today. But one of the important questions the peacemakers of Westphalia did not address was how such principles would work to bring about peace within a nation-state. Political thinkers and activist before and after the Peace of Westphalia who have devoted themselves to this question have put forth answers as convincing as they are conflicting, and as influenced by their cultural circumstances as they have influenced those since.

Among such prominent early modern polemicists was the Englishman Thomas Hobbes (1588–1679), upon whom the English Civil War had a profound effect. The son of a vicar, he graduated from Oxford and worked as a tutor to higher-born children, including the future King Charles II, translated Greek classics and wrote scientific, philosophical and political treaties. He accompanied his students on "grand tours" of the continent, during which he earned the respect of luminaries like René Descartes. Back in England, a split had occurred between Parliament and King Charles I over his abuses of power, including declaring wars and levying taxes to fund them without Parliament's consent. Before civil war broke out, Hobbes, whose political writings already showed strong monarchical tendencies, fled to Paris. As Cromwell's forces defeated the Royalists, Hobbes was writing his best-known book, *Leviathan* (1651), which perhaps more than any other has jaded modern views on the history of peace. While the idea that only autocratic governments can maintain peace was previously proposed and practiced, his articulation of why was shockingly novel:

> during the time men live without a common power to keep them all in awe, they are in that condition which is called war; and such a war as is of every man against every man (*bellum omnium contra omnes*). . . the nature of war consists not in actual fighting, but in the known disposition thereto during all the time there is no assurance to the contrary. All other time is peace.[1]

All *other* time is peace. The chaos of war in both individual and social senses is thus in Hobbes' view humanity's natural condition, so only what he calls an "artificial man" or autocrat can keep the order of peace.[2] He continues: "The passions that incline men to peace are: fear of death; desire of such things as are necessary to commodious living; and a hope by their industry to obtain them. And reason suggesteth convenient articles of peace upon which men may be drawn to agreement."[3] First among such articles, later called *natural laws*, is "that every man ought to endeavour peace, as far as he has hope of obtaining it; and when he cannot obtain it, that he may seek and use all helps and advantages of war." The second stems from the first, later known as a *social contract*, "that a man be willing, when others are so too, as far forth, as for peace, and defence of himself he shall think it necessary, to lay down this right to all things; and be contented with so much liberty against other men, as he would allow other men against himself." By the time Hobbes returned to England, recent events had proved his points: Cromwell died and just as anarchy was setting in, order was restored by King Charles II, who granted his former tutor a pension for his teachings, and for justifying the monarchy's Restoration.

The ruler who best represented the artificial peace of Hobbes' artificial man is Louis XIV of France, and the writer who presented the most compelling alternative yet was his subject, Montesquieu. During the Sun King's 72-year reign (1642–1715), the longest of any European monarch, France became the richest and most powerful nation on the continent. France's large population of nearly twenty million was leveraged by the acumen of Louis' ministers. Mazarin's replacement, Jean-Baptiste Colbert (1619–1683), introduced fiscal reforms that became bases of mercantilism, the economic policy that national prosperity and peace depend upon a favorable balance of trade, discussed in Chapter 8. This policy amplified the burdens of production and taxation on the lowest classes, called the Third Estate, the other two being nobility and clergy, who had the time and wherewithal to lead destructive armies and wield creative forces such as the world has rarely known. While the Glorious Revolution in England, also though inaccurately called Bloodless, turned the country into a constitutional monarchy, absolute power was vested in Louis. The saying "L'État, c'est moi" ("I am the State"), is apocryphally attributed to him, and his luxury and glory-seeking in five major wars each would have undone Colbert's fiscal goals by themselves. Together, they increased the Third Estate's burden to the point of destitution and, within decades, revolution. As a witness to these events, Charles-Louis de Secondat, Baron de Montesquieu (1689–1755) wrote silently but without staying so.

His major political treatise, *The Spirit of the Law*, was a direct response to Hobbes and an indirect critique of Louis. Agreeing that peace is the first natural law, Montesquieu conceived humanity's natural state not as war or chaos, but as individual weakness. Power, prosperity and peace are products of association, and republican government the means of producing them. However, as Louis' reign had shown, absolute power can be absolutely detrimental to prosperity and peace: "As fear is the principle of despotic government, its end is tranquillity; but this tranquillity cannot be called peace: no, it is only the silence of those towns which the enemy is ready to invade."[4] Thus, the "spirit of monarchy is war and enlargement of dominion: peace and moderation are the spirit of a republic," in which class disparities and conflicts are mitigated by universal equality under the law.[5] In calling for the rule of law, Montesquieu drew on Chinese legalism and the recent English constitution; for efficient legislatures and effective executives, on Spartan, Athenian and Roman examples. Only by separating the powers of government into legislative, judicial and executive branches can an intra-national balance of power secure peace and prosperity for all citizens. In this way, laws can reflect the will of the people, tribunals can resolve disputes and governments render public services without interference between branches. Inaugurating liberal political-economic theory, Montesquieu goes on to write that

"Peace is the natural effect of trade" by creating interdependencies and fostering trust.[6] Coolly received in monarchical France, the *Spirit of the Laws* was lauded in England and its colonies, and became one of the primary sources of the American Constitution.

At the same time in England, John Locke (1632–1704) was spearheading an intellectual movement known as the Enlightenment, whose proponents held that applications of reason and experience could be used to solve all problems, including those of peace. Like Hobbes, Locke received degrees from Oxford, but shared with Montesquieu a deep disdain for despotism. After serving as doctor to the soon-to-be Lord Chancellor Shaftesbury, Locke fled to France then the Netherlands when unfounded suspicions arose that he was involved in a plot to kill the king. There, he finished two works published upon his return, which also had a profound influence on the liberal tradition of intra-national peace and peacemaking based, among other things, upon individual rights and freedoms and equal opportunities for all: *A Letter Concerning Toleration* and *Two Treaties on Government*. In the *Letter*, Locke argues that autocratic measures against the practice of diverse religions rather than their proliferation are the cause and consequence of religious conflicts. Only a secular policy of religious toleration can secure intra-national religious peace, by which persuasion is promoted and coercive force punished. In parallel, the first of the *Two Treaties* refutes with reasoned arguments divine and hereditary rights of absolute monarchs. The second is Locke's positive theory of intra-national peace.

He puts forth this theory to dispel the Hobbesian belief that "all government in the world is the product only of force and violence."[7] Instead, he argues that "all peaceful beginnings of government have been laid in the consent of the people," who have inalienable rights to liberty, which he defines as the absence of restraint – but only insofar as it coincides with the absence of violence.[8] To achieve this social condition, he proposes that

> whoever has the legislative or supreme power of any commonwealth, is bound to govern by established standing laws, promulgated and known to the people, and not by extemporary decrees; by indifferent and upright judges, who are to decide controversies by those laws; and to employ the force of the community at home, only in the execution of such laws. . . And all this to be directed to no other end, but the peace, safety, and public good of the people.[9]

Unlegislated and unjust coercion by those with too much power create civil wars, rooted in the desertion of reason, "which is the rule given between man and man."[10] Thus, "civil society being a state of peace" in which collective reasoning resolves all conflicts, the diverse "members of a commonwealth are united, and combined together into one coherent living body."[11] Locke goes this far: any government which takes or keeps power by conquest, usurpation or tyranny is *a priori* illegitimate, and therefore can be legitimately overthrown, preferably non-violently but with violence if it is necessary to preserve civil society's state of peace. By these propositions, Locke sowed the seeds of two late eighteenth-century revolutions, in France and the United States, as well as the communist revolutions of the nineteenth and twentieth, far from peaceful affairs.

The catalyst in the case of France was Jean-Jacques Rousseau (1712–1778), who can be credited with instigating Romanticism in peace and peacemaking as he did in art, literature and philosophy. Sharing many of Locke's views, Rousseau emphasized emotion rather than reason in the making and maintenance of intra-national peace. A proud citizen of the then-independent republic of Geneva by birth, Rousseau lived most of his life in France, going into exile when his controversial writings made him a target of the monarchy. Also opposing Hobbes, Rousseau posited in the *Social Contract* (1762) that "Men, from the mere fact that, while they are living in their primitive independence, they have no mutual relations stable enough to constitute either the state of peace or the state of war, cannot be naturally enemies."[12] By primitive independence he meant a more imaginary than actual pre-societal human condition, in which individuals were in communion with nature, at liberty in it and equal with each other except in physical strength. These conditions fall short of peace because relative individual and group physical strengths are the only safeguarding forces. As his previous publications expounded, only when societies and civilizations entered the scene did individuals have the collective resources and inclination to join in unitive peace or oppress one another, and he emphatically states: "I prefer liberty with danger to peace with slavery."[13] Like Hobbes, Montesquieu and Locke, for Rousseau peace prospects are predetermined by human nature before human history, when in actuality they have proven to be products of our combined conceptions of and reactions to them.

Social contracts, as an expression of the people's will, are meant to ensure that isonomic peace prevails over oppression. Seldom when oppression prevails have social contracts been agreed upon and, when they have, "this convention, so far from destroying the state of war, presupposes its continuance."[14] Contracts enhance primitive independence by making permanent peace a political possibility rather than resorting to outright or structural violence. Yet, "peace, unity and equality are the enemies of political subtleties" because they are shared and innate emotional impulses that have been corrupted by the institutions of blind faith, reason or private property: "Man is born free but everywhere is in chains."[15] Hence, in a Locke-like validation of revolt in the name of peace, these institutions must be reformed or rejected. But where Locke saw secular state-backed religious diversity as an integral part of intra-national peace, Rousseau saw homogeneity: "For the State to be peace-able and for harmony to be maintained, all the citizens without exception would have to be good Christians. . . It is impossible to live at peace with those we regard as damned; to love them would be to hate God who pun-ishes them: we positively must either reclaim or torment them."[16] This perilous logic was later applied to race, language and other identity markers in defining who belongs to a nation-state to the detriment of intra-national peace and the individual freedoms Rousseau sought to secure thereby.

Rousseau's passion and prescription for peace were put into action during the French Revolution (1789–1799), which when legislative means failed made the feudal monarchy into a constitutional republic by mob violence. The slogan "Long live the King," competed with "Long live the Nation" until "Liberty, Equality and Fraternity" quieted both. The height of violence came with the Reign of Terror, during which the so-called Committee of Public Safety headed by Maximilien Robespierre ordered thousands of counter-revolutionaries killed, while authorizing the military mobilization of the masses to impose its Constitution. In their midst, a movement called the Thermidor after the revolutionary cal-endar month in which it took place (July 1794) sought to restrain the Reign of Terror so as to restore civil order and, if possible, peace through the rule of law called for by the Constitution. Although, having exhausted all alternatives, they tried to do so by beheading Robespierre, historians and theorists of revolutions have used the term *Thermidor* to describe the replacement of radical revolutionary regimes based on force with a moderate regime based on institutions. Radical factions soon regained leadership and decided to export their principles and tactics, doing so under the parvenu general Napoleon Bonaparte's military banner. Under pretexts of bringing liberty to the tyrannized, equality to the oppressed, and unity to the divided, Napoleon invaded and became dictator of most Europe, invalidating the intra-national principles of the Peace of Westphalia in the process. The pervasive, self-imposed limita-tions on intra-national peace by early political theoreticians and practi-tioners stemmed from their misconstrual of it along solely social lines. Nation-states were not and are never single-constituent groups but rather constellations of different constituent groups, making joint social-collective approaches to intra-national peace more plausible. In this sense, international peace and roles of individuals within and between (un)peaceful nation-states become reflective of what was irreplaceably missing from nation-states themselves.

International Peace and Peacemaking

On an international level, the Peace of Westphalia enacted the principle that nation-states are equals in legal and diplomatic terms regardless of what their relative weaknesses or strengths in economic, military or other terms may be. To take these actualities into account, the notion of a *balance of powers* had come in currency, by which equilibrium between competing nation-states was sought to keep each in check and prevent one from overriding the others. Such peace-oriented propositions were put forth in many ways at different times, and implemented with highly volatile degrees of success. One of the earliest practical proposals for a balance of power was put forth by Filippo Visconti in 1443. He sought joint diplomatic action by Florence, Venice and Milan to end the war between the condottiere Francesco Sforza and the Pope, efforts followed by meetings of major Italian city-states' representatives to settle outstanding issues and exchange mutual guarantees, culminating in the Peace of Lodi (1444–54).

After citizens of Milan named Sforza their Duke for his mercenary might and leadership skills, he set up permanent embassies in other city-states, the first to do so since Roman times. By means of alliances and counter-alliances, the Sforza and Medici saw to it that no one city-state grew strong at the others' expense on the weakest link principle. As one later historian puts it, with Italian city-states temporarily "at peace among themselves," they were "free from foreign intervention, and their resources could be devoted to improvement of their own dominions."[17] Successful balances of power achieved by these city-states were emulated during the emergence of nation-states, but proved difficult to duplicate on international scales. In 1461, the King of Bohemia contacted European rulers to set up a federation of states with a permanent congress of representatives, to no avail. The purported Grand Design of France's King Henry IV proposed to divide Europe proportionately between fifteen rulers so as to eliminate envy by equality and fear by equilibrium. A Treaty of Alliance and League (1596) with England's Queen Elizabeth I may have been geared towards this end, but her death and his assassination killed the plan.

During the seventeenth and eighteenth centuries, several European intellectuals put forth international peace plans. An early exponent was a monk and private school teacher in Paris, Eméric Crucé (1590–1648). His *New Cyneas* (1623) was published during the wars leading up to the Peace of Westphalia. The title indicates the book's intended audience by referring to an ancient counselor to kings, but its subtitle is more indicative of its content: *Discourse on Opportunities and Means for*

Establishing a General Peace and Freedom of Trade throughout the World. Crucé first critiques what he sees as the root causes of war: bigotry, profit, reparation and glory-seeking. He then proposes that humanity is a body "the organs of which are in such sympathy with each other that the sickness of one affects the other."[18] Since "Inveterate tradition alone is responsible for the fact that man often sees in his fellow-man a stranger," what is necessary above all is "to uproot the most common vice which is the source of all the others:" inhumanity.[19] He moves on to show how this can be done in worldly ways: by bring people into closer relations by physical means such as safer roads, seaways, canals and bridges; by economic means such as a common currency and chamber of commerce; and by political means such as a permanent congress composed of – and here Crucé is most clearly ahead of his time – delegates from all the world's nations, not just European. Disputes between them would be arbitrated by delegates not party to the conflict, and decisions made by majority votes. Crucé's visionary solutions to pressing problems of international peace still make for improvements on some contemporary actualities, and ever since world peace plans have been en vogue.

Seventy years later, William Penn published *The European Diet, Parliament or Estates*, in which he proposed a similar deliberative and judicial body that would meet regularly instead of permanently to set rules of international intercourse, settle differences unresolved by ongoing diplomacy, and whose decisions could be militarily enforced by members. In 1701, the English economist Charles Davenant published *The Balance of Power* in which he formalized the notion, enacted during the peace congresses at Utrecht of 1713 that ended the Europe-wide War of the Spanish Succession by partitioning Spain's continental and colonial territories, resolving trade disputes and clearing up claims to thrones. The peace plan of another French monk, Abbé Saint-Pierre, circulated during the same congress at which he was the French secretary, and published a year later in English as *A Project for Settling an Everlasting Peace in Europe*. Written in treaty form, Saint-Pierre proposed to unite European nation-states in a representative federation based on population rather than power and strictly limit the size of national militaries. Committees would be formed to discuss and pass resolutions on political, diplomatic, financial, and military matters with the support of a senate, supplemented by reconciliation committees to resolve disputes. Although these international peace plans and practices were never fully adopted, they were among the earliest of their kinds in modern times and so formed conceptual foundations of today's multinational bodies such as the United Nations (UN) and European Union (EU).

On a connected front, concerted efforts began to be made to create a legal framework in which wars and warfare could be contained or even eliminated as means to international peace. The groundbreaking Dutch jurist Hugo Grotius (1583–1645) put the problem this way in the prolegomena to *On the Laws of War and Peace* (1625):

> I observed a lack of restraint in relation to war, such as even barbarous races should be ashamed of; I observed that men rush to arms for slight causes, or no cause at all, and that when arms have once been taken up there is no longer any respect for law, divine or human; it is as if, in accordance with a general decree, frenzy had openly been let loose for the committing of all crimes.[20]

To counteract this lack of restraint, Grotius proposed a "common law among nations, which is valid alike for war and in war," voluntarily adopted but compulsory after that. He begins by reaffirming the validity of Cicero's *just war* (for self-defense, reparation and punishment) and its applicability in the age of nation-states. But Grotius' major contribution is his elaboration of this definition to include *just warfare*, that is, war conducted according to the principle of doing the least harm possible. Montesquieu echoed Grotius a century later, writing that the "law of nations is naturally founded on this principle, that different nations ought in time of peace to do one another all the good they can, and in time of war as little injury as possible."[21] Even with the advent of gunpowder weapons during their lifetimes, their advice went unheeded.

Only in the mid nineteenth century, as explosive, mechanized and chemical weapons became humdrum, was the idea of just warfare resuscitated. A Swiss businessman, Henri Dunant, was horrified by the devastation he accidentally witnessed at the Battle of Solferino (1859) and the total lack of care for the wounded. He roused citizens of nearby towns to their aid and requested that care be given without partisan considerations. Upon his return to Geneva, he published a book on his recent experience in which he proposed the formation of a neutral international organization to care for those wounded in war regardless of nationality, impressing a councilman who decided to implement it in the city, and so the International Red Cross was born in 1863, now one of the largest and most distinguished humanitarian groups in the world. A year later, on Dunant's initiative, the Swiss Parliament invited representatives of European nations, fourteen of which accepted, to sign an agreement geared towards the Red Cross' objectives, known as the Geneva Convention. The original Geneva Convention has been ratified several times since by nearly all the world's nations, and includes the wartime welfare and humane treatment of sailors, civilians, prisoners of war and humanitarian workers. Apogees of Grotius' and Dunant's line of peace work came at The Hague Peace Conferences of 1899 and 1907, discussed in Chapter 9, at which signatory nation-states agreed on rules and regulations governing the commencement and conduct of warfare, the status of neutral nations, and the prohibition of certain types of weapons, most of which were thrown out the window in the First World War.

Whereas Grotius and Dunant tried to establish principles of war limitation on the basis of humanity's best interests and historical experience, the first professor of international law, Samuel Pufendorf (1632–94), did the same on the basis of what he argued were universally valid and applicable natural laws revealed by reason. In *On the Laws of Nature and Nations* (1674), he argued that international law regulating relations between nations, including the limitation of war, is "instituted and sanctioned by nature herself without any human intervention, and that it rests, therefore, upon that obligation of natural law, by which all men are bound, in so far as they are endowed with reason, and which does not owe its original introduction to any convention of men."[22] Such conventions are aids to, not replacements of, natural laws upon which he believed international peace through restricted warfare or otherwise rests. A more analytical approach to international war and peace was put forth by a German professor of philosophy, Christian Wolff (1679–1754), in his *The Law of Nations Considered Scientifically*. He divided the validation of international law into four categories, each with its benefits and drawbacks: 1. *Voluntary laws* like those of Grotius are mutually agreed to between nations, such law governing ocean travel, but can be easily disagreed to; 2. *Natural laws* like those of Pufendorf are universal, such as self-determination, but are difficult to implement: 3. *Implicit customary laws* dependent on traditions of groups of nations, such tributary and allegiance systems, which can be detrimental to certain parties; and 4. *Explicit treaty laws* between nations, but binding only on the parties involved. Parallel to these natural and scientific approaches came ones practiced by lawyers, judges and diplomats in the burgeoning fields of international relations.

The thrust of their efforts was and is that practical knowledge can be gained by the trials and errors of peace's past. In 1789, German law professor George Frederic de Martens wrote:

> On the example of two nations, all the nations of Europe might, by common consent, make treaties to regulate their different rights; and, then, these general treaties would form a code, which might be called the positive law of nations.[23]

Further, "by comparing the treaties that the powers of Europe have made with one another, we discover certain principles" applicable in other circumstances.[24] Thus, "the aggregate of the rights and obligations established among the nations of Europe (or the majority of them), whether by particular but uniform treaties, by tacit convention, or by custom" forms "the general positive law of nations." For example, the Treaty of Osnabrück (1648) required "all and each of the contracting parties to this treaty shall be held to defend and maintain all and each of the dispositions of this peace."[25] Two centuries later, the Declaration of London (1871), stated "it is an essential principle of the law of nations that no Power can liberate itself from the engagements of a treaty, or modify the stipulations thereof, unless with the consent of the contracting Powers by means of an amicable arrangement."[26] Although the words used to represent principles do not always represent their implementation, they can and do represent their progress.

A challenge to this approach lay in the number of treaties that had to be sorted through, as one list from 800 to 1873 contained some 7,500 entries. To deal with such issues, *The Journal of International and Comparative Law* was launched by Gustave Rolin-Jacquemyns (1873), who also founded the extant Institute of International Law. Its distinguished jurists members apply de Martens' approach to codify international law in non-official capacities, offer legal advice in controversial cases and through publications. A similar organization, founded in Brussels the same year, is the International Law Association, which encouraged business people as well as legal professionals to join. Then as today, its members concentrate on "the study, clarification and development of international law, both public and private."[27] *Public law* refers to those binding on nation-states, *private* on individuals. International laws the Association helped formulate, including on transportation and shipping regulations, postal charges, copyrights and credit, continue to tangibly contribute to world peace by reducing day-to-day frictions.

A case-by-case approach based on relevant precedents became a custom for non-violently settling international disputes from the sixteenth to eighteenth centuries by so-called Prize Courts, which sought to resolve international conflicts within intra-national jurisprudence. In a prominent case between Sweden and England (1799), the presiding judge crystallized their functions:

> The seat of judicial authority is, indeed, locally here, in the belligerent country, according to the known law and practice of nations; but the law itself has no locality. It is the duty of the person who sits here to determine this question exactly as he would determine the same question if sitting at Stockholm; to assert no pretensions on the part of Great Britain which he would not allow to Sweden in the same circumstances, and to impose no duties on Sweden, as a neutral country, which he would not admit to belong to Great Britain in the same character.[28]

Standards for intra-national resolution of international disputes was set during negotiations between the United States and Great Britain over issues relating to the War of Independence, leading up to the Jay Treaty of 1794. A judge was chosen by the legislatures of each country, and a third by common agreement. The parties presented their cases to the judges on specific issues, such as reparations, borders and trade terms, and their decisions were binding. As one historian puts it, "Prior to this time arbitrations were irregular and spasmodic; from this time forward they assumed a certain regularity and system."[29] This system of international arbitration, in more or less modified forms, prevails but only works when conflicting parties want it to, rarely the case. Realizing this pitfall and drawing upon past peace plans, French and British parliamentarians established the Inter-Parliamentary Union (IPU) in 1889 as a permanent forum for negotiation and mediation, which has since grown to over 140 member-states.

At its first meeting, founder Frédéric Passy proclaimed "Civilization is peace; barbarism is war," and announced the IPU's purpose as promoting high-level negotiations and arbitration within a legal framework, first as a substitute then a replacement for war.[30] The current IPU Statute states its mandate as working "for peace and cooperation among peoples and for the firm establishment of representative institutions."[31] It does so by fostering contacts, coordination and exchange of experience among parliaments, parliamentarians and their international equivalents; considering questions of international interest and expressing its views on such issues with the aim of bringing about concerted action by its parliamentary members; contributing to the defense and promotion of human rights; generating and disseminating knowledge about representative institutions; and strengthening their means of action by way of recommendations. An outcome of these efforts towards international arbitration was the Permanent Court of International Justice established under the League of Nations after the First World War and its successor in the UN, discussed in Chapters 9 and 10, respectively. Yet, according to a historian of nation-state neutrality, after the Peace of Westphalia "either war had to become general to the point of excluding neutrality, or neutrality had to be imposed to the point of abolishing war by rendering it practically impossible. One was bound inevitably to do away with the other," and his view war won out.[32] In some ways this statement is true, in others not.

Taking the example of neutrality in maritime affairs, it is easy to see how a nation-state without naval capabilities could remain neutral in a naval war between nation-states. Indeed, this principle was codified early on in the jurisprudence of *Consolato del Mare* or Maritime Court of Barcelona, dealing with Mediterranean seafaring disputes in the sixteenth century. But on land, where national economies are mixed with one another, borders coterminous and interests intertwined, neutrality is difficult to define, let alone actualize. The Russian Empress Catherine II pioneered the practice of strategic or "armed neutrality," abstaining from war with any allied parties while reserving the rights to self-defense and attack others.[33] To resist the threats of England's already extensive naval capabilities, she formed the First League of Armed Neutrality in 1780, which eventually had over ten member-states, followed by a less successful Second League in 1800, also on Russian initiative. Modern neutrality norms became those adopted by President George Washington's Neutrality Act (1794) regarding US non-involvement in ongoing Franco-English wars. First of its kind, the Act declared criminal anyone who, in American jurisdiction, attempted to augment the armed forces of, or participated in hostilities against, any nation formally at peace with the US. The Neutrality Act was used as a model for the English Foreign Enlistment Acts of 1819 and 1870, which went one step further by outlawing the armament of and assistance to nations at war with those at peace with England. Together, these Anglo-American Acts inspired similar pro-peace legislation in other countries.

Sweden has not taken part in warfare since 1814, the longest running neutrality policy and a decisive part of its modern state formation. Switzerland, like Sweden, has armed forces for defensive purposes, but has not taken part in war since 1815, and it is the only European state never to have employed mercenaries. Similarly, after Belgium gained its independence from the Netherlands by armed revolt in 1830, King Leopold I declared the country neutral and it did not take part in a European war until the First World War, though this did not prevent its atrocities in Africa. In other cases, neutrality was imposed from without, as with Luxemburg when France and Russia agreed to its neutral status to avert war between themselves, and which lasted until 1948. Of course, these neutral nation-states are exceptions, but nonetheless prove the viability of neutrality as a peace policy. However, *neutrality* as a peace policy must be distinguished from *isolationism*, which is based on selective refusals to make any international commitments, as did the US vis-à-vis European affairs, England vis-à-vis continental European affairs, and Japan vis-à-vis world affairs in the 1800s. On a practical level, isolationism negatively secures one nation's peace with others by eliminating relations between them; neutrality positively secures peace by promoting all relations except military ones. On a theoretical level, universal isolationism would preclude international peace by ending relations among nation-states, and universal neutrality would bring about international peace by ending war among them.

By the nineteenth century's end, the term "benevolent neutrality" came into use with the Triple Alliance Treaties between Italy, Germany and Austro-Hungary from 1882–1912, and the League of Three Emperors between the last two and Russia. Actually, benevolent neutrality was a veiled term for parties' option to go to war in aid of its allies, and to "dedicate its attention to the localization of the conflict."[34] By the turn of the twentieth century, through a series of secret *ententes*, Britain and her former rivals France and Russia also became benevolently neutral towards each other. These arrangements made "the system of European alliances extremely complex, and this very complexity kept Europe and the world from becoming involved in war. No one nation dared to go too far in the absence of unconditional assurances of support in case of difficulty"– for a short time.[35] By 1914, this near-medieval convolution of political entanglements had become an anachronistic absurdity and turned out to be one of the driving factors behind the failures of diplomacy leading up to the First World War, despite the valiant efforts of individuals and groups who early on realized and reacted to dangers nation-states in themselves pose to peace, and courageously took it upon themselves to make and maintain peace despite them.

Peace and Peacemaking Despite Nation-States

At the *Symposium on the Political Relevance of the Peace of Westphalia* in 1998, the Secretary General of the North Atlantic Treaty Organization (NATO) noted that "the principle of sovereignty relied on produced the basis for rivalry, not community of states."[36] A historian a century earlier wrote that as nation-states "acknowledge no superior. . . they have not organized any common paramount authority."[37] These remarks draw attention to two fatal flaws of the Westphalian System, an overdependence on sovereignty and an underestimation of the need for effective supra-national bodies. Combined, these two flaws have led to a third, that nation-states may abuse their sovereignty internally due to a lack of external checks. Peace workers have tried to overcomethese flaws with great insight and innovation surpassed only by the tremendous and entrenched difficulties they faced. The leading Enlightenment thinker in Germany, Immanuel Kant (1724–1824), presents a compelling first case in point.

In his *Critique of Pure Reason*, Kant claimed that criticism can further the cause of peace where reason and open dialogue fail, as they did in the Peace of Westphalia's wake:

> Without the control of criticism, reason. . . can only establish its claims and assertions by war. Criticism, on the contrary, deciding all questions according to the fundamental laws of its own institution,secures to us the peace of law and order, and enables us to discuss all differencesin the more tranquil

manner of a legal process. In the former case, disputes are ended by victory, which both sides may claimand which is followed by a hollow armistice; in the latter, by a sentence, which, as it strikes at the root of all speculative differences, ensures to all concerned a lasting peace.[38]

Kant also proposed that inter-personal peace could be achieved if everyone acted "according to the maxim which can at the same time make itself a universal law," known as the *categorical imperative*.[39] So in terms applicable to our sphere of interest: if everyone acted peacefully, the world would be at peace, but if everyone acted in a warlike manner, there would be no one to be at peace with. Thus, "The morally practical reason utters within us its irrevocable veto: *There shall be no war.*"[40] Synthesizing Sophist peace practices, Christian peace principles and then-emerging political peace paradigms, he substantiated pragmatic roles criticism and categorical imperatives can play to secure peace politically despite or against nation-states.

In *Perpetual Peace* (1795), Kant criticized the scientific approach to international law for being "without substance, since it depends upon treaties which contain in the very act of their conclusion the reservation of their breach."[41] That is, in the words of the Preliminary Articles he sets forth to prepare the way for perpetual world peace:

1. No Treaty of Peace Shall Be Held Valid in Which There Is Tacitly Reserved Matter for a Future War;
2. No Independent States, Large or Small, Shall Come under the Dominion of Another State by Inheritance, Exchange, Purchase, or Donation;
3. Standing Armies Shall in Time Be Totally Abolished;
4. National Debts Shall Not Be Contracted with a View to the External Friction of States;
5. No State Shall by Force Interfere with the Constitution or Government of Another State;
6. No State Shall, during War, Permit Such Acts of Hostility Which Would Make Mutual Confidence in the Subsequent Peace Impossible.[42]

According to Kant, once these Preliminary Articles have been implemented, then his Definitive Articles can be put in place to maintain world peace perpetually:

1. The Civil Constitution of Every State Should Be Republican;
2. The Law of Nations Shall be Founded on a Federation of Free States;
3. The Law of World Citizenship Shall Be Limited to Conditions of Universal Hospitality.

By "republican," Kant, like others before him, meant states that safeguard individual rights and liberties by representative legislatures and isonomic legal systems. He criticizes previous peace plans for not having "the least legal force, because states as such do not stand under a common external power." Yet the federation of states he calls a "league of peace" has no dominion over the internal affairs of members, vested only with the authority and given the means to make and maintain peace between them. World citizenship is meant to end human rights abuses within nation-states by allowing individuals to appeal to a higher authority than national governments. Without the precondition of hospitality, "the right of a stranger not to be treated as an enemy when he arrives in the land of another" or what we would call refugee status today, perpetual peace is no less of a mirage than it was before. In more ways than one, the history of peace after the publication of Kant's *Perpetual Peace* is a series of unacknowledged footnotes to it.

In the English-speaking world during the first half of the 1800s, the primary propagandist for instituting peace plans similar to Kant's were the "friends of peace," formalized by 1815 as British and American Peace Societies. Their public lectures, private meetings, campaigning and lobbying got the ball rolling for what is called in contemporary peace studies the *organized peace movement*, which sought to institute international peace outside, in the cracks of as well as through the by-now prevailing nation-state system. England's *The Herald of Peace*, France's *La Paix des Deux Mondes*, Belgium's *La Paix* and the American *Advocate of Peace* were among the mouthpieces of the movement. By the First International Peace Congress, held in London in 1843, similar Societies had sprung elsewhere in Europe, notably in Paris and Geneva. Papers were presented by leading pacifist intellectuals on the economic and social benefits of nation-states not being at war, but aside from making a few national headlines speakers were preaching to the choir. A Second Congress took place in Brussels in 1848. While the number and diversity of attendees increased from the First, and issues such as disarmament, international arbitration and the creation of a federation of states were debated, the networking of European and North American peace activists at the Congress remained its only significant result. These early forums were markedly highbrow affairs and served to reinforce existing assumptions about peace and its insoluble ties to war rather than act as catalysts for any kind of change. Still, the effects of their galvanization can be traced through the twentieth and into the twenty-first century.

Paris officials permitted the Third International Peace Congress to take place in 1849 only when prominent statesmen and literati gave their support, including historian-statesman Alexis de Tocqueville and romantic novelist Victor Hugo. Hugo presided over the meeting of six hundred delegates and two thousand spectators, among whom were leading politicians, diplomats, scholars and economists in positions to influence affairs of state. In his opening address, Hugo urged his small audience to work towards a United States of Europe and, by attaching his name to the Congress, he brought the organized movement to the attention of the wider audience his pen commanded, somewhat broadening its base. Another Congress was held in Frankfurt the next year, but that of Paris is generally considered the organized peace movement's mid-century gem. In 1867, the largest peace conference yet took place in Geneva, organized by the new International League for Peace and Liberty, with more than six thousand attendees of nearly all political, religious and economic creeds. The organizers' stated aims were to execute a peace plan close to Kant's by establishing a permanent organization capable of implementing it across national borders. Its president explained: "The International League of Peace and Liberty never follows the example of the Peace Societies, the chimera that the direct establishment of absolute and universal peace can be realized by the efforts of existing governments. . . To expect good will from existing governments seems to be the mad hope of naive candour."[43] That Giuseppe Garibaldi, leader of nationalists in Italy, presided over the meeting is indicative of crosscurrents among its attendees. But Garibaldi's renowned support for democracy also signalled another trend: the organized peace movement's growing lower class appeal.

Before joining the British Peace Society, Richard Cobden (1804–65) was a leader of the Anti-Corn Law League, which sought the repeal of tariffs the government imposed on imported foodstuffs, starving the poor to protect pocketbooks of the rich. A major factor in the League's success was its dual renewal in approaches to peace and peacemaking, prompting Cobden to seek their wider application through the Society. First was opening the hearts and minds of the lower classes to the ideas that their struggles to improve their living conditions could be carried out nonviolently, and that international policies and relations directly benefit or harm their wellbeing. Second was an infusion of free trade principles, discussed more fully in Chapter 9, into longstanding middle- and upper-class liberal peace traditions so as to circumvent political barriers to international peace by eliminating economic ones. In brief, free trade according Cobden would decrease costs and raise standards of living, securing intra-national peace from poverty-based uprisings while cementing commercial links between nation-states as guarantees of international peace. Now leader of the British Peace Society, at the Paris Peace Conference Cobden proposed that banks and other credit institutions should be prohibited from lending funds for war purposes, overlooking the fact that for the German Krupp family who dominated the arms race, advance purchases superseded the need of such loans.

After learning of Cobden's Anti-Corn Law League and meeting him at the Frankfurt Congress, Edmond Potonié (1829–1902) founded the French League of Public Good in 1850, which pioneered what are now called *social justice* approaches to peace addressing underlying causes of its prevention such as inequality. On business trips throughout Europe, Potonié gained support of entrepreneurs, politician and labour activists who rightly saw the League as a liberal, non-violent vehicle of peace-oriented change. But in the next decade, he lost faith in liberalism and expanded the League's mandate to include lobbying for state-run elementary education, the abolition of the death penalty, collective self-help programs, community credit associations, international workers' groups and gender equality. This radical mishmash of platforms alienated many of Potonié original supporters like the political economist and parliamentarian Frédéric Passy (1822–1912), who then formed the International and Permanent League for Peace and later the International Parliamentarian Union. A popular lecturer, he made academic peace studies appealing to all by what can be called *pacifist pedagogy*: teaching peace both as a field in itself and through parallel fields that make peace possible. Denouncing the ineffectiveness of military solutions to intra- and international problems, he called for a "permanent congress to oversee the general interests of humanity" empowered with a police force.[44] At the first meeting of his League, Passy declared "war on war," arguing that if resources nations expend on their militaries were redirected towards improving living conditions instead, the two major causes of modern wars would be cut off at their source.[45] Passy's League also ran a publication series called The Library of Peace, aimed at educating the public about the history and aims of peace movements, which arguably inaugurated widespread disseminations of modern peace studies.

As Sandi Cooper recounts in *Patriotic Pacifism: Waging War on War in Europe, 1815–1914*, peace organizations thus transformed from Anglo-American initiatives to pan-European projects to worldwide movements including hundreds of local, regional and global groups. Once dominated by white, upper-class men, women and minorities of all classes began to play an ever-larger role in the organized peace movement. As Cooper relates, they

> traveled lecture circuits, published and catalogued libraries of books and brochures, raised money from governments and private donors, confronted politicians, challenged military budgets, criticized history curricula, combated chauvinist and establishment media, lobbied diplomats, questioned candidates for office, telegraphed congress resolutions to foreign ministries.[46]

Members of peace organizations often worked with other activist groups advocating human, women's and workers' rights, among others, leveraging their networks and resources but perhaps also diluting peace causes. Contemporary conflicts, such as the American Civil War and Franco-Prussian War, made clear the horrors modern war machines could wreak, invigorating rather than disheartening peace activists. An international arms-reduction campaign led by Britain's Henry Richard began in 1869 and, as a result, resolutions were proposed in the parliaments of France, Prussia, Italy, Spain, Sweden and the Netherlands, though not passed. To coordinate such efforts in different though all peace-oriented directions, a Universal Peace Congress was held yearly from 1889 to 1939 except during the First World War, and to present a unified pacifist front, the International Peace Bureau was established at Berne in 1892. Similar coordinating bodies were created at national levels, like the Permanent Delegation of French Peace Societies in 1897 and the British National Peace Council in 1905. In 1908, an American peace conference delegate exclaimed: "If you had been told, ten years ago, that we should have an international tribunal, an international Parliament assured, sixty treaties of arbitration, and an international prize court, I say that the boldest of dreamers would not have believed it."[47] In the effectiveness, such disbelief was not misguided.

A driving force behind these successes was that peace organizations at the end of the nineteenth and early twentieth centuries received unprecedented endowments from private sources and support from public officials. Belgian King Leopold II hosted the 1894 Universal Peace Congress in Antwerp, indicating his support for the cause. Alexander Millerand, the first French socialist to hold a parliamentary post, opened the Paris Congress of 1900. President Theodore Roosevelt, who had just brokered peace between Russian and Japan after their war of 1904, invited Inter-Parliamentarians to the White House to hold high-level peace talks. The self-made railroad baron Ivan Bloch, who wrote an influential critique of modern warfare, founded a Museum of War and Peace at Lucerne and left large sums to the Berne Bureau and other groups for scholarly and educational purposes. Steel magnate and arbitration advocate Andrew Carnegie gave away almost all of his self-made millions to peace-oriented and philanthropic organizations, funding constructions of the Pan-American Union Building in Washington, the Peace Palace at Hague, and the Central American Court of Justice in Costa Rica, and creating a trust that has ever since sponsored major studies and conferences on the past, present and future of peace: the Carnegie Endowment for International Peace. Yet the best-known bequest to the promotion of peace and peace-making is that of the Swedish inventor of dynamite and hundreds of other products who came to own an arms manufacturing plant. In his will, he designated a sizeable donation to be distributed annually as prizes recognizing individuals who have made significant contributions to scientific, medical and literary fields, but also to one who "shall have done the most or the best work for fraternity between nations, for the abolition or reduction of standing armies and for the holding of peace congresses."[48] There are hundreds of peace prizes in the world today, but none has a higher profile than that named after Alfred Nobel. His narrow definition of peace exhibits the limited scope of the word for most similarly situated Europeans of his day, due in no small way to the organized peace movement. In the end, however, historically unamtched financial and political backing fuelled rather than resolved ongoing ideological and logistical disputes among peace factions, fragmentations that proved to be the organized peace movement's greatest single internal impediment to achieving its aims, then but hopefully not today.

The question most proposals for intra- and international peace left unanswered is what individuals acting alone can do when nation-states abuse their powers against their own people and go to war against their wishes. Answers American Transcendentalists and the Russian Leo Tolstoy put forth not only provided ways for individuals to contest and change nation-states non-violently but also to find inner peace in doing so. Although not a Transcendentalist, Unitarian Minister William Ellery Channing (1780–1842) influenced Ralph Waldo Emerson, who was *par excellence*. Sermonizing, he proposed that there "can be no peace without but through peace within," allowing for war if individual consciences believed it was just.[49] However, just because governments go to war does not mean they are justified, requiring that individuals decide for themselves whether they should participate, "bound to withhold" if "conscience condemns the cause."[50] Emerson (1803–82), a Harvard graduate and schoolmaster, travelled in Europe before returning to Boston. Adopting Channing's perspective, in the belief that what is good for one is good for all he made it universal, a hallmark of his Transcendentalism. Because we are united in one "over-soul" encompassing humans and nature alike, he claimed, "he who kills his brother commits suicide."[51] In a lecture to the American Peace Society on "War" (1838), he compared it to epidemics that must be contained first and eliminated second. Failing this, in "Self-Reliance" (1841), "Nothing can bring you peace but yourself. Nothing can bring you peace but the triumph of principles."[52] During the Mexican-American War (1846–48), he criticized Abolitionists who did not act on their principles by resisting and going to prison "on their known and described disagreements from the state."[53] The example he had in mind was a former housemate who actually did, as well as eloquently argued for doing, exactly that.

Henry David Thoreau (1802–62), also a Harvard graduate, lived most of his life in Concord, Massachusetts, working odd jobs while reading, writing and taking nature walks. For two years starting in 1845, he lived in a cabin on Walden Pond, receiving visitors and running errands in town but otherwise withdrawing from society to practice self-reliance and develop intuition. A year into the project, he was stopped by the local tax collector in town who reminded him that he had not paid his taxes in years. When Thoreau said he had not done so on purpose, he was taken into custody, grudgingly released when someone paid them for him. After inadequate response to inquiries as to why he was arrested, he gave a lecture entitled "Resistance to Civil Government," published as "Civil Disobedience" in 1866. In it he explained he refused to support a state that supported slavery, which he saw as a motive for the Mexican-American War. If the law "requires you to be the agent of injustice to another," he contended, then "break the law. Let your life be a counter friction to stop the machine."[54] He goes on: "If the alternative is to keep all just men in prison, or give up war and slavery, the State will not hesitate which to choose."[55] Although he remained unrenowned in his lifetime, soon after his death Thoreau's works somehow reached and influenced one of the most famous living writers in the world, who gave book royalties to a group of persecuted, civilly disobedient conscientious objectors to relocate to Canada.

The son of a prominent nobleman, Tolstoy (1828–1910) was raised on his family's estate south of Moscow. He attended the University of Kazan at age sixteen, studying languages and law and considered a diplomatic career. After enlisting in the army and finding combat immoral and degrading, he split his time between managing his estate and leading a profligate intellectual's life, later regretting the latter. Bringing him literary fame was his graphic depiction of the Siege of Sevastopol (1854), in which he participated, exposing the terrors of war rather than glorifying it, the preferred literary treatment at the time. He then contrasted the benefits and drawbacks of progressive materialism with natural simplicity in *The Cossacks* (1862) before contrasting two other states of humanity, *War and Peace*, written 1862–9. Arguably the most famous novel ever written on the topics, it is also probably the least read due to its length and reduced here at great loss. Napoleon's disastrous 1812 invasion of Russia, described by Tolstoy as "opposed to human reason and to human nature," is the backdrop for a panorama of characters whose lives are affected by it in various ways. "Millions of men," he continues, "perpetrated against one another such innumerable crimes. . . but which those who committed them did not at the time regard as being crimes."[56] Yet his critique conflicts with the novel's core historical determinism, by which individual action "performed at a certain moment in time becomes irrevocable and belongs to history, in which it has not a free but a predestined significance."[57] Pierre Bezukhov, the story's focal point, shares Tolstoy's own biography and articulates views he would later assert in the first person. Also a reformed noble-born dilettante who fails in emancipating his serfs, Pierre is attracted to philosophies of Freemasons who tell him "Every violent reform deserves censure, for it quite fails to remedy evil while men remain what they are, and also because wisdom needs no violence."[58] Horrified by a battle he witnesses, Pierre decides to kill Napoleon himself. Captured and freed after the siege of Moscow, he finally finds love as the city is rebuilt.

Tolstoy's late-life spiritual crisis led him to channel his work evermore towards peace. In *What is Art?* (1897) he posited artists as peacemakers, arguing the "task for art to accomplish is to make the feeling of brotherhood and love of one's neighbor. . . the customary feeling and instinct of all men."[59] He put forth his philosophy of non-resistance in *The Kingdom of God is Within You* three years earlier, and that of non-cooperation in his last book, *The Law of Love and the Law of Violence* (1908). The point of *The Kingdom* is that "To offend another, because he offended us, for the specious reason of removing an evil, means to repeat an evil deed, both against him and against ourselves."[60] *Non-resistance*, the radical form of pacifism practiced by Jesus, breaks cycles of violence by liberating and empowering both inflictors and inflicted: "by this very relation to violence he not only frees himself, but also the world from external power." *The Law of Love and Violence* espouses a more activist approach. Non-resistance can end cycles of violence, but only non-violence can prevent it: *non-cooperation* with militarism by defection, objection and civil disobedience can bring about "the complete transformationof the existing order of things . . . among all the peoples of the globe."[61] With the same historical determinism permeating *War and Peace*, he holds that the law of love will triumph over the law of violence or else all laws will lose validity and with this loss, all our lives. A month before he died, Tolstoy responded to letters from Gandhi, praising "However insignificant may be the number of your people who practice non-resistance and of our people in Russia who refuse military service," they are cosmically significant.[62] Weeks later, he gave up all worldly concerns and embarked on what turned out to be a pilgrimage to nowhere, dying of pneumonia in train station.

A renewed religiosity was also at the heart of the final peace movement to be covered in this chapter, one based on the belief that humanity can still be spiritually united despite the geo-political borders of nation-states by which we are now divided. "The earth is but one country and mankind its citizens," is the most famous statement of Baha Ullah (1817–92), founder of the Baha'i faith.[63] But it begins, "It is not for him to pride himself who loveth his own country, but rather for him who loveth the whole world." He declared himself the Promised One prophesied by the Persian Ali Muhammad, known as the Bab ("living door"), originally a Shiite who split with the tradition in 1840, for which he was imprisoned and martyred. During his incarceration, the Bab's disciples gathered in Khurasan, for centuries a hotbed of religious integrations. After his execution, some made an attempt at the Persian Shah's life, for which all were imprisoned. Amongst them was Baha Ullah, who had always practiced and preached non-violence and which he continued to do in Baghdad and Kurdistan upon release, cleared of wrongdoing. His books, emphasizing gender equality, universal higher education, the unity of all religions and personal empowerment attracted many followers of all faiths, including Jews, Muslims, Christians and Zoroastrians. Fearful of his growing sect, the Persian authorities requested that the Ottomans extradite him. He was restricted from travelling out of the environs of Acre, Palestine, where he lived the rest of his life, sought out by scholars and spiritualists alike.

It was during this time that he wrote to the secular and religious rulers of Europe, urging them to "Be reconciled among yourselves that ye may need no more armaments. . . for thereby will the tempest of discord be stilled amongst you, and your people find rest."[64] They scoffed at his warnings about catastrophes that would occur if they did not. In his will, he reaffirmed his overarching principle, that "The religion of God is to create love and unity; do not make it the cause of enmity and discord," and named his son successor as the Baha'i leader to expound the teachings he had only begun to reveal.[65] Abdul Baha (1844–1921) was released from the captivity he shared with his father on harsher terms after the Young Turks seized power from the Ottoman Sultan in 1908. He then began a speaking tour in Europe and North America to promulgate his father's non-nationalistic, inter-religious peace. In Paris, he preached: "It is the outward practices of religion that are so different, and it is they that cause disputes and enmity – while the reality is always the same, and one."[66] In California, he warned that "The European continent is like an arsenal, a storehouse of explosives ready for ignition," writing elsewhere that

> religious, racial, national and political bias: all these prejudices strike at the very root of human life; one and all they beget bloodshed, and the ruination of the world. So long as these prejudices survive, there will be continuous and fearsome wars.[67]

Having thus sowed the seeds of what he called "World Faith" aimed at world peace, he returned to his home in Haifa, where he died. Today, Baha'i has over five million adherents globally, sharing with Kant, the organized peace movement, Transcendentalists and Tolstoy unwavering beliefs in and commitments to a transformative non-violence powerful enough to counteract the warmongering tendencies of nation-states. Concurrently, other peace traditions emerged to counteract proliferations of these tendencies within and between the worldwide empires some nation-states came to control, and to which we now turn.

7

Colonial and Imperial Peace and Peacemaking

Peaces of the World: Colonial Peace and Peacemaking

The Indian writer and activist Arundhati Roy recently made the provocative statement that debating the pros and cons of imperialism is like "debating the pros and cons of rape."[1] Certainly, it is impossible to explain away centuries of atrocities committed by colonizers to the peoples they colonized or violence their victims have used to overcome exploitative oppression – and it is the opposite of our purpose to do so here. But to ignore the innovative forms of peace and peacemaking put forth and practiced by colonizers and colonized at and shortly after first contact, then by imperial powers and their subjects as consolidations and resistances took place, is to discount the vital roles they have played in shaping those of today in both productive and counterproductive ways. In fact, contemporary means of and motives for making, maintaining and breaking international peace would not have evolved as they have without colonialism and imperialism. Parallel to and in conjunction with nation-states, colonial peace and peacemaking were proposed and implemented on three linked levels: among the colonizers, between the colonizers and the colonized, and among the colonized, best explored, analyzed and assessed in tandem as a second major vehicle towards modernity.

The early history of European colonialism is dominated by Spain and Portugal, each of which used scientific knowledge gained from the Islamic peoples of the Iberian Peninsula and the crusading zeal summoned to expel them to further their aims. Aside from spreading Christ's kingdom, by which they gained Popes' backing, their primary motive was the profit of trade in goods from spices and silk to grains and gold originating from east of Constantinople, controlled by Italian city-states, and south of the

Sahara, controlled by Muslims. By 1450, Portuguese explorers established a network of garrisoned trading posts down the west coast of Africa. Settlers from Castile, united with Aragon in 1481 as Spain, founded crop colonies on the Canary Islands, which Portugal actively competed for with native help. In the next decade, piratical warfare between the colonizers reached critical levels and fed into the Iberian War of Succession (1474–79) over the Castilian throne. The conflict was halted by the Treaty of Alcazovas (1479), the first modern European peace treaty regarding overseas possessions. Spain's Isabelle and Ferdinand's legitimacy was affirmed and all Canary Islands claims granted to them; Portuguese possession of all lands south thereof and their monopoly on all African trade were recognized. Natives were neither consulted nor taken into account in the peace other than as property, a precedent that later colonial peacemakers would replicate all too perfectly. Further "discoveries" like that of the Cape of Good Hope on the southern tip of Africa (1487), which promised a direct sea route to India, and Columbus' misidentified landing there, actually the Caribbean Islands, posed serious geo-political challenges to the Treaty's premises.

Portugal's King John II used the Alcazovas arrangements to claim Columbus' finds, made in the name of the Spain. In response, Isabella and Ferdinand convinced the Spanish-born Pope to issue papal bulls that first divided the colonial world between Spain and Portugal, favouring the former, then divested Portugal of all its colonial possessions by transfer to its rival. John strategically ignored these diplomatic shenanigans and continued colonial business as usual, forcing Spain to renegotiate. The result was the Treaty of Tordesillas (1494), providing for a line of demarcation 370 leagues west of Cape Verde: all lands east would be Portuguese and all lands west Spanish, with guarantees of safe passage for each. By splitting the world in this way, "peace was maintained between Portugal and Spain,"so that they directed their efforts "toward exploration and development of the discoveries rather than war;" to be precise, war between themselves, for both continued to wage wars on the colonized.[2] Limited geographical knowledge left large loopholes, such as whether the demarcating line ran from pole to pole or circled the globe, which worked to Spain's advantage in claims to the Philippines and Portugal to Brazil, making ambiguity an ally of peace. The expeditions of Vasco de Gama and Ferdinand Magellan compounded these geographical issues, so a second form of colonial peacemaking was put in place by the Treaty of Saragossa in 1529, by which Spain's King Charles V released his claims to the Moluccas Islands for a large sum from the Portuguese. Other European powers, by this time aware of Spain's South America mines and Portugal's lucrative trade in luxuries, found it more expedient to disregard their colonial peace treaties than to dispute them, though in different ways they influenced nearly all those that followed.

The first tract of land to be settled in the "New World" of the western hemisphere was an Antillean island called Hispaniola by the Spanish, now divided between the Dominican Republic and Haiti. In his diary of the 1492 voyages, Columbus noted on the first day he met natives that they "neither carry nor know anything of arms," and on the third that "with fifty [European] men they can all be subjugated and made to do what is required of them."[3] Less than a year later, the Pope ruled that these peoples "being in peace, and, as reported, going unclothed, and not eating flesh," were human and so capable of being Christianized by colonizers.[4] By 1502, a young man from the "Old World" named Bartolomé de las Casas (1484–1566) arrived in Hispaniola seeking fortune, which like his conquistador compatriots he secured by acquiring farmlands, mines and native slaves, collectively called *encomiendas*. Annoyed by a priest whose sermons denounced how Spaniards treated natives as unchristian, las Casas obliquely replied by obtaining more lands and slaves in what is Cuba today. But three years later, for unknown reasons, he sold his lands, freed his slaves, became a priest himself and dedicated the rest of his life to peacemaking between the Old and New Worlds. Upon his return to Spain in 1516, he pleaded with Catholic authorities, who named him "Protector of the Indians." He then presented a plan directly to King Charles V, who demanded practical and profitable alternatives to encomiendas: the establishment of communal associations of free Old World peasants and New World natives under the direction of priests on monastic models. This peace plan was shown to Erasmus, a member of the Royal Council, who lent it to More, after which he wrote *Utopia*. Charles found the plan appealing, but Spanish landlords killed it in fear of losing labourers. Disheartened, las Casas retreated to a Dominican monastery, where he wrote a *History of the Indies* over the next ten years.

His seclusion ended as his treaties urging conversion by persuasion rather than violence, *The Only Method of Attracting Men to the True Faith*, began circulating. In 1537, he issued a challenge to the Spanish authorities to allow him to implement his peace plans in Guatemala, dubbed the "Land of War" by the fierce native resistance to colonization, which was surprisingly accepted. Las Casas' experimental pacification methods, including preaching in native tongues, were so successful that the region was redubbed the "Land of True Peace." Years later, in his last testament, he described his newfound mission of peace in these words:

> To act here at home on behalf of all those people out in what we call the Indies, the true possessors of those kingdoms. . . To act against the unimag-
> inable, unspeakable violence and evil and harm they have suffered from our

people, contrary to all reason, all justice,so as to restore them to the original liberty they were lawlessly deprived of, and get them free of death by violence, death they still suffer.[5]

Unrelenting conquistadors soured the fruits of peace before they had a chance to ripen, but news of las Casas' non-violent victories had already crossed the ocean. Popes admonished deprivations of natives' liberty and property as unchristian and threatened to excommunicate enslavers, and Charles' New Laws prohibited native enslavement and abolished encomiendas, under politico-economic pressure retracted by 1545. Las Casas' last push for peace took place upon his return to Spain during the Valladolid Debates with Juan Gines de Sepulveda, who argued natives were divinely preordained slaves and lacked souls to convert. In line with his lifework, the gist of las Casas' response was that this view is not only unchristian, but inhuman. To expose the results of such views, Las Casas wrote the widely translated *Very Brief Recital of the Destruction of the Indies* (1552), staining Spain's international reputation and prompting other emerging colonial powers to at least try and keep the appearance of peaceful colonial strategies.

The colonial trajectories of the Netherlands and England differed significantly from those of Portugal and Spain, especially as paths to peace and profit. The Dutch, ruled by Spain until the mid sixteenth century, gained their navigational knowledge and used it against them. An Anglo-Dutch fleet defeated the legendary Spanish Armada which now had a strong Portuguese component in 1588, marking the start of the eclipse of the first two major European empires. Within a decade, Dutch merchant and military ships were circumnavigating the globe, trading and settling in the West Indies (Atlantic Islands) and East Indies (Pacific Islands). The Dutch sought the shortest routes to riches in that they attempted to displace the Spanish and Portuguese from their profit centers, making conflicts with them more likely than peace. For example, by 1543 Portuguese missionaries and merchants had established relatively peaceful and productive relations with China and Japan, acting as intermediaries between them when Chinese Emperors forbade trade after rampant Japanese piracy. Unlike with Africans or South Americans, the Portuguese dealt with Asians as equals or even superiors, probably because subjugation was not an option due to their large and advanced armies. The Japanese called them *nanban* ("barbarians"), after which a century of economic and cultural exchange until 1643 is sometimes named. Japanese diplomats with Portuguese escorts were welcomed at courts of South American and European rulers as curiosities but also as potential trading and military partners throughout this period. However, after the Dutch arrived in Asia, they systematically routed out key Portuguese trading posts and settlements in the region, eventually being granted exclusive trading rights in Japan on account of their less obtrusive ways. Wars against other colonizers for peaceful and profitable relations with natives, colonized or not, soon became commonplace.

Dutch colonialism was nowhere near as rosy elsewhere in the world. As they annexed Spanish and Portuguese possessions elsewhere in Asia and in Africa, they also took up the slave trade. Following this pattern, they moved into North America only after English and French explorers had made headway. In establishing New Amsterdam on Manhattan Island in 1614 (renamed New York after becoming an English possession in 1674) and several other fur-trading colonies, the Dutch gained competitive advantages over other Europeans by adopting native diplomatic and negotiation styles. The Iroquois, for instance, used ritualized gift exchanges to maintain mutually beneficial relationships with other tribes, to which Dutch traders were invited and in which they eagerly participated. But piggybacking colonial policies ultimately proved lethal for the Dutch by triggering a series of wars with England after which they lost many of their colonies. The series of peace treaties that ended each of these wars' instalments (Treaties of Westminster in 1654 and 1674, of Breda in 1667) codified pretextual principles of *uti possidetis* ("as you possessed") or *status quo ante bellum* ("existing conditions before the war") in colonial peace terms. Vesting each party with the properties under its previous control unless otherwise stipulated, events subsequent to these treaties showed how capricious such status quo peaces can be.

As the Dutch star rose, England already had a centuries-old colonial plantation system in nearby Ireland: dispossessed native Catholics were forced to work for Protestant newcomers. The British had found that this method could improve domestic peace prospects by satisfying disgruntled nobles, exporting overzealous proselytizers, expelling prisoners and recompensing soldiers. Doing so without interfering in the affairs of other European powers became the boon of early British colonial strategy, mitigating conflicts in two ways. First was by new routes to old destinations, such as John Cabot's failed 1494 attempt to find a northwest passage to Asia, during which he landed on a western coastal island of what is now Canada. Claiming territories there not already claimed by the French exemplifies the second: establishing presences in places other colonial powers had not, such as Jamestown in 1607, England's first overseas settlement. Within two generations, many more settler colonies and trading posts were established on the North American mainland, in the Indies and India, some explicitly for peace, others exclusively for profit.

Tying our discussion of reformed Christian peace practices with colonial trends, the Quaker William Penn inherited Irish estates from his father, to whom the newly restored King Charles II owed a large debt. In exchange for its cancellation, Penn asked for and received one of the largest tracts of land ever owned by a private person, now the US state of Pennsylvania, inaugurating one of the grandest experiments in the history of peace. Fleeing persecution in England and finding it again in the colonies, Quakers and other peace church members now had a place to carry out what has since been referred to as the "Holy Experiment," or the only known state officially founded on pacifist principles, set out by Penn. Natives were to be treated as equals, for as Penn proclaimed to them:

> I and my friends have a hearty desire to live in peace and friendship with you, and to serve you to the utmost of our power. It is not our custom to use hostile weapons against our fellow creatures, for which reason we have come unarmed . . . We are met on the broad pathway of good faith and goodwill, so that no advantage is to be taken on either side, but all is to be openness, brotherhood, and love.[6]

The Code of Handsome Lake, named after the Seneca tribe's leader (c. 1733–1815), combined Quaker pacifism with traditional tribal emphases on kinship and land in a legal and spiritual code focusing on interpersonal behaviour, still practiced today as the Longhouse Religion. Penn made two two-year trips to the colonies, during which he founded Philadelphia, the "city of brotherly love." At first the Experiment was quite successful: Pennsylvania was among the first colonies to outlaw slavery, abolish capital punishments and use arbitration to resolve disputes. However, the Experiment sputtered within a few generations as settlers with monetary and military rather than missionary motives took over Pennsylvania's administration, as England now had to contend with another power both on the European continent and in the colonies.

From the start, France pursued the same dual paths-of-least-resistance colonial policies as England, leading colonists of both countries to some of the same places, notably North America, making friction between them inevitable and forcing natives to take sides. Early French explorers arrived in Canada in the 1530s with scant supplies and could not have survived winters without native help, which they received in exchange for trinkets and muskets. Thus, in stark contrast to colonies where slave systems already prevailed, of necessity French colonies in North America began on a cooperative footing with natives, who acted as translators and guides in exchange for trading privileges. Marriages between French fur-traders and native North Americans were more common than with English or Dutch. Children of such unions, called *métis*, had counterparts in Spanish and Portuguese South America called *mestizos*; where Africans were brought, as in the Indies, they were called *creoles*. They often spoke native and newcomer languages which later turned into distinctive blends and so could act as intermediaries between colonial cultures when they were not subjected to the ever-elaborated structural violence based on skin color and class, or precisely because they were. In other cases, they were the result of unions of ruling natives and powerful newcomers, and so could act as intermediaries between the cultures of each continent, when they were not rejected outright by both.

Deaf to language and blind to color and class was disease, an early form of biological warfare when intentionally inflicted and the single most deadly weapon in both European (in North and South America) and native (in Africa and Asia) arsenals. No peace yet devised could deal with diseases that wiped out populations, except living bodies of mixed or immunized blood whose survival is a testament to the power of passive resistance, if it can be so called. In times of active resistance like during King Philip's War (1675–76) between New Englanders and natives, alliances between natives were broken and new ones created with colonial rivals like the French as with former native rivals. This pattern was repeated on ever-larger scales in a series of inter-colonial wars tied to international wars in Europe, as shown in the table on the following page. The debt and devastation caused by the French and Indian War, the Seven Years War and the Treaty of Paris prompted England to levy heavy taxes and tariffs on the North American colonies without seeking their consent, setting gears in motion that would revolutionize war, peace and peace-making the world over by creating the United States.

Often recognized by colonists but rarely used by them other than for survival and gain, native North Americans had their own longstanding peace and peacemaking traditions. Three prominent examples are the calumet, the League of Peace and Power and Condolence Councils. The calumet or peace pipe may have originated with the Pawnee of Nebraska, but by the time Europeans arrived it was in use across the continent, through which they were introduced to tobacco. In 1672, French Jesuit missionary Jacques Marquette and explorer Louis Joliet were given and carried a calumet as they mapped the Mississippi river basin, with which they formed "peaceful relations with all the tribes along the way."[7] In Pawnee culture, peace pipes were centerpieces of elaborate ceremonies through which inter-tribal trading and political relationships were made and maintained. Hosts were called "children" by their visitor "fathers," and brought with them a wide range of food and goods for exchange. Negotiations were initiated and closed by smoking the calumet in common "as a sign of peaceful intention and thus a safe-conduct pass through alien territory," extended to Europeans deemed worthy.[8] Many tribes recognized peace chiefs and war chiefs, and non-violent codes of intra-tribal conduct were widespread, such as the Cherokee Harmony Ethic by which tribesmen were required to walk away from a conflict and

Colonial Wars	European Wars	Peace Treaties
King William's War (1689–97)	Nine Years War (1688–97)	Treaty of Ryswick (1697)
Between British and French colonists and their native allies in northeastern North America for territory and trade; English Protestants and native Catholics in Ireland.	Between the Grand Alliance (England, Dutch, Holy Roman Empire, Austria, Portugal, Spain, Sweden) and France across Europe to contain French expansionism.	Restitution of colonial and European territories and religious rights; recognition of William III as King of England by King Louis XIV of France; inconclusive.
Queen Anne's War (1702–11)	War of the Spanish Succession (1701–14)	Peace of Utrecht (1713–4)
Between British and French colonists and their native allies in northeastern North America for territory and trade. As in King William's war, massacres of natives carried out by both sets of colonists to "pacify" the frontiers.	Between the same antagonists as the Nine Years War as well as Italian and Eastern European principalities. Anglo-Dutch allies first seek to prevent the union of France and Spain by royal marriage then split the spoils.	Series of treaties by which France/Spain cede colonies and trade rights to England; France gives up Spanish throne and other European territories for trade deals; marks English ascent in world affairs; shift from dynasties to balance of powers begins.
King George's War (1744–48)	War of the Austrian Succession (1740–48)	Treaty of Aix-la-Chapelle (1748)
Between British and French colonists and their native allies in northeastern North America and India for port towns.	Between Austria, Bavaria, Poland, England, Spain and France over the Austrian throne and territories.	*Uti possidetis* in North America and Europe, England strengthens positions in India; economic issues unresolved.
French and Indian War (1754–63)	Seven Years War (1754–63)	Treaty of Paris (1763)
Between British and French colonists and their native allies in central and northeastern North America and India over key cities and trade control.	France, Austria, Russia, Saxony, Sweden and Spain vs. Prussia, Great Britain and Hanover. Aimed at crippling France and boosting England.	French and Spanish cede North American colonies to English, who also gain Indian possessions; French European Power wanes until Revolution.

resolve it through generosity rather than bellicosity. But the League of Peace and Power was one of the first and few inter-tribal bodies Europeans encountered whose sole aim was to promote *cooperative peace* among its otherwise autonomous communities.

The League was and is a matrilineal alliance of Mohawks, Oneidas, Onondagas, Cayugas and Seneca of north-eastern North America, enduring "to this day as one of the oldest forms of participatory democracy on earth."[9] According to oral history, it was founded by Deganawidah (*c.* 1100–50), The Great Peacemaker. A stutterer, he enlisted the orator Hiawatha to his cause of bringing peace to the region's warring tribes by spreading a Great Law of Peace, both spiritual and legal. His first axiom was to balance stable minds and healthy bodies so that harmony within and between individuals and groups could flourish. Second was that humane thought, speech and action were the basis of equity and justice, so individual acts of violence were prohibited. Lastly was an extended series of ceremonial and civil procedures for inter-tribal relations, which as an oral tradition could take days to recite in full and by using *wampum* or rope-writings, accessed article-by-article. Each tribe had its own council. Male leaders were selected by women holding hereditary titles to the offices. The Grand Council of these tribal councils convened as necessary to debate, resolve and pronounce on pressing or ongoing issues and popular proposals, which could then be ratified or amended. Rites and rituals sometimes referred to as "Forest Diplomacy" served to widen bases of Great Council deliberations.[10] Among them were Covenant Chains, in which weapons were linked in symbolic circles of friendship, and Condolence Council rites, in which the dead were mourned, new chiefs named and inter-tribal ties and histories celebrated by storytelling, song and dance. Although for the most part lost to Europeans, many of these native North American peace traditions survived their colonialism and imperialism.

The World in Peaces: Imperial Peace and Peacemaking

Transitions from colonialism, by which relations among colonizers and colonized were made, to imperialism, by which they were maintained, took place at different times, in different places and in different ways. In all cases, however, these transitions transformed colonial into imperial peace and peacemaking in both overall trends and ones specific to the inter-cultural conditions in which they occurred. The earliest European imperial governments were aimed directly at curbing colonial violence by adapting Old World practices to New World conditions. As conquistador and viceroy brutalities became evident, the Spanish Council of Castile created supervisory bodies to allay them, up and running even before las Casas' protests for peace. The Chamber of Indies Commerce regulated emigration and trade, the Council of the Indies in Spain and *Audiencas* in the colonies analogously functioned as courts, advisory boards and policy-makers. "In checking the ill-treatment of natives by the colonists, in keeping watch upon the activities of colonial," peace- and profit-oriented services of these bodies soon spread throughout the Spanish Empire, from the Americas to the Philippines.[11] However, as early as the mid-1500s, conquistadors rebelled against the viceroy at the capital of what is now Bolivia, once named Our Lady Peace in reference to a Catholic title for Jesus' mother, often depicted with an olive branch and dove in her hands, sometime after which its name was shortened to La Paz ("The Peace"), to signify the restoration of peace after this early intra-colonial war.

Epitomizing imperial peace traditions are the works of a theologian and jurist, Francisco de Vitoria (1492–1564), who witnessed the shift to them from colonial traditions and expounded a realist approach to the problems of empires similar to a contemporary's approach to those of city-states, Machiavelli. In *The Law of War on Indians* (1532), he states that

> a prince ought to subordinate both peace and war to the common weal of his State and not spend public revenues in quest of his own glory or gain, much less expose his subjects to danger on that account. Herein, indeed, is the difference between a lawful king and a tyrant, that the latter directs his government towards his individual profit and advantage, but a king to the public welfare.[12]

Vitoria considers natives as part of the public whose welfare imperial sovereigns ought to serve, as did Spanish imperial government at first. As he points out, the New World is new only to the Old, so forceful possession of inhabited lands is armed robbery, though uninhabited lands are fair game. Natives, he goes on, "undoubtedly had true dominion in both public and private matters," unlawfully taken from them by colonists, which imperial governments could not only restore but also make amends for. While just war principles apply to New-Old World relations, he also articulated renewed principles for peaceful global relations, later taken for granted or which may still bear implementation: universal use and protection of ambassadors; compulsory participation in peace talks before war and mandatory acceptance of just peace terms afterward; interventions on behalf of those suffering or oppressed; respect for the lives and properties of neutral parties; rights of safe passage; restraint in warfare and sanctuary for civilians; the right to citizenship by standards of *jus solis*, birth within a country; and the right to become a naturalized citizen of any another country. Vitoria thus paradoxically provided both the basis for imperial governments to entrench and extend their control over their colonies and the grounds upon which non-violent anti-imperial movements were launched.

In contrast to the Spanish, Portuguese colonialism favoured trading posts over permanent settlements, a preference which in Brazil led to historically unique occurrences in cross-cultural collaboration and imperial government. Landing there accidentally in 1500, at first Portuguese traders found little of value on the coast other than bark that could be made into dye. But within two generations, Brazil was made the world's leading sugar producer by entrepreneurial families with royal charters under governor-generals fitting Vitoria's definition of tyrants to a tee. Facing labor shortages, they began importing African slaves, eventually totalling three million. Revolts brutally supplanted, Africans fled inland to a region called Palmares after its vegetation where their captors had no control, which then lent its name to the *quilombo* or "slave republic" formed in 1603. Soon twenty thousand refugees strong with an area a third of Portugal's size, Palmares became the first self-sufficient, post-colonial state in South America by practicing diversified agriculture of African origin rather than European single-crops. Loose associations of small communities trading among themselves, Palmarians welcomed those persecuted by Portuguese, including natives, mestizos, Jews, Muslims and Christians considered heretics. To keep peace, chiefs acted like Vitoria's kings, enforcing strict penal codes and granting all equality in law and opportunity. In 1678, Palmarians agreed to peace terms with hostile Portuguese. When attacks continued, they armed and retreated in defence, an early form of guerrilla peace tactics. Defeated in 1684, twice-over refugees formed a new *quilombo* and actively resisted until 1797. Ten years later, Napoleon invaded Portugal and its regent fled to Brazil, where he re-established his court and declared the colony equal with Portugal. He remained until 1821, when a pressing political crisis prompted his return, leaving his son behind as representative. After an attempt to abrogate the imperial state's new status, the son in defiance of his father declared the country independent. Backed by Brazil's elite, in 1822 he became Emperor of the first colony in the hemisphere to gain independence without a violent revolution on the US model. A minor one did occur when the monarchy became a republic seventy-five years later, but even this shows to what extent Brazilians, native and newcomers, had danced to their own drums.

As if shooting for the best and worst of Iberian peace strategies, second-wave imperialists formed joint-stock or charter companies, from which modern corporations derive, initially as commercial vehicles for royalty and merchants to jointly establish monopolies. By the 1600s, a flurry of English, Dutch and French companies were in operation, providing collective capital to finance colonial ventures while limiting the liabilities of private investors, but also invested with war- and peacemaking powers once reserved by public officials. The Dutch East India Company, for example, was empowered "to conclude treaties of peace and alliance, to wage defensive war" and to these ends enlist civilianand military personnel who would take loyalty oaths to the firm as to the state.[13] The Dutch West India Company was likewise authorized to make war and peace with "indigenous powers, to maintain naval and military forces, and to exercise judicial and administrative functions."[14] Peace was thus placed in the precarious position of a prerequisite for and perquisite of conducting booming imperial business.

The exemplar by far of such duplicitous complementary incorporations was the British East India Company (EIC), chartered in 1600 by Queen Elizabeth I, the peace policies of which were crucial to its short-term survival and long-term success. On his third spice-seeking voyage to India in 1608, EIC Captain William Hawkins approached the Muslim Mughal Emperor Jahangir with a proposal to set up a coastal warehouse at Surat for continuous trade. He agreed as long as tariffs were paid and his subjects well-treated. Seven profitably peaceful years later, a much broader agreement was reached between Jahangir's son and the King's ambassador, Sir Thomas Roe, by which several more coastal trading posts were set up and tariffs reduced, in the end eliminated altogether. While failed military manoeuvres against the Portuguese and Dutch threatened the EIC's existence in the East Indies, these productive mixes of business and peace negotiations ensured its survival in India, moving Roe to give the following advice to the EIC:

> It is the beggaring of Portugal, notwithstanding his many rich residences and territories, that he keeps soldiers that spends it; yet his garrisons are mean. . . It hath been also the error of the Dutch, who seek plantation here by the sword. They turn a wonderful stock, they prowl in all places, they possess some of the best; yet their dead payes consume all their gain. Let this be received as a rule: that if you will profit, seek it at sea, and in quiet trade: for without controversy it is an error to affect garrisons and land wars in India.[15]

By following this policy, the EIC had permanent representatives at the Mughal courts in 1639, through which it secured England's first territory on the subcontinent, Madras, de jure for the King but de facto for the Company.

However, the EIC abandoned this policy when it began operating in Bengal, where ongoing Muslim-Hindu power struggles resulted in an absence of a central authority with which to make and maintain peace. Skirmishes with locals prompted the EIC to create militias of natives and newcomers, which increased rather than diminished tensions on all sides and led to a Mughal–EIC war in 1689. Mughals won, but allowed the EIC to resume its mutually profitable commerce in a peace that did not keep. After several seesaw battles, the declining Mughal powers granted the EIC authority to appoint a *nawar* charged with formerly separated civil functions in addition to a monopoly on trade. As *subdar*, this EIC employee was responsible for law and order; as *diwan*, for collecting taxes and all other revenues. By the eighteenth century's end, the Company had assumed direct rule. In two hundred years, the EIC thus evolved from an exclusively economic entity seeking to make peace with native rulers to further trade, to an unrestricted ruling entity seeking to maintain peace among its native subjects to further direct rule and derivative income. While EIC "rule by the pen" or administrative rule had not replaced "rule by the sword" but merely displaced it, in the Western Hemisphere a former British colony found that it could come close to ruling it peacefully by doing comparatively next to nothing.

A decade after victory in its Revolutionary War against the British, the newly formed United States embarked upon a pragmatic but paradoxical policy of anti-imperial and imperial peace on a hemispheric basis. US War leader and first President George Washington hoped that "America will be able to keep disengaged from the labyrinth of European politics and wars;" another founding father, Alexander Hamilton, called for a "great American system superior to the control of all trans-Atlantic force of influence, and able to dictate the terms of connection between the Old and the New World."[16] In 1803, President Thomas Jefferson completed the Louisiana Purchase of French territory west of the Mississippi River from Napoleon, who was in desperate need of war funds, putting into practice a policy somewhere between that of Washington and Hamilton: "peace, commerce and honest friendship with all nations, entangling alliances with none."[17] The deal effectively ended France's imperial presence in North America, doubling the size of the original thirteen US states without war between contracting parties. A diplomat sent to Paris to negotiate the purchase, James Monroe, became president in 1817 and soon entered into similar talks with Spain to purchase Florida, tendered in 1819. In the next few years, the US quickly recognized newly independent South American states inspired by its Revolution, including Mexico, Chile, Peru, Argentina and Colombia. Fearing the spread of republicanism, a Holy Alliance of Austria, Russia, Prussia and Britain was formed in 1822 "to put an end to the system of representative governments, in whatever country it may exist in Europe, and to prevent its being introduced in those countries where it is not yet known."[18] In 1823, Monroe announced a new hemispheric foreign policy, designed by John Quincy Adams, which denounced European imperialism as "dangerous to our peace and safety."

The principle of the Monroe Doctrine, as the policy is now called, was at once isolationist and interventionist: the US would not allow European monarchical empires to spread in the Americas and would not otherwise intervene in Europe. Closing the western hemisphere to further European expansion, the Doctrine was used to justify American expansion westwards in the 1840s by a mix of wars and strategically broken peaces with natives. The US, now a bicoastal nation, then turned the Doctrine into a global policy. By the 1850s, the US was using imperial peace tactics, called gunboat diplomacy, in the Pacific, where the presence and warning shots of its navy intimidated Japan into reopening its markets, ushering in the Meiji Era (1868–1912) in which a pro-modernization monarchy was restored and Japan became an imperial force itself. In 1888, Germany, Great Britain and the US established joint rule over Samoa, which even the US Secretary of State acknowledged as a departure from the "traditional and well-established policy of avoiding entangling alliances with foreign powers in relation to objects remote from this hemisphere."[19] By the nineteenth century's end, the Doctrine was expanded to prevent Europeans from transferring imperial territories to one another, on the basis of US self-appointment as "impartial arbiter" in South American border disputes. The Doctrine proved so successful that Secretary of State Richard Olney, who in 1895 claimed to act as such an arbiter between Great Brittan and Venezuela over Guyana's borders, boasted that "today the United States is practically sovereign on this continent, and its fiat is law upon the subjects to which it confines its interposition."[20] The Doctrine also paved the way for unprecedented US investments in Central and South America, eventually surpassing the British. In Cuba, which the US failed to purchase from Spain in several attempts, business interests were threatened by a rebellion against Spanish rule, so US officials tried to broker ceasefires and Cuban independence. But when a battleship mysteriously exploded just off of Cuba in 1898, US forces were deployed, as well as to Guam, Puerto Rico and the Philippines, the stated aim being "the forcible intervention of the United States as a neutral to stop the war."[21] Spain, defeated, ceded these territories to the US, making it an imperial power just over a century after gaining independence from one, both by following a foreign policy aimed at anti-imperial peace and by knowingly contravening it.

Meanwhile, third-wave nineteenth-century European imperial expansions were punctuated by two major peace congresses in Vienna (1814–15) and Berlin (1884–5). In continental affairs, the Congress of Vienna sought to redraw Europe's map and rebalance its powers after Napoleon's wars, occupations and defeats. These goals achieved, the so-called Concert of Europe of Austria, England, Prussia, Russia and France was formed in pledges to preserve peace by diplomacy and periodic meetings, a score they often read but rarely played. The first German Confederation was also created which, after Prussia's defeat of Austria and France, became the First Reich in 1871. In imperial affairs, the Vienna Congress' outcomes were more one-sided because no conceivable counter-alliance could by this time redraw the map or balance the power of the British Empire, the imposing seaward supremacy of which is referred to as the Pax Britannica. However, having suffered serious losses in the Western Hemisphere as a result of the US Revolutionary War, the British were in the midst of shifting their imperial emphasis east. In Vienna, they secured global territories from the Portuguese, Dutch, and French for specie, privileges and promises. The next two decades' intensified competition for African territories not already under European control was branded the Scramble for Africa. Characterized by beliefs in cultural and racial superiority, backed by relatively advanced technologies and financial institutions, and aimed at direct rule, the Scramble also involved new or renewed approaches to imperial peace.

The American Colonization Society was founded in 1817 to repatriate freed black slaves to Africa. With Congress' financial support, ironically granted during Monroe's administration, the Society established Liberia with native consent but it remained in the Society's hands for nearly a century. Belgium's King Leopold II held a conference in 1876 to discuss "opening up" and "elevating" Africa to Europe and its standards. An International African Association was created to this end and, on its behalf, explorer Henry Stanley charted the Congo and negotiated hundreds of "peace" treaties with native chieftains for resource rights and trading posts, which became Leopold's personal possessions. The native African Kongo Empire (c. 1400–1914) had already signed several similar treaties with Portugal, which the British now recognized to stem the Association's expansion. France occupied huge tracts of North and West Africa, including what became Algeria, Tunisia and Morocco, and Indochina, later called Vietnam, Cambodia and Laos. Newly unified Italy seized parts of Eritrea and later Ethiopia, Russia and Austria took apart the Ottoman Empire in Eastern Europe and the Balkans, while the British took control of Egypt, formally still Ottoman, and with it the Suez Canal. Germany claimed Togo, Cameroon, West Africa (now Namibia) and East Africa (now Burundi, Rwanda and Tanganyika) by Otto van Bismarck's extension of *realpolitik* into *weltpolitik* or "world politics." Shortly after the Berlin Congress, aimed at settling the "Balkan question," a new balance of European imperial powers emerged: on the one hand were Germany, Austria and Italy, and the other France, Russia and England, close to the reverse of that before the Congress of Vienna. Arguably, it is at this point in history that peace and peacemaking became exclusively synonymous with the machinations of nation-states and their empires, short-sighted limitations from which they still suffer.

Contemporaneous European imperialism elsewhere in Asia was more commercial than territorial, leading to different peace prerogatives. The British found the Chinese had sufficient stores of bullion, little interest in their goods and slightly more in their missionaries. However, one thing they could not get enough of was opium. Late Qing Dynasty Emperors realized the threat the drug posed to their peoples, but when they barred its trade the British forced it upon them after the winning the Opium Wars (1839–42). Included in the peace terms was the mandatory opening of extraterritorial "treaty ports" under foreign protection, later extended to Germans, French, Russians and Americans. One Qing diplomat still claimed "the various barbarians have come to live in peace and harmony with us."[22] Less than a decade later, native dissatisfaction with the Qing reached a climax when a schoolmaster named Hong Xiuquan under missionary influence developed a large and loyal following by proposing to establish a Heavenly Kingdom of Peace (*Taiping Tianguo*), calling himself the brother of Christ. Like the Yellow Scarves two millennia earlier, he convinced tens of thousands of his poor followers to overthrow the ruling regime in what is now known as the Taiping or Great Peace Rebellion (1850–64). After capturing Nanking they made it their capital, from which they instituted gender equality in the civil service of their theocratic Kingdom for the first time in Chinese history, transferred all property to the state and outlawed opium, prostitution and gambling. By 1860, Western powers began to fear that if the Qing fell, so would foreign trade, so they backed their Imperial army as they crushed the Second Great Peace, which had cost twenty million lives.

Though the Qing still ran the civil service, following the First Sino-Japanese War (1894–95) nearly all of China was partitioned into foreign spheres of influence. The Emperor sought to modernize state and education systems but his efforts were stifled by an uprising sponsored by the Empress dowager aimed at expelling foreigners once and for all, called the Harmonious Fists or Boxers in the West. Their leader declared that "only when one can fight can one negotiate for peace," and proved that they could live up to the first part of his statement by attacking treaty ports, killing missionaries, diplomats and civilians.[23] As Boxers besieged Beijing, rickshaws or *dongyangche* ("eastern vehicles") with the characters for "foreign" in them were all relabelled *Taipingche* ("Great Peace Vehicles"). The Boxer Rebellion makes explicit a principle only made implicitly so far: xenophobic conditions are not conducive to peace, especially when foreigners get involved. Governors of southern provinces signed separate peaces with Western powers, and for the first and last time in imperial history, British, French, Russian, American, German and Japanese cooperated in crushing the Boxers, ushering China into the twentieth century as a subject nation. The capitulation treaty (1901) between the Western powers and Qing Emperor contained humiliating and debilitating articles, including public apologies, an immense indemnity, treaty port concessions and the stationing of foreign troops throughout the country to protect foreigners. Germany's representative noted that in peace the "interests of the European Powers are entirely different and a co-operation. . . is quite impossible."[24] Upon a remark that during the joint battle against the Boxers nationality distinctions between Western soldiers were never mentioned, he simply and accurately replied "It is not so now."

Nevertheless, during the Qing capitulation negotiations, US Secretary of State John Hay circulated among the victors his "Open Door Note" (1900), urging them to still work together to

> bring about permanent safety and peace to China, preserve Chinese territorial and administrative entity, protect all rights guaranteed to friendly powers by treaty and international law, and safeguard for the world the principle of equal and impartial trade with all parts of the Chinese Empire.[25]

Fearing possible outcomes of acting otherwise, they nominally agreed. Far from the first to link peace and free trade, discussed in the next chapter, Hay only applied existing general principles to the particular case of China. James G. Blaine had already articulated a distinctively American take on such principles in accepting the Republican Party's presidential nomination in 1876: "We seek the conquests of peace. . . While the great powers of Europe are steadily enlarging their colonial domination in Asia and Africa. . . our foreign policy should be an American policy in its broadest and most comprehensive sense – a policy of peace, of friendship, of commercial enlargement."[26] Although not elected President, he became Secretary of State and his proposed foreign policy prevailed. US intelligence officers stationed worldwide began reporting not only on military matters to the Department of Defense, but also on investment opportunities to the Department of Commerce, while government officials abroad doubled as solicitors for American investors. A financial journal later stated that "trade follows not the flag but the dollar – and the pound sterling, and the yen," when in actuality they and peacemaking with them went together.[27] As monetization of peace became as rampant as state collaborations with businesses, the validity of previous ideological principles was called into question.

For the US, the Monroe Doctrine thus had to be reinterpreted or rejected. When, in 1902, Italy, Britain and Germany blockaded Venezuela to collect debts, the US pressed for arbitration. Britain and Italy agreed and withdrew; Germany only did so when President Theodor Roosevelt threatened to send out the navy. Two years later, Roosevelt put forth his activist Corollary to the passive Monroe Doctrine, introducing the world to the notion of a Pax Americana, as if reversing history by enacting imperialism before colonialism:

> Chronic wrongdoing, or an impotence which results in a general loosening of the ties of civilized society, may in America, as elsewhere, ultimately require intervention by some civilized nation, and in the Western Hemisphere the adherence of the United States to the Monroe Doctrine may force the United States, however reluctantly, in flagrant cases of such wrongdoing or impotence, to the exercise of an international police power.[28]

The Roosevelt corollary was the "beginning of a diplomacy which was to serve the requirements of American investments in foreign countries, as the old diplomacy served the requirements of territorial expansion and of commerce," which took on two parallel forms.[29] One is referred to as "big stick," the other as "dollar diplomacy." US relations with Santo Domingo, later renamed Dominican Republic, show how the two could work concurrently for and against peace. In 1906, they tendered a treaty by which, in exchange for paying off Santo Domingo's foreign debt, the US would control its customs on foreign trade – dollar diplomacy at its best. But American investors soon acquired monopolies on fruit and sugar trade and, when guerrilla warfare erupted, US armed intervention followed – big stick diplomacy at its worst. Put metaphorically, dollar diplomacy was walking through the Open Door with foreign economic partners peacefully hand in hand, while big stick diplomacy was dragging them through the Open Door unwillingly, in certain cases slamming it in their face after crossing the threshold.

The US put diplomatic pressure on Honduras in 1911 on behalf of the banking syndicate of J. P. Morgan & Co. to secure its investments there; in 1912 another US protectorate on the Santo Domingo model was established in Nicaragua, followed by one in Haiti in 1915. The US, which had rocked the imperial world with its Declaration and War of Independence, redefined it for its protectorates, which now spanned the globe:

> It would appear that 'independence' as a technical term employed in treaties relating to such protected States does not mean full freedom of action as a positive attribute, but rather the absence of any such restrictions upon the protected State as would amount to an infringement of its international personality and take from it a certain theoretical legal competence to be the arbiter of its own destiny.[30]

Having propagated anti-imperial peace by the Monroe Doctrine in ensuring independence from European monarchical imperialism, the US by the Roosevelt Corollary reduced independence to a technicality in the interests of its economic imperialism, non-violent as dollar diplomacy, violent as the big stick. In 1912, President William Taft reaffirmed that US foreign policy "may well be made to include active intervention to secure for our merchandise and our capitalists opportunity for profitable investment which shall inure to the benefit of both countries concerned."[31] Growth in economic interests abroad, at first with the pacific pretext of mutual profit, spurred diplomatic and military support provided by the state; but as state concern for foreign economic affairs grew, this pretext was discarded and benefits became asymmetrical – a variation on longstanding patterns in the modern economics of peace.

8

Modern Economics of Peace and Peacemaking

Capitalism: The Profitability of Peace and the Cost of War

No development since that of agriculture has influenced the relationship between peace and plenty – historically among the most important of all – on individual, social and collective levels more than the industrial revolution of the eighteenth and nineteenth centuries. Theorists and activists of *economic imperatives* for peace and peacemaking have since been trying to channel, reform or reject industrialism's effects in contrasting and competing ways. With one eye on their past and the other on their future they fall into two categories, capitalist and socialist, each of which will be examined in turn. Of the many economic systems humans have devised, the consensus is that mercantilism is the least conducive to peace. Its principles congealed during and supported the rise of European nation-states, colonialism and imperialism from the sixteenth century onwards, and were inseparable from the peace- and war-making of their paradigms. The first modern economic theories and practices of peace were direct responses to mercantilism, and only later took into consideration the development of industrialism and its outcomes on producers and consumers, with which they have remained predominantly preoccupied.

Mercantilists took what is called a zero-sum economic view embedded with bellicosity: as there are a fixed number of resources (commodities, metals, territories, etc.), the only way one country or empire can increase its wealth is at another's expense, making conflict inevitable and perpetual. Mercantilist policies, less land-based than the feudal policies of the recent past, thus encouraged state intervention in the economy to foster favorable trade balances (more exports than imports), protectionist tariffs, state-granted or held monopolies on markets and goods, and the accumulation of gold and silver in national treasuries. Reflecting British mercantilist aims was the series of Navigation Acts enacted from the seventeenth to early nineteenth century. Prohibiting all non-British trade in and by the colonies, they required that goods like tobacco, sugar, cotton and metals be exported in unfinished forms to England, where they were finished and sold in Europe. Protectionist policies such as these ostensibly promoted peace among colonies insofar as they aligned colonists' interests. But by subordinating them to the metropole, seeds of colonial dissent and covetousness between colonial powers were sown and repeatedly reaped with violence. The purposes of mercantilist policies, aside from enriching the individuals involved, were to increase the powers of an imperial nation-state relative to others by using its wealth to fund permanent navies and armies for defending and advancing national interests at home and abroad. Growing classes of merchants and manufacturers paid more and more taxes to states for the military, legal and administrative services and infrastructures they provided on ever-larger scales, cementing civil and uncivil symbiotic relationships that continue to this day, monthly to the detriment of peace.

As the historical examples of the previous two chapters show, mercantilist theories made economic motives sufficient in themselves for countries and empires to go to war with another, even if religious and political justifications were and still are invoked. Clausewitz's well-known maxim, "war is a mere continuation of politics by other means," took on its full meaning with mercantilism.[1] No peace, an *a priori* transitory illusion according to mercantilists, could be made or maintained between countries and empires without economic considerations first being taken into account. Mercantilist peacemaking is analogous to cutting a coveted pie, where participants politely try to negotiate for larger pieces before resorting to violence, requiring the ceremonial repetition of the process without enduring peace ever becoming more probable or plausible: zero sums equal zero peace. In mercantilism's circular logic, imperial commerce provided material support to national governments the militaries of which backed imperial commerce, a broken business model that made peace an instrument of war and war an instrument of economics. Yet, as early as the late 1500s, mercantilism's inherent bellicosity was already being challenged, though certain of its tenets are alive but unwell today.

French political theorist Jean Bodin (1530–96) countered that commerce is always an agent of peace by its ongoing solidifications of mutually beneficial relationships between people who might otherwise go to war. His insight, that economic development can be a peacemaking activity, was explored by the school of French physiocrats a century later, the first to hold that economies are governed by immutable laws correlated to peace, rather than pragmatic measures opposed to it as mercantilists contended. Tying social welfare to individual wellbeing, the father of physiocracy François Quesnay (1694–1774) held that agriculture is the key to higher standards of living, the strongest safeguard of intra- and international peace. Quesnay and his followers gave shape to the idea of "laissez faire, laissez passer" ("let work, let pass") in arguing that selective non-interference by governments in economic affairs would increase production, innovation and trade by eliminating restrictions and barriers. Peace prospects would "naturally" improve through material abundance, while providing for state services, limited to protecting the peace, with a single uniform tax. Physiocrats after him also noted that breaking economic laws by nepotistic interventions leads to war, as Saintard did in asking "How can peace prevail among nations when there is abundance only for a few of them. . . when the riches of the earth, the commodities, flow into one or two centers of Europe, leaving outlying parts in want of them?"[2]

This line of questioning led some physiocrats to an anti-war stance on purely economic grounds, highly productive since. For example, Louis VXI's finance minister Jacques Necker advised that "to make war is to sow ten grains in order to gather one," the Quesnay correlative being that to make peace is to sow one grain in order to gather ten.[3] Although the nineteenth-century socialist statesman Louis Blanc advocated state regulation as necessary to mitigate economic crises that cause conflicts, he held a physiocratic position on standing armies. He denounced them as drains on resources that reduce productivity in peacetime and increase destructivity in war, as well as using them to suppress, arguing that only a peacekeeping force of loyal citizens is capable of maintaining order and distinguishing "a revolution from a riot."[4] Thus, as Elizabeth Souleyman explains in *The Vision of World Peace in Seventeenth and Eighteenth-Century France* (1941), physiocrats gave voice to the idea of ending wars from within nations outwards by eradicating their economic causes, stressing that wise uses of natural as national resources make peace and prosperity coterminous, not contradictory as with mercantilism. Although physiocrat perspectives on the economics of peace were ridiculed in France in their day, they influenced British theorists fully aware that they were living at the cusp and in the cradle of an industrial revolution and who, in turn, shaped all subsequent views on the subject.

The shift away from mercantilism's innate bellicosity and towards the notion of free trade friendliness was furthered by Adam Smith's *Wealth of Nations* (1776). Whereas the zero-sum thinking of the past and present made peace both implausible and improbable by construing all economic transactions as win-lose, he proposed that voluntary, informed transactions are always beneficial to all parties. Reconfiguring the perception of commercial interactions as pacifically cooperative rather than competitively conflict-ridden, Smith's peace-oriented insight lies in the positive-sum view he put forth. With industrial economies, characterized by divisions of labor and mechanized production methods, the allegorical pie gets bigger for everyone because growth in capacities and exchange values of goods and services – not only stores of gold and standing armies – increases wealth. Individuals as nations must work with not against others to get what they need and want, making peace more plausible and probable. Thus, economic and diplomatic activities merge for the benefit of peace when what is given up in negotiations is of greater value to nations than what they already have or could otherwise get. Intra-nationally, industrialism likewise creates constructive inter-dependencies among individuals through labor specialization. Conceptualizing capitalism before the term had become popular, Smith suggested that the wealth of industrialized nations both feeds into and feeds off of peace among them.

For Smith, distinct resources and expertise lead nations to specialize in what they can do better or cheaper than others, creating constructive inter-dependencies between them as between individuals intra-nationally. Devoting resources to mercantilist militarism makes no sense when they could be used for trade or economic development instead, a mainstay argument for liberal anti-war activists, based upon which he proposed that England divest itself of its colonies:

> A great empire has been established for the sole purpose of raising up a nation of customers who should be obliged to buy from the shops of our different producers all the goods with which these could supply them. For the sake of that little enhancement of price which this monopoly might afford our producers, the home-consumers have been burdened with the whole expense of maintaining and defending that empire. For this purpose, and for this purpose only, in the two last wars, more than a hundred and seventy millions has been contracted over and above all that had been expended for the same purpose in former wars. The interest of this debt alone is not only greater than the whole extraordinary profit, which, it ever could be pretended, was made by the monopoly of the colony trade, but than the whole value of that trade, or than the whole value of the goods, which at an average have been annually exported to the colonies.[5]

The conditions for peaceful collaborative growth to occur are in Smith's view that rational self-interest motivates individuals, nations and empires to participate in economic activities of their volition, and that these economic activities are free of restrictions. In this way directing "industry in such a manner as its produce may be of greatest value," an individual like a nation or empire "intends only his own gain, and he is in this, as in many other cases, led by an invisible hand to promote an end which was no part of his intention." Smith describes the end towards which the invisible hand guides as society's "best interests," only implicitly including an overall decrease in conflicts by an overall increase in prosperity. But as the pointing finger of the invisible hand, peace is greater than the sum of its economic parts and cannot exist without them.

Like Smith, his friend Jeremy Bentham (1748–1832) held that "all trade is in its essence advantageous – even to that party to whom it is least so," and "all war is in its essence ruinous; yet the great employments of government are to treasure up occasions of war, and to put fetters upon trade."[6] He even went so far as to say that "peace may always be had by some unessential sacrifice."[7] However, a lawyer who preferred pursuing reform to practicing, he approached the economics of peace from a different angle than Smith. Bentham's famous principle, "the greatest happiness for the greatest number," made him the fountainhead of utilitarian perspectives on peace, which see the most promising peace as the one that can be spread widest, sometimes and to its detriment regardless of its qualities. This principle, as the foundation of morals, law and economics, was for Bentham the standard by which the utility of pubic policies and institutions ought to be judged, whether geared towards peace or not. By utility, he meant that which tends to produce benefit, advantage, pleasure, good, or happiness, or to prevent the happening of mischief, pain, evil, or unhappiness to the party whose interest is considered: "if that party be the community in general, then the happiness of the community; if a particular individual, then the happiness of the individual."[8]

Enhancing this definition into a process, Bentham presents pleasure and pain as governing forces of human activity, their properties as gauges of and guides to individual, social and collective decisions: the extent, intensity, duration, certainty or uncertainty, proximity or remoteness, fecundity (the probability of causing the same sensation) and purity (the probability of causing the opposite sensation) of pleasure and pain can be quantified to form qualitative opinions or strategies. Bentham applied his "hedonic calculus" to war, ranking it low on the utility scale as a "mischief" highest on the pain scale, impending "indiscriminately over the whole number of members in the community."[9] While, in countering prevailing notions of natural laws of nations that all must invariably obey, Bentham the legalist coined the term "international law" to convey utility-based consensus, Bentham the economist did not apply his calculus directly to peace. By doing so, distinctive definitional and analytical potentials emerge: in a general sense, peace and peacemaking are always useful because they maximize pleasure and minimize pain; in particular cases, they can always be comparatively evaluated by properties of pain and pleasure to develop optimal, conditional peace plans and learn from their implementations.

Smith's laissez-faire and Bentham's utilitarian perspectives on the economics of peace were expanded as well as refined by Bentham's close companion James Mill (1773–1836) and other members of the "classical school" of British economics, classical insofar as capitalists are concerned. Mill also condemned war for its disastrous economic consequences, and mercantilist imperialism for being an aggressive economic system infused with militarism, arguing for its replacement by mutually beneficial free trade among independent international partners. Only defensive armed forces would then be needed and would in time become unnecessary. Even in economically motivated wars, nations expend wealth accumulations and productive capabilities (capital), decreasing their post-conflict economic capacities; perpetual industrial peace could, in theory and contrast, indefinitely increase nations' economic capacities. For Mill, capital's utility thus lies in providing for (a) productive conditions of prosperity in which peace is most likely, and (b) contingencies that may threaten existing peaces within or between nations. The idea that, through free trade and the utility of capital, enrichment without conflict is possible was more fully explored by Mill's friend, David Ricardo (1772–1823). His innovative analyses of the value of labor led him to the notion that economic competition can diffuse or act as a substitute for war and support peace by a conscious consumerism. Taking others' needs, resources and means into consideration along with their own, individuals like nations can use "comparative advantages" to produce and trade goods that are in demand:

> Under a system of perfectly free commerce, each country naturally devotes its capital and labor to such employments as are most beneficial to each. This pursuit of individual advantage is admirably connected with the universal good of the whole. By stimulating industry, by regarding ingenuity, and by using most efficaciously the peculiar powers bestowed by nature, it distributes labor most effectively and most economically. . . by increasing the general mass of productions, it diffuses general benefit, and binds together by one common tie of interest and intercourse, the universal society of nations throughout the civilized world.[10]

Competitiveness, then, need not mean the militaristic mercantilist ability to monopolize or take away, but the pacific capitalistic ability to meet needs and keep customers.

The leading liberal of the times, John Stuart Mill (James' son, 1806–73), argued further that free trade and unrestrained economic development can end war and guarantee world peace by the individual liberties and private property they presuppose:

> Before, the patriot, unless sufficiently advanced in culture to feel the world his country, wished all countries weak, poor, and ill-governed, but his own:

he now sees in their wealth and progress a direct source of wealth and progress to his own country. It is commerce which is rapidly rendering war obsolete, by strengthening and multiplying the personal interests which are in natural opposition to it. And it may be said without exaggeration that the great extent and rapid increase of international trade, in being the principal guarantee of the peace of the world, is the great permanent security for the uninterrupted progress of the ideas, the institutions, and the character of the human race.[11]

Hence, interdependencies created by specialization lead to reciprocal relationships in diversified, integrated economies, local or global, which act as guarantees of peace. The Mills' and Ricardo's unabashed optimism regarding capitalist economics of industrial peace stands in stark contrast to the pessimism of Thomas Malthus (1766–1833). He held that scarcity of resources and national territorial limits combined with unchecked population growth lead to civil and international wars, which by eliminating large numbers of people prevent further ones, but only temporarily. Only when population levels are optimized on an ongoing basis, according to Malthus, will intra- and international peace be assured. The idea that peace could be a result of widespread death or other undue hardships was denounced in a statement by statesman Benjamin Disraeli (1804–81) regarding the principle of *peace at any price*. "That doctrine," he proclaimed in an 1844 speech, "has done more mischief than any I can well recall. . . It has occasioned more wars than any of the most ruthless conquerors. It has disturbed and nearly destroyed that political equilibrium so necessary to the liberties and the welfare of the world."[12]

By the mid nineteenth century, free trade liberalism had become a mainstream in British policy and a defining characteristic of the Pax Britannica, heralded by the Frenchman Michel Chevalier as a practical model applicable worldwide. Still other approaches to improving peace prospects through economics were put forth in France and Germany during the same period. In working out the laws of supply and demand, Jean-Baptiste Say (1767–1832) proposed that the science of economics can aid in establishing and maintaining the material conditions of peace. Economists can in this way take up the roles of peacemakers by raising public awareness of, giving shape to, negotiating and implementing such material conditions within and between nations or empires. A *science of peace*, as a sub-field of economics, could for example aid in exposing the wastefulness of war and provide arguments for eliminating military expenditures, which would decrease the likelihood of invasions by the formation of alliances impossible at current levels of militarism. Say also identified economic war tactics such as sanctions, trade restrictions, embargos, boycotts, as alternatives to armed forces, but renounced them as self-defeating measures: in diversified and integrated economies based on free trade, disrupting chains of supply and demand affects the economically derived peace of all market participants negatively. What Say suggested, arguably for the first time, is that quantifying the conditions, causes and attributes of peace and its absence not only makes peace measureable, but in so facilitating evaluations and continual improvements of policies and their implementations, makes peacemakers into scientists in that they can draw upon the process of trial and error through experimentation.

Along these scientific peacemaking lines, progressive in the dual sense of a necessary series of steps and ongoing betterment, the leading member of the historical school of economics in Germany, Gustav von Schmoller (1838–1917), contended that:

> The progress of the nineteenth century beyond the mercantilist policy of the eighteenth depends – keeping to this thought of a succession of ever larger social communities – on the creation of leagues of states, on alliances in the matter of customs and trade, on the moral and legal community of all civilized states, such as modern international law is more and more bringing into existence by means of a network of international treaties. . . The struggle of social bodies with one another, which is at times military, at other times merely economic, has a tendency, with the progress of civilization, to assume a higher character and to abandon its coarsest and most brutal weapons. The instinct becomes stronger of a certain solidarity of interests, of a beneficent interaction, of an exchange of goods from which both rivals gain.[13]

Frédéric Bastiat also argued that competition and conscious consumerism are conducive to peace in *Economic Harmonies* (1863): "Superficial minds accused Competition of introducing antagonism among men. This is true and inevitable as long as one considers them only as producers; but if one takes the consumption point of view, then Competition itself will bring together individuals, families, classes, nations and races, united by universal brotherhood relations."[14] In his *Peace and Freedom, or the Republican Budget* of a year later, he proposed an immediate and complete disarmament of France to place the country on a sound economic and political footing which other countries could look to for inspiration. Free trade, for Bastiat, is in everyone's best interests, especially the working classes whom war affects most, because it ensures peace better than political solution can. Léon Walras, in *Peace Through Social Justice and Free Trade* (1907), combined Say's, von Schmoller's and Bastiat's views, proposing that economists act as advisors to government, giving politicians "the means to establish absolute free trade and, by this very fact, to ensure universal peace."[15] In the same spirit, Passy predicted that "One day, all barriers will fall; one day the human race, continually united by ceaseless transactions, will constitute a single workshop, a single market, a single family."[16] However, by this time, mercantilism was on the rise again, and a new set of economic principles with old roots was being proposed to make and maintain peace.

Who Owns Peace? Socialist Perspectives

The myriad of movements and plethora of prescriptions that fall under the umbrella term "socialism" share certain characteristics, but each has a distinct perspective on peace. Whereas capitalists from Smith to Say tended to sanctify private property and competition as the optimal peace paradigm, socialists tended to consecrate collective ownership and cooperation as the only conditions in which peace is possible. Ever-enlarging rifts between capitalists and socialists thus had, from the start, as much to do with what peace is as how to achieve it. In hindsight, cenobite monastic practices show strong affinities with socialist ideals, a difference being that the former were based on religious and the latter on economic principles. Further distinctions must be made between agrarian and industrial, and revolutionary and gradualist, positions on socialist peace, which came in either non-violent or violent persuasions.

A forerunner of non-violent, industrial gradualist approaches is that of Henri Saint-Simon (1760–1825). Having experienced firsthand the destruction caused and hope inspired by the American and French Revolutions, he proposed societies be peacefully reorganized on empirical principles by studying the past to inform the present and shape the future. As the "philosophy of the [eighteenth] century was revolutionary; that of the nineteenth century must be organizational," he argued, geared towards establishing cooperative, productive and stable social orders that secure social peace through individual wellbeing.[17] He argued further that "governments will no longer command men" in war if leaders are scientists and industrialists whose functions are "limited to ensuring that useful work is not hindered," united with working classes by a materialist morality that would gradually become a *New Christianity*, the title of his last, unfinished book.[18] Saint-Simon's principles and methods developed a cult-like postmortem following. Though none of his plans were immediately implemented, his student Auguste Comte started the "positivist" science of "sociology," terms he coined, likewise aimed at non-violent, peace-oriented transformations of societies by acting on empirical knowledge. Unlike Saint-Simon and Comte, François Babeuf (1760–97) was a revolutionary agrarian who condoned violence. Executed for founding a secret society called the Conspiracy of Equals, he sought to broaden the French

Revolution to include overthrowing economic as well as political systems and institutions so land, wealth and votes alike are equally distributed, the sole way he believed social peace could be sustained. Justifying short-term uses of violence as vehicles of long-term peace prospects became hallmarks of later revolutionary socialists, who taking into consideration the rise of industrialism focused more on the division of labor and ownership of means of production than land and distribution.

Similarly "utopian" schemes, as Karl Marx would later try to discredit them, were put forth by Richard Owen in England, Charles Fourier in France, and their American followers. Owen (1771–1858), a saddler's son, began working in Manchester's booming textile industry at the age of ten, by twenty-five was a manufacturer, and by thirty had purchased mills with other investors in Scotland. There, he spearheaded cooperative organizations by reinvesting portions of profits in improving the working conditions, housing, schools, sanitation and non-profit stores for his employees, increasing industrial productivity and peace. His maverick model instigated the social reforms passed by the British Parliament as the Factory Acts (1802–91). At around the same time, German immigrants to the US State of Indiana were running an agrarian collectivist community called Harmony, in which all property was held and all work done in common. They agreed to sell the property to Owen in 1825 to finance other such enterprises. Although New Harmony was under his direction for only three years, the first free kindergarten, free school for boys and girls, and free library in the US were established. Returning to England in 1829, Owen at first sought to combine the growing trade union and cooperative movements, but the unions' increasingly militant stance was at odds with his lifelong commitment to non-violent change, and he soon broke with them. As working class violence reached epidemic proportions throughout Europe, he spent his remaining years popularizing the idea that as social conditions are formative of individual characters, cooperatives can form peaceful individuals and so peaceful societies.

Like Owen, his contemporary Fourier (1772–1837) belonged to what was now called the bourgeoisie, merchant and entrepreneurial classes between aristocrats and laborers. His proposal for a cooperative community championed channeling people's interests and passions rather than restricting them, as he condemned the day's socio-economic systems for doing. Instead, he designed what he ironically named "phalanxes" after Ancient Greek army units: self-sufficient agrarian and manufacturing villages in which work is allotted based on individuals' inclination and all members live communally. Although unimplemented in his life, Fourier's followers established phalanxes across the US. The best-known is Brook Farm, Massachusetts, founded as an experimental joint-stock farm by Unitarians in 1841 and converted into a phalanx three years later, visitors of which included Ralph Waldo Emerson. The key similarity between Owen's and Fourier's propositions is that the immediate changes they considered necessary to end class struggles were revolutionary in their means and ends, but not in any violent sense; the key difference is that, for Owens, the peace-oriented change he proposed took place within the existing industrial socio-economic system and for Fourier from without it.

Gradualist, in opposition to revolutionary socialists, advocated change through reforms of existing socio-economic systems and their supporting political infrastructures rather than outright rejection, overhaul or overthrow. An early example is the British Chartist movement, named after the People's Charter published in 1838 by the London Working Men's Association. Tying fairer political processes to more equitable economic systems, Chartists called for universal male suffrage, annual elections, equalized electorates and payment instead of property qualifications for members of Parliament. Since in this way working classes would be better represented within government, putting them in a position to change laws that regulate industrialism, their economic interests could be politically advanced. Government could thus be an ally of working classes in the cause of industrial peace rather than an instrument of the bourgeoisie and aristocrats, and improvements in the economic conditions of working classes could be made without resorting to violence. But after Parliament twice threw out the Chartists' motions, riots broke out and their suppressions ended the movement. In response, Christian socialists like Charles Kingsley (1819–79), chaplain to Queen Victoria, tried to peaceably resolve class conflicts by aligning religious aims of churches with the economic aims of trade unions through workshops that would steadily and simultaneously uplift laborers' spiritual and material wellbeing. However, speculators on the roles secular states could play in balancing class interests soon eclipsed the influence of Christian socialists throughout Europe, such as the Fabian Society, which included prominent intellectuals like George Bernard Shaw and later H. G. Wells, opposed to revolutionary socialism.

Fabians advocated for the gradual permeation of economic equality within existing socio-political infrastructures. They rejected the violent class conflicts that had become part of urban European life by their times and, to help mitigate it, formed the Labor Representation Committee with the many active British labor unions in 1900, which evolved into the extant Labor Party. Along similar lines, Ferdinand Lassalle (1825–64) co-founded the German Workers' Association in 1863, which like the Chartists campaigned for universal suffrage but for the implementation of state socialism – the use of national government capital to de-class society by reorganizing industries so that they are owned and run, directly or indirectly through the state, by the workers themselves. Two collaborators, the avowed pacifist Wilhelm Liebknecht and the anti-militarist August Bebel, formed the Social Democratic Party into which the Association was absorbed. For openly opposing Chancellor Bismarck's war policy in the Reichstag, in their view benefitting the upper classes at the lowers' expense, they were imprisoned for two years. Their protests did not prevent the Franco-Prussian War, but did galvanize gradualist socialist movements. In the next three decades, dozens of similar parties were founded in Western and Eastern Europe and North America advocating non-violent intra-national reform via existing industrialized states instead of violent international revolutions against them, as advocated by Karl Marx and his followers.

While Marx opposed his "scientific" socialism to previous "utopian" ones by claiming a primacy of observation over ideals in determining its socio-economic strategies and goals, the idealist logic he adapted from Friedrich Hegel (1770–1831) rubbed off. Hegel had proposed that history unfolds in a dialectical process by which deficiencies of one idea, a thesis, are overcome by another, its antithesis. Thesis and antithesis are then synthesized to produce a new thesis and antithesis, progressing to intellectual and social perfection and so universal peace. For instance, in Hegel's time, revolutions from monarchical to constitutional states gave rise to constitutional monarchies, all towards intra-national peace. Hence, for him, "in war, war itself is characterized as something which ought to pass away," temporarily at first and permanently in the end.[19] Marx concretized Hegel's premises but kept his teleology intact, taking the economic conditions in which peace can and/or cannot be produced as determining factors of his dialectical materialism. As Marx observed, land ownership as the basis of feudal agrarian societies, in which aristocrats exploit peasants, was being displaced by capital as the basis of industrial societies, in which the bourgeoisie exploits working class proletariat. Human history is "the history of class struggles" for Marx because the inexorable structural violence of capitalism and all class-based economic systems precludes peace, and will do so for as long as classes exist.[20] Revolt against the classes that keep classes in place, then, is not only advisable but also an unavoidable step towards peace. In their passionate call-to-arms analysis, The Communist Manifesto (1848), Marx and colleague Friedrich Engels argued that capitalism had set the stage for the proletariat to seize control of the very economic conditions used to exploit them. They must unite to recreate an industrial society in which private property has ceased to exist, individuals contribute according to their abilities and receive according to their needs, in a word: communism.

A classless communist state, the only one that can be peaceful in Marx's terms, was to be the final outcome and cessation of all class struggle, guarantor of individual freedoms. Proletariat revolution and provisional dictatorship are thus predetermined birth pangs of communist peace:

> as the exploitation of one individual by another will be ended, the exploitation of one nation by another will also be ended. . . . as the antagonism between classes within the nation vanishes, the hostility of one nation to another will come to an end.[21]

In the meantime, socialists should prepare for the inevitable: in a revolution that would run along class lines, unity across national lines was required for lasting results, "a state of war which can only end with the final destruction of all pre-existing social structures."[22] In 1863, Marx and others founded the First International Workingmen's Association to unite, organize and mobilize workers worldwide from the capital of capitalism, London. When asked if socialists should participate in the day's organized peace movements, Marx condemned them as futile bourgeois enterprises aimed at placating the proletariat. Yet, the International splintered in 1875 in a power struggle during which Marx refused to endorse the terrorist tactics proposed by Mikhail Bakunin to abolish governments and their armies first, and classes later. While Marx's socialist stance cannot be called peaceful, the paradigm for and analysis of social peace he put forth has been immeasurably influential, to the extent that the history of peace and peacemaking in the next century and a half cannot be understood without them.

The global revolutions of 1848, launched on economic but not always socialist grounds, were brutally suppressed by government militias. These events renewed the urgency of resolving class conflicts and intensified debates over using revolutionary violence in the name of peace or peacefully bringing about change from the start, either along or across national lines and through or against national governments. An innovative proposal, called "non-violent anarchism," came from Paris, where in 1861 Pierre-Joseph Proudhon published his *War and Peace*, from which Tolstoy got more than the title of his novel, arguing that nation-states founded on the principles of private property and state-sponsored industrial socialism are both obstacles to social peace for self-interested reasons.[23] Mutualism, the alternative socio-economic system he put forth decades ahead of the socio-biological system given the same name and sharing certain principles, would replace government with freely associated, self-managed socio-economic units and decentralized labor-controlled firms to fill all state roles, eliminating without violence central authorities and the standing armies in place to protect them. Oxymoronically, the organized anarchy Proudhon proposed could taper static disadvantages and harness dynamic advantages of its terms, a model for social peace that has only lately begun to be re-explored.

A similar plan but on an agrarian platform was propagated at about the same time by the Russian *narodniki* (from "going to the people") movement. When it began using terrorist tactics shortly after it was formed, a young man named Georgi Plekhanov split, travelled abroad and brought Marxist socialism to Russia for the first time. With Vladimir Lenin and others, he then transformed the League for the Emancipation of Labor into the Russian Social Democratic Labor Party. In a debate later echoed around the world, Plekhanov held that industrial capitalism was not advanced enough in Russia to warrant the violent revolution Marx envisioned, and so it must be peacefully developed first, the Menshevik position when the Party split. Conversely, Lenin held that the interests of peasants and workers were sufficiently aligned for the revolution to be successful, the position of the Bolsheviks he came to lead. By 1889, socialists across Europe and North America reunited to form the Second International with its permanent headquarters in Belgium, which unlike the First was composed of and sought to direct existing local and national bodies. To the dejection of revolutionaries like Lenin, who now called themselves communists for contrast, socialists of the Second International were gradualist in their approach, inciting like Fabians practical political reforms in participating countries. But their departure from the First International's unitive stance of workers worldwide became clear when the Second broke apart as members supported their own nations in the First World War. By this time yet another approach to industrial peace had surfaced, in which governments were mediators rather than mediums.

A coordinating body of British trade unions, the Trades Union Congress, was established in 1868 to formulate and articulate common policy so as to avoid further violence. Three years later, unions were legally recognized by the Trade Union Act, and immediately and successfully began using non-violent tactics to achieve the better wages and working conditions. Strikes, or worker non-cooperation with employers until their demands are met, and lockouts, the same by employers with workers, at first displaced then replaced the violence that previously permeated relations between them. In the US, two competing organizations emerged, the Knights of Labor (1869–1917) comparable to Fabians, and the American Federation of Labor (AFL, 1886), which gave autonomy to its member-unions and did not enter politics directly. A militant organization, the Industrial Workers of the World, was formed in 1905, but after government crackdowns it collapsed as the Knights' Fabianism fizzled. Unions were legally recognized in the US with the National Labor Relations Act of 1935. Dissident AFL unions formed a Congress of Industrial Organizations (CIO) in the late 1930s, conflicts occurred, but after extensive negotiations they merged to form the extant AFL-CIO in 1955. In the words of a labor theorist, such "associations exert pressure on each other and on the government; the concessions which follow help to bind society together; thereafter stability is maintained by further concessions and adjustments as new associations emerge and power shifts from one group to another."[24]

Collective bargaining, as "a system of industrial jurisprudence. . . seeks to settle disputes short of industrial warfare, without resort to strikes and lockouts. It seeks to maintain industrial peace."[25] Opponents argue it deprives workers of individual liberties and hinders labor markets; proponents argue that without it employers and labor markets become oppressive dictators; but all seem to agree that it is better than industrial warfare. Even strikes and lockouts function "as both inducing and restraining factors in collective bargaining" as they become "a more passive and potential force, rather than an active one."[26] Collective bargaining has taken place at national and local levels (particularly in Europe), at industry levels (particularly in Asia), and at enterprise levels (particularly in North America, increasingly worldwide). In communist countries, unions tend to be transformed from worker vehicles into state instruments without collective bargaining mechanisms, which may explain why labor violence has been more prevalent. The International Labor Organization (ILO) founded in 1919 and which became the United Nation's first special agency in 1946, defines collective bargaining as all negotiations between employers and workers to (a) determine working conditions and terms of employment, (b) regulate relations between employers and workers, and/or (c) regulate relations between their respective organizations. The ILO Constitution states one of its aims as "the effective recognition of the right of collective bargaining" for the pacific settlements of disputes.[27] In 1949, it adopted a Collective Bargaining Convention, ratified by 140 states, a strong statement about the power of collective bargaining and the value of industrial peace it makes possible. But what are effective negotiation techniques at the collective bargaining table and can they apply at other ones?

In concluding *The Quest for Industrial Peace* (1966), renowned labor negotiator David Cole states "conflict is undeniable – industrial peace in the absolute sense is impossible," which does not mean that striving for it is pointless.[28] For centuries, a standard approach to negotiations in labor, diplomatic and other disputes was *advocacy*, seeking to reach a position without other parties leaving the table. With collective bargaining developed negotiation techniques based on interests underlying positions, a classic illustration being two sisters fighting over an apple, one to make juice and the other a pie from the pulp. Like mercantilism, focusing on their positions (possession of the apple) allows for accord only at the other's loss; by focusing on interests (juice and pie), mutually beneficial accord is possible. Early in the twentieth century, organizational theorist

Mary Follett stressed creativity, coordination and information-sharing as continuous processes in avoiding and resolving conflicts because common ground is thereby already actionable. Gerard Nierenberg's *The Art of Negotiating* became a bestseller in the 1960s, arguing that as negotiating determines outcomes, a win-win basis is always most successful, and he founded the Negotiation Institute in New York (1966) to offer training in collaborative dispute resolution. By the 1970s the field of Alternative Dispute Resolution (ADR) emerged to reduce growing costs of lawsuits by arbitration between individuals and entities. Directors of the Harvard Negotiation Project (est. 1979), Roger Fisher and William Ury, pioneered Principled Negotiation in the 1980s: separating people from problems while privileging interests over positions, objective over subjective criteria and mutual over one-sided gain. Recently, emphasis in negotiation studies has been on the role of emotions. Imagining modernity had negotiation been more widely used would be revisionist, and how the world could be if it were now, utopian. But imagining the uses of negotiation for individual peace in daily situations, social peace in group decision-making, and collective peace in inter-group relations is pragmatic. The history of peace in the twentieth century, subject of the next two chapters, can be taken as series of lessons in doing and failing to do so.

9

Peace in the Twentieth Century, Part I: 1900–1945

The "War to End all Wars"

Two opposing views regarding the outbreak of the First World War prevail among historians. One is it "was never supposed to have occurred;" the other, that there was "something inevitable about it."[1] Two opposing views on peace and peacemaking in the late nineteenth and early twentieth centuries thus emerge: either they failed in themselves and in their implementations, or they were proactively part of its causes. Each of these four scenarios is inseparable from the intertwined abornings of nation-states, colonialism-imperialism and industrialism previously discussed, which both set the stages for and structured the stories of peace and peacemaking in the periods covered in this and the next chapters. But such panoptic perspectives overlook complexities of pacific and bellicose forces then and now at work, which examined as continuums confirm that what was called the "war to end all wars," though far from being one, was a catalytic rather than cataclysmic event in the history of peace and peacemaking, perhaps second only to its sequel.

The first two milestones in twentieth-century peacemaking were the Hague Peace Conferences. That the first began in 1899 is suggestive of the nineteenth-century peace traditions in which they were both rooted. The motives of Russian Tzar Nicholas II for convening it, upon the urging of his foreign ministers, were mixed at best. Politically, prospects for peace in Europe never seemed brighter thanks to the organized peace movement and entangling alliances. Militarily, Germany and England were rearming at unprecedented rates with which Russia could not then compete. In these contexts, the Conference's failure in achieving its aim of arms reductions and its unplanned successes in international arbitration and arms limitations are explicable. Delegates from twenty-six nations negotiated and those from peace groups observed. General populations weighed in via petitions. Russians stated their objectives on the first day: "non-augmentation of the present number of troops" and "the maintenance, for the term of five years, of the amount of the military budget in force at the present time."[2] Nothing close to these terms was contracted, but by the Conference's end agreements were reached regarding the pacific settlement of international disputes at a newly formed Permanent Court of Arbitration; laws and customs of war on land; adaptations of the Geneva Conventions of 1864 to maritime warfare; and the prohibition of launching explosives from aerial balloons, and using asphyxiating gases and bullets inextricable from the human body. At the signing of the Convention, ratified in September 1900, Conference participants pledged to meet again about disarmament.

At the Second Hague Peace Conference in 1907, called for by Theodor Roosevelt upon the urging of Inter-Parliamentarians and convened by the Tzar, Russians pressed for furthering international arbitration and limitations on warfare rather than status quos on armaments, having recently lost a war with Japan and barely suppressed revolutionary soviets. Again, peace groups' delegates observed; petition signatories jumped from thousands to millions. Their disarmament demands went unanswered. This time, achievements in failure included limits on armed forces used for debt collection; rules for opening hostilities; rights and duties of neutrals; regulations regarding naval warfare; prohibitions on aircraft bombing; and the obligation of arbitration before war. A Third Conference was scheduled for 1916, but by 1914 Europe was engulfed in war, which statesmen justified by entangling alliances Conferencees had, in theory, disentangled. On one side were the Central Powers, Germany, Austro-Hungary and the Ottomans; on the other were the Allies, Britain, France, and Italy. Each was backed by decades of arms build-ups which Conferencees failed to stop but had, in theory, circumscribed. Within three years the world was engulfed in war, and the Conferences were explained away when convenient, ignored when not. A Third Conference did take place, a century after the First.

During the First World War, prior peace traditions were renewed while prior war traditions were forever changed. As one British soldier put it, "this war is not as past wars; this is everyman's war, a war of civilians, a war of men who hate war, of men who fight for a cause, who are compelled to kill and hate it."[3] Among the popular causes fought for, the most pervasive was nationalism, a form of patriotism placing the interests of one's nation not only above those of all others, but also above the interests of individual nationalists themselves. Even as the war began, 60,000 Germans protested for peace as their nation's best interest in Berlin to no avail. Within a year of its start, the Concert of Europe was playing nationalist strings to the terminal tune of twenty million dead, half civilians. Although the grand illusion that the War would be over in 1914 was shattered, on December 25 British and German soldiers on the Western Front put their nationalisms aside, called an impromptu ceasefire and emerged from their trench shelters to share a holiday meal. Stalemated massacres along national lines resumed the next day. Yet, a new kind of non-violent nationalism materialized in England with *conscientious objectors* who extended the religiously motivated pacifism of peace churches to include secular, moral and political motives. Upon the proposal of Fabian economist John Maynard Keynes to productively accommodate conscientious objectors, often accused of being unpatriotic, the British government allowed them to substitute combat for services of "national importance."[4] Unpredictably, "everyman's war" had become an agent of everyman's peace, up to a point. A special committee was established under the Board of Trade to review conscientious objector cases, assign work to those willing and imprison those not. Of about 16,000 known British conscientious objectors, 6000 went to jail at least once and 1500 absolutists refused to cooperate at all.

By 1915, the national No Conscription Fellowship (NCF) was providing support to those who refused to enlist. The NCF Manifesto recognized the different motives for objecting, such as to war in general or this War in particular, uniting them under a banner of defending non-violent individualism against violent nationalism. The chairman of a local NCF chapter noted that conscientious objectors were people "from every conceivable angle of life . . . a sort of cross-section of every type," but identified a "very curious group" of "artistically minded" people who "had a terrific repugnance at war which could only express itself individually."[5] The most prominent member of this group became a Cambridge philosopher and mathematician, Bertrand Russell (1872–1970), who before the War started collecting signatures from leading intellectuals for a statement proposing British neutrality, all of whom reneged once it began except him. It may be no coincidence that the man who first proved that one plus one equals two also articulated the fundamentals of secular pacifism in periodicals, books (notably the *Philosophy of Pacifism*, 1915) and lectures. "Hatred, cruelty, injustice, untruthfulness, love of violence," he inveterated, "are all recognized as vices in time of peace; but as soon as war breaks out, they are universally praised and stimulated, while lukewarmness in any one of them is denounced as a form of treachery," for which he was imprisoned for six months.[6] He pointed out that "what is wrong with mere opposition to war is that it is negative," so it should be complemented with positive contributions towards actualizations of peace.[7] Whereas organized peace movements worked *en masse* against war and for peace as systems, conscientious objectors like Russell on both sides of the Atlantic worked individually against war and for peace as conditions.

When the US entered the war in 1917 despite fierce political and popular opposition, objectors followed similar patterns on larger scales, with the significant difference that many isolationists did not want to get involved in the first place, though not always on pacifist grounds. On such grounds, professor and preacher A.J. Muste led protests against the War and, with social worker Jane Addams and other pacifists, founded the interfaith Fellowship of Reconciliation (FOR), which provided support to conscientious objectors through its Emergency Committee for Civil Liberties, from which the American Civil Liberties Union evolved. Muste and Addams became central figures in many twentieth-century peace movements. French-speakers in the Canadian province of Quebec contested what they saw as a British war by refusing to enlist on political grounds, spurring their nationalist separation movement. While short-term numbers of objectors was small relative to those who actively or passively agreed to the War, their long-term impact has been disproportionately large by pacifist, non-violently resistant and non-cooperative models they made. And while first-generation organized peace movements broadened worldwide activist bases, by the second and third generations these new bases' members became peace leaders.

Bertha von Suttner (1843–1914) was the first woman awarded the Nobel Peace Prize in 1906, which may have been created on her suggestion to her former employer, Alfred Nobel. She came to fame with a novel entitled *Lay Down Your Arms* (1889), depicting the tragic plight of a woman who lost two husbands to war, and which became the title of a peace activism journal she edited. *The Machine Age*, published that year, drew upon Darwin's evolutionary theory to argue that modern warfare, by killing the fittest, leads to a degeneration of our species. Nonetheless, in a speech to the American Federation of Women in 1912 she wryly remarked:

> The half of humanity that has never borne arms is today ready to struggle to make the brotherhood of man a reality. Perhaps the universal sisterhood is necessary before the universal brotherhood is possible.[8]

She founded the Austrian Peace Society and was a star attendee at many of the peace congresses previously discussed, advocating for a European confederacy in which arbitration could be used to prevent or quickly end wars. Dying a week before the First World War, her collected essays, *The Battle for the Prevention of World War* (1917), were banned in Austria. Inspired by Suttner, a Women's Committee of the South Africa Conciliation and South African Women and Children's Distress Fund were established in London to lobby for ending the Boer War

(1899–1902) and help those it left destitute. They noted governments started the war without people's consent, which the Union for the Democratic Control of Foreign Policy futilely sought to change. A leader of the aligned suffragettes, then in full swing, Maude Royden (1876–1956) was a pacifist Oxford graduate and the first woman ordained by the Church of England. She was an organizing member of British FOR, which published her popular pamphlet *The Way to Peace*, arguing that non-violence could victoriously end the War. In the early 1930s, she formed an Army of Peace which never went to war, and like many others renounced pacifism in the Second World War. But for decades another woman had brightened and basked in the limelight of feminist-and-beyond peacemaking.

Daughter of an Illinois State Senator with Quaker inclinations, Jane Addams (1860–1935) travelled to Europe after graduating from a local women's college. Shocked by London's slums, she was impressed with Toynbee Hall, the first "settlement house" where social and recreational services were provided to urban poor free of charge. Upon her return, she and a friend founded Hull House in Chicago's immigrant working class south side (1889), which apart from providing similar services became the birthplace of major US social reform movements, bringing Addams to national prominence. *Newer Ideals of Peace* (1907), Addams' third book, was critical of city governments' use of violence against the working and immigrant classes, which she attributed in part to their and women's lack of political representation. She proposed a novel cosmopolitan approach to international via inner-city peace: building upon shared experiences and worldwide networks of working class immigrants to bring about an integrated, trans-national society. With Hull House ongoing, she served as vice president of the National American Woman Suffrage Association from 1911 to 1914 when, with the outbreak of the First World War, she committed herself to peace activism. At a meeting in Washington with 3000 of her Association colleagues, Addams helped organize the Women's Peace Party (WPP) early in 1915, an extraordinary year in the history of peace, showing again that war stimulates desire, for its cessation.

The WPP's multifaceted but unidirectional platform included pressuring government officials through public and private channels; taking independent action towards a conference of neutral nations "in the interest of early peace;" the limitation of armaments; organized opposition to militarism; educating youths in the ideals of peace; democratic control of foreign policies; "humanizing of governments" through women's voting rights; superseding the balance of power system with a "concert of nations" by substituting laws for warfare; replacing national militaries with an "international police;" eliminating economic causes of war; and "the appointment by our Government of a commission of men and women, with an adequate appropriation [funding and support] to promote international peace."[9] Along with its platform, Addams, as chairman of the WPP headquartered in Chicago, attracted some 25,000 women who joined within a year. Later in 1915, Addams received and accepted invitations from European women's rights activists aware of the WPP who were organizing a Women's Peace Congress at The Hague the next year. The Congress delegates from 150 women's groups created an International Committee of Women for Permanent Peace (ICWPP) and elected Addams president. Its statement of purpose was close to that of the WPP and was signed by nearly 100,000 women worldwide. The ICWPP, of which the WPP became one of dozens of national chapters, sent delegates to meet governments currently or prospectively at war within weeks of its formation.

They were often ridiculed, but when Addams met US President Woodrow Wilson, he echoed several of his European counterparts in saying their plan for peace was the best proposed. Successful at first, belligerent governments had no objections to a conference of neutral nations, of which four agreed to attend. By 1916, even belligerent nations were considering attending, but when the US declined in preparation for war, it fell through. At the ICWPP's first post-war meeting in 1919, its name was changed to the Women's International League for Peace and Freedom (WILPF). Between the wars, the WILPF promoted disarmament in petitions signed by millions and high-level mediation, and campaigned for humanitarian aid to war-torn countries, among many other activities. When Germany invaded Czechoslovakia (1938), the WILPF issued a powerful statement in favor of non-violent intervention, part of which reads:

> Pacifism is not the quietistic acceptance of betrayal and lies for the sake of 'peace.' Pacifism is the struggle for truth. . . the struggle for clear political aims, for firm political will and action. Pacifism is not weak acceptance of 'faits accomplis' achieved by brute force. Pacifism is courageous initiative for a constructive policy of just peace.[10]

Leaders of the WILPF, oldest and largest international women's peace organization today, have been awarded the Nobel Peace Prize and the first was Addams in 1931. Her achievements as the head of a comparatively mainstream, international peace activism group were extensions of her work for workers, immigrants and women at societal margins. Other women, working from other margins but still against war, rejected mainstream internationalism outright.

Simone Weil (1909–43), a radical French socialist intellectual, graduated at the top of her class from the prestigious École Normale Supérieure. In a 1933 essay, "Reflections on War," she argued that because war gives governments more power over people than any ideology they may be based on, they can and do use wars to keep themselves in power. As this inbuilt conservatism of war remains hidden by destruction and reconstruction, competitive military buildups prevent ideological and material progress. Revolutions that become wars thus cease to be revolutions and genuinely revolutionary ideologies must perforce be pacifist. Weil was one, but did not stay one. After briefly serving in Spain's fight against fascism in the 1930s, she published another potently critical essay in which she elaborated an anti-war argument along different lines, again exhibiting an uncanny foresight of the Cold War era and our own:

> What a country calls its vital economic interests are not the things which enable its citizens to live, but the things which enable it to make war; petrol is much more likely than wheat to be a cause of international conflict. Thus when war is waged it is for the purpose of safeguarding or increasing one's capacity to make war.[11]

To hide these militarist–materialist aims, governments use abstractions such as national interests, security and any ideology one can name to deceive the masses into mobilization. Weil supported negotiating for peace with Hitler in 1938, the year she had mystical experiences in Francis of Assisi's church and her writings turned to religious topics. When the Nazis occupied France in 1942, she fled to the US with her family, then flew back to Europe to work with the Resistance government in England, where she died a year later of anorexia. Certainly unfamiliar with Weil's arguments against revolutionary war, the hundreds of ambassadors who created what came to be called the Commonwealth of Nations evidently shared her aversion to it.

Unlike revolution-based decolonization movements, the Commonwealth of Nations that grew out of British Imperial Conferences from 1907 to 1931 provided an unprecedented, non-violent path to post-colonial independence. At the first Conference in London, delegates from Canada, Australia, New Zealand, South Africa and India met to discuss defenses and clarify their statuses as partially self-governing states. The term "colony" was dropped, "dominion" adopted, and a balance between national military autonomy and coordinated imperial strategy reached. At the 1911 Conference, the hot topic was the constitutional basis of cooperation among dominions and Britain. The New Zealand premier proposed the establishment of an imperial parliament to debate and decide a common foreign policy, shelved by Britain's Prime Minister on the basis that it would infringe upon autonomy. But he conceded that dominions would be consulted on all imperial foreign policy issues, and agreed that all international treaties affecting them would be circulated before being signed. On these terms, Australia was consulted on naval matters before Britain treated with Japan, as was South Africa on territorial matters in British negotiations with

Germany. The term "commonwealth" was first used by British officials to refer to dominions as a whole during the First World War, and that it continued to be used thereafter indicates that ties made closer by war can be maintain afterwards if the willpowers involved are sustained. And though the Commonwealth ignored Britain's many other colonies worldwide cannot be denied, it must be acknowledged that for those concerned the process was peaceful.

In respect of their contributions to its First World War victory, Britain agreed to Canada, Australia, New Zealand and South Africa but not India acting independently at the 1919 Paris peace talks and as members of the League of Nations, discussed below. The first post-war Conference in 1921 aimed at creating a federated imperial government, but ended indecisively. The next year Britain called upon the dominions for military support against Turkey. Canada and South Africa refused and the rest only grudgingly agreed. When Britain made peace with Turkey by the Treaty of Lausanne in 1923 without consulting the dominions, Canada led them in declaring the Treaty binding only on Britain, and defiantly made commercial treaties with the US. The two countries are now the largest bilateral trading partners, and their border is the longest militarily undefended one in history. At the Conference that year, de facto independent control over foreign policy was recognized and pledges made to cooperate and not harm among dominions. Another Conference was called in 1926, at which British Prime Minister Lord Balfour made even more concessions: "Commonwealth" was officially adopted to designate the new voluntary union of its member "nations," whose autonomy was confirmed by the Statute of Westminster in 1931, without arms against imperialism ever being raised. Just as the First World War was the impetus for this first wave of non-violent decolonization, so the Second World War would be for a second, both within the extant framework of the cooperative and consultative Commonwealth and without it through the UN.

A different path to post-colonial peace was proposed and practiced by Mohandas Gandhi (1869–1948), given the honorary title Mahatma ("Great Soul") by the Indian people he dedicated his life to serving. He attended the University of Bombay before going to England to study law. In London, he became familiar with the Fabians and felt an affinity with their commitment to non-violent change. In 1893, after an unsuccessful attempt at establishing his own law firm in India, Gandhi went to Natal (Durban, South Africa) on a two-year contract with another firm. There, he witnessed and experienced the structural violence inflicted on natives and immigrants by local and British imperial governments, selectively choosing his struggle. He founded the Natal Indian Congress with other Indian émigrés a year later to publicize their plight and agitate for its improvement. Although he planned on returning to India when his contract expired, upon learning that the legislature would revoke Indian voting rights, he decided to stay and work for peaceful change, which he did for twenty years with trips to India and England to further the South African Indian cause. After the Boer War, during which he formed an ambulance corps, he had high hopes that Indians' support for Britain against the now-annexed Afrikaner states would improve their status. Instead, it got worse with the new South African dominion's partial self-rule: Indian marriages were invalidated, a tax was imposed on indentured Indian workers, their travel rights restricted and fingerprint registration cards required. In response, Gandhi developed and began employing the tactics of what he soon called *Satyagraha*, which he advised only when dialogue fails, translated by him from the Sanskrit as "truth-force."

In theory, Satyagraha is an innovative combination of ahimsa, civil disobedience, non-cooperation, ascetic self-discipline and selective non-resistance that proved to be one of the most effective methods of peaceful incitements to change ever conceived. In practice, Satyagraha in South Africa took the forms of marches, protests, strikes and symbolic acts such as burning registration cards, which led to the imprisonment of thousands of Indians, including Gandhi. As the First World War broke out, a victory for transformative non-violence was thus secured with the Indian Relief Bill of 1914, repealing the discriminatory laws. His goal partially achieved, Satyagraha's effectiveness evidenced, Gandhi was welcomed as a hero upon his return to India the following year, leaving indelible imprints behind. Paying homage, South African civil rights leader Nelson Mandela wrote: "The Gandhian influence dominated freedom struggles on the African continent right up to the 1960s because of the power it generated and the unity it forged among the apparently powerless."[12] Gandhi found agitation for Indian self-rule was rising. The National Congress, founded to foster dialogue among British and Indian elites, was now the focal point of the independence movement. But it was split along crossed lines Gandhi became determined to overcome: moderate gradualists and revolutionary radicals along one line, and Hindus and Muslims along the other. He would die trying.

Whereas the end of the First World War saw peaceful increases in autonomy for other British colonies, India's was further restricted by laws allowing imprisonments of sedition suspects without trial. Gandhi was propelled to the forefront of independence politics when he announced a Satyagraha against these laws, in which millions participated and hundreds were killed while protesting non-violently. But the Satyagraha led directly to the Government of India Act (1919), granting limited local autonomy within the country but none without. With this victory Gandhi became a driving force behind the Congress, which he restructured for involvement of all Indians rather than just the elite, broadening its missions to include improving living conditions and abolishing the caste system, like Ashoka had done millennia earlier. When protests turned violent despite Gandhi's best efforts, he called off the Satyagraha and was sentenced to six years imprisonment for sedition, of which he served two on account of appendicitis. In his absence, the moderate-radical and Hindu-Muslim rifts in the Congress and at large deepened. So he dedicated the next few years to reconciling the conflicting parties, using self-imposed fasts to draw attention to the harm disunity was causing and bring them together to resolve their differences. He sought autonomous dominion status as an alternative to independence, but when the constitutional reform committee formed by the British lacked even one Indian member, he called another Satyagraha and acceded to the Congress' commitment to full independence in 1929.

With Gandhi's guidance, the goal of independence was extended beyond rejecting British rule and became *Swaraj*, or national independence through non-violent individual liberation from all forms of oppression: religious, racial, gender, economic and otherwise. Britain involved India in the Second World War without consultation, to which Gandhi and other Congress leaders responded with calls for immediate imperial withdrawal and were imprisoned. Gandhi fasted against the incarceration, and as his health declined pro-independence and Hindu-Muslim violence increased and did not cease upon his release in 1944. He then met with but could not dissuade the leader of the Muslim League, Mohammad Ali Jinnah, whose calls for a separate state were supported by the British post-war government. In 1947, India gained independence and the new Muslim state of Pakistan was created, the greatest achievement and disappointment of Gandhi's life. In the next year, he successfully fasted to end religious violence in Calcutta, and in tours of regions so torn it was reported that his arrival relieved tensions. During his last fast in New Delhi for the same reasons, while on an evening walk, he was shot dead by a Hindu extremist who resented this reconciliation. Gandhi's influence on the subsequent history of peace cannot be underestimated. In 2007, the UN declared his birthday, October 2, the International Day of Non-Violence to raise awareness that "non-violence, tolerance, full respect for all human rights and fundamental freedoms for all, democracy, development, mutual understanding and respect of diversity, are interlinked and mutually reinforcing."[13]

The Peace to End all Peace?

In October, 1917, Lenin and his Bolshevik Party overthrew the Russian Tzar and formed a new government. In December, he withdrew Russia from the First World War, denouncing it as a bourgeois imperialist enterprise holding back his modified Marxist revolution, and in March 1918 made a separate peace with the struggling Central Powers. On November 11 of that year, Armistice Day (now Veterans' Day in the US), the Allies signed an armistice with the defeated Central Powers. However, the War was formally ended only six months later at the Paris Peace Conference (1919–20) and ensuing Treaty of Versailles. Neither the Central Powers nor Russia were invited to attend the Conference, so while the terms of Treaty were heatedly debated, debates were among the victorious Allies themselves. What began as a meeting of seventy delegates from twenty-six nations soon boiled down to a struggle between three: French Prime Minister Georges Clemenceau of France, British Prime Minister David Lloyd George and US President Woodrow Wilson.

Clemenceau openly sought revenge on Germany, the formerly French territory of Alsace-Lorraine, French control of German industries, elimination of its military, its political impotence by a ban on alliances with Central Powers, and reparations that would cover both France's First World War costs and those of the Franco-Prussian War. Though Lloyd George also sought reparations and coveted the Central Powers' colonies, he feared that without a viable German economy or military and with Russia in Bolshevik hands, France would become a threat to Britain once again. Ten days prior to the Conference, before Congress, Wilson put forth his famous Fourteen Point Plan, his position at the Conference, summarized as follows:

1. "Open covenants of peace," i.e. no secret or separate ones;
2. Freedom of navigation upon the seas outside territorial waters;
3. Free trade on equal terms for parties to the peace;
4. The reduction of national armaments consistent with domestic safety;
5. Adjustment of imperial claims with equal weight given to colonist and colonized;
6. Evacuation of and assistance to Russia and its self-determination;
7. Likewise with Belgium;
8. Restoration of Alsace-Lorraine to France;
9. Re-adjustment of Italy's borders along "recognizable lines of nationality;"
10. Autonomous development for the peoples of Austro-Hungary;
11. Economic independence, territorial integrity and old alliances for Balkan States;
12. Autonomous development for former Ottoman peoples and open Dardanelles;
13. An independent Polish state inhabited by "indisputably Polish populations;" and

14. A general association of nations to guarantee political independence and territorial integrity to great and small states alike.[14]

In the end, the Treaty held Central Powers wholly responsible for the War; imposed crippling reparations on Germany; restored Alsace-Lorraine to France; made all Central Power colonies mandates under Allied control; made Poland a state and Danzig a free city; provided for plebiscites in which residents chose their state, resulting in the growth of Belgium, Denmark and Poland at Central Power expense; placed the industrial Saarland and Rhineland under French control for fifteen years; demilitarized the right bank of the Rhine; and reduced the German army to 100,000 soldiers, its navy to insignificance, forbidding its manufacturing, import or export of weapons. At first Germany rejected the Treaty of Versailles, but with no alternatives accepted it in futile protest, and it became effective in January of 1920.

A British delegate, John Meynard Keynes, resigned from the Conference after his calls for moderation went unheeded. His *Economic Consequences of the Peace* (1919) disparaged the Treaty as ill-conceived for its malevolence, its return to mercantilist militarism, and above all for the malicious reparations Germany was forced to pay. The book radicalized the anti-Treaty US Republican Party, which after defeating Wilson never ratified it. Keynes, calling the peace terms "Carthaginian" referring to the devastated ancient city after losing wars with Rome, nevertheless predicted that the economic hardships the Treaty inflicted on Germany would preclude the peace it was meant to restore and ruin Europe again. After a brief and uneven reconstruction boom in the 1920s, hardships spread around the world during the 1930s Great Depression. Keynes, now a Labor Party economist, advocated government-funded public works programs for employment to prevent civil strife. Lenin's successor in the new Union of Soviet Socialist Republics (USSR), Joseph Stalin, attempted the same in his Marxist Five-Year Plans for rapid industrialization and collectivization. US President Franklin Roosevelt engaged in similar tactics with his New Deal of relief, recovery and reform, as did the rising stars of Depression-era German politics, Hitler's National Socialists (Nazis). A French economist refuted Keynes' arguments in *The Carthaginian Peace, or the Economic Consequences of Mr. Keynes*, published after he died fighting Nazi Germany, which he held had come into existence precisely because they had not been paid enough by the Treaty of Versailles, contrasting interpretations historians continue to ponder.

As one of them put it, "The Paris peace settlement reveals more than any other episode of the twentieth century the tension between the ideal and real in history," and particularly in the history of peace.[15] More than an ideal, less than a reality was the League of Nations, among the few non-retaliatory results of the Treaty of Versailles, except for the Central Powers' exclusion and the distribution of their colonies among Allies through a mandate system, as if as prizes. The League was organized during the Paris Conference, its governing Covenant was part of the Treaty and, unfortunately but not unpredictably, they shared similar fates. The League's stated purpose was to promote international cooperation, peace and security by (a) the acceptance of obligations not to resort to war; (b) regularizing open and just relations between nations; (c) the establishment of international law as the rule of conduct among governments; and (d) respect for all treaty commitments in the dealings of organized peoples with one another. In all, some sixty nations around the globe became League members, nearly half of which withdrew at different times, usually either in protest or circumvention of the League's resolutions. Wilson was the driving force behind the League's creation, but the US was the only major power not to join the League due to partisan domestic opposition. The only nation expelled from the League was the USSR for its unprovoked attack on Finland (1939), following the green light of a non-aggression pact with Nazi Germany, which like other wars the League proved unable to prevent.

The League was composed of three bodies: an Assembly of delegates from all members which met yearly; a Council of permanent major-power and non-permanent members elected by the Assembly for three-year terms which met as needed; and a Secretariat for year-round civil services such as meeting preparation and report publication at League headquarters in Geneva. The Assembly and Council were empowered to discuss "any matter within the sphere of action of the League or affecting the peace of the world."[16] Unanimity was needed for resolutions to be binding on members, and enforcement by them was on a voluntary basis. Special Agencies were also formed to achieve League missions from several angles simultaneously. The Disarmament Commission aimed at reversing ongoing arms races by reducing national militaries. The Health Committee focused on preventing the spread of infectious diseases. The International Labor Organization sought to improve working conditions and end child labor. The International Office for Refugees supervised resettlements of those war and other catastrophes displaced, provided material and legal support, and issued passports for stateless persons. The Slavery Commission's goal was the eradication of slavery and forced labor. The League's *multi-pronged approach to world peace* arguably made it actualizable for the first time and is its greatest legacy. Proposals for world peace had been advanced for centuries; that it took a calamity of world war proportions to implement one is one of the greatest misfortunes in world history.

Highlighting the League's limits were the Locarno Pact of 1925 and the Kellogg-Briand Pact of 1928, both negotiated outside its framework, incongruously because they were landmarks in inter-war disarmament and conflict resolution efforts. In 1924, British foreign minister Austen Chamberlain shocked the world at the annual meeting of the League's Council by rejecting the Geneva Protocols prohibiting the use of certain bio-chemical weapons. He did so based on the contradictory principles that it was the Council's responsibility to decide on policies and that the League's Covenant should be supplemented, not replaced, "by making special arrangements in order to meet special needs."[17] The first special arrangement of this kind was the Locarno Pact. On the initiative of the German Weimar Republic's Chancellor Gustav Stresemann, and with the support of French foreign minister Aristide Briand, delegates from Britain, France, Germany, Italy, Belgium, Czechoslovakia and Poland met in the Swiss town of Locarno to work out post-war borders, commit to arbitration for resolving future disputes, and admit Germany into the League. The seeming success of this cooperative reconciliatory effort led to the popular phrase "spirit of Locarno," which Briand sought to extend to the US in a second special arrangement to outlaw war between the two countries. US Secretary of State Frank B. Kellogg responded with an offer of a much broader agreement involving other countries, which was again negotiated in Paris beginning in 1927 and signed the next year.

The resulting Kellogg-Briand Pact had fifteen original signatories and later sixty-four. Pact parties agreed that all conflicts of any cause would be resolved only by arbitration and that war would be renounced as an instrument of their national policies. But questions as to the role the League would play in such mediated disarmaments and how decisions would be enforced were fatally left unanswered. Although ratified by all signatory nations and still technically in effect today, for these reasons the Kellogg-Briand Pact proved impotent in preserving peace and preventing wars during the 1930s when Japan invaded Manchuria, Nazi Germany invaded or annexed Poland, Austria and Czechoslovakia, and Italy invaded Ethiopia and Albania. Each of the aggressors had rearmed and withdrawn from the League, which they argued had let them down or could not stop them. The benevolent spirit of Locarno became a back-stabbing ghost by further special arrangements, also outside the League's forum, in the inter-war years. Known as appeasement policies, they undid prospects for peace by purportedly doing what the two Pacts prescribed. Blurring peacemaking and pandering, the underlying logic of appease-ment was peace at any price, which in actuality meant giving actual or potential aggressors what they wanted, or unofficially already had, for empty promises of non-aggression. Successful appeasements can be claimed for the Commonwealth. Appeasement also helped temporarily diffuse the armed revolt of the nationalist Irish Republican Army (1916–21) by offering Catholic separatists the autonomy they sought as the Irish

Free State and Protestant loyalists had the option to remain part of Britain. But positive appraisals of inter-war appeasement policies end there.

Disregarding that these Pacts were *fait accompli*, in 1932 the League's Disarmament Commission hosted the World Disarmament Conference in Geneva. There, Hitler argued that because other European powers refused to reduce their militaries as the Pacts required, let alone to the level the Treaty of Versailles had reduced that of Germany, he had a right to rearm his country up to their levels, which he did after withdrawing from the Conference and the League in 1933. While "saying all of the things that peaceful people want to hear," by 1935 Hitler had abrogated the Treaty of Versailles, and Nazi armed forces quintupled.[18] Meanwhile, Britain and France, according to the latter's ambassador to Germany, were "prisoners of our internal discords and dominated by our love of peace" even when, in 1936, Hitler renounced the Locarno Pact and remilitarized the Rhineland.[19] Over the next two years, the Axis with Italy and Japan, foes of Germany in the First World War, was formed. As it became clear that the Nazis had similar plans for resource-full regions of Czechoslovakia, British Prime Minister Neville Chamberlain, Austen's half-brother, held abortive meetings with Hitler. After appeals from Franklin Roosevelt and support from France and Italy on each side, the anti-climax of appeasement policies was reached at a third, inauspicious meeting in Munich in 1938.

Hitler was allowed to occupy the Sudetenland in exchange for promises to respect the territorial integrity of nations from now on. Upon his return to London, Chamberlain pronounced "peace for our time," and almost everyone seemed willing to believe except Winston Churchill. Most European nations then began rearming at unprecedented rates. That appeasement was a war strategy, not one of peace, aimed at buying time, may have been the case on the British side and certainly was on the Nazi's side from the start. Within a year of the Munich Pact, Hitler broke a previous non-aggression pact with Poland, which had also signed similar pacts with England and France, by a blitzkrieg invasion of the country, at which point the policy of appeasement was put to a deserved rest. Hitler had signed a similar non-aggression pact with Stalin and also broke it. What appeasing the Nazis failed to do on the European continent, namely prevent war, appeasing the Japanese failed to do in the Pacific region by another string of special arrangements, which one later historian aptly called a "parchment peace."[20] Japan emerged from the First World War as an imperial power by occupying large parts of China formerly under German control, putting the future of the Open Door policy in jeopardy. After rejecting the Versailles Treaty and League membership, the US government under President Warren Harding called a conference in Washington (1921–22) to discuss naval and territorial issues in the Pacific.

The result was a series of special arrangements called Power Pacts that succeeded in preserving peace in some ways, but prepared for war in others. The first was the Four Power Pact among Britain, France, Japan and the US, by which the parties agreed to maintain the territorial status quo, committed to negotiations to resolve disputes, and to discuss joint or separate action should any party's Pacific interests be threatened. The Five Power Pact, also known as the Naval Limitation Treaty, among these parties and Italy is considered the only inter-war agreement to have effectively curbed rearmament, albeit for less than a decade, because it dealt specifically with battleships by a ratio based on quantified relative security needs, to which all the signatories agreed. Third and lastly was the Nine Power Pact, among the preceding Five Powers as well as China, Belgium, Portugal and the Netherlands to "respect the sovereignty, the independence, and the territorial and administrative integrity of China" and not to take advantage of its political instability in the wake of its nationalist revolution under Ching Kai-shek, while China agreed to leave all foreign economic interests intact and treat them equally.[21] In fact, the Nine Power Pact was almost identical to the Open Door note of 1900, neither the first nor the last time the US made a multilateral agreement out of a unilateral decree.

Together, the Power Pacts permitted the US to continue on its isolationist course vis-à-vis Europe and Asia for twenty years. They also allowed the other Powers to turn a blind eye as Japan raised armed forces unmatched in Asia at the time. With these, it invaded Manchuria in 1931, breaching the Pacts. A ten-year military pacification of the Chinese resistance and the formation of the puppet Manchukuo government followed, just as Nazis would do with Vichy France. Japan withdrew from the League in 1933 to form what it called the Greater East Asia Co-Prosperity Sphere, supposedly a bloc of independent countries free from Western influence. Actually, the Sphere was part of Japan's propaganda used to justify the attacks on Pearl Harbor in 1941 that brought an end to this line of inter-war appeasement by directly involving the US in a world war it could no longer ignore. In an appraisal of how the League responded to the Manchurian invasion, a Harvard professor of international law politely but accurately summed up the reasons why the first world government, born after the First World War, died in the Second:

> In this instance, the world's peace machinery has been put to a laboratory test in unfavorable conditions; but conditions may frequently be unfavorable to its success, and the severity of this test may have served to reveal latent defects in that machinery. It has been shown to operate in a cumbersome fashion, and its operation consumes a great deal of time. It remains incomplete so long as fact-finding agencies must be created ad hoc, so long as they are not at hand for more immediate use. It lacks a worldwide

support, and the necessity of securing the cooperation of "non-member" states introduces elements of perilous uncertainty. At best, it serves to create and to crystallize a world opinion; but even if that process were less difficult, even if it were more prompt, opinion may not be effective to bring hostilities to an end. The clearest treaty obligations do not execute themselves, and each test is likely to disclose new ambiguities in the phrasing of the words on paper. Nor do the institutions which have been created operate automatically. The Council and the Assembly of the League of Nations can function only as the governments represented wish them to function, and in any crisis some government may have interests or commitments which will lead to its hesitation. International agencies must of necessity deal with the established government in each country; yet events have shown that even an established government may not hold the reins of power.[22]

The League was reborn as the UN during the Second World War in a chain of charters, pledges, declarations and conferences among anti-Axis countries, renamed Allies. They were geared towards securing the total defeat of the Axis, the only means the Allies found viable in securing post-war peace. Taking the racial, ideological and territorial goals of their enemies into account as well as their renewed military capabilities, Allied priorities were first to cooperate to win total war and second to cooperate to win total peace. In other words, without victory there could be no peace, and without peace there could be no victory. But while definitive military victory was achieved in a matter of years, decades have since passed without definitive peace.

10

Peace in the Twentieth Century, Part II: 1945–1989

Cold War/Hot Peace

The greatest and most fortunate of many ironies in the history of peace between 1945 and 1989 is that the two superpowers involved not once entered into armed conflict with one another directly in fear of nuclear war. Deterrence, as we have seen, is the oldest and crudest means of avoiding war, yet there seemed to be no other choice as modern societies became "aware that the 'old' problem of survival reappears as the imperatives of peace."[1] The US, a major power since the century's start, reemerged as one after the Second World War by reinforcing its position as the world's largest economy and introducing the world to atomic bombs. The USSR, a relatively weakened power at the turn of century and US ally during the Second World War, reversed both positions at the start of the Cold War between them by its politico-economic prowess and becoming the world's second nuclear nation a few years after the first. US imperatives were based in the peace traditions of liberal capitalism, those of the USSR in socialist traditions, and both developed nuclear arsenals to back them in a balance of power that brought the world to the brink of annihilation. This dichotomy was antithetical to yet formative of renewed multi-pronged approaches to world peace pioneered by the League of Nations in new conditions by new participants, contrasted below.

The term "hot peace" has recently been used to describe the resurgence of using military force to end armed conflicts after the Cold War.[2] As used in here, however, the term refers to individual, social and collective efforts to prevent the Cold War from becoming hot or, in other words, to avoid a nuclear World War Three, which in fact they did. But how did they?

Economic diplomacy was perhaps the primary non-military way for each superpower to attract and retain states into its sphere of influence without giving the other a reason for war. The US Marshall Plan, extending the lend-lease policy of supplying Allies in the Second World War, provided billions of dollars to rebuild Western Europe and stop Soviet advances there. The USSR established a Council for Mutual Economic Assistance (COMECON) to do likewise in Eastern Europe. An early climax of conflicting Cold War economic diplomacies came in 1948, when the USSR blockaded western parts of Berlin; the US airlifted supplies until the blockade was lifted a year later. By the 1950s President Truman's Point Four Program provided know-how, funds and equipment to developing nations worldwide (i.e., so they could develop into aligned countries), forming the grounds of the later US Peace Corps; the COMECON began doing the same. Containment policies for keeping external status quos intact and internal ones inviolable were embodied in the Berlin Wall, built by the USSR in 1961 to stem East-to-West migrations. Yet without the military organizations and technologies to support them it is doubtful the superpowers would have agreed to disagree.

Also originating with the Cold War were the North Atlantic Treaty Organization (NATO) and the Warsaw Pact Organization (WPO). As collective defense alliances based on coordinated armed forces, they politically formed decisive and divisive blocs in the UN, and militarily maintained the balance of power that ultimately checked the superpowers. NATO was created in 1949 by Western European and North American countries to counter threats of Soviet expansion in Europe. In 1955, the USSR and its Eastern European allies created the WPO to counter NATO on similar principles. In accordance with the Truman Doctrine of limiting communism's spread, with force if necessary, NATO considered an attack on one member as an attack against all, as did the WPO. No such attack ever occurred, no armed operation against the other took place, and their drills pushed rather than crossed the precipice. However, unlike NATO, WPO forces were put into action twice in accordance with Premier Brezhnev's Doctrine of keeping Soviet satellite states lockstep with the USSR, with force if necessary. The first was to suppress the Hungarian Revolution (1956), instigated by the USSR's refusal to allow withdrawal from the WPO, turning peaceful protests violent. The second was to suppress Czechoslovakia's liberalization movement (1968). In this case, widespread non-violent resistance to and non-cooperation with WPO forces led to withdrawal, though repressive measures followed. In each case, some WPO members refused to supply troops and Soviet troops were the majority, indicating an effective high-level opposition which NATO members never showed. Ironically, NATO and WPO troops worked together in several UN peacekeeping missions. The WPO was disbanded after the USSR's collapse and its members have since joined NATO, still struggling to redefine its purpose.

As economic diplomacies were backed by these military organizations, the latter were backed by the arms races upon which their success was predicated. Nuclear deterrence, the most costly and potentially deadly war strategy ever practiced, paradoxically was also among the most effective peace strategies ever implemented. As soon as Soviets developed nuclear weapons (1949), they reciprocated the US policy of "massive retaliation" should they attack anywhere outside their sphere. Vacant notions of "first strike" and "second strike" capabilities came into vogue by the 1960s when US Secretary of State Robert McNamara put forth the theory of and put into practice Mutually Assured Destruction (MAD) in a nuclear war scenario, by which each superpower continued to increase first-strike destructive capabilities so as to make a second strike by the other impossible. Based on the premise of an interminable nuclear proliferation, the deterrent in these strategies was their elimination of the possibility of winning a nuclear war for either side because the only possible outcome could be total annihilation. Nuclear deterrence blurred the line between war and peace strategies at great costs but priceless benefits. MADness can be discerned in the development of missiles called "Peacekeepers" capable of carrying a dozen warheads multiple times stronger than the original atomic bomb. Sanity can be discerned in a small group of scientists who, while MADness was in the making, countered that eliminating not multiplying nuclear weapons is the only way to assure peace. In so doing, they propelled later worldwide anti-nuclear movements, turning them and themselves into peacemakers.

Albert Einstein and Leo Szilárd, whose work on particle physics made nuclear weapons feasible, founded the Emergency Committee of Atomic Scientists shortly after the first ones were deployed. Its eight members publicized the total annihilation made possible by nuclear war, drew attention to peaceful purposes for which atomic energy could be used, and promoted world peace as the only guarantee that nuclear weapons are never be deployed again in lectures, radio talks, and popular and academic publications. In four years of existence, the Committee effectively got anti-nuclear movements rolling. In 1955, two anti-nuclear statements were signed by prominent scientists and intellectuals. One was a Manifesto penned by Russell and seconded by Einstein days before he died, in which they and nine other renowned academicians affirmed that because of the advent of nuclear weapons, and to prevent the need for keeping hot peace cold,

> We have to learn to think in a new way. We have to learn to ask ourselves, not what steps can be taken to give military victory to whatever group we

prefer, for there no longer are such steps; the question we have to ask ourselves is: what steps can be taken to prevent a military contest of which the issue must be disastrous to all parties?[3]

Recognizing that doing so "will demand distasteful limitations of national sovereignty," they called on governments to publicly renounce violence and legally commit themselves to peaceful conflict resolution methods, highlighting the role scientists could play. The Manifesto called for a conference of scientists crossing Cold War lines, first held in 1957 at its sponsor's hometown of Pugwash in eastern Canada. The ongoing Pugwash Conferences on Science and World Affairs have informed several UN nuclear-related treaties, have over forty global branches and received the Nobel Peace Prize fifty years after the first deployment of atomic bombs.

Days after the Manifesto, fifty-two renowned scientists met in Mainau, Germany, to sign a Declaration highlighting long-lasting repercussive dangers of nuclear weapons even aside from their destructivity. Acknowledging "perhaps peace is being preserved precisely by the fear of these weapons," they asserted that "all nations must come to the decision to renounce force as a final resort. If they are not prepared to do this, they will cease to exist."[4] The Declaration, widely covered in newspapers and on television worldwide, was a sharp nail in the coffin of nuclear hazard disbelievers. An American chemist, Committee member and signatory of the Manifesto as well as the Declaration, Linus Pauling, went on to publish *No More War!* (1957), in which he described in detail what the Declaration only hinted at, to show that "it is the development of great nuclear weapons that requires that war be given up, for all time. The forces that can destroy the world must not be used."[5] The popularity of the book and the subsequent petition circulated by Pauling, signed by 2000 American scientists, led to the first resolution in the US Congress to halt nuclear testing. Pauling's petition then circulated internationally and, with over 9000 signatures, was presented to the UN in 1958. The scientist-as-peacemaker approach has been adopted by other professional groups, from teachers to lawyers, who use their expertise and influence as weapons against the wars and injustices that make peace impossible.

MADness may have prevented, and scientist sanity steered public opinion against, direct attacks between the two superpowers, but did not prevent "proxy" wars within and between their potential or actual satellite states. The Greek Civil War (1946–49), acid test of this new take on an old kind of conflict, was like others ideologically supported by the visions of world peace the superpowers had to offer: the US, global capitalism based on independent democratic states; the USSR, global communism based on centrally coordinated socialist states. Within proxy states, economic diplomacy and military aid made a bigger difference than ideologies of world peace, though without openly adhering to one neither would have been received. While these ideologies became stale rhetorics of peace and were often sufficient within the superpowers to start proxy wars, they just as often proved insufficient in sustaining them. As costs in lives and resources increased, public support decreased. In the US, for which data is available, 20 percent of people asked in a poll disagreed with the Korean War (1950–53) when it started. When Dwight Eisenhower won the Presidency on a "peace ticket" in 1953, disagreement was up to nearly 40 percent. After negotiations broke down, he threatened nuclear war, and an armistice lasting to this day, but not officially peace, was reached. Public opinion polls not only reflected the civilian disagreement with the war, but also helped change politicians' proxy war into peace policies. A periodic poll started in 1965 shows that 24 percent of respondents believed that sending troops into the Vietnam was a mistake and 64 percent did not. By 1973, when the Paris Peace Accord ending US involvement was signed, these figures had nearly reversed.[6] What MADness and sanity did help do, however, was to prevent hot proxy wars from escalating into direct cold war.

A considerable force in shifting US public opinion was that peace became part of its popular culture and thereby disseminated around the world, which it arguably never had before. In 1965, a consortium of anti-war and pro-peace groups issued a "Declaration of Conscience against the War in Vietnam" signed by 6000 people, in protest at the proxy wars for hot peace, part of which reads:

> We hereby declare our conscientious refusal to cooperate with the U. S. government in the prosecution of the war in Vietnam. . . We shall encourage the development of other nonviolent acts, including acts which involve civil disobedience, in order to stop the flow of American soldiers and munitions to Vietnam.[7]

Boxing champion Muhammad Ali became a conscientious objector on Islamic grounds, for which he lost his title and was banned from the sport for three years. Draft-dodging by leaving the country, declaring an inability to serve or objecting soon reached epidemic proportions. After testifying in Congress, a group of former soldiers returned the war medals they had received and formed Vietnam Veterans Against the War. But it was students who transformed relatively marginal anti-war, pro-peace activism into a nationwide movement, remaking universities into the peace hubs they were in Europe centuries before.

At the University of California, Berkeley, students burned their draft cards, and others across the country began doing the same. Professors and students at the University of Michigan, Ann Arbor, held teach-ins to debate the war and what to do about it, a mixed model combining education and protest that also spread quickly. Within a year after many relatively small campus demonstrations, the first of several large anti-war marches took place in Washington, inspiring similar events around the country and world, including Rome, Paris and London. The largest of these occurred in Washington in 1967, where over 100,000 demonstrators marched from the Lincoln Memorial to the Pentagon, novelized by Norman Mailer in *The Armies of the Night*. The term "flower power" came into vogue after these protesters shot petal canons on the Pentagon. The *New York Review of Books* published linguist Noam Chomsky's "The Responsibility of Intellectuals," in which he critiqued their complacency, shooting him to the forefront of the anti-war movement along with historian Howard Zinn, whose *Vietnam: The Logic of Withdrawal* was a rallying cry. In the course of their collaborative and separate careers as academics as well as peace and social justice activists, Chomsky and Zinn have distinguished between non-violent resistance aimed at stopping violent policies or regimes, and peace-oriented dissent aimed at exposing them as such, having admirably practiced both.

In the late 1960s and early 1970s, many mass protests were held near the Haight Ashbury neighborhood in San Francisco, which became a center of the "hippie" youth movement, today's "baby boomers." Combining anti-war protests with displays of free love (sex without marriage), drug use, drinking and music (mostly folk, rock and jazz), they confirmed that the cause of peace is part of America's purpose, chanting the well-known slogans "make love not war," "draft beer not boys," and "fighting for peace is like fucking for virginity." Bob Dylan's "Blowin' in the Wind" (1963), John Lennon's "Give Peace a Chance" (1969) and "Imagine" (1971), Black Sabbath's "War Pigs" (1970), and Cat Stevens' "Peace Train" (1971) became peace anthems. At concerts and while marching, hippies often held up their middle finger and index in a "V," the sign for Allied victory in the Second World War and now one of peace worldwide. However, hippies' radical stances and demonstrations on several issues at once tended to dilute their anti-war and pro-peace messages and alienate those who did not share their other views. Generations since have yet to make such a concerted call to action, maybe because they have seen their parents back-step, maybe because their governments have stopped giving reasons for hope.

After the end of the Korean War and before Vietnam, the superpowers entered into what is known as a *détente*, from the French for "relaxation," of Cold War political tensions. USSR Premier Nikita Khrushchev and US President John F. Kennedy improved relations, encouraged disarmament and promoted peace initiatives, turning the ongoing arms race into a short race for peace. In 1959, Khrushchev gave a speech at the UN suggesting peace through disarmament, and the next day a Declaration of the Soviet Government on General and Complete Disarmament was filed, which opened the way to an agreement on the use and testing of nuclear weapons in Antarctica. A Disarmament Administration was created within the US Department of State and, with its Soviet counterpart, presented a Joint Statement of Agreed Principles for Disarmament Negotiations, in which they agreed to "multilateral negotiations on disarmament and to call upon other States to cooperate in reaching early agreement on general and complete disarmament in a peaceful world."[8] Kennedy then gave a speech at the UN in which he famously pronounced "Mankind must put an end to war – or war will put an end to mankind."[9] On his suggestion, negotiations resulting in the Treaty Banning Nuclear Weapon Tests began, broken by both sides within years of it taking effect. In 1962, the USSR put forth a plan for UN consideration calling for complete disarmament, and a month later the US presented a rival plan. Close to reaching a final agreement, negotiations were derailed by the Cuban Missile Crisis, ending the détente and halting concerted political efforts towards disarmament.

During these races for and against war, a "space race" was taking place with implications for the history of peace literally beyond this world. The USSR wowed the world with Sputnik, the first earth-orbiting satellite, in 1957. Stunned, the US revamped its space exploration program, and the next year launched the satellite Explorer. When the Soviets sent the first human into orbit (1961), the US pledged to send one to the moon by the decade's end. Several dozen satellites and moon probes later, the Outer Space Treaty (1967) was signed by the US, USSR and other states, prohibiting all weapons in Earth's orbit, their installation on the moon, any other celestial body and in outer space while exclusively limiting the use of outer space for peaceful purposes. In this light, Neil Armstrong's statement as he became the first human to walk on the moon takes on new meaning: "One small step for a man, one giant leap for mankind."[10] Humanity thus established extraterrestrial peace before peace on earth, although it did not last long. Inextricable from the military enterprises of both superpowers, notably in espionage and long-range missiles, competitive space exploration was also a peaceful alternative to the arms race with powerful propaganda value. When tactical nuclear weapons and interception capabilities emerged in the 1970s, the deterrence equation changed. "Acceptable losses" and nuclear weapons falling into the hands of "rogues states" became concerns, inciting President Ronald Reagan's Strategic Defense Initiative (1983) from space, popularly known as Star Wars. New initiatives for extraterrestrial peace such as the International Space Station have since emerged, but the Orwellian motto of the US Strategic Air Command remained "Peace is Our Profession."

Exposing the limits of this professionalized peace, extolling peace as a way of life and its absence as the way to death, were activists who extended and refined organized peace movement strategies and Gandhian Satyagraha tactics, combining them with Pugwash urgency. Towards the end of his presidency, Eisenhower stated that

> the people in the long run are going to do more to promote peace than our government. Indeed, I think that people want peace so much that one of these days government better get out of the way and let them have it.[11]

Anti-nuclear movements since the end of the Second World War make his point clear by pointing to the plain but powerful principle that only by efforts of individuals and groups can peace and the world with it be passed on to future generations because in the atomic age without peace there can be no world and without a world there can be no peace. Ironically, then, the logic that led to the use of atomic weapons to secure victory and peace in the Second World War was the same used to safeguard the world and peace from atomic weapons. With the proliferation of nuclear capabilities, for the first time since the origin of our species, survival of the peaceful applied equally to individuals and groups as to humanity as a whole. Actualizations of this bio-genetic and cultural imperative could not have been accomplished without deterrence and détente, but they would not have taken the forms that they did without two concurrent types of anti-nuclear movements.

One was non-violent direct action, which like the other is explicable by way of examples. In the 1950s Dorothy Day and the Catholic Workers in New York refused to participate in civil defense drills aimed at preparing citizens for nuclear war, which by the logistical impossibility of the task may have simply served to inflame fear. They were popularly demonized for their civil disobedience, but in so being ignited anti-nuclear activists already incited by the scientists-as-peacemakers' informational campaigns. The next year, a pioneering anti-nuclear group as much about individual consciences as collective consciousness was formed by longtime peace activist A. J. Muste, a former Navy Commander turned Quaker named Albert Bigelow and others. Their Committee for Non-Violent Action (CNVA) established the basic patterns of peace activism still in place today, holding non-stop protest vigils and being purposefully arrested for trespassing or obstructing traffic by sit-ins at nuclear-related government facilities across the US. In the 1960s, the CNVA organized two cross-continental Walks for Peace, bringing the issue of nuclear arms reduction door-to-door. A CNVA activist and University of Chicago student founded the Student Peace Union, which became one of the largest groups of its kind. Bigelow's publicity-stunt sea voyage into a nuclear test site in the Pacific inspired another group in to carry out similar stunts, which became Greenpeace, today the largest environmental activist group in the world, and its campaigns later successfully pressured the super-powers to withdraw atomic weapons from their surface ships. Always the nonconformist, Russell started a non-violent direct action group called the Committee of 100, which with their thousands of supporters held disruptive demonstrations at the War Office in London for which many were arrested, ironically, for breaching the peace. The value of non-violent direct action when the forces against which it is immediately addressed are exponentially greater lies more in making a point than making a difference. However, when non-violent direct actions reach critical mass, the point becomes the difference.

Other anti-nuclear activists focused their efforts on nuclear power, as did farmers in West Germany who prostrated before bulldozers to prevent the construction of a nuclear power plant, only to be water-cannoned away by police, but returning with larger numbers secured a judicial ruling against its construction. Similar peaceful obstructions occurred at the construction sites of nuclear power plants in the US. More than a thousand members of the Clamshell Alliance were imprisoned for so protesting in the 1970s, using their captivity to network and train members in new non-violent direct action techniques, such as working in small, autonomous, consensus-based *affinity groups* to respond to confrontations with authorities, reducing risks of mass violence breaking out. Two plants were proscribed by state legislatures when Clams attracted national media attention. The anti-nuclear power Abalone Alliance put forth a Nonviolence Code adopted by many non-violent direct action groups, prescribing openness and friendliness, abstention from physical and verbal violence, respect for property, abstinence from intoxicants while on duty, and a commitment not to flee nor carry weapons of any kind.[12] Christianity also resurged as a focal point for anti-nuclear activity as one US bishop convinced workers at a weapons assembly plant to quit on moral grounds, and another refused to pay half of his income taxes on the grounds that they were being used for war purposes, prompting many others to do the same. Direct action of questionable non-violence broke new grounds in the 1980s, when eight people broke into a Pennsylvania warhead facility, damaged specimens and poured blood over documents. A movie they inspired in turn led to similar *plowshare* action around the world, so-named after a sharp steel wedge used to cut loose top layers of soil. Their destruction of property and dubious intents were condemned by many peace activists, but none of the hundreds of ploughshare actions that have since been taken have been against individuals as they thereby lose their meaning.

The second type of anti-nuclear movement was mass action, the value of which lies in its awareness-raising mobilization and the political influence such mobilization makes for. In 1957, the National Committee for a Sane Nuclear Policy (SANE) was formed by distinguished civil rights, peace and health activists. SANE's provocative anti-nuclear newspaper ads also increased its membership to 25,000 in a year. When a famous talk-show host formed a Hollywood chapter in 1960, celebrities as big as Marilyn Monroe flocked to SANE, the same year it began holding huge anti-nuclear rallies. In a matter of months, Eisenhower offered to stop nuclear testing if the USSR agreed to do the same, and did. An international SANE petition signed by philosophers and artists urged Kennedy to extend the moratorium, which he did. SANE lobbied in its Voter's Peace Pledge Campaign (1966) by sponsoring candidates who committed to peace and with its support the US War Powers Resolution and Act (1973) was passed, limiting presidential war powers without Congress' explicit support. In 1961, a SANE member formed a parallel group also aimed at empowering women, which decided that a single-day strike by women would be a practical way to start, set for November 1. Their slogan, "End the Arms Race, Not the Human Race," soon gained national media attention, along with what has been referred to as their maternity-based appeal, calling on women to assure not only their children's immediate safety, but also that they have a future to be safe in. An estimated 50,000 women participated in the worldwide Women's Strike for Peace. Thereafter, the Un-American Activities Committee, a federal anti-communist body, called Strike leaders in for questioning, sardonically represented by a cartoonist asking whether they were un-American for being women or peace activists. The Clearing House on the Economics of Disarmament was established by them in 1963, which published seminal research. That year, the UN thanked the Strike for the pivotal role it played in the run-up to the Partial Test Ban Treaty. What SANE and the Strike show is that mass action moves the public, policies and before them its participants in the direction of peace.

By this time, the British Campaign for Nuclear Disarmament (CND) had been staging mass action anti-nuclear demonstrations across England for years. The globally recognizable symbol of peace (see the following page) was designed for the CND to use in a protest march against nuclear weapons research. The symbol superimposes the semaphores of "N" and "D," for Nuclear Disarmament: "N" is formed by holding two flags in an upside-down "V" and "D" by holding one flag pointed straight up and the other straight down. After the CND became a general anti-war advocacy group, as it is today, the European Nuclear Disarmament (END) led by E. P. Thompson held yearly international conventions on the topic. "We must protest if we are to survive," he wrote, "Protest is the only realistic form of civil defense."[13] END ended with the Intermediate-Range Nuclear Forces Treaty (1987) between the

US and USSR that removed missiles from the region. Back in the US, the Nuclear Weapons Freeze Campaign was initiated in 1980 by Randall Forsberg, who received her PhD in defense policy from MIT then worked at the Stockholm International Peace Research Institute, the same year she started the Institute for Defense and Disarmament Studies in Cambridge, Massachusetts. The Freeze sought to achieve nuclear arms reductions by ballot initiatives through a network of affiliated grassroots groups, prompting local and states legislatures to pass Freeze resolutions. In 1986, SANE merged with the Freeze, which became Peace Action in 1993, with a much broader mandate and now over 100,000 members worldwide.

A successful synergy of non-violent direct and mass action came in West Germany. Anti-nuclear and environmental activists, united by the belief that a healthy peace is dependent on a healthy world, joined forces to form the world's first Green Party, which gained nearly ten percent of the national vote in 1983 even while carrying non-cooperation campaigns against the government. One of its founders, Petra Kelly, put the Party's mixed methods in this way:

> When we talk of nonviolent opposition, we do not mean opposition to parliamentary democracy. We mean opposition from within parliamentary democracy. Nonviolent opposition in no way diminishes or undermines representative democracy, in fact it strengthens and stabilizes it. It is expressed in all kinds of local groups operating outside parliament, in work councils, and other self-governing bodies. Nonviolent opposition is one way, among others, of forming political opinion within that infrastructure. [14]

As Kelly indicates, the German Green Party's mass action sought to simultaneously change public policy and opinion from both inside and outside government, whereas SANE, the Strike, the CND, END and the Freeze sought to do the same solely from outside. Nonetheless, faced with the Freeze's mass action, Reagan proposed a Strategic Arms Reduction Treaty (START), a two-phased deal between the US and USSR to reciprocally reduce warhead counts. START's final implementation resulted in the removal of 80 percent of nuclear weapons in existence as of 2001. That these anti-nuclear movements took place in only one of the two super-powers' sphere is neither purposeful nor without coincidence, but serves as a sign of the leeway they had compared to people in the other. While it is beyond the scope of this book to compare the actualities of peace within the superpowers and their spheres with their own peace ideals, it is within its range to suggest that in neither did the actualities match the ideals to different degrees.

Just as these anti-nuclear movements attest to how bottom-up approaches to bridging the gap between actualities and ideals could be effective, Mikhail Gorbachev's career (b. 1931) attests to how top-down approaches can be likewise, and maybe even more so. After studying law at Moscow State University, he steadily rose in the Communist Party administration, holding posts ranging from Secretary of Agriculture to Youth Affairs. By the 1970s, he was an integral part of the powerful Communist Party Politburo and was selected by superiors as head dele-gate on diplomatic missions in the early 80s. Upon the death of his pre-decessor, for whom Gorbachev acted as Politburo liaison, he became the Premier of the USSR in 1985. He immediately began implementing reforms under the *glasnost* ("opening") program, making government operations more transparent and lessening restrictions on civil liberties such freedoms of speech and press. He also announced an end to the arms race that had debilitated the Soviet economy and the abolition of nuclear weapons altogether. To this end, he met with Reagan in Geneva in 1985, pointedly asking why new nuclear weapons were being built when old ones never deployed. They met again in Iceland a year later and, for the first time in the Cold War, superpower leaders openly discussed disarma-ment together. Perhaps the Chernobyl nuclear power plant disaster a few months earlier reminded them of what was at stake.

In 1987, Gorbachev published *Perestroika* ("restructuring"), referring to Soviet domestic and foreign affairs. In theoretical terms, he explained: "We want peaceful competition between different social systems to develop unimpeded, to encourage mutually advantageous cooperation rather than confrontation and an arms race."[15] He proposed creating societies that are more peaceful, productive and integrated, not dogmati-cally based on one ideology, but by combining principles with proven results regardless of origin. Practicing Perestroika, he decreased military spending to revitalize the now-more decentralized economy, freed politi-cal prisoners, removed press restrictions, and met again with Reagan to discuss disarmament. Perestroika was admired abroad, but domestic opponents feared the reforms as too rapid or slow. In 1988, he announced that Soviet troops in Afghanistan, fighting there for a decade in a failed attempt to occupy, would be withdrawn. Speaking at the UN at that year's end, he announced further overall reductions in the USSR's standing army, particularly those stationed in Eastern Europe. Peaceful protests against repression in Hungary went undisrupted and led to multi-party elections. The ban on Poland's Solidarity Party was lifted and its leader, Lech Walesa (Nobel Peace Prize, 1984, for keeping worker strikes against Soviet interference non-violent), became President. Gorbachev said that he would not block further reforms; other Eastern European and Central Asian countries followed suit. Revolutionary violence occurred, but as an exception not the rule. The dramatic destruction of the Berlin Wall in 1989, which for many worldwide symbolized the Cold War, signaled the beginning of its end. But the superpower dichotomy that changed what peace meant by changing how it could be made and maintained had always competed with another paradigm it also framed that, after the end of the Cold War and its hot peace, remains.

One World, Many Peaces

The "one world" paradigm, a combination of ideology and global geography, was first actualized with the extension of colonialism into imperialism. At that time, nation-states and religion, backed by zero-sum mercantilism, were driving forces behind conflicts aimed at control of land, labor and resources worldwide. As a result, and as for the Romans in antiquity in more limited geographical and ideological senses, the sole way for one world to be and stay at peace was by the unquestioned domination of one peace on the basis of a nation-state, an empire and an economy. These confluences were a recipe for disaster from the start because they attempted to make compulsory for many groups the peace of one, a misconstrual of social as collective peace that, in effect, made "one world, one peace" impossible. The world wars made this recipe into a two-course meal, and the Cold War was its desserts, but did not change the fact that it was poisonous to begin with. Some peacemakers tried to make themselves antidotes or digestive aids, others into emetics, and they succeeded as such to the extents of one world, one peace allowed. Only during the Cold War did they collectively cook a new recipe with old ingredients, and in so doing put forth a paradigm along Ancient Eastern harmonic lines: one world, many peaces.

Still directly related to the Cold War but in stark contrast to its primary multinational military organizations, NATO and the WPO, was the explicitly peace-oriented Non-Aligned Movement (NAM) of states. The term "Third World," based on parallels with the French Third Estate, became a broad term referring to all developing nations not part of the first two, US or Soviet, "worlds." In affirming that this other world existed, the NAM also affirmed that another paradigm for peace did too. The NAM's origins are sometimes traced to a series of agreements reached between India and China in 1954, aimed at easing tensions between them after China's occupation of Tibet. Hoping to avoid conflict that would cripple the two new countries' development, their leaders adopted a policy of Panchsheel, Five Principles: 1. Mutual respect for territory; 2. Mutual non-aggression; 3. Mutual non-interference; 4. Mutual equality and benefits; ultimately, 5. Peaceful coexistence.[16] More than containment, less than complete cooperation and conflict resolution, this bilateral agreement was formative of a multinational movement that proposed collectivity as a basis of world peace.

In 1955, an historic conference of newly independent African and Asian countries was held in Bandung, Indonesia, to promote economic and cultural cooperation and affirm opposition to the old European colonialism and any new colonialism by the superpowers. Six years later, the NAM as an organization was established on principles similar to Panchscheel at a summit in Belgrade, led by Tito of Yugoslavia, Jawaharlal Nehru of India and Gamal Nasser of Egypt. African, Asian and Latin American leaders agreed their countries would cooperate in exerting political pressure to ease Cold War tensions and stimulate economic development. The NAM did not and could not reflect socio-political systems of its members because they were heterogenous, defining its novel collective approach to world peace but also allowing its membership to include oppressive states under military regimes in no way internally peaceful. Soon forming a majority in the UN Assembly and representing a majority of the world's population, NAM countries proposed and passed resolutions calling for the independence of all remaining colonies and declared the 1960s a "decade of development" to be backed by global financial institutions such as the International Monetary Fund and the World Bank, in theory not practice free from Cold War motives. As it became clearer that increasing numbers of supposedly non-aligned states were now superpower satellites, and disparities between quickly and slower-developing nations became evermore acute, the Bandung's spirit of collective unity dissipated. By highlighting the possible benefits of one world, many peaces, the NAM also underscored its challenges.

Disputes arose at NAM summits and a splinter group of 77 states, the G-77, was formed to pursue limited, definite economic aims, such as fixed commodities prices to boost economies of developing nations, but its result disappointed. A G-7 of developed states created a counterorganization whose aims were similarly one-sided. Another NAM offshoot, the Organization of Petroleum Exporting Countries (OPEC), tried using the growing reliance of developed nations on oil to influence world affairs in favor of developing nations. Culminating collective efforts was a UN proposal for a New International Economic Order in which NAM nations would play greater global and regional roles. A resolution to this effect was passed in the Assembly, but in response the US refused to pay its UN dues and the resolution was unimplemented. By the late 1980s, the paradigm of harmonized, coordinated development the NAM had originally offered as an alternative to discordant Cold War militarism had become polarized on a hemispheric North–South line, along which debts due to developed from less developed countries turned into instruments of control. What the NAM and its offshoots achieved, if indirectly, was heightened competition between developed nations for the benefits the markets and products developing nations had to offer, though with little concern with welfares of their populations. Within NAM nations, this competition tended to amplify rather than overcome structural violence and all but ended the use of violence between some of them.

If the NAM, NATO and the WPO were stages upon which their underlying paradigms of world peace played out, the UN was the theater. Formed a year after the Second World War at a conference in San Francisco, its purpose was essentially to prevent a Third, and by this standard it has so far triumphed, though it did not do so on its own. It could not do so by its design coupled with the Cold War conditions in which it was born and raised, only one of which has changed. The unequivocal terms of the UN Charter's preamble outlines its goals:

> to unite our strength to maintain international peace and security, and to ensure, by the acceptance of principles and the institution of methods, that armed force shall not be used, save in the common interest, and to employ international machinery for the promotion of the economic and social advancement of all peoples.[17]

How the UN surpassed the League of Nations and made many contributions to world peace becoming more of an actuality is explored below. But its victories and losses in peacemaking may make more sense by first explaining three of its inherent limitations, easily distinguishable from its problems then and now. For example, problems during the UN's formation included the roles of regional organizations, and it was agreed that they could be agents of settlements and enforcements. Another was the status of treaties of outside origin, and it was agreed that they could be registered with, ratified and amended through the UN. Still another was the jurisdiction of the International Court of Justice, and it was agreed that it would be voluntary but only on a compulsory basis. In contrast to these problems the UN's limitations were also extensively debated but inadequately resolved because they have added to difficulties of completing its intrinsically difficult missions.

One limitation the UN shares with its defunct predecessor is a self-inflicted inability to take independent action from its member nation-states, stemming from a self-perpetuating total dependence on the wills of and support from them. Of course, this limitation was a practical impracticality since there were no other wills and support to depend on since this was, after all, a United Nations, but it was also an outgrowth of longstanding principle. A second limitation of the UN it shares with the Westphalian System is the inviolability of state sovereignty, to the point that historically nearly no violation of peace of any kind within states has been reason enough for the UN to intervene without governments' permission, even when governments are responsible for the violations. The rock and a hard place between which this limitation puts the UN is understandable, as doing so would call into question the basis upon which its members exist and therefore its own existence, a position perhaps impossible to get out of. The third and last limitation to be mentioned here is the veto powers of the "Big Five" permanent members of the UN Security Council, the US, Britain, France, Russia and China, also the largest arms-producing nations in the world. The most contentious issue by far in San Francisco, delegates from the other countries contended, was that veto power would render the Security Council powerless if one of its members became a menace to peace and that they could act in their own interests regarding matters between non-Big Five nations. The Big Five gave other nations two choices: either accept the veto or forsake the UN. They chose the former, and within years their prescient nightmare came true within their magnanimous dream.

The Security Council was designed to be the UN's primary decision-making body with regards to the preservation of international peace. Composed of the Big Five permanent members and six temporary members elected by the General Assembly on an equitable regional basis for two-year terms (increased to ten in 1965), non-member nations may also participate in Council discussions affecting them upon its request but may not vote. The Council is continuously in session and one of its members' delegates must be present at UN headquarters in New York at all times in case of emergency, measures aimed at improving the League of Nations' slow response time. Article 33 of the Charter, dealing with "Pacific Settlement of Disputes," states

> The parties to any dispute, the continuance of which is likely to endanger the maintenance of international peace and security, shall, first of all, seek a solution by negotiation, enquiry, mediation, conciliation, arbitration, judicial settlement, resort to regional agencies or arrangements, or other peaceful means of their own choice.[18]

If a member nation fails to comply with this or other peace-preserving provisions, the Council is empowered to investigate the infringement, make recommendations, and to enforce political and economic sanctions or use voluntary member-state force to uphold the Charter. By the letter, then, world peace was to be maintained one conflict resolution at a time.

The Council passes Resolutions in two ways. In cases of disputes between nations, any nine votes of the Council suffice; where peace has been breached or is threatened, the nine votes must include those of the Big Five. The latter mechanism embodies the Big Five veto, which has often prevented peace-related Resolutions from being passed, as when France and the UK vetoed measures to resolve the Suez Crisis (1956). Since the Council's inception, the veto has been used five times by China, 18 by France, 32 by the UK, 81 by the US and 122 by the USSR/Russia. Reasons have ranged from blocking admission of new member states to the UN to refusing to issue statements against aggressors based on politico-economic interests. During the Eastern European revolts against Soviet rule in the 1950s and 60s and wars for independence in Northern Africa in the 1960s, the Big Five sometimes based their vetoes on the Charter's clause stating that the Council may not intervene in internal affairs of member states. In other cases, the Council has decided to intervene in the internal affairs of countries to promote intra-national peace upon their request as during the Greek Civil War, and has imposed sanctions aimed at the removal of structurally violent intra-national policies, as against apartheid in South Africa. However, abstentions have not always been considered vetoes, as when the Council went ahead with its planned operations in Korea, led by American armed forces, even though the USSR was then boycotting the Council. Yet despite Cold War frictions, the UN did achieve a number of its peace-oriented objectives when the Council failed, thanks to the Assembly.

The Assembly, in which all member states are represented, was intended as a deliberative and advisory body, but like the office of the Secretary General it soon developed the capability to circumvent Council deadlocks through its agencies. For example, in 1950 the Assembly passed a Uniting for Peace Resolution asserting that it may take action on peace-threatening issues if the Council is veto-paralyzed. Thus, although Britain and France used vetoes in the Suez Crisis, they heeded Assembly calls for cease-fires and troop withdrawals. Pursuant to the Charter, it may discuss and make recommendations on peace, security and UN operations issues except if they are not under Council consideration, then only upon its request. In 1948, a committee headed by Eleanor Roosevelt presented a Universal Declaration of Human Rights asserting "the inherent dignity and the equal and inalienable rights of all members of the human family is the foundation of freedom, justice and peace in the world," passed unanimously by the Assembly.[19] Today comprising 192 voting members and non-voting observer non-governmental organizations in a wide variety of fields, aside from the unparallel international forum it provides, the Assembly has also initiated studies and sponsored agencies on human rights, economic, political, education or health issues affecting its member states, vastly improving on the multi-pronged approach to world peace pioneered by the League of Nations, beginning with disarmament. One world, many peaces were thus also to be achieved by simultaneously actualizing each of their components.

The Assembly's first resolution dealt with atomic power, not yet used when the UN was formed, creating the Atomic Energy Commission to abolish atomic weapons, which it has not, and to ensure that atomic energy would be used only for peaceful purposes, which it has. A year later the Assembly further resolved to regulate to reduce all weapons, for which the Security Council convened the Commission for Conventional Armaments. Within five years, all the Big Five except China had growing nuclear arsenals, and China would a decade later, and it became evident that the two Commissions' proposals were being systematically rejected along Cold War lines. So in 1952, the Commissions were united in a comprehensive Disarmament Commission of five USSR-aligned, five US-aligned and eight non-aligned nations charged with drafting mutually acceptable treaties for monitoring, controlling and eventually eliminating all militaries. Significant progress towards disarmament was made in treaties of which numbers of signatories continue to increase, generally along with the size of their militaries. At the Assembly's First Special Session on Disarmament in 1978, the Disarmament Commission increased to forty members and a periodic Conference on Disarmament was initiated. The Special Session produced a Final Document consisting of a Declaration of Principles, a Program of Action, and Machinery for Disarmament, guiding lights of contemporary demilitarization efforts. With the Final Document, every UN member state became part of the Disarmament Commission as an advisory body, and the Conference became the single multilateral negotiating forum on the issue.

While delegates in San Francisco openly approved of disarmament, most were just as openly opposed to granting the UN legislative powers to enact or enforce international laws, putting it in binds, because they would impinge on state sovereignty. Instead, the Charter allows the Assembly to initiate studies and make recommendations for "encouraging the progressive development of international law and its codification" without the power to enact or enforce them.[20] The International Law Commission (ILC) was created in 1947, which unlike many other UN bodies is composed exclusively of field experts, not necessarily Assembly delegates. As the International Military Tribunals at Tokyo and Nuremberg headed by Allied jurists prosecuting Axis officials were winding down, the ILC published its Principles of International Law based on their charters. In them were legally defined in detail for the first time in history:

> **Crimes against peace:** i. Planning, preparation, initiation or waging of a war of aggression or a war in violation of international treaties, agreements or assurances; ii. Participation in a common plan or conspiracy for the accomplishment of any of the acts mentioned under (i); and
>
> **War crimes:** Violations of the laws or customs of war which include, but are not limited to, murder, ill-treatment or deportation to slave-labor or for any other purpose of civilian population of or in occupied territory, murder or ill-treatment of prisoners of war or persons on the seas, killing of hostages, plunder of public or private property, wanton destruction of cities, towns, or villages, devastation not justified by military necessity.

The ILCs takes progressive development mandate to mean "the preparation of draft conventions on subjects which have not yet been regulated by international law or in regard to which the law has not yet been sufficiently developed in the practice of States."[21] Its mandate of codification is taken as "the more precise formulation and systematization of rules of international law in fields where there already has been extensive State practice, precedent and doctrine." Within these frameworks, the ILC has produced an extensive body of research. But the Assembly's inability to enact or enforce their findings or recommendations is, to stress the point, among the primary weaknesses the UN has inherited from the League of Nations, which no longer exists.

Post-conflict peacekeeping is, in contrast, an area in which the UN greatly surpassed the League, but again only when the Council and Assembly have taken concerted decisions and the conflicting parties have agreed to cooperate. Since 1945, over sixty missions have been carried out by the UN's peacekeeping forces, recognizable by their light blue helmets, which have also negotiated 172 conflict-ending settlements. But a distinction must be made between diplomatic peacemaking that must be well underway before peacekeeping forces under UN command can be deployed. In other words, without a peace treaty or other accord already in place, there is no peace for the UN to keep, which is why peacemaking always precedes peacekeeping. Early UN operations make this distinction clear and intimate how the organization works. Days after Japan's defeat in the Second World War, Indonesia declared independence from its wartime occupiers only to see its pre-War colonizer, the Dutch, attempt to regain control. Two years into war, the conflict was brought to the Council, which called on them to end hostilities and enter arbitration. They agreed and an international Consular Commission of diplomatic observers from six neutral states was sent to monitor the peace that had thus been made. Fighting resumed a year later, so the Council replayed its peacemaking role by arranging another ceasefire. With only sixty-three "military observers" working at any one time, neutral zones between the conflicting forces were defined and implemented, and supervised troop withdrawals were complete in months.

This first, unofficial UN peacekeeping operation demonstrated limits and potentials of post-conflict intervention. It and many other post-Second World War conflicts originated with imperialism, as does one of many peaces that have yet to be fully kept. After the Second World War, Palestine and its rapidly growing Jewish population were still a British colony. On Britain's request, the UN created a committee to review and make recommendations on decolonization, which proposed partitioning the territory into two states, one Arab and one Jewish, with Jerusalem as an international city. Despite fierce protests, the Assembly voted the plan into effect and by 1948 civil war between Palestinian Jews and Arabs was raging. On the day Britain announced its withdrawal, Israel declared independence. In less than a week, the civil war escalated into an international conflict. Several UN ceasefire calls went unanswered and a truce was finally reached. To oversee its implementation the Council created the UN Truce Supervision Organization (UNTSO), the first official UN peacekeeping operation. Showing initial promise, UNTSO kept the peace but only for a month due to support constraints and the unwillingness of the parties to cooperate. After a week more of fighting, a second truce was reached as talks for a new peace plan began. When the UN mediator was assassinated by Jewish radicals in September, negotiations fell through, and war resumed by October. In December, the Assembly formed the UN Conciliation Commission for Palestine, which facilitated Armistice Agreements (1949) between Israel and Egypt, Lebanon, Jordan and Syria, respectively. The Commission also held a conference that formally ended this Arab–Israeli War, though no final territorial agreement was reached. The ongoing conflicts in the region, still monitored by UNTSO, can be traced back to these events.

The fact that this UN peacekeeping mission is also its longest-running testifies to the determination of the early organization to overcome the impotence of the League of Nations and its ongoing commitment to seeing them through. The fact that the conflict has yet to be resolved makes evident the magnitude of the problems the UN is willing to tackle. The UN now recognizes UNTSO as its first peacekeeping operation, but the term "peacekeeping" as an umbrella term also covering peacemaking and peace-enforcement only gained currency after the Suez Canal Crisis. In 1954, the US and the Britain withheld funds for a Nile dam when Egypt bought arms from Soviet satellites. In retaliation and need of revenue, Egypt nationalized the Canal halfway into 1956, and England, France and

Israel invaded. The US sponsored a Council resolution calling for a cease-fire. Britain and France vetoed, and the US brought the matter to the Assembly. Under a Uniting for Peace measure, the Assembly called a ceasefire, successfully negotiated by Canadian foreign minister and later Prime Minister Lester B. Pearson. He proposed a UN Emergency Force (UNEF) to secure the ceasefire, supervise troop withdrawals and patrol buffer zones along armistice lines, which became a model for future UN post-conflict operations. For this proposal, Pearson is considered the father of modern peacekeeping, which still seeks to secure one world, many peaces one peace at a time.

However, it was UN Secretary General Doug Hammarskjöld who, acting on Pearson's proposal, defined the roles, responsibilities and structure of UNEF and was its chief executive. Egypt accepted UNEF in its territory, Israel did not. At its peak, over 6,000 UNEF peacekeepers from ten neutral countries were on the ground. Within months of UNEF's deployment, all foreign troops had left Egypt, and buffer zones were secure. The first victory for the so-called "soldiers of peace" lasted ten years, when Egypt's request for their withdrawal, in preparation for an attack on Israel, was granted. Following the quick though temporary successes of UNEF, the UN carried out several other peacekeeping operations on the same basic premises, with varying objectives tailored to the conditions and participants, including: the UN Observation Group in Lebanon (1958), the UN Operation in the Congo (1960–64), UN Security Force in West New Guinea (1962–63), UN Yemen Observation Mission (1963–64), the Second UN Emergency Force (1973–79) along the Israeli–Egyptian border, UN Disengagement Observer Force (1974–Present) along the Israeli–Syrian border, and the UN Interim Force in Lebanon (UNIFIL, 1978–Present). UN peacekeeping forces were awarded the Nobel Peace Prize in 1988, which they certainly deserve. But as this summary list of UN peacekeeping operations shows, while UN post-conflict interventions have on the whole been effective, they are limited by the UN's peacemaking efforts which are in turn limited by its inability to take independent action from its member-states, making the success of post-conflict interventions dependent upon their often fickle wills, those of the parties involved and Big Five consent. In the end, the merits and defects of the UN with regards to world peace stems from its aspiration to and partial actualization of a world government on the nation-state model and system of its members.

The UN makes clear that one world, many peaces requires international cooperation as long nation-states exist. Social justice movements, generally holding that isonomic laws only work within isonomic socio-economic systems, likewise make clear that one world, one peace also requires intra-national transformation as long as discrimination exists.

Two of many social justice movements have had particularly profound but polarizing influences on how non-violence is now perceived. On the one hand, social justice movements like that for civil rights in the US show that non-violence is not only the way for them to succeed, but that the absence of non-violence could lead to their non-existence. Martin Luther King, Jr. (1929–68), a theology student from the US State of Georgia, heard A. J. Muste speak about Gandhian Satyagraha and how its methods had been successfully applied to challenge and change discriminatory laws on local and national levels. King, already leaning in this direction since reading Thoreau and Tolstoy, was enthralled with the possibilities and results transformative non-violence like civil disobedience and non-cooperation had to offer to the ongoing US civil rights movement.

After receiving his doctorate, King joined a Baptist church in Montgomery, Alabama, as preacher and became involved with the National Association for the Advancement of Colored People (NAACP), the country's largest civil rights group. There, in 1955, Rosa Parks refused to give up her seat on the bus to a white man and was arrested. King helped organize a bus boycott that drew national media attention. When his house was bombed he prevented a riot by convincing an angry crowd not to give in to hate. A year later, with the boycott ongoing, the Supreme Court declared the state's separate but equal policies, by definition not isonomic, unconstitutional and they were lifted. Reflecting on the bus boycott in *Stride Toward Freedom* (1958), in which he advocated trans-formative non-violence as a platform for civil rights movements world-wide, King wrote "True peace is not merely the absence of tension; it is the presence of justice. . . Today the choice is no longer between violence and nonviolence. It is either non-violence or non-existence."[22] He then formed the Southern Christian Leadership Conference, which sponsored a Student Nonviolent Coordinating Committee, and together with the NAACP they organized civil disobedience campaigns throughout the country. Soon after extending the transformative non-violence civil rights platform to end poverty and war, he was assassinated.

On the other hand, social justice movements like that against apartheid in South Africa show that non-violence has its limits. After a university dismissal for protesting against its racial policies, Nelson Mandela (b. 1918) committed himself to the cause of the African National Congress (ANC), which was to present a united front against racial discrimination. He helped launch the ANC's Youth League in 1944 to mobilize next-generation activists and in two years was an executive of the ANC itself. At the time, Mandela was for a non-violent approach to change towards social justice through boycotts and non-cooperation campaigns and against non-black ANC membership; he would reverse both of his posi-tions in the coming years. The openly white supremacist National Party began enacting apartheid laws prohibiting permanent residency in cities to non-whites, forcing them to set up outskirt shanty towns, and outlawing mixed marriages and sexual relations. At this point, Mandela adopted a multi-racial ANC membership position. The ANC worked with the Indian National Congress Gandhi had founded and other non-black groups in a general strike on May 1, 1950, after which the National Party made protests of state policies illegal under pretexts of suppressing communism, an excuse which with the Cold War had become a common practice within the Capitalist bloc.

The ANC then began a Defiance Campaign, including civil disobedience such as black use of white-only facilities and remaining in cities permanently, which led to the imprisonment of ANC leaders but also the quintupling of its membership. But the Campaign only triggered further suppressive and discriminatory laws, so Mandela founded a support group to aid those arrested in the anti-apartheid movement. The NAM was by this time not only speaking out against apartheid, but advising its members not to trade or maintain political relations with South Africa. The UN soon did the same. In 1953, a Freedom Charter was issued by a coalition of South African civil rights groups including the ANC, declaring "people have been robbed of their birthright to land, liberty and peace by a form of government founded on injustice and inequality."[23] Officials responded by arresting Congress members; mass protest marches, sit-ins and boycotts were carried out but to no avail. The ongoing ineffectiveness of non-violence in bringing about social justice led some ANC members to consider using violence, including Mandela. The ANC was banned by the National Party government, though it continued to work underground. Mandela was arrested, tried for what he intended as a ploughshare but became an act of sabotage in which one person was killed, and sentenced to life imprisonment in 1964.

Two decades later, yearly deaths from riots and police attacks had risen to the thousands, and still-imprisoned Mandela emerged as the most likely candidate to provide peaceful solutions. The Minister of Justice held talks with him and he referred a Commonwealth delegation to the ANC president, proposing that the road to negotiations lay in the apartheid state removing their armed forces so that the anti-apartheid movement could renounce violence. Amidst ongoing violence, talks continued for another five years. In 1990, National Party leader F.W. de Klerk announced that bans on the ANC and other organizations was lifted, and Mandela would be released. Talks to form a new government began almost immediately. Mandela traveled the country to resolve conflicts between rival anti-apartheid groups, and went on international tours to speak with heads of state to ask them to continue or start sanctions on South Africa. In 1993 South Africa held its first free elections: the ANC won a majority with Mandela as its President. A Truth and Reconciliation Commission addressed the human rights violations that had occurred during the apartheid. Longtime activist and priest Desmond Tutu chaired the Commission, which with few exceptions granted amnesty in exchange for full confessions. Recapping his experiences in the anti-apartheid movement and, coincidentally, one of many invaluable lessons to be drawn from the history of peace in the twentieth-century, Tutu wrote: "Even after the agreements are signed, peacemaking is never finished. Peace is not a goal to be reached but a way of life."[24]

11
The Presents of Peace

Globalization: Peace at the End of History

Where have five millennia of peace history brought us? In a controversial essay entitled "The End of History?" published in 1989, American political scientist Francis Fukuyama stated:

> What we may be witnessing is not just the end of the Cold War, or the passing of a particular period of post-war history, but the end of history as such: that is, the end point of mankind's ideological evolution and the universalization of Western liberal democracy as the final form of human government.[1]

He also noted "the fact that 'peace' seems to be breaking out in many regions of the world," but his lack of qualification of the quotation-marked term highlights his hesitation. His argument, that Marx's view of history as an ideological and actual class struggle leading inevitably towards war and peace has been superseded went far from unchallenged. French philosopher Jacques Derrida derided the idea, declaring "it must be cried out, at a time when some have the audacity to neo-evangelize in the name of the ideal of a liberal democracy that has finally realized itself as the ideal of human history: never have violence, inequality, exclusion, famine, and economic oppression affected as many human beings in the history of the earth and of humanity."[2] These provocative, antithetical perspectives are fruitful starting points for assessing both the presents the world history of peace has bequeathed upon humanity and aspects of its historical presents. What Fukuyama called the universalization of liberalism and Derrida a neo-evangelization in its name has, in a broader sense, been widely and no less contentiously discussed under the rubric of *globalization* – which by one of many definitions is "not something new," but rather and more significantly "a deepening of the extent to which relations transcending geographical borders are now possible; the increased speed with which such relations are now taking place; and the consequences of such intensification of relations on political, economic and social levels."[3] The questions to be briefly raised here are to what extent has the current stage of globalization, in the process, deepened, increased and intensified peace and peacemaking or not.

Politically, globalization has in fact increased the rate of democratization in former leftist and rightist autocratic regimes, which many scholars and activists see as giving rise to a worldwide "democratic peace."[4] While what the term means is debated, in general it refers to the notion that outright and structural as well as internal and external violence associated with autocracies diminishes after they become representative democracies. For example, once rife with domestic and regional strife during the 1970s and 80s, fermented by the US and USSR through what the US Navy called low-level "violent peace," since their autocrats have been removed, military spending for use inside and outside the country as percentage of gross domestic product declined from 8.4 percent in 1989 to 1.3 percent in 1996 in Honduras and from 28.3 percent to 1.5 percent in Nicaragua.[5] Critics, especially of the post-colonial persuasion, point to the plight of large numbers of disempowered individuals and groups they call subalterns who are still voiceless and suffer structural violence in all representative democracies today. Holding fast to non-violent principles of participatory democracy, they contend, can subvert existing socio-political boundaries and make the best of what globalization can do politically, or at least limit the worst economically.

From its supporters' perspective, globalism has also made capitalism the most plausible solution to reduce, stop and prevent strife within states through development or modernization, and war between them along the lines discussed in Chapter 8, other than or in addition to democratization. Some take this argument to the point where the nation-state system itself may become obsolete. Thomas Friedman put forth the wry propositions that no two states with a McDonalds franchise have ever gone to war with another, and no two states part of a major global supply chain such as Dell computers ever will.[6] The basis of the first proposition is that higher standards of living, somehow equated with fast food chains, decrease national appetites for war; the basis of the second is that the economic, particularly labor, benefits tied to being part of a major global supply chain vastly outweigh the risks of jeopardizing them by engaging in war. In other words, peace is seen as both "a requisite for successful establishment of global capitalism" and as "a free-enterprise system serving buyers and sellers through market signals" that "cannot withstand the pervasive intervention of government in wartime."[7] One world, many peaces then is to be achieved one economic market at a time.

Much of anti-globalist discourse and action is dominated by the equation "modernization = Westernization = capitalism = globalization = imperialism."[8] In this view, globalization is not a solution to contemporary problems of peace, but the problem itself, because of the

> power of the rich world's governments and their appointed institutions (the IMF, the World Bank, the World Trade Organization) to wage economic warfare and the power of the same governments, working through a different set of institutions (the UN security council, NATO) to send in the Bombers. . . the grotesque maldistribution of power which permits a few national governments to assert a global mandate.[9]

At one end of the spectrum, anti-globalists have countered globalism with localism: practices that lead to autonomy and peace along the lines of Proudhon's mutualism. At the other end, the massive polycentric and open conferences of the World Social Forum (WSF) aims, as its "Call of Social Movements" states, at "Resistance to Neoliberalism, War and Militarism: For Peace and Social Justice."[10] First held in 2001 in Porto Alegre, Brazil, as a counter to the World Economic Forum, the WSF has grown into several yearly events around the globe attended by hundreds of thousands of activists. The term subaltern cosmopolitanism has been used to describe these diverse, non-violent, counter-hegemonic movements that seek to build upon differences rather than erase them, and challenge instead of accept the status quo.

Taking a long retrospective view on a smaller scale, parallels to today's globalization can be drawn with the eras of Romanization, Sinicization and Arabization that occurred on regional levels. In this case the transformation is generally seen as an Americanization, even if multi-way flows of cultural commodities and practices are ongoing. Taking a shorter view on a similar scale, the domination of the US in world politics and economics – despite its slips in the new millennium – is comparable to Britain's in the imperial era. The periods in and/or after which these hegemonies occurred have, worthy or not, been associated with a "Pax," and resistances to them have been violent and non-violent, effective or not. Although debates have already started, historians of the future will be in better positions to judge whether globalization does or does not correspond to a Pax Americana. But what can be painted in broad and preliminary strokes is what world peace may look like for its supporters and critics as of 2009 (see the table on the following page).

With the Fukuyama–Derrida polemic and the facts behind them still unsettled, in 1993 Samuel Huntington put forth another theory that roiled academics and activists and has since been a major influence on the

Globalization and Alter-Globalization Perspectives on World Peace

Issue	Globalization	Alter-Globalization
Domestic Economy:	Equal Opportunity	Equal Distribution
Domestic Politics:	Democracy	Socialist Democracy
	Limited Government	Interventionist Government
Global Economy:	Competitive Free Trade	Cooperative and
	Economic Aid	Coordinated Development
Global Politics:	Absolute State Sovereignty	Social Justice in/for all States
Role of Global Bodies:	Supervisory:	Enforcement:
	Promote Free Trade	Protect Rich From Poor
	Monitor Human Rights	Ensure Human Rights
Role of Regional Bodies:	Forum for Discussion	Decision-Making Forum
	Formulation of Policy	Implementation of Policy
Globalization in History:	End and Ideal of History	Stage in History as Step in the Wrong/Right Direction

rhetoric, if not the thinking, of foreign policymakers: "The great divisions among humankind and the dominating source of conflict will be cultural. . . The clash of civilizations will dominate global politics. The fault lines between civilizations will be the battle lines of the future."[11] Globalization's reformation of proximity is, in Huntington's view, neither a benevolent opportunity for economic cooperation nor a hostile one for ideological expansion, but simply a predestined source of friction. The implication is that cultural groups must guard against both internal and external enemies, not only those who threaten their interests, but also those who just do not belong. Anyone who is not one of "us" is transformed from a potential into an actual threat to "our" peace. Two possible endgames of this clash-of-civilization theory are: one culture subsumes or supplants all others, or cultures somehow manage to peacefully coexist. In the first case, conflict is inevitable unless cultural groups cave in of their own volition, and even if it were accomplished non-violently, it is in no way "a formula for peace, as throughout history some of the most vicious wars have taken place within civilizations."[12] For how the second case can happen and be sustained, other schools of thought must be sought.

A perspective poles apart in respect to peace prospects comes from the famed Frankfurt School of critical theory. "Peace," wrote Theodor Adorno during the Cold War, "is the state of differentiation without domination, with the differentiated participating in each other," which within the context of our discussion means that it is both possible and necessary for cultures to peacefully coexist and interact with one another.[13] Taking this line of thought leaps further and making it more concrete, Jürgen

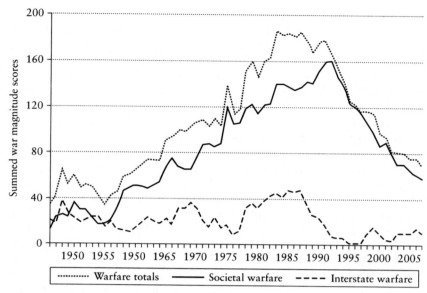

Global Trends in Armed Conflict, 1946–2006

Habermas has proposed that collaborative identities conducive to peace during globalization can, are and must be created within what he calls a "post-national" framework. Over a decade before Huntington put forth his hypothesis, Habermas wrote that "new conflicts no longer arise in areas of material reproduction. . . new conflicts arise in areas of cultural reproduction, social integration, and socialization."[14] While conflicts over energy and water resources call their common view into question, where Habermas departs from Huntington in his post-Cold War theory is that he sees the dynamics of negotiating systems for democratic national and regional international institutions (such as the European and African Unions) and non-governmental bodies (such as professional associations and not-for-profit humanitarian organizations) as being inherently able to prevent, resolve or make obsolete violence of any kind through ongoing critical dialogue. But have they?

Monty Marshall and his colleagues at the Center for Systemic Peace have been conducting quantitative-qualitative studies with some startling, some reinforcing and some inspiring results. Using extensive data from 126 countries, they have found that since 1991, the levels of both intra- and international warfare have declined dramatically, falling from their peaks at the end of the Cold War by over 60 percent, as the graph shows above. According to their studies, one in every three countries was engaged in armed conflict in 1991, dropping to less than 15 percent in 2006.[15] In terms of the onset of new warfare, intra-national conflicts have outnumbered international ones in the same period, fluctuating between one and thirteen. Rates of intra-national onsets are near unchanged, while international rates have been cut in half. As of 2007, 24 states are directly affected by ongoing wars, half of which have lasted more than ten years. The three longest are Myanamr (60 years), India (56) and Israel (43). The studies also show that while poor*er* countries are more likely to be at war, the highest levels of warfare are not in the poor*est* countries, but those in the quintile just above because they have more means to engage in it. The researchers also note that the increase in displaced persons since the onset of the Cold War is due to the inability of countries in protracted wars to meet basic needs and a breakdown in distinction between combatants and civilians. However, one could add that in countries like the US, being *at* war is experientially dissociated from being *in* war for the vast majority of its residents, who are thereby made more complacent.

Another study, the Global Peace Index by the British financial journal *The Economist*'s Intelligence Unit and a large international team of peace researchers and statisticians, is the first to rank countries worldwide according to their peacefulness and its drivers. Using data from 121 states, the Index considers both internal factors such as crime, homicide and imprisonment rates and respect for human rights, and external ones such as arms sales and production and troop deployment. Norway, New Zealand, Denmrk, Ireland and Japan are the top five most peaceful states according to the study; Nigeria, Russia, Israel, Sudan and Iraq are at the bottom. Striking features are that both Japan and Russia are in the G-8, and that states with unquestionable twentieth-century war credentials like Ireland and Germany are near the top of the list. The US ranks 96th – just above Iran. The Index found that peace is correlated to high levels of incomes, schooling, regional integration and government transparency. Its President says the aim is to provide a "quantitative measure of peacefulness that is comparable over time," hoping it "will inspire and influence world leaders and governments to further action."[16] What the Index depicts but does not sufficiently account for are violence, peace and peace-making internal to new and established states that have been the result or cause of democratic-capitalist systems. Three emerging areas of peace research and practice that do are the management and resolution of ethnic, secessionist and post-autocratic conflicts, which are in most cases intertwined, but can be split for heuristic purposes and to expose a lack of foresight that has cost millions of lives.

While some academics have gone so far as to call battles on the scale of the world wars things of the past, few disagree that small-scale armed conflicts are and will be the norm. Since 1989, among the most prevalent of these have been ethnic, which have proven hard to resolve in part because they have such a diversity of causes. Racial, kinship, linguistic, religious, lifestyle and location characteristics have all been linked to ethnic conflicts from Rwanda and Burundi to Georgia and Azerbaijan. Common denominators include ascriptive and exclusivist, subjective and objective cultural traits defined or magnified at the whims of war leaders who manipulate them to mobilize sometimes already peaceful populations. Two dominant ways to deal with such conflicts by national and international bodies have been reducing or eliminating differences by forced migration, new borders, assimilation, genocide, etc., and/or by managing them through arbitration, third-party intervention such as the UN, reconciliation, incentives, etc.[17] Obviously, some of these methods are as far from peaceful as possible, which underscores the urgent need for more creative thinking, critical dialogue and concerted action in this still gladiatorial arena.

The aims and bases of secessionist movements are usually clearer: the separation from one nation and the formation of another, based on predefined cultural, historical, ideological and/or geographic characteristics. In some cases, notably Czechoslovakia's "Velvet Revolution" from the USSR and its "Velvet Divorce" into the Czech Republic and Slovakia, democratic and diplomatic reform through intra- and international systems has successfully met the needs of the parties involved with little violence. Václav Havel, the playwright and President of the unified state between these two events as well as the Czechs afterwards, asserted:

> Without free, self-respecting, and autonomous citizens there can be no free and independent nations. Without internal peace, that is, peace among citizens and between the citizens and the state, there can be no guarantee of external peace.[18]

Another example is the Quiet Revolution in the French-language-dominated Canadian province of Quebec, which has unsuccessfully held two referendums on separation without resorting to state-sponsored violence, with intermittent talks on reconfiguring the confederation. However, there has also been no shortage of violence by secessionists and the states from which they wish to secede, particularly when population bases are split between two existing states: Kurds caught between Turkey and Iraq, and Basques between France and Spain, fit this model. Violence also erupts when existing states refuse to take the requests of the aspiring ones seriously, as between Chechens and Russia and potentially between China and Taiwan. In these cases, it is the neglect of established political processes rather than their absence, the inflexibility of participants in conjunction with their desperation, and the intricacies of reaching multi-lateral agreements – not their impossibility – which makes peace through succession or more autonomy difficult.

Post-autocratic violence, peace and peacemaking are very delicate topics because they are either ongoing or in the works, and they stir up deep-seated beliefs. Two recent cases, the former Yugoslavia and Iraq, are the most debated today, and the closest historical parallels in peace terms are ancient Sparta and Athens. The six federated republics of Yugoslavia, formed with the support of both the communist and capitalist blocs after the Second World War, were ruled with an iron fist by strongman Tito until his death in 1980. His oppressive peace – still the most liberal of any communist country during the Cold War – defines the term in modern times, stifling dissent and repressing rebels in the republics while providing for them. His contributions to the Non-Aligned Movement and strategic alliances outside NATO and the WPO run alongside these efforts. Tito's twenty-two chosen replacements proved unable to do what he did. Many observers held that this inability was nonetheless a positive change, even when ethnic nationalists in the republics began "cleansing" (i.e., massacring) themselves of each other in the early 1990s under the direction of elected officials. In less than a decade, Tito's unitive oppressive peace had disintegrated through democracy into divisive war, after which six new states emerged, aided by UN mediators and sanctions as well as NATO bombs, and Yugoslavia is no more. In this case, unpeaceful forces internal to the state were at work, in others it has also been those from outside.

Saddam Hussein's regime began in 1979 when he assumed control of the Iraqi Ba'ath party. Once supported by Soviets, Iraq now received US aid against Iran's new Islamic regime. Hussein used it to boost oil production as well as the army, which he used to contain Kurdish and Shiite rebels after UN-brokered peace with Iran, making his rule more oppressive than peaceful. After invading Kuwait in 1991, he rejected UN calls for withdrawal. A coalition led by the US quickly forced him to. He was not removed from power and continued to contain the internal revolts while refusing to adhere to peace terms like UN arms inspection, which led to more US bombings. After September 11, 2001, President George Bush declared war on terror, discussed below. Within a year this was extended to depose with NATO forces the elected Islamic Taliban party in Afghanistan, which the US supported against the USSR, and another to eliminate weapons of mass destruction never found, brushing aside UN and international opposition. The 2003 "Summer of Protest" included millions around the world, to no avail. Hussein was captured and killed, but the invading, predominantly Anglo-American forces have remained as haphazard occupiers. Conflicts between Shiites, Sunnis and Kurds that Hussein was able to contain have become a civil war protracted by outside interference. "The invaders came with a minutely detailed war plan," which has since been changed several times, "but without a peace plan other than protecting oil and other critical facilities."[19] How the war in Iraq will ultimately be resolved will undoubtedly be a defining moment in the twenty-first-century history of peace.

As the peace metrics above show, the UN has made great strides towards the reduction of international conflicts, as its Charter mandates. But the sovereignty and veto issues discussed in Chapter 10, compounded by tactical non-payment of dues, has rendered UN performance in the face of intra-national conflicts poor, to be polite, and impotent in stopping or preventing non-sanctioned wars by the Big Five and their allied organizations. Declaring the year 2000 as one of a "Culture of Peace" was more a public relations measure than a practical act aimed at creating one. The fact that the number of UN peacekeeping missions since 1989, many geared towards intra-national peace though by invitation only, outnumbers the total of the fifty years before is an indication both of its willingness to meet these challenges and their enormities. The UN Peace-Building Commission, established in 2005, was a year later invested with a Peace-Building Fund aimed solely at "reconstruction, institution-building and sustainable development, in countries emerging from conflict" – in an advisory role.[20] That NATO has taken up more peacekeeping than war-making missions in the same period also suggests that international bodies, even strictly military ones, have begun to realize that in incremental steps: conflict management leads to conflict resolution leads to peacemaking leads to peace-enforcement leads to peacekeeping leads to peace-building leads to peace.

Threatening Opportunities: Terrorism, Technology, New Media and Peace

Can peace be made or maintained with terrorists and rogue states? This is a pressing and in some circles unpopular question facing the world today – but it is far from the only one. Terrorism, like globalization, is not something new but which has in correlation with it increased and intensified. Maybe even more than ethnic conflicts, a diversity of causes and effects have made individual, group and state-sponsored terrorism and rogue states difficult to understand, let alone non-violently transform into peace. Indeed, terrorists and rogue states challenge principles and practices of peace in ways few occurrences in history have. One of many general definitions of terrorism serves our purpose here, which is to note some perils to and imperatives for peace and peacemaking that terrorism in some of its current forms presents: "the threat or use of violence, often against the civilian population, to achieve political or social ends, to intimidate opponents, or to publicize grievances."[21] That acts of terror have not yet triggered a third world war is a clear indication of how far world peace has come, but that they still occur and can still be a trigger is an equally clear indication of how far there is to go.

The highly problematic axiom "one man's terrorist is another's freedom fighter" can be extended to peacemakers insofar as Nobel Peace Prize laureates such as Nelson Mandela, to name one, have at different points in their careers labelled both. But the axiom's underscoring of perspectives in determining who is what is universally valid. Teenagers toting machineguns in high schools or refugee camps may or may not be terrorists, but they are as great a danger to micro-level peace as atomic bombs are to macro. Idiosyncrasies of individual terrorists not directly motivated by an affiliation with a group or common cause make their acts of violence hard to prevent, deter or diffuse because they are hard to predict. Peacemaking with them is equally impractical because their acts of violence tend to start and end quickly, even if planned a long time in advance, and often their aims preclude the possibility. With theories and practices of pacific violence prevention still in their infancy, it may be fruitful along with personal causes and situational determinants that have been identified as manipulatable to investigate metrics of inner peace and how it can be monitored and enhanced as a means of removing motives of individual terrorists. Otherwise, it may be that "the militant is the one who best expresses the life of the multitude: the agent of biopolitical production and resistance" because some continue to hold that "militancy today is a positive, constructive, and innovative activity."[22]

Today's terrorist groups are more easily categorized, broadly falling into two sets, and peace prospects easier to identify though historically not to implement. Again, these groups are heroic to some, but violence does not depend on perspective. A first set is political, one of the largest being the Liberation Tigers of Tamil Eelam (LTTE) which began in 1975. They attacked rival groups in addition to government officials seeking to secede from Sri Lanka, and the state's army fought back. India intervened in the late 1980s, a federal state structure was proposed and a ceasefire agreed to. Suspicions mounted and both peace projects fell through. Attacks continued as the state waged a War for Peace; in 2001 the LTTE announced that autonomy would do and another ceasefire was called. When a Sri Lankan president was elected on a crackdown platform, it was broken and remains so. Politically motivated groups like the LTTE, the Irish Republican Army (IRA) and the Palestinian Liberation Organization (PLO) have tended to use violence as means to an end, not as an end in itself. They are not terrorist *movements*, but find it necessary or expedient

to use terrorist *tactics*, opening up the possibility of negotiation and compromise, of course easier said than done as these tactics have also been
used to shape or call off peace efforts and in retaliation for peaces deemed
unfair. Conducting a worldwide "war on terror," especially when what
"winning" it means has not yet been concretely set out, escalates rather
than diffuses tensions and conflicts that lead to political terrorism. As a
result, peacemakers and keepers are targeted not for what they are or are
not doing, but for who they do or do not represent.

A second set is religiously based, giving rise to the sense that an "Age
of Sacred Terror" is upon us.[23] The international fundamentalist Islamic
Al Qaeda, operating in semi-autonomous cells wherever its leaders believe
Muslim interest are threatened, hence Osama bin Laden's Jihad, is best-
known. But fundamentalist Christians in the US have used terrorist tactics
against abortion clinics and Aum Shinrikyo, which released nerve gas in
Tokyo's subway and claims a Buddhist basis, have acted violently on religious convictions. The means these groups use are often coterminous with
their ends, putting the feasibility of negotiation and compromise on both
their and their victims' side in peril. Counter-terrorism measures based on
bolstered surveillance, investigative agencies and police forces may
prevent religious acts of terror but they cannot in themselves eliminate
their motives. A recent, unprecedented conciliatory initiative by Muslim
to Christian leaders gives both reason for hope and sets a precedent for
future practices. In 2007, 138 potentates from across the Islamic spectrum
presented their Christian counterparts with a letter entitled "A Common
Word Between Us and You," urging closer and collaborative ties by building on common interests and traditions and warmly received. "Given that
there's no simple one-off solution to terrorism," noted Cambridge
University's Interfaith Program director, "this letter does have all the elements necessary to move in that direction."[24]

In addition to these drivers of terrorism's threats to peace, state-
sponsored and state-run terrorist programs, by which governments
support, protect or use terrorists to further their aims, have been recognized. In conjunction with these phenomena the notion of rogue states
willing to use violence in disregard of established international forums
and procedures has emerged. Along these lines President Bush declared in
2001 that the nuclear ambitions and terrorist links of Iraq, Iran and North
Korea formed an "Axis of Evil," and Nobel Peace Prize laureate Sean
McBride stated at a conference on terrorism: "The terrorist who holds a
hostage for ransom is not very different from the head of a government
who threatens to use nuclear weapons to force another State to yield to
its demands."[25] By the same token, a majority in Britain (2005), currently
the US' closest ally, saw the US as "a greater threat to global peace than
Al Qaeda;" so more than just terrorists believe it to be a rogue state

itself.[26] Economic and diplomatic sanctions on UN or bilateral levels have been and are widely used to punish and prevent state-related terrorism and oppression that breeds terrorism on smaller – but not superpower states – to varying degrees of success. Most notably, North Korea has agreed to end its nuclear program and has entered into permanent peace talks with the South in 2006–7 after its economy was crippled – at its citizens more than its leaders' expense, and with outcomes all but certain.

In 1999, after a string of terrorist attacks on US embassies, the UN Security Council called for international cooperation to "fight" terrorism, as if it were an enemy in itself rather than a tactic enemies use against each other. After 9/11, it adopted a resolution calling on states to criminalize assistance for terrorist activities, deny financial support and safe haven to terrorists and share information about groups planning terrorist attacks. Important steps as these are, they are also an extension of the pattern by which the US made unilateral into multilateral policy, as with the Monroe Doctrine and Open Door. In the case of terrorism, the unilateral policy is called the Shultz Doctrine, put forth in 1984, which instituted counter-terrorist tactics of pre-emptive attacks, forceful retributions and anti-terrorist military aid; its world correlative today is the "war on terror." National and global counter-terrorism measures remain directionless unless endgames of peace are predefined and prepared for, and retrogressive until coordinated with proven peace principles and practices on ground and high levels, among them:

1. Recognizing and addressing terrorist motives as well as acts;
2. Meeting the needs of victims of terrorism to avoid its perpetuation;
3. Incentivizing the replacement of violence with negotiation;
4. Pre-determining interests in and purposes of negotiation, not outcomes;
5. Negotiating with those who have the authority to end violence on all sides;
6. Planning for and implementing post-negotiation peace scenarios;
7. Inducing weapon handovers and cessation of incitement to violence;
8. Reconciliation-based trial and punishmentof terrorists, including re-integration;
9. Transforming (counter-) terrorist infrastructures into productive non-violent ones;
10. Preventing terrorism through rather than around legal systems.[27]

Terrorism's chief challenge to peace may be one identified in the Cold War, and which applies to terrorist and counter-terrorist forces alike: "The infrastructure knows no boundaries and observes no borders: the battlefields are virtually everywhere. Scores of nations are linked. . . all of them are on the front lines. Just as the distinction between war and peace is blurred, so is the distinction between military and civilian."[28] As an extension of Adorno's definition of peace, the most effective response to terrorism may prove to be one based on a "new universalism, both recognising and promoting plurality. . . based on a relational ontology, in which universalistic principles dominate procedures."[29] Thinking about it and actually doing so requires a "dialogic ethic, in which procedures allow for the possibility of developing a common discourse between different and unequal partners." Among the greatest vehicles and inhibitors of this kind of discourse are technological innovations in peace and peacemaking.

Vital to understanding and maximizing recent technological innovations in peace and peacemaking are metaphors and methods put forth by media theorist Marshall McLuhan in *War and Peace in the Global Village* (1968) and two previous works. "Electronic interdependence recreates the world in the image of a global village," that is, new media, in his day television, cinema and radio, in ours, satellite communication and the internet, are able to reflect, shape and integrate cultures on scales and with speeds compared to which print pales.[30] Coining "the medium is the message," he argued further that these media shape not only the messages they convey, but the societies in which they do.[31] But in *War and Peace* he tempered positive connotations many began to ascribe to these notions early on, just as many do today to the point of triteness, by drawing attention to the fact that the mobilizations and integrations new media vs. old allow can be military- as well as peace-oriented. Other critics have argued that disparities in technologies, communicative or otherwise, are in themselves obstacles to peace.

New media may be the sharpest double-edged swords regarding peace and peacemaking in our times. Magnitudes and targets of terrorist attacks are correlated to the media attention they get because they assure higher viewer ratings, which in turn brings in more advertising revenue for media outlets. To symbiotic relationships between merchants, manufacturers and mercantilist governments have been added those of terrorists, counter-terrorist operations and the media. At the same time, however, the ability to nearly instantaneously become aware of threats and breaches of peace around the planet allow for reaction times and dimensions aimed at peace-maintenance and against war previously unimaginable, let alone implementable. United for Peace and Justice, a US anti-war umbrella group, reported that its webpage listing hundreds of planned local demonstrations even before the Iraq War was declared received over 1.5 million hits daily in March 2003. MoveOn.org, an internet-based anti-war campaign, has carried out non-violent "virtual protests," bombarding government offices with e-mails, faxes and phone calls urging peace, and raising $400,000 in 48 hours through online fundraising. A Canadian backpacker in Myanamr who witnessed the Buddhist-led protest for democracy began a blog, and in days had over 100,000 signatories to his petition, causing the autocratic regime to shut down national internet access. New media's hazards to and opportunities for peace and peacemaking are just starting to be documented, analyzed and employed. But there can be no doubt that "Cyberspace subverts spatial boundaries, including those of territorial political communities at all levels. It empowers affinity groups that cut across jurisdictions, and vastly increases the possibilities of forming temporary or longer-lasting collectivities," peaceful and not.[32]

Other technological innovations that cannot be overlooked or overemphasized in relation to the presents of peace and peacemaking are developments in means of transportation. Like long-range ships forever transformed peace in the colonial-imperial eras, trains since the nineteenth century, automobiles since the first half of the twentieth century and airplanes since the second have not only made modern peacekeeping possible, but have allowed for persistence and deepening of personal interactions between policymakers as well as peace activists otherwise impossible. Even outside these small circles and despite their use in warfare, these new transportation means are *sine qua non* of globalization's commercial and cultural networks, and any alternatives however peaceful that do not take equally full advantage of them will probably not prevail. But the boons of modern transportation to peace and peacemaking cannot be accurately assessed without considering their banes in the overconsumption of natural resources as well as the detriments to the environment. As tensions related to control over energy resources mount between nations, so has the awareness that the ecological harm their exploitation is causing may parallel that which specters of nuclear war do only potentially, thus similarly putting not only the survival of peace at risk, but also the survival of humanity itself. This parallel partially explains why sustainability organizations today are recognized as being intrinsically and increasingly explicitly aligned with contemporary peace organizations, to which we now turn in closing.

There are thousands of peace-related organizations in the world today, and no complete, up-to-date register and analysis of all of them or their precursors exists. Such a project would be invaluable to understanding and making the most of the human and material resources globally devoted to peace and is vital to the purposes of this book but far beyond its scope. Instead, what follows is a summary of three major types of peace organizations today. The first is research-based and activities include funding peace-related studies by individual and groups of scholars, organizing forums to present their research to each other and the public, otherwise disseminating results and serving as advisors to policymakers. Usually structured as foundations, institutes or centers, they include think tanks which tend to be highly partisan, university departments which tend to pretend that they are not partisan, and *a priori* partisan government bodies. The second type of peace organization fulfils peace advocacy functions, serving as watchdogs of threats to peace, promoting particular approaches to peace, popularizing the results of research-based organizations, sometimes collaborating with them or conducting research themselves. The main difference between the first and second type is that experts and knowledge are the bases of the one while actual or aspiring political or other kinds of leaders and causes are the driving forces of the other, though distinctions are often blurred. The third and last type of organization to be discussed here continues the tradition of peace activism, i.e., doing things for peace in addition to or aside from thinking and talking about what can or should be done, specialties of the first two. Demonstrations, grassroots and door-to-door campaigns, ploughshares, coordinated publicity and mobilization, voter initiatives, non-violent direct action, civil disobedience, non-cooperation, providing for needs which if unmet could threaten peace, are just a few of their purposes and tactics, most of which is done on a voluntary basis by their members.

One movement adeptly combining elements of all three of these organizational types, as most do to varying degrees, is the global Department of Peace Initiative. Its aim is to establish such bodies, wholly dedicated to peace programs, within national government frameworks so that tax funds can directly supplement the donations and endowments required to support all these organizations and synchronize their efforts for maximum effect, just as is done for national and international military organizations and in the hopes of replacing them. The Solomon Islands was the first to create a Department of Peace, Nepal the most recent. What these organizations taken together suggest is an ever-widening acknowledgment that "violence among humans has never solved any problem without creating new ones; enduring solutions arise from continuous voluntary co-operation."[33] The emergence of peace professionals such as researchers, advocates and activists, paid to advance peace in different ways even aside from governmental mandates, does not take away but adds to the spirit of voluntarism vital to peace as a condition of survival since the origins of humanity. What remains to be seen is whether they will meet the fragmented fate of the nineteenth-century organized peace movement or collectively rise to meet the challenges of a new millennium and make it one in which the final chapter of this world history of peace can serve as an introduction to a history of world peace.

Conclusion

The Pyramid of Peace: Past, Present and Future

Among the purposes of this book has been to challenge the notions that peace is solely the absence of war and that writing history is an exclusive privilege of the mightiest militarily. Without the victories of peacemakers and the resourcefulness of the peaceful, I have tried to show, not only would there be no history to write, but there might not even be a world in which to write it. Learning from them, as the most successful have from those before, is perhaps the safest way to ensure that the only constraints to peace and peacemaking are those beyond our control. As mentioned in the introduction, the analytical narratives presented in the preceding chapters are meant less as guidelines than as signposts; the opposite applies to this conclusion. Its purpose is in no way to draw the world history of peace recounted and still unfolding through us to a close, but to reopen certain of its lessons in redoubled directly applicable ways.

To recap and attempt to make a small contribution to pasts, presents and futures of peace, I present this Pyramid adapted from Abraham Maslow's pyramid of human needs and motives, summarizing and prag-matizing some salient peace principles and practices already covered in more depth.[1] Defining the Pyramid's terms theoretically and by way of key historical examples will, I hope, not limit but rather inform the meanings and applications they may take on in different contexts. The structure, in which the levels below are supportive prerequisites for those above, is likewise not intended to limit their scopes or functions but to expose rela-tionships and interdependencies that may be difficult to see outside of it. That the Pyramid is based on peace strategies with track records is indica-tive only insofar as they can transcend their original circumstances through constant re-qualifications within cultural contingencies and

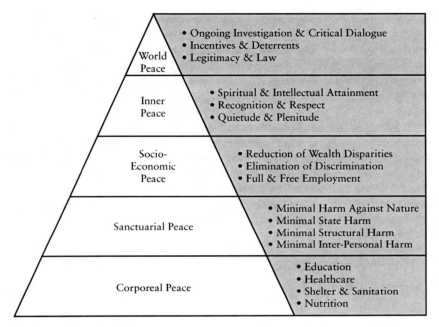

Pyramid of Peace Principles

diversities as evolving conditions and participants require. The point is less to offer a definitive plan for world peace, of which there is no shortage, than to propose for ongoing debate and action an alternative framework in which it becomes additionally actualizable and sustainable.[2]

Items linked to each level, like the levels themselves, are applicable in individual, social and collective ways demonstrated by the selected examples given. They are purposefully limited in number because a less suggestive, fuller exposition would require a separate book, which new generations could rewrite with levels, items and examples relevant to their times. Cumulatively, differences and similarities in version chains would thus provide prosperity with more and more complete historical guides to world peace, analyzable and implementable as experimental scientific models. World peace requirements discovered in or expressed through the Pyramid are intended to be pertinently holistic for humanity for now not forever, that is only as suitable to unaccounted-for idiosyncrasies. If not, such requirements can be catered to fit the needs of situations at hand, in which case the Pyramid and the lessons of the world history of peace it represents would stand amended. Conversely, they can be wantonly rejected outright and the Pyramid falls if it is not restructured by item, by level or from the ground up as necessary.

Climbing the Pyramid, so to speak, means actualizing each item of each level from the bottom up on a continual, progressive basis. Reaching any level except the top at any one place and time does not necessarily depend on it being reached everywhere by everyone, but surely would not hurt. Likewise, reaching any level once does not mean it will always be held, as the Pyramid embodies a static dynamism by which its structure can stay intact even if its levels and items are periodically unactualized, though each must be actualized before or in tandem with the next. Extents to which items and levels are actualizable individually, socially and/or collectively depend in large part on the specificity of the meanings attributed to them, which must perforce be substantiatedly general for our purposes here. The set of imperatives previously discussed are part of the Pyramid as binds that tie together its items and levels. On these premises and those set out below, the Pyramid is both a description of world peace and a way to achieve it.

Corporeal Peace

The premise of corporeal peace is that without the wellbeing of our bodies and minds world peace is an irrelevancy. As obvious as this premise may be when pointed out, a prevalent pitfall of peacemakers historically and contemporarily has been failing to take it into account. If true, then nothing is more relevant to world peace than components of corporeal peace such as nutrition, shelter and sanitation, healthcare and education. Individual experiences concretize this level as the Pyramid's base in ways history cannot, and make self-evident that corporeal peace is a precondition of world peace. Nevertheless, history does provide examples of how instinctual and bio-genetic imperatives were made into systematic measures consciously taken to secure or enhance corporeal peace as the basis of all other peaces.

Nutrition

Starvation precludes the peace of an individual just as, on wide enough scales, it does for society. In addition to the suffering empty stomachs cause to individuals and societies, they are like ticking time bombs inadvertently targeted at collective peace. Efforts to secure enough food have been starting points of peace since primordial times, when gathering and hunting were the norms. Advents of agriculture and hydraulic revolutions were expansions of this base, which the Ancient Chinese and Japanese rightly believed to be the source of any and all kinds of peace. Similarly in Ancient Greece, first-generation Horae who represented how peace was made and maintained were agricultural goddesses the worship of whom was intended to ensure plentiful harvests. Industrialism changed the way food is produced and distributed, but not its being the foundation of world peace. What individual nutrition needs are and how they are met depends on cultural traditions as much as economic systems, and world peace depends on nutrition needs being met in consideration of cultural traditions and economic systems.

Shelter and Sanitation

Shelter was as necessary for the corporeal peace of prehistoric nomads as it is for us now, though only with transitions to sedentary life in the home base structure of hunter-gatherers can the idea of home originate. The first meanings of Shalom for the Jewish tribes of the Torah related to protection from hostile natural elements, the basic sense in which shelter is taken here. Metaphorically, their perennial search for the Promised Land as a prerequisite of peace can be seen as an indication of the significances of such a permanent dwelling for aspiring or currently sedentary peoples. The violence used in stealing peoples' homes as a way to the Promised Land may have been justified by Yahweh, but within our context serves only to show how for people so lacking, no place is more precious to peace than home. In Ancient India, pre-Vedic societies and, millennia later, Ashoka sought to secure sanitation for all as a step towards peace because diseases terminally infecting people otherwise at peace can thereby be curtailed. Reconstructions that have occurred after destructive wars attest to the importance of shelter and sanitation as a second step **after nutrition** in rebuilding peace; world peace cannot be actualized **before everyone** everywhere who so wants to has taken these two steps.

Healthcare

The Hippocratic Oath, a non-violent code by which doctors' duties are combined with doing no harm and protecting their patients from injustice, and Henri Dunant's efforts to assist the wounded in war regardless of the nationality, may be the only specifiable healthcare items in this book. But implications of the Oath and the Red Cross which Dunant founded, that healthcare is a birthright linked to justice and necessary to corporeal peace because of its upholding role, are logical extensions of nutrition, shelter and sanitation. Once available only to the high-born, the well-off and the poor as charity, universal healthcare was made actualizable with industrialism coupled with the social planning developed to stem civil strife along antithetical ideological lines during the Great

Depression, a sign that universal healthcare can be part of any political position. Efforts towards universal healthcare are made more difficult by meanings it has in different parts of the world. While debates in some places are about providing health services more equally or cost-effectively, in others they are about how to provide it to begin with. Universal healthcare would not be necessary for world peace if everyone was always healthy; as this is an unfortunate improbability universal healthcare is required for world peace.

Education

Education is a form of healthcare for the mind. In Clement of Alexandria's view, peace is the point of education and war a result of its absence, but education itself can create absences of peace depending on what is taught. Enculturation processes, such as those of simple societies like the Tasaday, can both extend past peace practices into the present and prepare youths to deal with future problems in peaceful ways. Universities have been places where peacemakers have converged and emerged when they have not been instruments of bellicose status quos. Peaceful catalytic examples can be drawn from US universities in the 1960s and 1970s and European in the eighteenth century; counter-examples would be early medieval universities in servitude of momentary militant powers. Today's University for Peace in Costa Rica may not be historically related to the School of Prosperous Peacein Tokugawa Japan, but they share an impulse that, if more widespread, would put the power and influence of intellectuals at the disposal of peacemakers and/or make peacemakers out of intellectuals themselves, as was the case with atomic scientists in the mid twentieth century and the Pugwash Conference to this day. More than for other items of corporeal peace, what constitutes education for peace thus depends as much on how it is done as on if it is done.

Sanctuarial Peace

The premise of sanctuarial peace is that without tangible assurances and reason to believe that intentional harm is unlikely to be done to us as individuals or groups, world peace is no less a mirage than the promise of bodily and mental wellbeing. Indeed, breaches of sanctuarial peace often originate in violations of corporeal peace at the level below and result from contraventions of socio-economic peace at the level above. The "minimal" before each item in this level serves to indicate that regardless of longstanding cultural and categorical imperatives aimed at curbing and eliminating intentional harm, it has, does and is likely to continue to occur despite best efforts. Though beyond our scope to explain why this is, what can and has been done about it is not. The use of "harm" instead of "violence" is intended to denote that damage can be done in more ways than physically. Minimalization as a goal for social and collective mechanisms for averting harm, ending it quickly and equitably is thus more probable and plausible than permanent eradication, as history makes painfully clear. Sanctuarial peace is not absolute in the same way as corporeal peace and perhaps cannot be, even if to actualize it we must believe it is.

Minimal Interpersonal Harm

Intentional interpersonal harm has been proportionally less prevalent in primate behavior than help, an equation equally applicable to human prehistory and history. Sympathy, mutual aid and social cohesion as evolutionary advantages; Confucius' passive rule not to do to others what you do not wish for yourself; Jesus' active rule to do to others as you would have done to you; and Kant's categorical rule to do only that which could bear being universally done are just three of many exemplary imperatives to prevent interpersonal harm so far proposed, which of course would be pointless to posit if it never happened. Interdependencies like those put forth by capitalists and cooperatives put forth by socialists each served the same purpose: making interpersonal harm unnecessary by meeting individual and social needs. Conflict may or may not be inevitable but using harm to resolve conflicts certainly is not, and doing so creates retaliatory cycles much more difficult to end than start. Interpersonal harm prevention as a discipline is still in its infancy, but as an unevenly studied practice is as old as humanity.

Minimal Structural Harm

No social, political or economic system yet implemented has been devoid of structural violence, again redubbed harm to broaden its senses, despite the fact that without those on whom it has been inflicted they could not have existed. The Indian caste system, citizenship in Ancient Greece and Rome, European feudalism and Chinese Fengjian, and industrial societies' classes show that many such systems have nonetheless survived for centuries. However, they did so only because social strife stemming from structural harm was effectively mitigated and, when not, it brought about their downfall either from internal collapse or restructuring, or external invasion or amalgamation. Counter-dominant behavior such as non-violent removals from power, ostracism, coups, popular revolts and factionary feuds are answers to questions about why structural harm is perpetuated, but not solutions to the problem in themselves. Power vacuums like power struggles have historically closely coincided with periods of broken peace for two reasons. One, external powers have no authority with which to make and maintain peace, as with Bengal and the British East India Company in colonial times. The other, crises of legitimacy by which wannabe powers lack the authority to internally make and maintain peace, a driver of the Thermidor during the French Revolution. Intra-national peace theories and practices across the political spectrum and collective bargaining have sought to mitigate structural harm when it cannot be minimalized, upon which world peace relies until it can be eliminated.

Minimal State Harm

That states must be adequately defended from external threats and properly equipped to deal with internal threats for peace to be secured is not tantamount to affirming that states have always been and must always be war machines. Cicero's conceptions of just war as self-defense and unjust for those without provocation were held even by the imaginary residents of Utopia, who also practiced Spartan discipline for protection and order. The key difference between Romans and them is that Utopians subscribed to Grotius' notion of just warfare, or doing the least harm possible, a version of "civilized" warfare as with the Bushido in Shoen Japan. Deterrence, the oldest and crudest means of preserving peace between states, was in the end what kept the Cold War cold, culminating in traditions of states and their leagues decreasing frequencies of warfare by increasing its specter's scale. International law, balances of powers, neutrality and isolationism, arbitration and coordinated disarmament have been successful in varying degrees in moderating harm between states. Harm caused by states internally is predicated on and perpetuated by their unchecked sovereignty, against which transformative non-violence works but also has its limits. The organized peace movement's peace-despite-states approach shows that the only way to absolutely guarantee the end of state harm is to eliminate or pacify states altogether. For now, the surest path to world peace is to globally secure minimal use of minimal force.

Minimal Harm to Nature

Depletions of natural resources are far from new concerns, and have been related to peace since before humans were humans. Bio-genetic imperatives or peace instincts such as restorative behavior and tension relief in primates have human correlates such as reconciliation and détente, and have as much to do with how we relate to each other as how we relate to ecological systems to which we owe our existence. The Minoan Peace, the longest lasting in European history, ended with an ecological catastrophe of some kind, and inaugurated the fractious First Intermediary Period in Ancient Egypt after a unitive peace of some 700 years. Malthus' proposition that only checked populations can secure peace within and between nations because if unchecked, nature cannot support them is pessimistic insofar as it is realistic. The doctrine of peace at any price, he suggests, applied to the environment shows how ludicrous it is, as terminal harm to the earth would mean the ruination of the only place we have to be at peace. This simple logic was lent an added intensity in the second half of the twentieth century when nuclear energy was harnessed and burning oil became ubiquitous, reunifying the causes of environmental and peace activists. The non-violent direct action and awareness campaigns of Greenpeace and politicizations of peace and sustainability in Green Parties are thus two recent manifestations of age-old concerns.

Socio-Economic Peace

The premise of socio-economic peace is that how we live and work with each other (or not) as individuals and groups is a determining factor of whether peace is actualizable, as well as forms it takes if so. No historical socio-economic system has *a priori* made peace impossible other than mercantilism because each conceives of peace in a different sense based on its means and ends. That many participants would agree that their socio-economic systems preclude peace for them by misusing its means and misconstruing its ends is a fact worthy of fiction. In some cases the ways or conditions in which socio-economic systems are implemented, rather than any one fault in them, preclude the peace they strive for. Thus using the peace proposed by one system to evaluate others would produce radically different results than evaluations of quality and degree of peace based on criteria common to all and distinct to one. Doing the latter provides critically safer comparative grounds for making one more like another, substituting one for another, or combining the best features of all. The point is not to give immunity to a socio-economic system for the positions it places and hardships it confers to the disempowered, upon whom the peace of every system so far set in place has rested, but to put the disempowered in a position to non-violently empower themselves as individuals and groups.

Full and Free Employment

Mozi, Hesiod and Bentham concurred that useful labor is constituent of peace for individuals as for societies, and tied it to justice in socio-economic systems. For eons before them, as in our stage of globalization, a lack of remunerative work made chances of survival slim, let alone chances of peace. Receiving just enough to survive was a rife, worldwide rationalization for keeping vast majorities of populations barely above the subsistence levels of prehistory, and had this not been done to some degree no socio-economic system could lay claims to any peace, however deficient. Colonialism exposed this rationalization by exploitative oppressions abroad that made irrefutable what the powerful rarely acknowledged at home. Las Casas' plan for a Land of Peace where native laborers work alongside foreign for their own benefit as for empire and god is a case in point. Another is Ricardo's analysis of labor, which led to the conclusion that economic competition among individuals and nations can diffuse or be a substitute for war while supplying for the welfare of all. Industrialism and the diversified interdependencies it sponsored provided means to overcome agriculturally based exploitation, though not without entailing exploitations of its own. From socialist perspectives, the answer to the question of who owns peace is everyone, or no one. Full and free employment here does not mean that everyone does what they want for a living, an un-Platonic ideal, but that everyone can make a contributive, self-satisfactory living with commensurate compensation without being forced.

Elimination of Discrimination

Discrimination has always been based in prejudiced minds and adversative to peace in situations created by their manifestations. Anti-discriminatory responses along three lines have been put forth, related to the absence of explicitly political levels and items in the Pyramid. One is to change minds first and situations second, an instance being Abdul Baha, who saw prejudice as a cause of war and preached its elimination as a path to peace. As politics is a reflection of our prejudices in his view, their removal must be carried out non-politically, in his cause religiously. A second is to change situations first and minds second, exemplified by social justice movements from the non-citizen Socii to the two Great Peace Rebellions, as for women's suffrage, civil and worker rights. Of course, changing situations involves changing at least the minds of policymakers, but not necessarily those of prejudiced masses who must thereafter cope, in which case politics is a means to an end not an end in itself. Lastly is to simultaneously change minds and situations, as in cultural homogenizations like Romanization, Sinicization, Arabization and Americanization, and heterogenizations against which they are directed, into which they invariably turn. Adorno's definition of peace as differentiation without domination with the differentiated participating in each other is egalitarian politics perfected in ways yet to be made fully actualizable.

Reduction of Wealth Disparities

Like structural harm to which they tend to be attached, wealth disparities are historically omnipresent obstacles to peace when they are prohibitive of individual or group actualization of items and levels in the Pyramid. Only when wealth disparities have been effectively assuaged from barring such actualizations can peace and prosperity, persistently linked in thought all through history, also be linked in practice. Partnership societies do not necessarily preclude wealth disparities and can exist despite them, but only insofar as they counteract the inclinations of dominator societies to abuse wealth disparities and the power asymmetries wealth disparities can cause. In Mesopotamia, balanced geo-social configurations were keys to stemming decline due to latifundization and over-privatization, accentuations of wealth disparities which like all others if unimpeded become threats to peace. The Third Estate in France as the vehicle of its Revolution, and the Third World as the vehicle of the Non-Aligned Movement, are two sides of the same coin on different scales and positions on the peace spectrum. Contemporary critiques of globalism based on the reduction of wealth disparities between and within nations are thus historically justified in pointing out its menaces. Yet, imagining the management of components of peace as product lines of global businesses, in which everyone has a stake and expects returns on their investments, comes close to how handling wealth disparities can work today. Competing to meet unmet needs, continually improving their products to increase their market share, such businesses of peace would monetarily enrich stakeholders beyond their wildest dreams while non-violently satisfying their highest pacific hopes.

Inner Peace

The premise of inner peace is, as the precursor to Transcendentalism Channing preached, there can be no peace without but through peace within. With few if any exceptions, corporeal, sanctuarial and socio-economic peaces are as essential for individuals to be internally at peace as for societies, just as peace within societies is essential for peace between them. In the same vein, inner peace on individual, social and collective levels are prerequisites of world peace even if by proportions and degrees more than for the Pyramid's previous items. Privileging one prescription for inner peace over others must be an individual choice for it to be actualized, and the best way to ensure optimal choices are made is for many options to be available, regardless of where they come from.

Unconditional acceptance and encouragement exponentially increases the probability of success once a choice for inner peace is made or changed, and compulsory choices not only invalidate the meaning of choice but the peace towards which choices are geared.

Quietude and Plenitude

Tranquility, calmness and stillness have long been and still are characteristics strongly associated with inner peace, as well as with the natural, social and collective states conducive to it. For example, the inner peace of Daoist inaction in wu-wei lies in the free-flow of inward and outward energy of which an individual can be a medium or impediment. Even samurai had their tearoom safe havens where weapons reminiscent of their livelihood were not allowed. Many share the desire for a few fleeting moments of quietude in the midst of everyday life's hustle and bustle; those systematically denied usually find peace difficult to attain. Eremite Christian monks and Shugendo practitioners made these fleeting moments ways of life, but may not have been able to without a degree of plenitude, a sense of completeness corporeal or otherwise. Fastings and moments of silence of different kinds prescribed by most religions serve to remind devotees of quietude's and plenitude's criticality for inner peace. The Epicurean Garden, Buddhist Sangha and cenobite monasticism are examples of how quietude and plenitude can be socially achieved while providing for their lack in societies of which they are a part and apart from. Stoic masteries of passions and loyal dedication make individual quietude and plenitude possible even when they are totally absent socially and collectively, a model though not a method for everyone.

Recognition and Respect

Mesopotamian issuance of coins by states was a way to non-violently assert their fiscal or political independence, cylinder seals cemented relationships between individuals and groups, and their value depended on recognition and respect. Medieval states were and modern states are recognized by one another through treaties and gain respect through mutually beneficial trade and/or protective alliances. Mohammed had a reputation for justice and honesty which allowed him to improve plights of the first Muslims. Trade unions were recognized by their states before they became effective collective bargaining bodies, as which they gained respect they lacked as militant bodies before. Individually, recognition and respect successively derive from or against family, community, education, professions, states, the media, and religious, regional and world bodies, without which the most successful peacemakers in world history could not have achieved what they did. The flipside: militants and terrorists gain recognition the same way but at others' expense, thereby losing the respect of their enemies while gaining that of their backers, creating a precarious asymmetry that makes (re)conciliation difficult, let alone peace. Whom to recognize and how, whom to respect and for what are central questions to world peace depending entirely on what point of view is taken and what is at stake.

Spiritual and Intellectual Attainment

The most elusive and yet most sought-after components of inner peace are probably spiritual and intellectual attainment. Religious imperatives of peace are related to but distinguished from spiritual imperatives. The former organize, systemize and make prescriptions of the latter only after the latter have been proven. The belief in karma as individual pursuits for peace made more achievable in social conditions insofar as the social reflects the prevalence of the individual rested on reincarnative peace, the idea that our peace or its absence in this life will continue in the next, shared by major monotheisms. The Buddhist Eightfold Path and Islamic Five Pillars are both passages to peace and its spiritual qua behavioral supports. Intellectuals such as Russell, Pauling and Forsberg were all eminent in their fields before becoming peacemakers, and peace writers throughout the ages have been able to articulate new ideas and principles inasmuch as they are versed in those of the past and present. This is not to say that everyone must have a PhD or be saintly for world peace to be actualized, but instead to suggest that striving for and reaching the spiritual and intellectual attainment within one's grasp is a stepping stone thereto more easily actualizable once the Pyramid's previous levels and items are met.

World Peace

The premise of world peace is to facilitate the Pyramid's previous peaces by aiding their adaptation to conditions and participants as circumstances require. Crucé's analogy between humanity and the human body, the organs of which are in such sympathy with each other that the sickness of one affects the other, takes on its full meanings in the levels below and culminates in world peace, not the other way around. No state or organization today has the expertise, authority or means to make world peace possible along the Pyramid's lines. UN agencies as a bettering expansion of the League of Nations' multi-pronged approach have been one of the few ways a global, centrally funded organizational approach to world peace along the Pyramid's lines has ever been effectively enacted. But it may be undesirable that a single one does because doing so puts all the proverbial eggs of world peace in one basket. Another possibility is the recent emergence of independent, specialized agencies which have taken on limited tasks not explicitly for world peace, and professional peace researchers, advocates and activists who have, which cumulatively can circumvent barriers to world peace political imperatives on their own cannot. The point of the items in the Pyramid's level of world peace is thus not to show how the levels below can be accomplished on a global scale, which must be worked out within the levels themselves, but rather to suggest what can be done to help and sustain them in the meanwhile and afterwards.

Legitimacy and Law

Wolff's scientific fourfold allotment of laws as voluntary, natural, implicit, customary and explicit treaties are applicable throughout world history and have each been crucial to peace. The legitimacy of both those in power and their agents, and laws to regulate relations and define penalties for contraventions, were as crucial for the peace of early civilizations as they are today even if in strikingly different ways. At the heart of Ancient Chinese legalism was that the law itself not people who apply it is the source of all legitimate authority capable of making and maintaining peace, which in conjunction with Confucian traditionalism and meritocracy became the longest-running governmental form in history. The second, Roman Republicanism, must be taken with a big grain of salt because Augustus was an autocrat who upheld republican forms as a matter of convenience more than of conviction. The Pax Romana he inaugurated is a testament to the fact that for peace political functions do not always follow their forms. Solon's reforms in Ancient Athens were meant to allay the dangers of direct democracy such as demagoguery with isonomic principles of equality in law. Representative democracy today has the added danger of officials saying one thing to get elected then doing another, or doing what they said they would do like Hitler and the last leaders of Yugoslavia. For Machiavelli, war and peace are indifferent instruments to get and keep power, but no one can do so by force alone because they thereby lose their legitimacy, wherein lie the powers of laws and periodic or emergency elections in making peace when broken and maintaining or enhancing it when not.

Incentives and Deterrents

Deterrence, the prevention of aggression by threat of retaliation, was one of the uses of large teeth in primates. Their smaller size in humans, a morphological modification providing the earliest evidence of peace, was made up for in the destructivity of our weapons from arrowheads to atomic bombs. Arms races that have always been part of the human race, then, have also always been peace races in part, a paradoxical absurdity fully exposed in the face of annihilation. Yet, for Spartans and Athenians as for Egyptians and Hittites, as for the Allies in the First and Second World Wars, as for NATO and the WPO, uniting to deter was an incentive to unite in peaces that may not have been feasible otherwise. Incentives go as far back as deterrence, from survival of the peaceful as a complement to survival of the fittest, to reciprocal tributary systems and non-military alliances, and to a certain extent the Monroe Doctrine and Open Door. Economic and political sanctions imposed bilaterally or multilaterally for policy change such as those imposed on Apartheid South Africa and Iran today, as well as food-for-peace programs, combine incentives and non-violent deterrents in ways that have yet to be fully explored. But the effectiveness of incentives and deterrents depends entirely on the capaciousness of the inflictors and inflicted, so that jeopardies of peace in sanctions may lie in self-deceitful self-defeat.

Ongoing Investigation and Critical Dialogue

The Pyramid's two topmost items are in some ways only practical when those below are met and in other ways need to be practiced for them to be met. Finding food is an investigation of some kind, and debating where to eat it is a form of critical dialogue, but these are only partial senses of how these items are taken here. Innovation, adaptation and perpetuation are the goals of ongoing investigation into, and critical dialogue about, what peaces are and how they are to be made, maintained and combined. The Socratic Method still stands as a model for investigation and critical dialogue, whether in impromptu teach-ins, diplomatic gatherings, court proceedings, parliamentary debates or around dinner tables. The complaints of Erasmus' personification of peace circle around replacing weapons with and expediting reconciliation through persuasion, and even bona fide Enlightenment thinkers such as Kant confirmed that criticism is the only way to prevent conflicting rationalities from going to war. Although the shadow of the figure of barbarians as a cultural other has with whom no peace is possible has loomed large, ongoing contact consistently fostered intercultural convergences permitting investigation and critical dialogue. Language as a barrier to peace is a pretext rather than an acceptable apology, and peace in all its senses can only be grasped multilingually in addition to its non-linguistic experiences.

Epilogue: The Puzzle of World Peace

Principles and practices of "one world, one peace" are fatally flawed because if the world history of peace teaches us anything it is that peace and peacemaking are contingent on conditions and participants that are perpetually evolving. If the world history of peace should teach us only one thing, it is this: like putting together a puzzle the design of which cannot be known because it is always already changing, actualizing world peace lies in continually configuring and reconfiguring the world's peaces into a dynamic whole rather than forcing all of them to fit into a static one. I undertook this book in the belief that coming closer to terms with how and why the world's peaces came or ceased to be what they are is a first, necessary step in renewed directions towards world peace – only to discover that, of necessity, there is no last.

Notes

Introduction: How Does Peace Have a World History?

1 I. Bloch, *The Future of War*, trans. R. Long (Ginn, 1903), lxv.
2 T. Livius, *Histories*, trans. A. de Selincourt (Penguin Classics, 2002), 401.
3 L. Lincoln, *Collected Works of Abraham Lincoln*, vol. 6 (Rutgers, 1990), 410.
4 C. Clausewitz, *On War*, trans. J. Graham (Penguin,1982), 197.
5 B. Fogarty, *War, Peace, and the Social Order* (Westview, 2000), 1.
6 M. Weddle, *Walking the Way of Peace* (Oxford, 2000), 7.
7 K. Jaspers, *The Origin and Goal of History*, trans. M. Bullock (Yale, 1953), 1–2.

1. Survival of the Peaceful: Prehistory to the First Civilizations

1 L. Sponsel, "The Natural History of Peace: The Positive View of Human Nature and its Potential," in *A Natural History of Peace*, ed. T. Gregor (Vanderbilt, 1996), 96–128, p. 100.
2 J. Goodall, *The Chimpanzees of Gombe: Patterns of Behavior* (Harvard, 1986), 357.
3 T. Kano, "The Bonobo's Peaceable Kingdom," *Natural History*, 11 (1990), 62–71, p. 70.
4 S. C. Strum, "Baboons may be Smarter than People," *Animal Kingdom*, 88: 2 (1985), 12–22, p. 22.
5 F. de Waal "The Biological Basis for Peaceful Coexistence: A Review of Reconciliation Research on Monkeys and Apes," in *A Natural History of Peace* (supra), 37–70, p. 58.
6 S. Kuroda, "Social Behavior of the Pygmy Chimpanzee," *Primates*, 21 (1980), 181–97, p. 190.
7 G. Kemp, "Nonviolence: A Biological Perspective," in *A Just Peace Through Transformation: Cultural, Economic and Political Foundations for Change*, eds C. Alger and M. Stohl (Westview, 1988), 112–26, p. 118.

8 M. Roper, "A Survey of the Evidence for Intrahuman Killing in the Pleistocene," *Current Anthropology*, 10: 4 (1969), 427–58, p. 448.

9 Sponsel, "The Natural History of Peace," 95–6.

10 H. Spencer, *Principles of Biology*, vol. 1 (Appleton, 1864), 14.

11 H. Kellerman, *Group Cohesion: Theoretical and Clinical Perspectives* (Grune and Stratton, 1981), 166.

12 C. Darwin, *On the Origin of Species* (Broadview, 2003), 524.

13 P. Kropotkin, *Mutual Aid: A Factor of Evolution* (Kessinger, 2004), 10.

14 R. Bigelow, *The Dawn Warriors: Man's Evolution Towards Peace* (Little, Brown, 1969), 4.

15 B. Knauft, "The Human Evolution of Cooperative Interest," in *A Natural History of Peace* (supra), 71–94.

16 R. Firth, *Primitive Economics of the New Zealand Maori* (E. P. Dutton, 1929), 422.

17 D. Fabro, "Peaceful Societies: An Introduction," *Journal of Peace Research*, 15:1 (1978), 67–83.

18 R. Eisler, *The Chalice and the Blade: Our History, Our Future* (Harper and Row, 1987).

19 R. Potts, *Early Hominid Activities at Olduvai* (Aldine de Gruyter, 1988), 251.

20 R. Leakey and R. Lewin, *Origins: What New Discoveries Reveal about the Emergence of Our Species* (Macdonald and Jane's, 1977), 248.

21 Knauft, "The Human Evolution of Cooperative Interest," 75.

22 Sponsel, "The Natural History of Peace," 109.

23 Church Missionary Society, *Proceedings of the Church Missionary Society for Africa and the East*, vol. 7 (Church Missionary House, 1836), 159.

24 L. Warner, *A Black Civilization: A Social Study of an Australian Tribe* (Peter Smith, 1937), 156–7.

25 I. Eibl-Eibesfeldt, *Human Ethology* (Aldine de Gruyter, 1989), 421.

26 B. Fogarty, *War, Peace and the Social Order* (Westview, 2000), 149.

27 R. Cohen, "Warfare and State Formation: Wars Make States and States Make Wars," in *Warfare, Culture and Environment*, ed. R. Ferguson (Academic Press, 1984), 329–58, p. 338.

28 C. Freeman, *Egypt, Greece and Rome* (Oxford, 2005), 20.

29 Isaiah 5:8.

30 D. Christie, "Reducing Direct and Structural Violence: The Human Needs Theory," *Peace and Conflict*, 3 (1997), 316–23. The concept of structural violence originates with J. Galtung, "Violence, peace and peace research," *Journal of Peace Research*, 3 (1969), 167–91.

31 S. Moscati, *The Face of the Ancient Orient: A Panorama of Near Eastern Civilizations in Pre-Classical Times* (Quadrangle Books, 1960), 25.

32 D. Snell, *Life in the Ancient Near East* (Yale, 1997), 109.

33 Freeman, *Egypt, Greece and Rome*, 107–8.

34 F. Heichelheim, *An Ancient Economic History: From the Palaeolithic Age to the Migrations of the Germanic, Slavic and Arabic Nations* vol. 1, tr. J. Stevens (Sijthoff, 1957), 166.

35 Snell, *Life in the Ancient Near East*, 106.

36 J. Hertzler, *The Social Thought of the Ancient Civilizations* (McGraw-Hill, 1936), 79.
37 S. Moscati, *Ancient Semitic Civilizations* (Putnam, 1957), 80.

2. Peace in the Ancient West: Egypt, Greece and Rome

1 E. James, *The Ancient Gods: The History and Diffusion of Religion in the Ancient Near East and the Eastern Mediterranean* (Putnam, 1960), 263.
2 R. Platt and M. Hefny, *Egypt: A Compendium* (American Geographical Society, 1958), 7.
3 T. Wilkinson, *Early Dynastic Egypt* (Routledge, 1999), 51.
4 V. Childe, *The Most Ancient East: The Oriental Prelude to European Prehistory* (Knopf, 1929), 218.
5 F. Heichelheim, *An Ancient Economic History: From the Palaeolithic Age to the Migrations of the Germanic, Slavic and Arabic Nations* vol. 1, tr. J. Stevens (Sijthoff, 1957), 446.
6 "The Maxims of Ptah-Hotep," in J. Lewis, *The Mammoth Book of Eyewitness Ancient Egypt* (Carroll and Graf, 2003), 17.
7 S. Glanville, *The Legacy of Egypt* (Clarendon, 1942), 73.
8 A. David, *The Pyramid Builders of Ancient Egypt: A Modern Investigation of Pharaoh's Workforce* (Routledge, 1996), 29, 33, 45.
9 A. Weigall (1923), *The Life and Times of Akhnaton Pharaoh of Egypt* (Kessinger, 2004), 27.
10 C. Lamberg-Karlovsky and J. Sabloff, *Ancient Civilization and Trade* (U of New Mexico, 1975), 105.
11 C. Ogden, *From Tribe to Empire: Social Organization among Primitives and in the Ancient East*, (Paul, Trench, Treubner, 1926), 331, my ital.
12 J. Modrzejewski, *The Jews of Egypt: From Rameses II to Emperor Hadrian*, tr. R. Cornman (Jewish Publication Society, 1995), 30, my ital.
13 R. Gabriel and D. Boose, *The Great Battles of Antiquity: A Strategic and Tactical Guide to Great Battles That Shaped the Development of War* (Greenwood, 1994), 85.
14 Modrzejewski, 325.
15 Ogden, *From Tribe to Empire*, 325–6.
16 Ibid., 295.
17 C. Kerényi, *Prometheus: Archetypal Image of Human Existence*, trans. R. Manheim (Bollingen Foundation, 1963), 100–1.
18 *Iliad*, 9.514–15.
19 *Iliad*, 5.889–91
20 R. Gabriel and K. Metz, *From Sumer to Rome: The Military Capabilities of Ancient Armies* (Greenwood, 1991), 132.
21 Epilogue of the *Odyssey*, 24.485–6.
22 Hesiod, *Works and Days*, 225–9.
23 E. Wilkins, *The Delphic Maxims in Literature* (University of Chicago, 1929), 1.
24 E. Cook, *The Odyssey in Athens: Myths of Cultural Origins* (Cornell, 1995), 132.
25 Xenophon, *Anabasis*, 3.1.38

26 G. Norlin, trans. *Isocrates*, vol. 1 (Heinemann, 1928), 185.
27 M. Finley, *The Greek Historians: The Essence of Herodotus, Thucydides, Xenophon and Polybius* (Viking, 1959), 482.
28 Plutarch, *Pericles*, 17.1.
29 Thucydides, *History of the Peloponnesian War*, 5.26.
30 G. Grundy, *Thucydides and the History of His Age*, vol. 2 (Blackwell, 1948), 220.
31 Thucydides, 5.26.2.
32 Thucydides, 8.132.
33 Porphyry, *De vita pythagorica*, 36.372.
34 *Herodotus*, vol. 1, trans. W. Beloe (H. Colburn and R. Bentley, 1830), 73.
35 B. Sandywell, *Presocratic Reflexivity: The Construction of Philosophical Discourse c. 600–450 BC* (Routledge, 1996), 264–5.
36 L. Edelstein, "The Hippocratic Oath: Text, Translation and Interpretation," in *Ancient Medicine*, eds O. and L. Temkin (Johns Hopkins, 1967), 60.
37 Alcidamas, *Rhetoric*, 3.3.4.
38 Xenophon, *Memorabili*, 4.2.15–16.
39 Plato, *The Republic*, 2.373a.
40 Plato, *The Laws*, 7.803d; 8.829a.
41 Ibid., 1.626a.
42 G. Zampaglione, *The Idea of Peace in Antiquity*, trans. R. Dunn (University of Notre Dame, 1973), 131.
43 C. Smith, *Early Rome and Latium: Economy and Society c. 1000 to 500 BC* (Clarendon, 1996), 212.
44 Tacitus, *Life of Agricola*, 3.25.
45 N. Machiavelli, *Discourses on the First Decade of Titus Livy*, trans. N. Thomson (K. Paul, Trench and Co., 1883), 219.
46 O. Thatcher, *The Roman World* (University Research Extension, 1901), 9–11.
47 Plybius, *Histories*, 4.74.3, my ital.
48 Cicero, *Pro Sestio*, 45.98. J. Johnson, *Just War Tradition and the Restraint of War: A Moral and Historical Inquiry* (Princeton, 1981), xxi–xxxv.
49 *De republica*, III, 23 and 25.
50 Seneca, *Epistola ad Lucilium*, 2.21.
51 Flavius Arrianus, *Discourses of Epictetus*, 3.13.40–1.
52 Ovid, *Fasti*, 1.711–22.
53 Eutropius, *Breviarium historiae romanae*, 9.17.
54 Falvius Vopiscus, *Vita Probi*, 20.
55 Velleius Paterculus, *Roman History*, 2.126.
56 J. Grainger, *Nerva and the Roman Succession Crisis AD 96–99* (Routledge, 2002), 47, 13ff.
57 A. Claridge, *Rome: An Oxford Archaeological Guide* (Oxford, 1998), 19.

3. Peace in the Ancient East: India, China and Japan

1 Kautalya, *The Arthashastra*, trans. L. Rangarajan (Penguin, 1992), op. cit.
2 W. Polk, *Neighbors & Strangers: The Fundamentals of Foreign Affairs* (University of Chicago, 1997), 232.

3 B. Nanamoli and B. Bodhi, trans., *The Middle Length Discourses of the Buddha: A New Translation of the Majjhima Nikaya* (Wisdom, 1995), 533–6.

4 G. Deng, *The Premodern Chinese Economy: Structural Equilibrium and Capitalist Sterility* (Routledge, 1999), 88, 99–103.

5 L. Chang *et al.*, *The Four Political Treatises of the Yellow Emperor* (University of Hawaii, 1998), p. 62.

6 Wei Z., *et al.*, eds. *Emperor Kangxi's Instructions on State Management* (Expatriates', 1995), 45.

7 R. Huang, *China: A Macro History* (Sharpe, 1997), 19.

8 M. Lewis, *Sanctioned Violence in Early China* (State University of New York, 1990), 92–3.

9 Y. Lo, "The Formulation of Early Confucian Metaphysics," in *Imagining Boundaries: Changing Confucian Doctrines, Texts, and Hermeneutics*, eds K. Chow *et al.* (State University of New York Press, 1999), 57–85, p. 70–1.

10 Confucius, *The Analects*, trans. S. Leys (Norton, 1999), 77.

11 W. de Bary *et al.*, eds, *Sources of Chinese Tradition*, vol. 1 (Columbia, 1960), 115; my rendition cf. E. Pound, *The Great Digest* and *The Unwobbling Pivot* (Peter Owen, 1968), 30–1.

12 J. Gernet, *A History of Chinese Civilization*, trans. J. Foster and C. Hartman (Cambridge, 1999), 81.

13 Chang, *Four Political Treatises* 175.

14 *Dao De Ching*, ch. 57.

15 B. Watson, *The Complete Works of Chuang Tzu* (Columbia, 1968), 191.

16 *Mozi*, trans. W. Mei (Probsthain, 1929), 2.

17 Gernet, *History of Chinese Civilization*, 145.

18 Ibid., 119.

19 Ibid., 132.

20 Ibid., 133.

21 M. Hane, *Premodern Japan: A Historical Survey* (Westview, 1991), 118.

22 K. Henshall, *A History of Japan: From Stone Age to Superpower* (Palgrave Macmillan, 2004), 16.

23 R. Borgen, *Sugawara No Michizane and the Early Heian Court* (University of Hawaii, 1994), 228.

24 H. Ichiro, "Japanese Folk-Beliefs," *American Anthropologist*, 61 (1959), 405–24.

25 M. de Visser, "The Tengu," *Transactions of the Asiatic Society of Japan*, vol. 36 pt. 2 (1908), n.p.

26 B. Burke-Gaffney, "Jaodori," *Harbor Light*, 2:9 (1987), 7.

27 C. Blomberg, *The Heart of the Warrior: Origins and Religious Background of the Samurai System in Feudal Japan* (Sandgate, 1994), 83.

28 Ibid., 81.

29 K. Friday, *Samurai: Warfare and the State in Early Medieval Japan* (Routledge, 2003), 29–32.

30 Ibid., 38.

31 H. Cortazzi, ed., *Mitford's Japan: The Memoirs and Recollections, 1866–1906, of Algernon Bertram Mitford, the first Lord Redesdale* (Athlone, 1985), 160.

32 J. Hall, "Japanese Feudal Laws III: The Tokugawa Legislation, Part I," *Transactions of the Asiatic Society of Japan,* vol. 38:4 (1911), 288.
33 K. Kawaiumi, *Japan and World Peace* (Macmillan, 1919), 13.
34 J. Behrman, "Transformation of Society: Implications for Globalization," *Making Globalization Good: The Moral Challenges of Global Capitalism,* ed. Dunning (Oxford, 2003), 121–45, 138.
35 C. Haguenauer, "La danse rituelle dans la ceremonie du chinkonsai," *Journal Asiatique* June(1930), 324–50.
36 Blomberg, *Heart of the Warrior,* 197.
37 W. de Bary, ed., *Sources of Japanese Tradition,* vol. 1 (Columbia, 1958), 347.
38 I. Nobutaka *et al., Shinto: A Short History* (Routledge, 2003), 170–1.

4. Monotheistic Peaces: Judaism, Christianity and Islam

1 Zampaglione, *The Idea of Peace in Antiquity,* 192.
2 Gen. 21: 22–32.
3 Josh. 9:15.
4 Isa. 27:5.
5 I Chr.; 28:3
6 Job 22:21.
7 Isa. 32:16–17.
8 Isa. 11:6 and 57:21.
9 Isa. 2:4.
10 Philo, "On the Change of Names," in *Philo,* trans. R. Marcus (Harvard), 267.
11 Luke 2:14.
12 Matt. 5: 9, 38–39, 43–5.
13 Matt. 7:12.
14 Luke 10: 5–6.
15 Matt. 26:52.
16 John 16:33.
17 John 24:27.
18 Eph. 2:17; Col.1:9–20.
19 Gal. 3: 28.
20 I Cor. 14: 33.
21 Eph. 2:14.
22 II Cor. 5:18–19.
23 Thess. 5:3.
24 Justin, "The First Apology," in *The Ante-Nicene Fathers: The Writings of the Fathers Down to A.D. 325,* vol. 1, trans. and ed. A. Roberts *et al.* (The Christian Literature Publication Co., 1885), 159–88, 163.
25 Tertullian, *Ad martyres,* quoted in Zampaglione, *The Idea of Peace in Antiquity,* 246.
26 J. Dymond, *An Inquiry Into the Accordancy of War with the Principles of Christianity* (Friends Books, 1892), 50.
27 Zampaglione, *The Idea of Peace in Antiquity,* 248.
28 Clement, *Christ, the Educator,* trans. S. Wood (Catholic University of America, 1954), 35.

29 Quoted in Zampaglione, *The Idea of Peace in Antiquity*, 251.
30 Ibid., 252.
31 Ibid., 257.
32 Ibid., 265.
33 Z. Karabell, *Peace Be Upon You: The Story of Muslim, Christian and Jewish Coexistence* (Knopf, 2007), 13.
34 Qur'an 20.47 and 14.23.
35 Qur'an 59.23 and 10.25.
36 Qur'an 2.224.
37 Qur'an 28:36.
38 Qur'an 8.61.
39 Qur'an 49.9.
40 Qur'an 49.10.
41 Qur'an 4.90.
42 Qur'an 2.11.
43 Qur'an 4.91.
44 Qur'an 4.94.
45 Ibid., p. 22.
46 J. Kelsay, *Islam and War: A Study in Comparative Ethics* (Westminster/John Knox, 1993), 47, orig. ital.
47 J. Kelsay and J. Johnson, eds., *Just War and Jihad: Historical and Theoretical Perspectives on War and Peace in Western and Islamic Traditions* (Greenwood, 1991), iii.
48 M. Bamyeh, *The Social Origins of Islam: Mind, Economy, Discourse* (University of Minnesota, 1999), 224.
49 M. Sicker, *The Islamic World in Ascendancy: From the Arab Conquests to the Siege of Vienna* (Praeger, 2000), 10.
50 Qur'an 2: 256.
51 G. Hawting, *The First Dynasty of Islam: The Umayyad Caliphate AD 661–750* (Routledge, 2000), ch. 1.
52 Sicker, *Islamic World in Ascendancy*, 2.
53 Ibid.
54 S. Qasha, *Christians in the Muslim State* (Dar al-Malak, 2002), 67.

5. Medieval, Renaissance and Reformation Peaces

1 Augustine, *City of God*, vol. 2, trans. M. Dodds (Edinburgh: Clark, 1871), 319; my rendition cf. Zampaglione, 301.
2 Ibid., 405.
3 Ibid., 57.
4 Quoted in Zampaglione, *The Idea of Peace in Antiquity*, 299.
5 E. Gibbon, *The Decline and Fall of the Roman Empire* (Collier, 1899), 270.
6 Saint Benedict, *The Rule of Saint Benedict* (Vintage, 1998), 62.
7 D. Alighieri, *On World-Government*, trans. H. Schneider (Liberal Arts, 1957), 13.
8 Ibid., 22.
9 Quoted in M. Bishop, *Petrarch and His World* (Indiana, 1963), 286.

10 N. Machiavelli, *The Prince*, trans. N. Thomson (Paul, Trench, 1882), 115–16.
11 Ibid., 57.
12 N. Machiavelli, *Discourses on the First Decade of Titus Livy*, trans. N. Thomson (Paul, Trench, 1883), 219.
13 Ibid., 431.
14 Erasmus, "On the War against the Turks," in *The Erasmus Reader*, ed. E. Rummel (University of Toronto, 1990), 316–19.
15 *The Adages of Erasmus*, ed. W. Barker (University of Toronto, 2001), 323.
16 T. More, *Utopia* (Rickerby, 1852), 174.
17 Ibid., 183.
18 Ibid., 156.
19 M. Mullett, *Martin Luther* (Routledge, 2004), 75.
20 M. Wagner, *Petr Chelcicky: A Radical Separatist in Hussite Bohemia* (Herald, 1983), 89.
21 P. Brock, *Political and Social Doctrines of the Unity of Czech Brethren* (Mouton, 1957), 55.
22 C. Grebel, Letter to Thomas Muntzer, September 1524.
23 J. Stayer, *Anabaptists and the Sword* (Wipf and Stock), 172.
24 A. Weinberg and L. Weinberg, eds, *Instead of Violence: Writings of the Great Advocates of Peace and Nonviolence Throughout History*, (Grossman, 163), 438l.
25 G. Fox, *Journal of George Fox*, ed. J. Nickalls (Cambridge, 1952), 65.
26 Ibid.
27 Ibid., 405.
28 Ibid., 398–404.

6. Peace, Peacemaking and the Ascent of Nation-States

1 T. Hobbes, *Leviathan* (Routledge, 1886), 64.
2 Ibid., 93.
3 Ibid., 65.
4 C. de Montesquieu, *The Spirit of the Law*, trans. T. Nugent (Colonial, 1900), 59.
5 Ibid., 127.
6 Ibid., 316.
7 J. Locke, *Two Treaties on Government* (Routledge, 1887), 191.
8 Ibid., 250, 219.
9 Ibid., 258–9.
10 Ibid., 287.
11 Ibid., 302.
12 J. Rousseau, *The Social Contract*, trans. G. Cole (Dutton, 1950), 9.
13 Ibid., 66.
14 Ibid., 12.
15 Ibid., 3.
16 Ibid., 140.
17 C. Ady and E. Armstrong, *A History of Milan under the Sforza* (Methuen, 1907), 62.

18 E. Crucé, *Le Nouveau Cynée*, trans. T. Balch (Allen, Lane, and Scott, 1909), 85.
19 Ibid., 9, 3.
20 H. Grotius, *On the Laws of War and Peace*, trans. F. Kelsey (Carnegie, 1925), 28.
21 Montesquieu, 5.
22 J. Scott, ed., *The Classics of International Law* (Clarendon, 1934), 175.
23 G. de Martens, *Summary of the Law of Nations Founded on the Treaties and Customs of the Modern Nations of Europe*, trans. William Cobbett (Philadelphia, 1795), 3–5.
24 Ibid., 5.
25 W. Grewe, *The Epochs of International Law*, trans. M. Byers (Walter de Gruyter, 2000), 380–1.
26 Ibid.
27 Constitution of the International Law Association, Article 3www.ila-hq.org/html/main_constitution_english.htm accessed June 1, 2008.
28 G. Finch, *The Sources of Modern International Law* (Hein, 2000), 77.
29 J. Ralston, *International Arbitration: From Athens to Locarno* (Stanford, 1929), 191.
30 *Bulletin du premier congrès universel de la paix* (Paris, 1889), 10–13.
31 Statutes of the Inter-Parliamentarian Union, Article 2, http://www.ipu.org/strct-e/statutes-new.htm accessed October 25, 2007.
32 N. Politis, *Neutrality and Peace*, trans. F. Macken (Carnegie, 1935), 12.
33 P. Schroeder, *The Transformation of European Politics, 1763–1848* (Clarendon, 1996), 25, 46.
34 F. Hartmann, ed., *Basic Documents of International Relations* (McGraw-Hill, 1951). 16.
35 Ibid., 11–12.
36 J. Solana, "Securing Peace in Europe," NATO Publications (November 12, 1998) www.nato.int/docu/speech/1998/s981112a.htm accessed June 1, 2008.
37 H. Wheaton, *Elements of International Law* (Philadelphia, 1846), 3.
38 I. Kant, *The Critique of Pure Reason*, trans. J. Meiklejohn (Collier, 1901), 548.
39 I. Kant, *Foundations of the Metaphysics of Morals* (Prentice Hall, 1997), 54.
40 I. Kant, *The Philosophy of Law. An Exposition of the Fundamental Principles of Jurisprudence as the Science of Right*, trans. W. Hastie (Clark, 1887), 229–30.
41 W. Phillips, *The Confederation of Europe: A Study of the European Alliance, 1813–1823, as an Experiment in the International Organization of Peace* (Longmans Green, 1920), 5.
42 I. Kant, *Perpetual Peace*, trans. L. Beck (Liberal Arts, 1957).
43 "The Herald of Peace," in *Les États-Unis d'Europe* 1:46 (1868), 182.
44 F. Passy, *Guerres et congrès ou le socialisme international: Extrait de l'Économiste belge*, (Paris, 1899), 5–6.
45 Passy "Ligue internationale et permanente de la paix" (Paris, 1868), 77–87.
46 S. Cooper *Patriotic, Pacifism: Waging War on War in Europe, 1815–1914* (Oxford, 1991), 61.

47 E. Mead, *Official Report* (London, 1908), 88.
48 A. Schou, *Nobel: The Man and His Prizes* (Norman, 1951), 477.
49 W. Channing, *The Works of William E. Channing* (American Unitarian Association, 1894), 673.
50 Ibid., 676.
51 R. Emerson, *The Journals of Ralph Waldo Emerson*, vol. 10 (Houghton Mifflin, 1914), 117.
52 R. Emerson, *Essays* (Houghton Mifflin, 1883), 87.
53 R. Emerson, *The Journals of Ralph Waldo Emerson*, vol. 7 (Houghton Mifflin, 1912), 221.
54 H. Thoreau, "Civil Disobedience," in *Walden and Other Writings* (Modern Library, 1950), 635–63, p. 644.
55 Ibid., 647.
56 L. Tolstoy, *War and Peace*, trans. L. and A. Maude (Oxford, 1998), 667.
57 Ibid., 669–70.
58 Ibid., 476.
59 L. Tolstoy, *What Is Art?* (London, 1924), 332.
60 L. Tostoy, *The Kingdom of God Is Within You and Peace Essays* (Oxford, 1951), 19.
61 L. Tostoy, *The Law of Love and the Law of Violence* (R. Field, 1938), 38.
62 R. Christian, trans. *Tolstoy's Letters* vol. 2 (Scribner, 1978), 707–8.
63 Baha Ullah, *Gleanings from the Writings of Baha'u'llah*, trans. S. Effendi (Baha'i Publishing), 250
64 Ibid., 119.
65 H. Balyuzi, *Baha Ullah: A Brief Life* (G. Ronald, 1963), 69.
66 *Paris Talks: Addresses Given by 'Abdu'l-Baha in 1911* (Baha'i Publishing, 2006), 120–1.
67 'Abdu'l-Baha, *The Promulgation of Universal Peace* (Baha'i Publishing, 1982), 371; *Selections from the Writings of 'Abdu'l-Baha* (Baha'i World Center, 1978), 249.

7. Colonial and Imperial Peace and Peacemaking

1 A. Roy, "The New American Century," *The Nation*, 278: 5 (2004), 11.
2 J. Olson *et al.*, eds, *Historical Dictionary of European Imperialism* (Greenwood, 1991), 627.
3 E. Bourne, eds, *The Voyages of the Northmen* (Scribner's, 1906), 112, 114.
4 O. Dickason, *The Myth of the Savage, and the Beginnings of French Colonialism in the Americas* (University of Alberta, 1997), 29.
5 F. Sullivan, trans., *Indian Freedom: The Cause of Bartolomé de Las Casas, 1484–1566, A Reader* (Rowman and Littlefield, 1995), 354.
6 B. Dobrée, *William Penn, Quaker and Pioneer* (Houghton Mifflin, 1932), 145.
7 G. Weltfish, *The Lost Universe: Pawnee Life and Culture* (University of Nebraska, 1977), 175.
8 Ibid.
9 B. Johansen, *The Encyclopedia of Native American Legal Tradition* (Greenwood, 1998), 81.

10 J. Roach, *Cities of the Dead: Circum-Atlantic Performance* (Columbia, 1996), 120.
11 J. Parry, *The Audiencia of New Galicia in the Sixteenth Century: A Study in Spanish Colonial Government* (Cambridge, 1948), 6.
12 J. Scott, *The Spanish Origin of International Law* (Clarendon, 1934), 348.
13 J. Thomson, *Mercenaries, Pirates, and Sovereigns: State-Building and Extraterritorial Violence in Early Modern Europe* (Princeton, 1994), 35.
14 C. Boxer, *The Dutch Seaborne Empire, 1600–1800* (Knopf, 1965), 24–5.
15 "Dead payes" are cash given to the families of those killed while on commission. P. Griffiths, *The British Impact on India* (MacDonald, 1952), 51.
16 J. Fitzpatrick, ed., *The Writings of George Washington from the Original Manuscript Sources 1745–79*, vol. 30 (Government Printing Office, 1939), 71; *The Federalist: A Collection of Essays by Alexander Hamilton, John Jay and James Madison* (Colonial, 1901), 58.
17 T. Jefferson, *Writings*, vol. 8, ed. P. Ford (Putnam, 1892–99), 4.
18 J. Elliot, Jonathan, *The American Diplomatic Code*, vol. 2 (Privately Printed, 1834), 179.
19 J. Foster, *American Diplomacy in the Orient* (Houghton Mifflin, 1903), 395.
20 A. Dennis, *Adventures in American Diplomacy, 1896–1906* (Dutton, 1928), 24.
21 *U. S. Congressional Record* v. 31 (Government Printing Office), 3789.
22 V. Purcell, *The Boxer Uprising: A Background Study* (Cambridge, 1963), 70.
23 D. Preston, *The Boxer Rebellion: The Dramatic Story of China's War on Foreigners* (Walker, 2000), 206.
24 Ibid., 307.
25 P. Clyde, *United States Policy Toward China: Diplomatic Public Documents, 1839–1939* (Duke, 1940), 216.
26 J. Blaine, *Political Discussions, Legislative, Diplomatic, and Popular* (Henry Bill, 1887), 429.
27 *The Annalist*, 23 (1921), 159.
28 *U. S. Congressional Record* v. 39, 19.
29 S. Nearing and J. Freeman, *Dollar Diplomacy: A Study in American Imperialism* (Viking, 1925), 247.
30 *Types of Restricted Sovereignty and of Colonial Autonomy* (Government Printing Office, 1919), 6–7.
31 *Foreign Relation* (1912), vxiii.

8. Modern Economics of Peace and Peacemaking

1 C. von Clausewitz, *On War*, trans. J. Graham (Penguin, 1982), 197.
2 *Le Roman politique sur l'état présent des affaires de l'Amérique ou Lettres de M * * * à M * * * sur les moyens d'établir une paix solide et durable dans les Colonies et la Liberté générale de Commerce Extérieur* (Amsterdam, 1756), 332.
3 J. Necker, *De l'Administration des finances de la France* (Dijon, 1784), vol. III, ch. 36, n.p.
4 L. Loubère, *Louis Blanc: His Life and His Contribution to the Rise of French Jacobin-Socialism* (Northwestern, 1961), 67.

5 A. Smith, *An Inquiry into the Nature and Causes of the Wealth of Nations* (Collier, 1909), 445.

6 J. Bentham, "Principles of International Law," in *The Works of Jeremy Bentham*, vol. 8 (Tait, 1839), 552.

7 Ibid., 556.

8 J. Bentham, *An Introduction to the Principles of Morals and Legislation* (Clarendon, 1879), 2.

9 Ibid., 215.

10 D. Ricardo, *On the Principles of Political Economy and Taxation* (Murray, 1821), 153.

11 J. Mill, *Principles of Political Economy, with Some of Their Applications to Social Philosophy*, vol. 2 (Appleton, 1897), 136.

12 H. Paul, *A History of Modern England*, vol. 4 (Macmillan, 1905), 85.

13 G. Schmoller, *The Mercantile System and its Historical Significance* (Kelley, 1989), 78–9.

14 F. Bastiat, "Harmonies économiques," *Œuvres complètes*, vol. 6 (Guillaumin et Cie, Paris, 1864), 385.

15 L. Walras, "La paix par la justice sociale et le libre échange," *Œuvres complètes*, vol. 7 (Economica, 1907), 467–70, p. 467.

16 F. Coulomb, *Economic Theories of Peace and War* (Routledge, 2004), 58.

17 H. Saint-Simon, *Selected Writings on Science, Industry, and Social Organization*, ed. K. Taylor (Holmes and Meier, 1975), 34.

18 Ibid., 36.

19 G. Hegel, *Philosophy of Right*, trans. T. Knox (Clarendon, 1942), 215.

20 D. Moellendorf, "Marxism, Internationalism, and the Justice of War," *Science and Society*, 58:3 (1994), 264–86.

21 Coulomb, *Economic Theories of Peace and War* 121.

22 J. Monnerot, *Sociology and Psychology of Communism* (Boston: Beacon, 1953), 27.

23 G. Woodcock, *Pierre-Joseph Proudhon: A Biography* (Routledge, 1956), 278.

24 H. Clegg, *A New Approach to Industrial Democracy* (Blackwell, 1960), 20.

25 J. Dunlop, *Collective Bargaining: Principles and Cases* (Irwin, 1949), 32.

26 D. Cole, *The Quest for Industrial Peace* (McGraw-Hill, 1963), 67, 96.

27 Ibid.

28 Ibid., 98.

9. Peace in the Twentieth Century, Part I: 1900–1945

1 G. Herman, *The Pivotal Conflict: A Comprehensive Chronology of the First World War, 1914–1919* (Greenwood, 1992), ix; R. Pearce, "The Origins of the First World War," *History Review*, 27 (1997), 12–31, p. 21.

2 J. Choate, *The Two Hague Conferences* (Princeton, 1913), 9.

3 B. Adams, *Nothing of Importance: A Record of Eight Months at the Front with a Welsh Battalion, October 1915 to June 1916* (Stevenage, 1988), 303.

4 J. Rae, *Conscience and Politics* (Oxford, 1970), 250.

5 J. Atkin, *A War of Individuals: Bloomsbury Attitudes to the Great War* (Manchester, 2002), 3.

6 B. Russell, *"The Philosophy of Pacifism,"* *Collected Papers* vol. 13, ed. R. Rempel *et al.* (Allen and Unwin, 1985), 147–8.

7 N. Griffin, ed., *The Selected Letters of Bertrand Russell: The Public Years, 1914–1970* (Routledge, 2002), 260.

8 B. Hamann, *Bertha von Suttner: A Life for Peace*, trans. A. Dubsky (Syracuse, 1996), xv.

9 J. Addams, *Peace and Bread in Time of War* (Macmillan, 1922), 8.

10 G. Bussey, *Women's International League for Peace and Freedom: 1915–1965* (Allen and Unwin, 1965), 163.

11 S. Weil, "Reflections on War," in *Formative Writings* (University of Massachusetts, 1988), 224.

12 N. Mandela, "The Sacred Warrior," *Time Magazine*, 100 Person of the twentieth Century www.time.com/time/time100/poc/magazine/the_sacred_warrior13a.html accessed June 1, 2008.

13 United Nations, Sixty-first General Assembly Plenary, 103rd Meeting (AM), June 15, 2007, GA/10601.

14 R. Baker, *Woodrow Wilson and World Settlement* (Doubleday, 1922), 23–42.

15 A. Link, *Wilson the Diplomatist* (New Viewpoints, 1974), 122.

16 Covenant of the League of Nations, Article 3.

17 Biography for the Nobel Peace Prize, http://nobelprize.org/nobel_prizes/peace/laureates/1925/chamberlain-bio.html accessed October 27, 2007.

18 G. Craig, *Germany, 1866–1945* (Clarendon, 1978), 685.

19 Andre François-Poncet, after a conversation with Adolf Hitler, ibid., 689.

20 J. Vinson, *The Parchment Peace* (University of Georgia, 1950).

21 W. Willoughby, *China at the Conference: A Report* (Johns Hopkins, 1922), 43.

22 M. Hudson, *The Verdict of the League: China and Japan in Manchuria* (World Peace Foundation, 1933), 15–16.

10. Peace in the Twentieth Century, Part II: 1945–1989

1 P. Hejl, "Communication and Social Systems: Evolutionary and Developmental Aspects," in *Human by Nature: Between Biology and the Social Sciences*, eds P. Weingart *et al.* (Lawrence Erlbaum, 1997), 392–417, p. 407.

2 A. Parsons, *From Cold War to Hot Peace: UN Interventions 1946–1994* (Penguin, 1994).

3 "The Russell-Einstein Manifesto" (1955), Pugwash Conference on Science and World Affairs www.pugwash.org/about/manifesto.htm accessed June 1, 2008.

4 In I. Abrams *et al.*, *Nobel Lectures: Peace, 1951–1970* (World Scientific, 1999), 262.

5 L. Pauling, *No More War!* (Dodd, 1958), vii.

6 USA Today/CNN Gallup Poll www.usatoday.com/news/polls/2005-11-15-iraq-poll.htm accessed June 1, 2008.

7 "Declaration of Conscience Against the War in Vietnam" in S. and A. Lynd, eds, *Nonviolence in America: A Documentary History* (Bobbs-Merrill, 1965), 270–1.

8 T. Dupuy and G. Hammerman, eds, *A Documentary History of Arms Control and Disarmament* (Bowker, 1973), 470–471.

9 D. Whittaker, *United Nations in Action* (UCL, 1995), 243.

10 R. Launius, *Frontiers of Space Exploration* (Greenwood, 1998), 9.

11 D. Eisenhower, British Broadcasting System television interview, August 3, 1959.

12 B. Epstein, *Political Protest and Cultural Revolution: Nonviolent Direct Action in the 1970s and 80s* (University of California, 1991), ch. 3.

13 E. P. Thompson, "1980s," *The Nation* (January 10, 2000), 44.

14 P. Kelly, "Women and Ecology," in *Women on War: Essential Voices for the Nuclear Age*, ed. D. Gioseffi (Simon and Schuster, 1988), 309–316, p. 312.

15 M. Gorbachev, *Perestroika: New Thinking for Our Country and the World* (Harper and Row, 1987), 247.

16 R. Thakur, *Peacekeeping in Vietnam: Canada, India, Poland, and the International Commission* (University of Alberta, 1984), 50.

17 L. M. Goodrich and E. Hambro, *Charter of the United Nations: Commentary and Documents* (World Peace Foundation, 1946), 53.

18 Ibid., 334.

19 J. Humphrey, *Human Rights and the United Nations: A Great Adventure* (Transnational, 1983), 53.

20 Charter of the United Nations, Article 13.

21 Statutes of the International Law Commission, Article 1, http://untreaty.un.org/ilc/texts/instruments/english/statute/statute_e.pdf accessed June 1, 2008.

22 M. King Jr., *Stride Toward Freedom: The Montgomery Story* (Harper and Brothers, 1958), 217.

23 L. Eades, *The End of Apartheid in South Africa* (Greenwood, 1999), p. 159.

24 D. Tutu, *God Has a Dream: A Vision of Hope for Our Time* (Random House, 2005), 120.

11. The Presents of Peace

1 F. Fukuyama, "The End of History?," *The National Interest*, 16 (1989), 2–18, p. 3.

2 J. Derrida, *Specters of Marx*, trans. P. Kamuf (Routledge, 1994), 9.

3 C. Kinnvall, "Analyzing the Global-Local Nexus, in *Globalization and Democratization in Asia: The Construction of Identity*, eds C. Kinnvall and K. Jönsson (Routledge, 2002), 1–19, p. 5.

4 B. Russett, *Grasping the Democratic Peace: Principles for a Post-Cold War World* (Princeton, 1993).

5 W. Perdue, *Terrorism and the State: A Critique of Domination through Fear* (Praeger, 1989), 198.

6 T. Friedman, *The Lexus and the Olive Tree: Understanding Globalization* (Farrar, Straus and Giroux, 2000), 248; and *The World is Flat: A Brief History of the 21st Century* (Farrar, Straus and Giroux, 2007), 491.

7 J. Behrman, "Transformation of Society: Implications for Globalization," *Making Globalization Good: The Moral Challenges of Global Capitalism*, ed. J. Dunning (Oxford, 2003) 108–44, p. 115.

8 J. Pieterse, *Globalization or Empire?* (Routledge, 2004), 164.

9 G. Monbiot, "Stronger than Ever," *Guardian* (28 January, 2003).

10 Europe Solidaire Sans Frontières' website, www.europe-solidaire.org/spip. php?article472 accessed June 1, 2008.

11 S. Huntington, *The Clash of Civilizations and the Remaking of the World Order* (Simon and Schuster, 1996).

12 J. Schmidt and J. Hersh, eds, *Globalization and Social Change* (Routledge, 2000), xiv.

13 T. Adorno, *Critical Models: Interventions and Catchwords* (Columbia, 2005), 247.

14 J. Habermas, "New Social Movements," *Telos*, 49 (1981), 33.

15 M. Marshall, "Measuring Systemic Peace" (Center for Systemic Peace and George Mason University) http://www.systemicpeace.org/conflict.htm accessed June 1, 2008. Graph used with permission.

16 "Global Peace Index," Vision of Humanity, www.visionofhumanity.com/ introduction/index.php accessed June 1, 2008.

17 J. Coakley, "The Resolution of Ethnic Conflict: Towards a Typology," *International Political Science Review*, 13 (1992), 343–58; J. McGarry and B. O'Leary (1993), "Introduction: The Macro-Political Regulation of Ethnic Conflict," in *The Politics of Ethnic Conflict Regulation: Case Studies of Protracted Ethnic Conflicts*, eds, ibid., (Routledge), 1–40.

18 V. Havel, "Peace: The View from Prague," *New York Review of Books* (November 21, 1985), 30.

19 Pieterse, *Globalization or Empire* 52.

20 UN Peace-Building Commission http://www.un.org/peace/peacebuilding/ index.html accessed June 1, 2008.

21 "Terrorism," *The Columbia Encyclopedia*.

22 M. Hardt and A. Negri, *Empire* (Harvard, 2000), 411.

23 S. Benjamin and S. Simon, *The Age of Sacred Terror: Radical Islam's War Against America* (Random House, 2003).

24 E. Vencat, "Giving Peace a Chance: In an Unprecedented Letter, Muslim Leaders Across the Globe Invite the World's Christians to the Table," *Newsweek* (October 11, 2007), www.newsweek.com/id/42707/output/print accessed June 1, 2008.

25 S. McBride, "Nuclear Terrorism," in *Terrorism and National Liberation*, ed. H. Koechler (Peter Lang, 1988), 35–40, p. 35.

26 N. Smith, *The Endgame of Globalization* (Routledge, 2005), 10.

27 Heavily adapted from J. Darby and R. MacGinty, "The Management of Peace," in *The Management of Peace Processes* (supra), 253–59.

28 W. Arkin and R. Fieldhouse, *Nuclear Battlefields: Global Links in the Arms Race* (Ballinger, 1985), 2.

29 P. Waterman, "Social Movement Unionism: A New Model for a New World Order?" *Review* 16:3. 1993.

30 M. McLuhan, *The Gutenberg Galaxy* (University of Toronto, 1962), 43.

31 M. McLuhan, *Understanding Media: The Extensions of Man* (McGraw Hill, 1964).

32 C. Raab and C. Bellamy, "Electronic Democracy and the 'Mixed Polity':

Symbiosis or Conflict?," in *Electronic Democracy: Mobilisation, Organisation, and Participation Via New ICTS*, eds R. Gibson *et al.* (Routledge, 2004), 17–43, p. 18.

33 Behrman, "Transformation of Society," 130.

Conclusion: The Pyramid of Peace: Past, Present and Future

1 A. Maslow, *Motivation and Personality* (Harper and Row, 1970).

2 S. Hembleben, *Plans for World Peace through Six Centuries* (Chicago: University of Chicago Press, 1943).

Selected Bibliography

A list of peace-related journals is available at the Peace and Justice Studies Association's website: http://www.peacejusticestudies.org/membership/journals. php.

Abrams, I. *et al.*, eds, *Nobel Lectures: Peace* (London: World Scientific, 1999).

Adams, R. *The Better Part of Valor: More, Erasmus, Colet, and Vives, on Humanism, War, and Peace, 1496–1535* (Seattle: University of Washington Press, 1962).

Alfred, T. *Peace, Power, Righteousness: An Indigenous Manifesto* (New York: Oxford University Press, 1999).

Alger, C. and M. Stohl, eds, *A Just Peace Through Transformation: Cultural, Economic and Political Foundations for Change* (Boulder: Westview,1988).

Angell, N. *The Great Illusion: A Study of the Relation of Military Power to National Advantage* (NY: McClelland and Goodchild, 1913).

Armstrong, H. *Peace and Counterpeace: From Wilson to Hitler* (NY: Harper & Row 1971).

Aruri, N. and M. Shuraydi, eds, *Reinventing Peace: The Influence of Edward W. Said* (Northampton: Interlink, 2000).

Asher, S. *et al.*, eds, *Nonviolent Social Movements: A Geographical Perspective* (Boston: Blackwell, 1999).

Axelrod, R. *The Evolution of Cooperation* (New York: Basic Books, 1984).

Barash, D., ed. *Approaches to Peace: A Reader in Peace Studies* (New York: Oxford University Press, 1999).

Barnaby, F. *The Gaia Peace Atlas: Survival into the Third Millennium* (New York: Doubleday, 1988).

Bigelow, R. *The Dawn Warriors: Man's Evolution Towards Peace* (Boston: Little, Brown, 1969).

Bainton, R. *Christian Attitudes Toward War and Peace: A Historical Survey and Critical Re-evaluation* (New York: Abingdon, 1960).

Beales, A. *The History of Peace* (New York: The Dial Press, 1931).

Bederman, D. *International Law in Antiquity* (Cambridge: Cambridge University Press, 2001).

Bhatia, H. *International Law and Practice in Ancient India* (New Delhi: Deep and Deep, 1977).

Bledsoe, R. and B. Boczek, *The International Law Dictionary* (Santa Barbara: ABC-Clio, 1987).

Bohman, J. and M. Lutz-Bachmann, *Perpetual Peace: Essays on Kant's Cosmopolitan Ideal* (Cambridge: Cambridge University Press, 1997).

Bonta, B. *Peaceful Peoples: An Annotated Bibiliography* (Metuchen: Scarecrow, 1993).

Boulding, E. *Cultures of Peace: The Hidden Side of History* (Syracuse: Syracuse University Press, 2000).

Breyman, S. *Why Movements Matter: The West German Peace Movement and US Arms Control Policy* (Albany: State University of New York Press, 2001).

Brierly, J. L. *The Law of Nations: An Introduction to the International Law of Peace* (New York: Oxford University Press, 1963).

Brittain, V. *The Rebel Passion: A Short History of Some Pioneer Peacemakers* (Nyack: Fellowship, 1964).

Brock, P. *Pioneers of the Peaceable Kingdom* (Princeton: Princeton University Press, 1968).

—— *Pacifism in Europe to 1914* (Princeton: Princeton University Press, 1972).

—— *Freedom from Violence: Sectarian Nonresistance from the Middle Ages to the Great War* (Toronto: Universtiy of Toronto Press, 1991)

—— and N. Young, *Pacifism in the Twentieth Century* (Syracuse: Syracuse University Press, 1999).

Cable, J. *Gunboat Diplomacy: Political Applications of Limited Naval Forces* (London: Palgrave Macmillan, 1986).

Carment, D. and A. Schnabel, *Conflict Prevention: Path to Peace or Grand Illusion?* (UN Publication, 2003).

Ceadel, M. *The Origins of War Prevention: The British Peace Movement and International Relations, 1730–1854* (Oxford: Oxford University Press, 1996).

Chatfield, C. *The American Peace Movement: Ideals and Activism* (New York: Twayne, 1992).

Cheah, P. and B. Robbins, eds, *Cosmopolitics: Feeling and Thinking beyond the Nation* (Minneapolis: University of Minnesota Press, 1998).

Choate, J. *The Two Hague Conferences* (Princeton: Princeton University Press, 1913).

Clark, G. and L. Sohn, *World Peace Through World Law* (Cambridge: Harvard University Press, 1958).

Claude, I. *Swords into Plowshares: The Problems and Progress of International Organization* (New York: McGraw-Hill, 1984).

Cobban, H. *The Moral Architecture of World Peace: Nobel Laureates Discuss Our Global Future* (Charlottesville: University of Virginia Press, 2000).

Coulomb, F. *Economic Theories of Peace and War* (New York: Routledge, 2004).

Craig Blohm's *An Uneasy Peace: 1945 to 1980* (Chicago: Lucent, 2002).

Crocker, C. et al., eds, *Turbulent Peace: The Challenges of Managing International Conflict* (Washington: US Institute of Peace, 2001).

Curti, M. *The American Peace Crusade, 1815–1860* (Durham: Duke University Press, 1929).

Degen, M. *The History of the Woman's Peace Party* (Baltimore: Johns Hopkins University Press, 1939).

Dennis, M. *Cultivating a Landscape of Peace* (Ithaca: Cornell University Press, 1993).

Derrida, J. "Globalization, Peace and Cosmopolitics," in *The Future of Values: 21st Century Talks*, ed. J. Bindé (New York: Berghahn, 2004), 110–123.

Dungen, P., *From Erasmus to Tolstoy: The Peace Literature of Four Centuries* (New York: Greenwood, 1990).

Dupuy, T. and G. Hammerman, eds, *A Documentary History of Arms Control and Disarmament* (NewYork: R. R. Bowker, 1973).

Einstein, A. *On Peace*, ed. O. Nathan and H. Norden (New York: Random House, 1988).

Epstein, A. *Political Protest and Cultural Revolution: Nonviolent Direct Action in the 1970s and 80s* (Berkeley, University of California Press, 1991).

Friedman, L. *The Law of War: A Documentary History* (New York: Random House, 1972).

Frost, J. *A History of Christian, Jewish, Muslim, Hindu, and Buddhist Perspectives on War and Peace* (Toronto: Edwin Mellen, 2004).

Galtung, J. "Violence, Peace and Peace Research," *Journal of Peace Research*, 3 (1969), 167–191.

—— *Peace by Peaceful Means: Peace and Conflict, Development and Civilization* (Oslo: International Peace Research Institute, 1996).

Glahn, G. *Law Among Nations: An Introduction to Public International Law* (New York: Macmillan, 1986).

Grewe, W. *The Epochs of International Law*, trans. M. Byers (New York: Walter de Gruyter, 2000).

Hatfield, C. and R. Ilukhina, eds, *Peace/Mir: An Anthology of Historic Alternatives to War* (Syracuse University Press, 1994).

Hershberger, G. *War, Peace, and Nonresistance* (Scottdale: Herald, 1944).

Heuser, B. *War, Peace and World Orders in European History* (London: Routledge, 2001).

Hinsley, F. H. *Power and the Pursuit of Peace: Theory and Practice in the History of Relations Between States* (Cambridge: Cambridge University Press, 1963).

Howell, S. and R. Willis, eds, *Societies At Peace* (New York: Routledge, 1989).

James, A. *The Politics of Peace-Keeping* (New York: Chatto and Windus, 1969).

Johnson, J. *Ideology, Reason, and the Limitation of War* (Princeton: Princeton University Press, 1974).

—— *Just War Tradition and the Restraint of War: A Moral and Historical Inquiry* (Princeton: Princeton University Press, 1981).

Kelsay, J. and J. Johnson, eds, *Just War and Jihad: Historical and Theoretical Perspectives on War and Peace in Western and Islamic Traditions* (New York: Greenwood, 1991).

Khadduri, M. *War and Peace in the Law of Islam* (New York: AMS, 1979).

Khatchadourian, H. *War, Terrorism, Genocide, and the Quest for Peace: Contemporary Problems in Political Ethics* (Lewiston: Edwin Mellen, 2003).

Kleidman, R. *Organizing for Peace: Neutrality, the Test Ban, and the Freeze* (Syracuse: Syracuse University Press, 1993).

Kurlansky, M. *Nonviolence: 25 Lessons from the History of a Dangerous Idea* (New York: Random House, 2006).

Lackner, S. *Peaceable Nature* (New York: Harper and Row, 1984).

Langholtz, H. ed. *The Psychology of Peacekeeping* (New York: Praeger, 1998).

Laszlo, E. and J. Yoo, *World Encyclopedia of Peace* (New York: Pergamon, 1988).

Leiter, D. *Neglected Voices: Peace in the Old Testament* (Scottdale: The Herald, 2007).

Lesaffer, R., ed. *Peace Treaties and International Law in European History: From the Late Middle Ages to World War One* (Cambrdge: Cambridge University Press, 2004).

Lowe, B. *Imagining Peace: A History of Early English Pacifist Ideas, 1340–1560* (Philadelphia: Pennsylvania State University Press, 1997).

Lynd, S. and A. eds, *Nonviolence in America: A Documentary History* (Maryknoll: Orbis, 1995).

Mackie, K. *A Handbook of Dispute Resolution: ADR in Action* (New York: Routledge, 1991).

MacNair, M. *The Psychology of Peace* (New York: Praeger, 2003).

Mattingly, G. *Renaissance Diplomacy* (London: Jonathan Cape. 1955).

Mayer, P. ed. *The Pacifist Conscience: An Anthology of Pacifist Writing* (London: Hart-Davis, 1966).

McNamara, R. and J. Blight, *Wilson's Ghost: Reducing the Risk of Conflict, Killing, and Catastrophe in the 21st Century* (New York: Public Affairs, 2001).

McAlister, P. ed. *Reweaving the Web of Life: Feminism and Nonviolence* (Philadelphia: New Society, 1982).

Meisler, S. *The United Nations: The First Fifty Years* (New York: Atlantic, 1995).

Melko, M. *52 Peaceful Societies* (Oakville: Canadian Peace Research Institute, 1973).

—— and R. Weigel, *Peace in the Ancient World* (Jefferson: McFarland & Co. 1981).

—— and J. Hord, *Peace in the Western World* (Jefferson: McFarland & Co.: 1984).

—— *Peace in Our Time* (New York: Paragon House, 1990).

Menocal, M. *The Ornament of the World: How Muslims, Jews and Christians Created a Culture of Tolerance in Medieval Spain* (New York: Little Brown, 2002).

Mitscherlich, M. *The Peaceable Sex: On Aggression in Women and Men* (New York: Fromm, 1987).

Montagu, A. *Learning Non-Aggression: The Experience of Non-Literate Societies* (New York: Oxford University Press, 1978).

Mote, C. *Industrial Arbitration: A World-Wide Survey of Natural and Political Agencies for Social Justice and Industrial Peace* (Indianapolis: Bobbs-Merrill, 1916).

Mott, W. *The Economic Basis of Peace: Linkages Between Economic Growth and International Conflict* (Westport: Greenwood, 1997).

Nagler, M. *The Search for a Nonviolent Future: A Promise of Peace for Ourselves, Our Families, and Our World* (Novato: New World Library, 2004).

Nolan, C. ed. *The Greenwood Encyclopedia of International Relations* (Westport: Greenwood, 2002).

Oliver, I. *War and Peace in the Balkans: The Diplomacy of Conflict in the Former Yugoslavia*, (New York: I. B. Tauris, 2005).

Palmer, R. *Rome and Carthage at Peace* (New York: F. Steiner, 1997).

Paris, R. *At War's End: Building Peace after Civil Conflict* (Cambridge: Cambridge University Press, 2004).

Patterson, E. *Economic Bases of Peace* (Port Washington: Kennikat, 1971).

Rahim, M. and A. Blum, *Global Perspectives on Organizational Conflict* (Wesport: Praeger, 1994).

Raimundo, B. *Peaceful Coexistence: International Law in the Building of Communism* (Baltimore: Johns Hopkins University Press, 1967).

Ralston, J. *International Arbitration: From Athens to Locarno* (Stanford: Stanford University Press, 1929).

Reves, E. *The Anatomy of Peace* (New York: Penguin, 1945).

Roetter, C. *The Diplomatic Art: An Informal History of World Diplomacy* (Philadelphia: Macrae Smith, 1963).

Rothschild, J. *Ethnopolitics: A Conceptual Framework* (New York: Columbia University Press, 1981).

Salomon, G. and B. Nevo, eds, *Peace Education: The Concept, Principles, and Practices Around the World* (Mahwah: Lawrence Erlbaum, 2002).

Samaddar, R. ed. *Peace Studies: An Introduction to the Concept, Scope, and Themes* (NewberryPark: Sage, 2004).

Sharp, G. *The Politics of Nonviolent Action*, vols 1–3 (Boston: Porter Sargent, 1973–85).

Schweitzer, A. *Peace or Atomic War?* (New York: Henry Holt, 1958).

Sheehan, M. *The Balance of Power: History and Theory* (London: Routledge, 2000).

Sponsel, L. and T. Gregor, eds, *The Anthropology of Peace and Nonviolence* (Boulder: Lynne Reinner, 1994).

Stanford, B., ed. *Peacemaking: A Guide to Conflict Resolution for Individuals, Groups, and Nations* (New York: Bantam, 1976).

Stawell, F. *The Growth of International Thought* (London: Thornton Butterworth, 1929).

Stephenson, C. "Peace Studies: The Evolution of Peace Research and Education," Occasional Papers no. 1 (Honolulu: University of Hawaii Institute of Peace, 1990).

Tracy, J. *The Civil Disobedience Handbook: A Brief History and Practical Advice for the Politically Disenchanted* (San Francisco: Manic D, 2002)

Utopian Novels: Bacon, *New Atlantis* (1624), Campanella, *City of the Sun* (1637); Harrington, *Oceana* (1656); Fénelon, *Telemaque* (1699); Cabet, *Voyage in Icaria* (1840); Bellamy, *Looking Backward* (1889); Morris, *News from Nowhere* (1890); Hertzka, *Freiland* (1891); and Wells, *A Modern Utopia* (1905) and *New Worlds for Old* (1908).

Vellacott, J. *Bertrand Russell and the Pacifists in the First World War* (New York: Palgrave Macmillan, 1980).

Viallate, A. *Economic Imperialism and International Relations* (New York: Macmillan, 1923).

Webel, C. *Handbook of Peace and Conflict Studies* (New York: Routledge, 2007).

Weinberg, A. and L. eds, *Instead of Violence: Writings by the Great Advocates of Peace and Nonviolence Throughout History* (Boston: Grossman, 1963).

Wells, D., ed. *An Encyclopedia of War and Ethics* (Westport: Greenwood, 1996).

Willetts, P. *The Non-Aligned Movement: The Origins of a Third World Alliance* (London: Pinter, 1983).

Wittner, L. *Rebels Against War: The American Peace Movement, 1933–1983* (Philadelphia: Temple University Press, 1984).

Wolfthal, D., ed. *Peace, Negotiation, and Reciprocity: Strategies for Co-Existence in the Middle Ages and Renaissance* (Brussels: Brepols, 2000).

Wright, Q. *et al.*, *Preventing World War III: Some Proposals* (New York: Simon and Schuster, 1962).

Ziegler, D., War, *Peace, and International Politics* (Boston: Longman, 1988).

Zinn, H., ed. *The Power of Nonviolence: Writings by Advocates of Peace* (Boston: Beacon, 2002).

Index